Perspectives on Deviance and Social Control

Michelle dedicates this book to her students, past and present, inside and outside, who offer inspiration, creative challenges, and, most importantly, real hope for a better future.

Kristin would like to dedicate this book to Jeff, William, and Christopher, who are a welcome reminder that the world can be a really cool place.

Randy would like to dedicate this book to Beth, the newest and loveliest deviant in his life.

Perspectives on Deviance and Social Control

MICHELLE INDERBITZIN

Oregon State University

KRISTIN A. BATES

Cal State University, San Marcos

RANDY GAINEY

Old Dominion University, Norfolk

Los Angeles | London | New Delhi
Singapore | Washington DC

APR 0 8 2015

PROPERTY OF SENECA COLLEGE LIBRARIES NEWNHAM CAMPUS

Los Angeles | London | New Delhi
Singapore | Washington DC

FOR INFORMATION:

SAGE Publications, Inc.
2455 Teller Road
Thousand Oaks, California 91320
E-mail: order@sagepub.com

SAGE Publications Ltd.
1 Oliver's Yard
55 City Road
London EC1Y 1SP
United Kingdom

SAGE Publications India Pvt. Ltd.
B 1/I 1 Mohan Cooperative Industrial Area
Mathura Road, New Delhi 110 044
India

SAGE Publications Asia-Pacific Pte. Ltd.
3 Church Street
#10-04 Samsung Hub
Singapore 049483

Library of Congress Cataloging-in-Publication Data

Inderbitzin, Michelle Lee.
Perspectives on deviance and social control / Michelle Inderbitzin,
Kristin Bates, Randy Gainey.

pages cm
Includes bibliographical references and index.

ISBN 978-1-4522-8885-7 (pbk. : alk. paper)

1. Deviant behavior. 2. Social control. I. Bates, Kristin Ann. II.
Gainey, Randy R. III. Title.

HM811.I533 2014
302.5'42—dc23   2014014621

This book is printed on acid-free paper.

Acquisitions Editor: Jerry Westby
Production Editor: Libby Larson
Copy Editor: Shannon Kelly
Typesetter: C&M Digitals (P) Ltd.
Proofreader: Theresa Kay
Indexer: Kathy Paparchontis
Cover Designer: Anupama Krishnan
Marketing Manager: Erica DeLuca

SUSTAINABLE FORESTRY INITIATIVE
Certified Chain of Custody
Promoting Sustainable Forestry
www.sfiprogram.org
SFI-01268
SFI label applies to text stock

14 15 16 17 18 10 9 8 7 6 5 4 3 2 1

Brief Contents

Detailed Contents

Foreword

Howard S. Becker

By the time sociology came to universities at the beginning of the 20th century, all the "good" topics had been snatched up by earlier arrivals: Historians got to write about wars and kings and queens, economists acquired the market as their special turf, and political science took control of the state and government. Sociology was left with whatever topics were left over, especially (chief among these less desirable subjects) the "bad behavior" nice people didn't like in the increasingly urbanized society they lived in: slums, gangs, prostitution, alcoholism, and crime. No one had to worry, then, about defining this field or justifying all these disparate topics being treated under one heading. It seemed obvious to all right-thinking people that these things were problems that needed looking into. Sociologists took them over as their own, and the nature of these problems (and the solutions to them everyone hoped the new science would provide) defined the nature of the field.

Since university disciplines like to make sense of what they are doing, sociologists soon began to look for a unifying thread, for what all these things had in common that justified calling studying them a scientific field. Once you question the commonsense idea that they all simply exemplified "bad behavior" or "social problems," you commit yourself to finding a more logical and scientifically defensible description of what you're doing. Sociologists worked hard to come up with that definition. What they came up with, in the end, was not a definition, but definitions, lots of them. Because to go beyond saying these were all simply differing versions of badness, to define what made bad people's behavior bad, created great difficulties because people don't agree on that kind of definition. The commonsense understanding of "badness" included a mixture of very different things: drunkenness, stealing, craziness—the definition really consisted of nothing more than a list of activities that the law banned. Because legislatures don't make laws to define the subject matter of a science but rather to satisfy constituents, the science part comes hard.

For many years, taking commonsense ideas of bad behavior at face value and accepting conventional definitions of what "bad" was, sociologists tried to make science by accepting and trying to prove and improve upon equally commonsense explanations of why people behaved badly. They mostly relied on one of two ideas. On one hand, some theories said that people did bad things because they were inherently bad—there were plenty of genetic theories in the early history of criminology, identifying potential criminals by physical markers of bad heredity—similar to the markers of feeble-mindedness, another topic that sociology and criminology had on their hands—or because they lived in bad circumstances, which turned otherwise normal children into delinquents, sane people into the mentally ill, and healthy people into alcoholics and drug addicts.

These general ideas, scarcely worth being dignified as general theories, for many years dominated the classes taught under such titles as "Social Disorganization" or "Social Problems." Textbooks and lectures proceeded along a well-marked path of problems, dominated by well-known kinds of crimes—starting with juvenile delinquency and following criminal types through more adult crimes like robbery, theft, burglary, and murder—and equally familiar kinds of personal pathologies, revolving around pleasurable forms of behavior that right-thinking people thought were wrong—sex, drugs, and alcohol, all three leading to mental illness. Teachers and books rehearsed the numerous and varied things that had been found to be correlated with bad behavior and presumably to cause them: living in a slum neighborhood, coming from a broken home (that is, a household not headed by a married heterosexual couple), low educational achievement, and a long list of other phenomena usually correlated with some measure of social class so that, in some fundamental sense, the cause of all this pathology seemed to be being poor.

Such an approach did not produce a lot of results. What one study found was often contradicted by another study, and eventually some sociologists and criminologists began to take a more neutral approach to these subject matters, seeing them not as signs of bad character or heredity but rather as signs of a mixed-up society, whose operations and organization made it likely that some sizable number of people would find it attractive and/or profitable to engage in behavior that led them into conflict with the law (as the gang members in *West Side Story* sang, "We're not depraved, we're deprived!").

Since finding the causes of bad behavior in society did not produce reliable results any more than genetic and psychological theories had, some sociologists began to look further. They asked about a larger spectrum of things and focused on what we might call "the crime industry," the agencies and organizations that made laws that defined what things were crimes, that devoted themselves to finding people who had violated these laws, adjudicating their cases, and administering the punishments and forms of supervision the resolution of those cases dictated: the legislatures that made the laws, the police who found the guilty parties, the courts where their cases were decided, the jails and prisons where they served their sentence, and the parole offices and officers that oversaw those who came out at the other end of this process.

All this research is best summarized, as the authors of this book have done, by considering the variety of theories that sociologists and criminologists have created to make sense of this confusing mass of ideas and of the research the variety of ideas has engendered. Reading their crisp, informative summaries of so many conflicting ideas, and then the wisely chosen illustrative examples of what you get from each approach, will give students the best possible introduction to a lively and still-developing field of research.

Preface

While there are many textbooks and readers on deviant behavior currently on the market, this book is unique because it is framed within and written entirely from a sociological perspective. We explain the development of major sociological theoretical perspectives and detail how those theories have been and are currently used to think about and study the causes of deviant behavior and the reactions to it. We find the theories fascinating, and we think you will, too. We have also provided many specific examples of deviant behavior and social control within the text so that students will have numerous opportunities to apply the concepts and theories and make connections to their everyday lives. In the following, we describe how *Perspectives on Deviance and Social Control* differs from existing texts on the market.

In contrast to most of the popular readers and textbooks on deviant behavior, this book is primarily organized around theories and perspectives of deviance, rather than types of deviant behavior or a singular approach to understanding deviance. We have aimed for a combination of both depth and breadth in this book; in taking a broad sociological perspective, we focus on theory but also include full chapters on researching deviance, the social control of deviance, deviant careers, and deviance and social control in global context.

We hope this book will serve as a guide to students delving into the fascinating world of deviance and social control for the first time, offering clear overviews of issues and perspectives in the field as well as introductions to classic and current research. *Perspectives on Deviance and Social Control* is intended to replace standard deviance textbooks or readers; it can be used in both undergraduate and graduate deviance courses.

◈ Overview of Features

Perspectives on Deviance and Social Control includes topics generally found in textbooks on deviant behavior, with significant focus on the major sociological theories of deviance and discussion of rulemaking and societal reaction to deviance. This book offers clear explanations and discussion of concepts and theories and carefully selected examples to illustrate relevant topics. This book features the following:

1. An introductory section explaining the sociological perspective on deviance and social control. This section provides an overview on the organization and content of the book and also introduces relevant themes, issues, and concepts to assist students in understanding the different

perspectives. Along with the introduction, we have full chapters on the diversity of deviance and methods of researching deviance to introduce students to the broader issues in the field.

2. Each chapter includes five different features or sections that prompt students to engage with the material, apply the concepts, and learn more about current research. These features include the following:

   a. *Deviance in Popular Culture*—offers several examples of films and/or television shows and encourages students to apply the concepts and theories to the behavior depicted in these examples.

   b. *Recent Studies in Deviance*—offers a brief overview of a recently published study on diverse types of deviant behavior.

   c. *Explaining Deviance in the Streets and Deviance in the Suites*—explores the impact of social class and status on different types of deviance and the reactions to such behavior.

   d. *Ideas in Action*—highlights examples of current policies or programs designed to address deviant behaviors from the perspective(s) covered in each chapter.

   e. *Now YOU . . .* —asks students to apply the material they learned in the chapter to specific questions or examples.

3. Each chapter includes discussion questions and exercises/assignments that will give students a chance to test and extend their knowledge of the material.

4. The book contains a glossary of key terms.

◈ Structure of the Book

We chose very deliberately to organize our book around sociological theories rather than around types of deviance. This is in direct opposition to most of the competing texts on the market, and it is one of the reasons you might consider using our book. We believe the theoretically based approach offers students fertile ground for learning and exploring the realm of deviant behavior and social control. Once they learn the different theoretical perspectives, students will be able to apply the different theories to virtually any type of deviant behavior and, furthermore, be able to compare and contrast the theoretical models and decide for themselves which offers the most compelling explanation for the behavior. This is the kind of understanding and flexibility we hope our students achieve—while studying types of deviance is certainly interesting, being able to consider both individual and macro-level causes and explanations seems to us the larger and more important goal.

The book is divided into 13 chapters that cover an overview of the field of deviance and social control, methods and examples of researching deviance, the major theoretical traditions used in studying deviance, a glimpse into the social control of deviance and deviant careers, and a discussion of deviance and social control in global context. The theory chapters each provide an overview of a theoretical perspective and its development, critiques of the perspective, and examples of current developments and research in that theoretical tradition. The chapters are as follows:

Chapter 1—Introduction to Deviance: We first provide the basic building blocks for studying deviant behavior from a sociological perspective. Different conceptions of deviance are described, and students are encouraged to develop and use their sociological imagination in studying deviant behavior. We explain the organization of the book and why we believe theory is so critical to understanding and researching deviance.

Chapter 2—The Diversity of Deviance: In this chapter, we offer an overview of some of the many types of deviance and show how our conceptions of deviance vary widely and change over time. We encourage students to think broadly about deviance and to always consider the culture, context, and historical period in which the "deviant" act takes place.

Chapter 3—Researching Deviance: This chapter addresses the many ways one might go about researching deviant behavior and social control. We highlight different research methods and the strengths and weaknesses of each approach. Examples are used throughout to make abstract concepts concrete for students.

Chapter 4—Anomie/Strain Theory: This chapter looks at one of the first sociological theories of deviance and traces the development of anomie and strain theories from Durkheim's, Merton's, and Cloward and Ohlin's macro-level ideas on how the very structure of society contributes to deviant behavior to Agnew's general strain theory and Messner and Rosenfeld's institutional strain theory, which offer contemporary views on individual and institutional strain and the resulting deviance.

Chapter 5—Social Disorganization Theory: We discuss another early sociological perspective on deviance in this chapter: social disorganization theory developed from early research on Chicago to explain patterns of deviance and crime across social locations such as neighborhoods. We offer an overview of the perspective and show how it is being used today to explain high levels of deviance and violence in particular neighborhoods.

Chapter 6—Differential Association and Social Learning Theory: How do individuals learn to become deviant? This chapter covers ideas and research that try to answer that exact question. We explain the key ideas of Sutherland's differential association and Akers' social learning theories and offer an overview of the development of a sociological perspective that argues that deviance is learned through communication with intimate others.

Chapter 7—Social Control Theories of Deviance: Social control theories begin by flipping the question; rather than asking why individuals deviate, social control theories ask, if we are born prone to deviance, what keeps us from committing deviant acts? In this chapter, we trace the development of social control and life course theories and look at the importance of the individual's social bonds to conforming society.

Chapter 8—Labeling Theory: In this chapter, we look at the importance of being labeled deviant. We begin with a brief overview of symbolic interactionism, which then leads to a discussion of the labeling process and how it can affect individuals' self-concepts and life chances.

Chapter 9—Marxist/Conflict Theories of Deviance: Within the conflict perspective, power and inequality are key considerations in defining who and what is deviant in any given society. In this chapter, we begin with the ideas of Karl Marx and go on to show how Marxist perspectives have been used to study lawmaking and how the process of defining and creating deviant behavior is used to maintain positions of power in society.

Chapter 10—Critical Theories: In this chapter, we focus on theories that examine deviance from a perspective that questions the normative status quo. We offer brief overviews of peacemaking criminology, feminist criminology, and critical race theory as alternative perspectives for studying deviance and social control.

Chapter 11—Social Control of Deviance: In this chapter, we offer a brief look into informal and formal social control of deviance. We discuss the medicalization (and medication) of deviance, mental hospitals, prisons and juvenile correctional facilities, felon disenfranchisement, and general effects of stigma on those labeled deviant.

Chapter 12 – Deviant Careers and Career Deviance: While much attention is focused on getting into deviance, in this chapter we consider the full deviant career, including desistance, or the process of exiting deviance.

Chapter 13 – Global Perspective on Deviance and Social Control: For our final chapter, we move beyond the United States to consider how deviance is defined and researched in other countries. Further, we briefly consider and discuss the many different forms of social control across the globe.

Each chapter offers original material that introduces students to the issues, concepts, and theories covered in that chapter and contextualizes the examples used to show the wide variation in deviance and social control.

◈ Ancillaries

To enhance the use of this text and to assist those using this book, we have developed high-quality ancillaries for instructors and students.

Instructor Resource Site. A password-protected site, available at www.sagepub.com/inderbitzin, features resources that have been designed to help instructors plan and teach their course. These resources include the following:

- An extensive test bank that includes multiple-choice, true/false, short-answer, and essay questions for each chapter
- Chapter-specific PowerPoint slide presentations that highlight essential concepts and figures from the text
- Sample syllabi for semester, quarter, and online courses
- Access to recent, relevant full-text SAGE journal articles and accompanying article review questions
- Class assignments and activities that can be used in conjunction with the book throughout the semester
- Links to Web resources, which direct both instructors and students to relevant Web sites for further research on important chapter topics

- Audio and video resources for use in class to jump-start lectures and emphasize key topics of your discussions
- Figures and tables from the text

Student Study Site. An open-access study site is available at www.sagepub.com/inderbitzin. This site provides access to several study tools, including the following:

- eFlashcards, which reinforce students' understanding of key terms and concepts presented in the text
- Web quizzes for student self-review
- Web resources organized by chapter for more in-depth research on topics presented in each chapter
- Access to relevant full-text SAGE journal articles that were selected by the authors
- Audio and video resources for a more in-depth understanding of the material covered in class and in the text

◈ Acknowledgments

First, we thank Jerry Westby for choosing to work with us a second time and for shepherding our stubborn ideas for a different kind of book on deviance and social control through the publication process once again. Jerry's faith in this book and our vision for it helped to sustain the project through difficult patches and busy schedules.

We would also like to thank our graduate school mentors and friends; our time with these people in the University of Washington sociology program contributed a great deal to our lasting understanding of deviant behavior and social control: Bob Crutchfield, George Bridges, Joe Weis, Charis Kubrin, Sara Steen, Rod Engen, Edie Simpson, Ed Day, and Tim Wadsworth—thanks to you all! We hope you recognize your influence in this book, and we hope that we have made you proud. We also thank Howie Becker for being a powerful figure in the field of deviance and social control generally, a supportive mentor for Michelle specifically, and for writing the foreword to this book.

Michelle would like to thank Kristin Bates and Randy Gainey for being wonderful coauthors and friends. It's a continuing joy to have colleagues who are like family and who even manage to make working on endless revisions enjoyable. Sincerest appreciation to you both for sharing ideas and laughs and for being there for every step of this journey. She also offers particular thanks to friends and colleagues Charis Kubrin, Chris Uggen, Scott Akins, Kristin Barker, Becky Warner, and Debbie Storrs for many, many thought-provoking conversations about teaching and writing. And, finally, she is endlessly thankful to her parents and sisters for giving her a strong and loving start to life and for their continuing support.

Kristin would like to thank her colleagues in the Department of Sociology at California State University, San Marcos, for sharing their critical perspectives, their intellectual energy, and their friendship. "The work isn't work when I get to do it with all of you. To my students who remind me every day why I love what I do. And all my love to my parents and sisters who taught, fostered, and lived relativist/social constructionist/critical perspectives of deviance long before the livin' was cool."

Randy would like to thank his colleagues at Old Dominion University, where going to work is like going out and "playing with friends." He would also like to thank all of the students that have kept him engaged in social science research, always asking great questions and offering unique solutions. Much love to my family and friends—you rock!!!

And Randy and Kristin would like to thank Michelle for her leadership and hard work and for asking them to take this adventure with her. We had fun!

We would also like to thank the reviewers:

Keith J. Bell, West Liberty University, West Virginia
Cindy Brooks Dollar, North Carolina State University
Angela Butts, Rutgers University
Seth Crawford, Oregon State University
Joseph Gallo, Sam Houston State University
George Guay, Bridgewater State University
Abdy Javadzadeh, Florida International University
Eric Jorrey, Ohio University
Lutz Kaelber, University of Vermont
Joachim Kibirige, Missouri Western State University
Ross Kleinstuber, University of Delaware, Newark
Carol Cirulli Lanham, University of Texas at Dallas
Timothy O'Boyle, Kutztown University of Philadelphia
Robert Peralta, University of Akron
Andrew Rochus, West Virginia University at Parkersburg
Julia So, University of New Mexico at Valencia
Lindsey Upton, Old Dominion University
Brenda Vollman, Loyola University New Orleans
Lisa Weinberg, Florida State University
Lester Howard Wielstein, California State University at Sacramento
Janelle Wilson, University of Minnesota Duluth

CHAPTER 1

Introduction to Deviance

Founded in 1972, the Fremont Fair is one of Seattle's most beloved neighborhood street festivals, featuring a weekend of eclectic activities that celebrate the quirky community of Fremont, the self-proclaimed "center of the universe." Held annually in mid-June to coincide with the Summer Solstice, the event draws more than 100,000 people to shop, eat, drink, mingle, groove, and enjoy all manners of creative expression. Artistic highlights include craft and art booths, street performers, local bands, wacky decorated art cars, the free-spirited Solstice Parade produced by the Fremont Arts Council, and many other oddities that personify Fremont's official motto "Delibertus Quirkus"—Freedom to be Peculiar.

—Fremont Fair (2010)

The Fremont Arts Council (FAC) is a community-based celebration arts organization. We value volunteerism; community participation; artistic expression; and the sharing of arts skills. The Fremont Solstice Parade is the defining event of the FAC. We celebrate the longest day of the year through profound street theater, public spectacle, and a kaleidoscope of joyous human expressions. We welcome the participation of everyone regardless of who they are, or what they think or believe. However, the FAC reserves the right to control the content presented in the Fremont Solstice Parade.

The rules of the Fremont Solstice Parade, which make this event distinct from other types of parades, are:

- No written or printed words or logos
- No animals (except guide dogs and service animals)
- No motorized vehicles (except wheelchairs)
- No real weapons or fire

—Fremont Arts Council (2010)

(Continued)

(Continued)

It is true that a parade with no logos, animals, or motorized vehicles is different from most parades that we experience in the United States. But one more thing sets the Fremont Solstice Parade apart from other parades—the public displays of nudity. Every year at the parade, a contingent of nude, body-painted bicyclists (both men and women) rides through the streets of Fremont as part of the parade. Rain or shine (and let's face it, in June in Seattle, there can be a lot of rain), a large group of naked adults cycles down the street as the crowds cheer and wave. The Fremont City Council estimates that more than 100,000 people visit the weekend fair, and pictures show that the streets are crowded with parade watchers, from the very young to elderly.

Contrast this event to the following story of a flasher in San Diego County. Between the summer of 2009 and the summer of 2010, there were numerous reports of an adult man flashing hikers and runners on Mission Trails near Lake Murphy in San Diego. An undercover operation was set in motion to catch this flasher, and on July 19, 2010, an adult man was apprehended while flashing an undercover officer who was posing as a jogger in the park. The man was held on $50,000 bail while waiting for arraignment (KFMB-News 8, 2010).

While both these events center around public displays of nudity, one is celebrated while the other is vilified. Why?

▲ Photos 1.1 & 1.2   When is a public display of nudity considered deviant? When is it celebrated?

Sources: Photodisc/ThinkStock; ©JMW Scout/iStockphoto.

◈ Introduction

You might expect that a book about deviance would start with a definition of what deviance is. But, like all things worth studying, a simple definition does not exist. For example, in the stories above, one public display of nudity was not only welcomed but celebrated by 6-year-olds and grandmothers alike, but another display led to arrest and possible jail time. Why? This chapter and this book explore how it can be that the Fremont Summer Solstice Parade can be celebrated in the same summer that a flasher is arrested and held on $50,000 bail until charged.

Conceptions of Deviance

All deviance textbooks offer their "conceptions of deviance." Rubington and Weinberg (2008) argue that there are generally two conceptions of deviance as either "objectively given" or "subjectively problematic." Clinard and Meier (2010) also suggest two general conceptions of deviance, the reactionist or **relativist conception** and the **normative conception**. Thio (2009) argues that we can view deviance from a **positivist perspective** or a constructionist perspective.

While none of these authors are using the same language, they are defining similar conceptions of deviance. The first conception—that of an "objectively given," normative, or positivist conception of deviance—assumes that there is a general set of norms of behavior, conduct, and conditions on which we can agree. **Norms** are rules of behavior that guide people's actions. Sumner (1906) broke norms down into three categories: folkways, mores, and laws. **Folkways** are everyday norms that do not generate much uproar if they are violated. Think of them as behaviors that might be considered rude if engaged in—like standing too close to someone while speaking or picking one's nose. **Mores** are "moral" norms that may generate more outrage if broken. In a capitalist society, homelessness and unemployment can elicit outrage if the person is considered unworthy of sympathy. Similarly, drinking too much or alcoholism may be seen as a lapse in moral judgment. Finally, the third type of norm is the **law**, which is considered the strongest norm because it is backed by official sanctions (or a formal response). In this conception, then, deviance becomes a violation of a rule understood by the majority of the group. This rule may be minor, in which case the deviant is seen as "weird but harmless," or the rule may be major, in which case the deviant is seen as "criminal." The obvious problem with this conceptualization goes back to the earlier examples of reactions to public nudity, where we see that violation of a most "serious" norm (law) can receive quite different reactions. This leads to the second conception.

The second conception of deviance—the "subjectively problematic," reactionist/relativist, **social constructionist conception**—assumes that the definition of deviance is constructed based on the interactions of those in society. According to this conception, behaviors or conditions are not inherently deviant; they become so when the definition of deviance is applied to them. The study of deviance is not about why certain individuals violate norms but instead about how those norms are constructed. Social constructionists believe that our understanding of the world is in constant negotiation between actors. Those who have a relativist conception of deviance define deviance as those behaviors that illicit a definition or label of deviance:

> Social groups create deviance by making the rules whose infraction constitutes deviance, and by applying those rules to particular people and labeling them as outsiders. For this point of view, deviance is not a quality of the act the person commits but rather a consequence of the application by others of rules and sanctions to an "offender." The deviant is one to whom that label has successfully been applied; deviant behaviors is behavior that people so label. (Becker, 1973, p. 9)

This is a fruitful conceptualization, but it is also problematic. What about very serious violations of norms that are never known or reacted to? Some strict reactionists/relativists would argue that these acts (beliefs or attitudes) are not deviant. Most of us would agree that killing someone and making it look like he or she simply skipped the country is deviant; however, there may be no reaction.

Sidebar: Be Careful Who You Are Calling Deviant: Body Ritual Among the Nacirema

In 1956, Horace Miner published an article on the Nacirema, a poorly understood culture that he claimed engaged in body rituals and ceremonies that were unique, obsessive, and almost magical. He highlighted several of these beliefs and actions:

- The fundamental belief of the Nacirema people is that the human body is ugly and prone to "debility and disease."
- The people engage in rituals and ceremonies in a "ritual center" considered to be a shrine. Affluent members of society may have more than one shrine devoted to these rituals and ceremonies.
- Each shrine has near its center point a box or chest filled with magical potions. Many believe they cannot live without these magical potions and so collect to the point of hoarding them, afraid to let them go even when it is determined they may no longer hold their magic.
- The people have an "almost pathological horror and fascination with the mouth, the condition of which is believed to have a supernatural influence on all social relationships. Were it not for the rituals of the mouth, they believe that their teeth would fall out, their gums bleed, their jaws shrink, their friends desert them, and their lovers reject them" (p. 505).

Miner never lets on that this fascinating culture that believes magic will transform its members' ugly, diseased bodies is actually American (Nacirema spelled backward) culture. But his point is made: Our understanding and interpretation of events and behaviors is often relative. If we step back from the everyday events in which we engage with little thought, our most accepted practices can be made to seem deviant.

Take a moment to examine some everyday activity that you engage in from the perspective of an outsider. What might watching television, going to a sporting event, babysitting, or surfing look like to those who have never experienced it? Can you write a description of this everyday event from an outsider's point of view?

Source: Miner, H. (1956).

A third conception of deviance that has not been advanced in many textbooks (for an exception, see DeKeseredy, Ellis, & Alvi, 2005) is a critical definition of deviance (Jensen, 2007). Those working from a **critical conception** of deviance argue that the normative understanding of deviance is established by those in power to maintain and enhance their power. It suggests that explorations of deviance have focused on a white, male, middle- to upper-class understanding of society that implies that people of color, women, and the working poor are by definition deviant. Instead of focusing on individual types of deviance, this conception critiques the social system that exists and creates such norms in the first place. This, too, is a useful and powerful approach, but there are still some things that the vast majority of society agrees are so immoral, unethical, and deviant that they should be illegal and that the system can serve to protect our interests against these things.

Table 1.1   Conceptions of Deviance

Conceptions of Deviance	Assumptions	Definition of Deviance	Example Research Question
Positivist/Normative	There is a general set of norms of behavior, conduct, and conditions on which we can agree.	A violation of a rule understood by the majority of the group	"What leads an individual to engage in deviant behavior?"
Relative/Social Constructionist	Nothing is inherently deviant; our understanding of the world is in constant negotiation between actors.	Deviance is behaviors that illicit a definition or label of deviance.	"What characteristics increase the likelihood that an individual or a behavior will be defined as deviant?"
Critical	The normative understanding of deviance is established by those in power to maintain and enhance their power.	Instead of focusing on individual types of deviance, this conception critiques the social system that exists and creates such norms in the first place.	"What is the experience of the homeless and who is served by their treatment as deviant?"

Given that each of these conceptualizations is useful but problematic, we do not adhere to a single conception of deviance in this book because the theories of deviance do not adhere to a single conception. You will see that several of our theories assume a normative conception, while several assume a social constructionist or critical conception. As you explore each of these theories, think about what the conception of deviance and theoretical perspective mean for the questions we ask and answer about deviance.

HOW DO YOU DEFINE DEVIANCE?

As Justice Stewart of the Supreme Court once famously wrote about trying to define obscene materials, "I shall not today attempt further to define the kinds of material I understand to be embraced within that shorthand description; and perhaps I could never succeed in intelligibly doing so. But I know it

(Continued)

(Continued)

when I see it" (*Jacobellis v. Ohio*, 1964). Those who do not study deviance for a living probably find themselves in the same boat; it may be hard to write a definition, but how hard could it be to "know it when we see it"?

Choose a busy place to sit and observe human behavior for one hour. Write down all the behaviors that you observe during that hour. Do you consider any of these behaviors to be deviant? Which conception of deviance are you using when you define each as deviant? Might there be some instances (e.g., places or times) when that behavior you consider to be nondeviant right now might become deviant? Finally, bring your list of behaviors to class. In pairs, share your list of behaviors and your definitions of deviant behaviors with your partner. Do you agree on your categorization? Why or why not?

◈ The Sociological Imagination

Those of us who are sociologists can probably remember the first time we were introduced to the concept of the sociological imagination. Mills argues that the only way to truly understand the experiences of the individual is to first understand the societal, institutional, and historical conditions that individual is living under. In other words, Mills believes that no man, woman, or child is an island. Below is an excerpt from C. Wright Mills' (1959/2000) profound book, *The Sociological Imagination* (Oxford University Press):

Men do not usually define the troubles they endure in terms of historical change and institutional contradiction. The well-being they enjoy, they do not usually impute to the big ups and downs of the societies in which they live. Seldom aware of the intricate connection between the patterns of their own lives and the course of world history, ordinary men do not usually know what this connection means for the kinds of men they are becoming and for the kinds of history-making in which they might take part. They do not possess the quality of mind essential to grasp the interplay of man and society, of biography and history, of self and world. They cannot cope with their personal troubles in such ways as to control the structural transformations that usually lie behind them.

The sociological imagination enables its possessor to understand the larger historical scene in terms of its meaning for the inner life and the external career of a variety of individuals. It enables him to take into account how individuals, in the welter of their daily experience, often become falsely conscious of their social positions. With that welter, the framework of modern society is sought, and within that framework the psychologies of a variety of men and women are formulated. By such means the personal uneasiness of individuals is focused upon explicit troubles and the indifference of publics is transformed into involvement with public issues.

The first fruit of this imagination—and the first lesson of the social science that embodies it—is the idea that the individual can understand his own experience and gauge his own fate only by locating himself within his period, that he can know his own chances in life only by becoming aware of those of all individuals in his circumstances. In many ways it is a terrible lesson; in many ways a magnificent one.

In these terms, consider unemployment. When, in a city of 100,000, only one man is unemployed, that is his personal trouble, and for its relief we properly look to the character of the man, his skills, and his immediate opportunities. But when in a nation of 50 million employees, 15 million men are unemployed, that is an issue, and we may not hope to find its solution within the range of opportunities open to any one individual. The very structure of opportunities has collapsed. Both the correct statement of the problem and the range of possible solutions require us to consider the economic and political institutions of the society, and not merely the personal situation and character of a scatter of individuals.

What we experience in various and specific milieux, I have noted, is often caused by structural changes. Accordingly, to understand the changes of many personal milieux we are required to look beyond them. And the number and variety of such structural changes increase as the institutions within connected with one another. To be aware of the idea of social structure and to use it with sensibility is to be capable of tracing such linkages among a great variety of milieu. To be able to do this is to possess the sociological imagination. (*The Sociological Imagination* by C. Wright Mills [2000] 527w pp. 3–11. By permission of Oxford University Press, USA.)

One of our favorite examples of the sociological imagination in action is the "salad bar" example. In the United States, one of the persistent philosophies is that of individualism and personal responsibility. Under this philosophy, individuals are assumed to be solely responsible for their successes and failures. This philosophy relies heavily on the notion that individuals are rational actors who weigh the costs and benefits of their actions, can see the consequences of their behavior, and have perfect information. The salad bar example helps those who rely heavily on this conception of the individual to see the importance of social structure to individual behavior.

No one doubts that when you order a salad bar at a restaurant, you are responsible for building your own salad. Every person makes his or her own salad, and no two salads look exactly alike. Some make salads with lots of lettuce and vegetables, very little cheese, and fat-free dressing. Others create a salad that is piled high with cheese, croutons, and lots and lots of dressing. Those who are unhappy with their choices while making their salad only have themselves to blame, right? Not necessarily.

A salad is only as good as the salad bar it is created from. In other words, individuals making a salad can only make a salad from the ingredients supplied from the salad bar. If the restaurant is out of croutons that day or decided to put watermelon out instead of cantaloupe, the individual must build his or her salad within these constraints. Some individuals with a great sense

▲ **Photo 1.3**   The salad bar can represent the restriction on choices that individuals have. We can only make our salad with the ingredients offered to us on the salad bar.

Source: Comstock/Thinkstock.

of personal power may request additional items from the back of the restaurant, but most individuals will choose to build a salad based on the items available to them on the salad bar. In other words, the individual choice is constrained by the larger social forces of delivery schedules, food inventory, and worker decision making. The sociological imagination is especially important to understand because it is the building block for our understanding of sociological theory.

DEVIANCE IN POPULAR CULTURE

Many types of deviance are portrayed and investigated in popular culture. Films and television shows, for example, illustrate a wide range of deviant behavior and social control. There are often several interpretations of what acts are deviant in each film—how do you know when an act or person is deviant? One way to develop your sociological imagination is to watch films and television shows from a critical perspective and to think about how different theories would explain the deviant behavior and the reactions portrayed. To get you started, we've listed a number of films and television shows that you might watch and explore for examples of cultural norms, different types of deviant behavior, and coping with stigma.

Films

Trekkies—a documentary following the stories of individuals who are superfans of *Star Trek.* Known as Trekkies, these individuals have incorporated *Star Trek* into their everyday lives. Some wear the uniforms or speak and teach the various languages from the show, one has considered surgery to alter the shape of his ears, and some have legally changed their names and incorporated *Star Trek* into their businesses and workplaces. The movie documents their fandom and experiences navigating these consuming obsessions while in mainstream society.

American Beauty—the story of a suburban family that, from the outside, appears to be "perfect." However, the characters are leading far from perfect lives filled with depression, lies, drug dealing, homophobia, and self-loathing.

Crumb—a movie about the cartoonist Robert Crumb, who was a pioneer of the underground comix. This movie offers a dark portrait of an artist besieged with personal and family demons.

Usual Suspects—a story of five men who are brought in for questioning for a crime they did not commit. While being held on suspicion of that crime, they agree to work together on another crime. They soon realize they are being set up by someone they had wronged in the past.

Television

Reality television and the TLC channel, in particular, feature a number of programs offering an inside view of people perceived as deviant or different in some way and showing how they deal with stigma from various sources:

Sister Wives—a look inside the world of a polygamist marriage. This reality show introduces viewers to a man, his four wives, and his 16 children. His motto: "Love should be multiplied, not divided."

My Strange Addiction—a reality show that highlights potentially deviant obsessions of individuals with addictions such as eating glass, plastic bags, household cleaners, or makeup; having dozens of surgeries in order to look like a living doll; and living as husband and wife with a synthetic doll.

Seinfeld—a situation comedy that is simply masterful at focusing on small behaviors or characteristics that break norms and are perceived as deviant. Episodes on the close-talker, the low-talker, and the high-talker, for example, all illustrate unwritten norms on interpersonal communication.

In each of the chapters that follow, we will offer suggestions of one or more films or television shows for you to watch from the theoretical perspective outlined in the chapter. We think you'll soon agree: Deviance is all around us.

◈ The Importance of Theory

The three of us (the authors of this book) spent many hours discussing the importance of **theory** as we wrote this book. Why did we choose to write a textbook about deviance with theory as the central theme? Many of you may also be asking this question and worrying that a book about theory may suck the life right out of a discussion about deviance. Really, who wants to be thinking about theory when we could be talking about "nuts, sluts, and preverts" (Liazos, 1972)? But this is precisely why we must make theory central to any discussion of deviance—because theory helps us *systematically* think about deviance. If it weren't for theory, classes about deviance would be akin to watching MTV's *Jersey Shore* or Bravo's *Real Housewives of New Jersey* (why is New Jersey so popular for these shows?)—it may be entertaining, but we have no clearer understanding of the "real" people of New Jersey when we are done watching.

Theory is what turns anecdotes about human behavior into a systematic understanding of societal behavior. It does this by playing an intricate part in research and the scientific method.

The **scientific method** is a systematic procedure that helps *safeguard*

Figure 1.1. The Scientific Method Allows Us to Systematically Examine Social Phenomena Such as Deviance

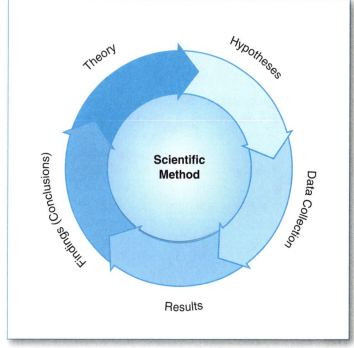

against researcher bias and the power of anecdotes by following several simple steps. First, a researcher starts with a research question. If the researcher is engaging in deductive research, this question comes from a theoretical perspective. This theory and research question help the researcher create hypotheses (testable statements) about a phenomenon being studied. Once the researcher has created hypotheses, he or she collects data to test these hypotheses. We discuss data and data collection methods for deviance research in detail in Chapter 3. The researcher then analyzes these data, interprets the findings, and concludes whether or not his or her hypotheses have been supported. These findings then inform whether the theory the researcher used helps with our understanding of the world or should be revised to take into consideration information that does not support its current model. If a researcher is engaging in inductive research, he or she also starts with a research question, but in the beginning, the researcher's theory may be what we call "grounded theory." Using qualitative methods such as participant observation or in-depth interviews, the researcher would collect data and analyze these data, looking for common themes throughout. These findings would be used to create a theory "from the ground up." In other words, while a deductive researcher would start with a theory that guides every step of the research, an inductive researcher might start with a broad theoretical perspective and a research question and, through the systematic collection of data and rigorous analyses, would hone that broad theoretical perspective into a more specific theory. This theory would then be tested again as the researcher continued on with his or her work, or others, finding this new theory to be useful and interesting, might opt to use it to inform both their deductive and inductive work.

RECENT STUDY IN DEVIANCE

The Poverty of the Sociology of Deviance: Nuts, Sluts, and Preverts

By Alexander Liazos, 1972, in *Social Problems, 20*(1), 103–120.

Liazos argues that the study of deviance used to be the study of "nuts, sluts, and preverts," a sensationalistic ritual in finger pointing and moralizing. The focus was on individuals and their "aberrant" behavior. This meant that the most harmful behaviors in society, the ones that affected us most thoroughly, were ignored and, in ignoring them, normalized. Liazos referred to these forms of deviance as *covert institutional violence.*

According to Liazos, the poverty of the study of deviance was threefold: First, even when trying to point out how normal the "deviance" or "deviant" is, by pointing out the person or behavior, we are acknowledging the difference—if that difference really were invisible, how and why would we be studying it? This meant by even studying deviance, a moral choice had already been made—some differences were studied; some were not. Second, by extension, deviance research rarely studied elite deviance and structural deviance, instead focusing on "dramatic" forms of deviance such as prostitution, juvenile delinquency, and homosexuality. Liazos argues that it is important to, instead, study covert institutional violence, which leads to such things as poverty and exploitation. Instead of studying tax cheats, we should study unjust tax laws; instead of studying prostitution, we should study racism and sexism as deviance. Finally, Liazos argues that even those who profess to study the relationship between power and deviance do not really acknowledge the importance of power. These researchers still give those in positions of power a pass to engage in harmful behavior by not defining much elite deviance as deviance at all.

The implication of this is that those who study deviance have allowed the definition of deviance to be settled for them. And this definition benefits not only individuals in power but also a system that has routinely engaged in harmful acts. While Liazos wrote this important critique of the sociology of deviance in 1972, much of his analysis holds up to this day. In this book, we examine theories expressly capable of addressing this critique.

As you explore each of the theories offered to you in this book, remember Liazos's critique. Which theories are more likely to focus on "nuts, sluts, and preverts"? Which are more likely to focus on elite deviance and new conceptions of deviance?

If we go back to our example of reality shows about people from New Jersey, we may see the difference between an anecdote and a more theoretically grounded understanding of human behavior. After watching both *Jersey Shore* and the *Real Housewives of New Jersey*, we may conclude that people from New Jersey are loud, self-absorbed, and overly tan (all three of which might be considered deviant behaviors or characteristics). However, we have not systematically studied the people of New Jersey to arrive at our conclusion. Using inductive reasoning, based on our initial observation, we may start with a research question that states that because the people of New Jersey are loud, self-absorbed, and overly tan, we are interested in knowing about the emotional connections they have with friends and family (we may suspect that self-absorbed people are more likely to have relationships with conflict). However, as we continue along the scientific method, we systematically gather data from more than just the reality stars of these two shows. We interview teachers and police officers, retired lawyers and college students. What we soon learn as we analyze these interviews is that the general public in New Jersey is really not all that tan, loud, or self-absorbed, and they speak openly and warmly about strong connections to family and friends. This research leads us to reexamine our initial theory about the characteristics of people from New Jersey and offer a new theory based on systematic analysis. This new theory then informs subsequent research on the people of New Jersey. If we did not have theory and the scientific method, our understanding of deviance would be based on wild observations and anecdotes, which may be significantly misleading and unrepresentative of the social reality.

In addition to being systematic and testable (through the scientific method), theory offers *solutions to the problems* we study. One of the hardest knocks against the study of deviance and crime has been the historically carnival sideshow nature (Liazos, 1972) of much of the study of deviance. By focusing on individuals and a certain caste of deviants (those without power) and using less than systematic methods, deviance researchers were just pointing at "nuts, sluts, and preverts" and not advancing their broader understanding of the interplay of power, social structure, and behavior.

Theory can focus our attention on this interplay and offer solutions beyond the individual and the deficit model, which is a model that focuses on the individual (or group) in question and blames the deviance on something broken, lacking, or deficient in him or her. Bendle (1999) also argued that the study of deviance was in a state of crisis because researchers were no longer studying relevant problems or offering useful solutions. One of Bendle's solutions is to push for new theories of deviant behavior.

Theoretical solutions to the issue of deviance are especially important because many of our current responses to deviant behavior are erroneously based on an individualistic notion of human nature that does not take into account humans as social beings or the importance of social structure, social institutions, power, and broad societal changes for deviance and deviants.

Explaining Deviance in the Streets and Deviance in the Suites

We have included a section in each chapter that discusses a "street" deviance and juxtaposes it against an "elite"/"suite" deviance. We have chosen to do this because in many instances street deviance is the focus of examinations (again, we gravitate to conversations of "nuts, sluts, and preverts" if we aren't systematic). We wanted to make sure for each street deviance we explored that we offered an exploration of an elite deviance, too. Depending on the chapter we have chosen to do this in one of two ways. Some chapters focus on a single deviance that, while engaged in by a variety of individuals, is interpreted differently depending on the characteristics of who is doing the engaging. For example, in Chapter 6 we focus on social learning theory and drug use and examine how class neighborhood characteristics impact drug use. In Chapter 8, we focus on labeling theory and how the class characteristics of individuals impact the likelihood that they will be labeled with a drinking problem. Both of these approaches show that a single behavior is impacted by class—either by affecting the likelihood of engaging in the behavior or the likelihood that the behavior will be perceived as deviant. Finally, in some of our chapters we choose to examine two separate forms of deviance, highlighting how a street deviance (one that often receives more attention, is perceived of as more detrimental, or is perceived as likely to be engaged in by the poor) compares to an elite/suite deviance (often an action or behavior that many cannot agree is deviant or that is engaged in by those who have substantial amounts of power). For example, in Chapter 10, we use critical theories to discuss how changing technologies have affected pornography (our example of street deviance) and illegal government surveillance (our example of suite deviance). In chapters such as this we want to highlight how a single theory may address behaviors that are often on very different ends of the power and class spectrum. In all of the chapters, we first offer a substantive discussion of the deviance before we analyze it from the perspective of the chapter.

◈ Ideas in Action

For the purposes of this book, we are expanding the discussion of public policy to include public and private programs, which is why we have titled this section in each chapter Ideas in Action. While a single, concrete definition of public policy is elusive, there is general agreement that public policy is the sometimes unwritten actions taken by the city, state, or federal government. These actions may be as formal as a law or regulation or be more informal in nature, such as an institutional custom. While public policy is often associated with government guidelines/actions, we also find it important to highlight the work of public/private programs, nonprofits, and non-governmental organizations (NGOs). For this reason, our Ideas in Action section may highlight a private program or entity or a public (state or federal) guideline, rule, or law that affects our understanding or control of deviance.

Some argue that tension exists between public policies and private programs created to address deviance, crime, and public well-being. These tensions are twofold. The first argument involves what some argue is an abdication of public well-being out of the public realm (the government) to a private and more likely profit-motivated industry (private programs). This shift is often referred to as neoliberalism:

> The term neoliberalism refers to a political, economic, and social ideology that argues that low government intervention, a privatization of services that in the past have predominately been the domain of government, an adherence to a free-market philosophy, and an emphasis on deregulation (Frericks, Maier, & de Graaf, 2009) is "the source and arbiter of human freedoms" (Mudge, 2008, p. 704). What may be one of the most important aspects of neoliberalism from the standpoint of those focused on social justice, then, is this link between the free markets and morality. While free markets have proven time and again to place the utmost emphasis on the profit motive (because this is what the free market is: an adherence to the notion of supply and demand)—this connection between free markets and "freedom" seems to intrinsically suggest that free markets, and, therefore, neoliberalism, have individual well-being as their focus.
>
> However, individual well-being in the form of a guarantee that individuals will have access to the basic human needs of shelter, food, clothing, good health care, and safety from harm is not always produced by two of the most central components of neoliberalism—privatization and deregulation. In some ways, privatization and deregulation are opposite sides of the same coin. Privatization means the "opening up of the market" and the loosening of the rules (regulations) that are often the purview of the government. But privatization, at its core, is also the introduction of the profit motive into services that, at *their* core, are about protecting the human condition. A reliance on a neoliberal philosophy and free market economy means that we begin to evaluate everything through the lens of profit and cost benefit analyses. We abdicate the responsibility of the state to private companies and then feign surprise when those companies defer to the profit motive. . . . In addition to the increased preference for free markets and profits, privatization both reduces state responsibility for the care of its citizens and masks the lack of preparation of the government to care for its citizens that quickly develops. (Mitchell, 2001) (Bates & Swan, 2010, p. 442)

As you read and evaluate the policies and programs we have chosen, keep this argument in mind. Does it play out with the programs we discuss?

The second argument is that public programs may more likely focus on **suppression** (the social control of deviance), while private programs may more likely focus on rehabilitation and prevention.

In general, suppression policies are those that focus on the punishment and social control of behavior deemed deviant. **Rehabilitation programs** focus on groups or individuals who are deemed likely deviant and involve attempts to change this assumed deviant behavior. **Prevention programs** may be either focused on groups or individuals who are assumed to be more "at risk" for deviant behavior, or they may be focused on decreasing the likelihood of deviance in all groups equally. Many argue that there has been a buildup of suppression policies in the state and federal government at the expense of rehabilitation and prevention programs:

> From the recently repealed Rockefeller drug laws through the expansion of the prison systems in Texas and Florida, onto the increasingly punitive response to poverty in the Clinton years, and the continuing disparity in sentencing laws, states and the federal government have chosen the Iron State over the Golden State. And whatever arguments there may be about the relative effectiveness of imprisonment in affecting crime rates (a topic of great controversy amongst scholars and analysts), one thing seems certain: a policy that exacerbates the brutalization of society is not one that will make us safer. Investing in prisons means investing in institutions that produce neither goods nor new opportunities (aside from the limited jobs available for prison employees and the one-time opportunities in construction); money spent on imprisonment is money taken from rebuilding our worn out infrastructure, our schools, our communities, and our economic future. Insofar as corrections remains at the heart of our social policy—rather than as a supplemental or marginal support as it was throughout most of United States history—it is the Iron State stealing from the future of the Golden State. (Meranze, 2009, n.p.)

Finally, according to Barlow and Decker (2010, p. xi), "Policy ought to be guided by science rather than by ideology." As we have already briefly discussed, a central part of the scientific method is theory. Therefore, a book whose primary focus is a theoretical examination of deviance and social control should have as one of its central themes an examination of public policy from the viewpoint of each of these theories.

The reaction to deviance has often been spurred by interests well beyond science:

> The pen remains firmly in the hands of politicians and legislators, whose allegiance is less to the products of science—for example, how to deal with the AIDS pandemic, warnings about global warming, and the ineffectiveness of the Strategic Defense Initiative, or SDI (otherwise known as "Star Wars")—than to the whims of voters and the personal agendas of their counselors and financial supporters. (Barlow & Decker, 2010, pp. xi–xii)

This means the reactions to deviance have often focused on the stigmatization and criminalization of a variety of behaviors and in many instances on the harsh punishment of those behaviors.

We offer a wide variety of public policies, or "ideas in action," that were designed to address deviant behaviors. It will be your job to evaluate these programs and policies for their intents and subsequent success.

NOW YOU . . . USE YOUR SOCIOLOGICAL IMAGINATION

In his 1972 article, "The Poverty of the Sociology of Deviance: Nuts, Sluts, and Preverts," Liazos argues that the sociology of deviance focuses too much attention on individual idiosyncrasies and not enough attention on structural dynamics and the deviance of the powerful. The following graph is taken from a Web page from the U.S. Energy Information Administration (part of the Department of Energy) explaining the U.S. energy consumption for 2009. Following this chart is a section taken from the Environmental Protection Agency (also a federal agency) explaining the effects of fossil fuels on climate change.

Using your sociological imagination, how might you discuss the figures and text as an example of deviance? How might the relationship between the U.S. government, lobbyists, and oil companies affect the conversation around climate change? Pretend you are an oil executive: Which might be more deviant in your view, the breakdown of U.S. energy consumption or the research on climate change? Why? Now pretend that you are an oceanographer studying changes in the Gulf of Mexico or a zoologist studying polar bear migration: What might you define as deviant? Why? Would both groups define the same information as deviant? Do you consider either the breakdown of the U.S. consumption of energy or the discussion of climate change to be deviant? Why or why not?

Figure 1.2   U.S. Energy Consumption by Energy Source, 2009

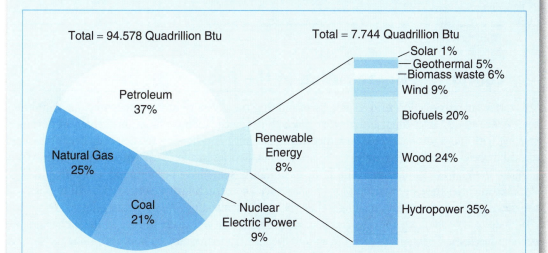

Source: U.S. Energy Information Administration, *Annual Energy Review 2009,* Table 1.3, Primary Energy Consumption by Energy Source, 1949–2009 (August 2010).

Note: Sum of components may not equal 100% due to independent rounding.

(Continued)

(Continued)

For over the past 200 years, the burning of fossil fuels, such as coal and oil, and deforestation have caused the concentrations of heat-trapping "greenhouse gases" to increase significantly in our atmosphere. These gases prevent heat from escaping to space, somewhat like the glass panels of a greenhouse.

Greenhouse gases are necessary to life as we know it, because they keep the planet's surface warmer than it otherwise would be. But, as the concentrations of these gases continue to increase in the atmosphere, the Earth's temperature is climbing above past levels. According to NOAA and NASA data, the Earth's average surface temperature has increased by about 1.2°F to 1.4°F in the last 100 years. The eight warmest years on record (since 1850) have all occurred since 1998, with the warmest year being 2005. Most of the warming in recent decades is very likely the result of human activities. Other aspects of the climate are also changing, such as rainfall patterns, snow and ice cover, and sea level.

If greenhouse gases continue to increase, climate models predict that the average temperature at the Earth's surface could increase from 3.2°F to 7.2°F above 1990 levels by the end of this century. Scientists are certain that human activities are changing the composition of the atmosphere, and that increasing the concentration of greenhouse gases will change the planet's climate. But they are not sure by how much it will change, at what rate it will change, or what the exact effects will be. (Environmental Protection Agency, 2011)

◈ Conclusion: Organization of the Book

We start your introduction to deviance by examining the diversity of deviance, how our definitions of deviance change over time, and how we research deviance. Then we focus on theories of deviance, starting with the traditional, positivist theories of deviance and moving to social constructionist and critical theories of deviance. We also try to present the theories in a fairly chronological manner. While all these theories are still in use in the study of deviance, some have been around longer than others. Positivist theories have been around longer than social constructionist theories, and, within positivist theories, anomie has been around longer than social disorganization. We think this offers you a general road map of how thinking and theories have developed about deviance. In each of these chapters, we present the classical versions of each theory and then the contemporary version, and, along the way, we explore several types of deviance that may be explained by each given theory. Finally, we examine our individual and societal responses to deviance and end with an exploration of global deviance, reactions, and social control.

This book has been written with a heavy emphasis on theory. We think you will agree as you read the book that theory is an important organizational tool for understanding (1) why deviance occurs, (2) why some behavior may or may not be defined as deviant, and (3) why some individuals are more likely to be defined as deviant. It is important to note that you probably won't have the same level of enthusiasm for every theory offered here. Some of you will really "get" anomie theory, while others might be drawn to labeling or feminist theory. Heck, we feel the same way. But what is important to remember is that *all* of these theories have been supported by research, and all help answer certain questions about deviance.

Along the way, we present examples of specific acts that may be considered deviant in both the research and pop culture. You will be introduced at the beginning of each chapter to a vignette that discusses a social phenomenon or behavior. As you learn more about theory, you can decide for yourself how and why these acts and actors may be defined as deviant. One of our goals for you is to help you start to think sociologically and theoretically about our social world and the acts we do and do not call deviant.

EXERCISES AND DISCUSSION QUESTIONS

1. Choose a behavior, action, or group that you consider to be deviant. Explain why you consider your example to be deviant and then explain which conception of deviant you are using when you make your determination.

2. Choose any half-hour sitcom. While watching the show, examine its treatment of "deviant" behavior. Is there a character that others treat as different or deviant? Why do others treat him or her this way? Is there a character that you would describe as deviant? Is he or she treated this way by others in the show? What conception of deviance are you using to determine the deviant behavior on the show?

3. Why is theory important to our understanding of deviance?

KEY TERMS

Critical conception

Folkways

Laws

Mores

Normative conception

Norms

Prevention programs

Rehabilitation programs

Relativist conception

Scientific method

Social constructionist conception

Sociological imagination

Suppression

Theory

CHAPTER 2

The Diversity of Deviance

What would you think if you were walking down the street and passed a man covered entirely in leopard spots? It would definitely make you look twice and would qualify as a deviant appearance. Would you wonder what he was thinking, how it felt to live within those spots, and why he would choose such a visible form of **body modification**? Tom Leppard once held the title of the most tattooed man in the world, with 99% of his body covered in tattooed leopard spots. For more than 20 years, Leppard lived as something of a hermit in a shack with no electricity or furniture on the Scottish island of Skye. Despite his solitary lifestyle, Leppard clearly enjoyed the attention of strangers, at least to some degree. He spoke of choosing his leopard appearance and his visible status: "I've loved every minute and when you're covered in leopard tattoos you certainly get noticed—I became a bit of a tourist attraction on Skye" (Irvine, 2008).

▲ Photo 2.1 What would you think if you were at the grocery store and ran into Tom Leppard, who has tattooed leopard spots over 99% of his body?

Source: ©Murdo McLeod/The Guardian.

◈ Introduction

Now that you've been introduced to the concept of deviance and the importance of understanding deviant behavior from a theoretical perspective, we want to spend some time exploring the various forms that deviance can take. When you think about deviance, what do you typically think about? Take a moment to quickly think of five types of deviant behavior. What immediately comes to mind? You probably came up with examples that reflect criminal behavior, such as drug dealing, assault, robbery, or homicide. These are quite common responses, especially given the way the media cover crime and deviance. Yet deviance is not always criminal in nature. Nor does it always reflect an act or a behavior. There is a much broader array of what constitutes deviance in our society. In short, deviance can take many forms.

In this chapter, we discuss the diversity and relativity of deviance and explore its many manifestations in American society. It is our hope that by introducing you to deviance in its varied forms, you'll gain a deeper understanding of its nature before we move on to learning about how deviance is researched (Chapter 3), explained (Chapters 4–10), and responded to in American society (Chapters 11–12) and in a global context (Chapter 13). This chapter on the different types of deviance is a good place to begin an analysis of the sociological field of deviance and the phenomena it investigates.

A chapter on types of deviance is difficult to write because deviance as a field of study is very subjective. Many textbooks offer a survey or overview of different types of deviant behavior, devoting entire chapters to such topics as **physical deviance**, **sexual deviance**, drug use, mental disorders, and corporate deviance. As authors of this text, we do not necessarily agree with those categories or characterizations of different behaviors, attitudes, and physical attributes as deviant. Rather than writing simply from our own points of view and trying to persuade you to adopt our perspectives, however, in this chapter we offer a glimpse into the field of deviance as it has been defined, studied, and treated throughout the years.

◈ Deviance and Its Varied Forms

While deviant behavior and crime certainly overlap, deviance encompasses much more than crime. Sociologists who have studied deviance have researched and written about a range of topics, including the disabled (E. Goffman, 1963), the mentally ill (Link, Phelan, Bresnahan, Stueve, & Pescosolido, 1999), the voluntarily childless (Park, 2002), the homeless (L. Anderson, Snow, & Cress, 1994), Jewish resisters during the Holocaust (Einwohner, 2003), topless dancers (Thompson, Harred, & Burks, 2003), bisexuals (Weinberg, Williams, & Pryor, 2001), anorexics and bulimics (McLorg & Taub, 1987), self-injurers (Adler & Adler, 2007), and gay male Christian couples (Yip, 1996), to name just a few. This research is in addition to the many studies of criminal deviance, too numerous to list here. You can get a sense of the range of deviant behavior and how it has been studied simply by exploring the contents of the academic journal that is devoted to this very topic: *Deviant Behavior*. In addition to this introductory chapter exploring the many forms of deviance, we include short summaries of recent research on different types of deviant behavior in each chapter of this book.

The diversity of deviance and how drastically norms and attitudes may change over time is attested to in research conducted by J. L. Simmons (1965), who, several decades ago, surveyed 180 individuals, asking them to "list those things or types of persons whom you regard as deviant." More than 250 different acts and persons were listed. The range of responses not only included expected items such as prostitutes, drug addicts, and murderers but also liars, Democrats, reckless drivers, atheists, the self-pitied, career women, divorcees, prudes, pacifists, and even know-it-all professors! The most frequent survey responses are listed in Table 2.1.

Imagine conducting a similar survey today. Which responses from this list might still occur with some frequency? Which might be less frequent? Whatever you imagined, there is little doubt that the list would look different today compared to 1965, reflecting the key point that what constitutes deviance changes depending on the historical context, something we discuss more later on in this chapter. For now, we want you to simply recognize the sheer range of deviance and its diversity.

Table 2.1   Most Frequent Responses to the Question, "What Is Deviant?"

Response	Percentage
Homosexuals	49
Drug addicts	47
Alcoholics	46
Prostitutes	27
Murderers	22
Criminals	18
Lesbians	13
Juvenile delinquents	13
Beatniks	12
Mentally ill	12
Perverts	12
Communists	10
Atheists	10
Political extremists	10

Source: Simmons (1965).

It would be nearly impossible to describe deviance in *all* its varied forms. Rather than try to provide an exhaustive list of the different realms of deviance, we have chosen to highlight a few to illustrate the broad spectrum of behaviors, attitudes, and characteristics that have been deemed deviant by at least some segments of the larger society.

THINKING LIKE A SOCIOLOGIST—STRICT CONFORMITY AS DEVIANCE

A student film, *55: A Meditation on the Speed Limit,* which can be viewed on YouTube (www.youtube .com/watch?v=1B-OxOZmVIU), illustrates a potential problem with strict conformity. In the 5-minute video, college students filmed an experiment where they managed to have cars in every lane of the freeway driving exactly the speed limit. This created a wall of traffic and frustrated drivers in the cars behind them, leading to visible road rage. Do you think strict conformity can also be a form of deviance? Why or why not? Can you think of other circumstances in which strict conformity might be considered deviant?

**Physical Deviance and Appearance:
Ideals of Beauty and Everyone Else**

Physical deviance is perhaps the most visible form of deviance, and it can evoke stereotypes, stigma, and discrimination. Sociologists have described two types of physical deviance: (1) violations of aesthetic norms (what people should look like, including height, weight, and the absence or presence of disfigurement) and (2) physical incapacity, which would include those with a physical disability (Goode, 2005).

Erving Goffman (1963) opens his book *Stigma* with a letter a 16-year-old girl wrote to Miss Lonelyhearts in 1962. The young girl writes about how she is a good dancer and has a nice shape and pretty clothes, but no boy will take her out. Why? Because she was born without a nose:

> I sit and look at myself all day and cry. I have a big hole in the middle of my face that scares people even myself. . . . What did I do to deserve such a terrible bad fate? Even if I did do some bad things, I didn't do any before I was a year old and I was born this way. . . . Ought I commit suicide? (reprinted in E. Goffman, 1963, first page)

As suggested by the letter to Miss Lonelyhearts, physical deviance may be viewed as a marker of other forms of deviance. In other words, passersby may notice people with numerous tattoos, heavily muscled female bodybuilders, or those with visible physical disabilities and may attribute other characteristics to those individuals. You may notice, for example, when talking to a person who is hard of hearing that others in the conversation may slow their speech considerably and use smaller words, as well as speaking louder than usual; this suggests an implicit assumption that the individual has difficulty understanding as well as hearing.

Our ideas of what is acceptable or desirable in terms of physical appearance vary widely depending on the context. You can get a sense of this by visiting a local museum or simply flipping through an art book showing paintings and photographs of women thought to be very beautiful in their time. From the rounded curves of the women painted by Peter Paul Rubens in the 1600s (which is where the term *Rubenesque* originated to describe an hourglass figure), to the very thin flappers considered ideal in the 1920s, to Marilyn Monroe in the 1950s, Twiggy in the 1960s, Cindy Crawford in the 1980s, Kate Moss in the 1990s, and Kim Kardashian in 2010, our ideals of beauty and the most-desired body types clearly change and evolve over time.

Along with professionally styled hair and makeup and the use of meticulous lighting and camera angles, editors can now touch up photographs to remove wrinkles and traces of cellulite and to make beautiful models' already thin limbs and waists trimmer and more defined. This is of concern to sociologists because setting a truly unattainable standard for the ideal physical appearance can lead to deviant behavior, including harmful eating disorders, such as anorexia nervosa or bulimia, or unnecessary plastic surgeries.

Another form of physical deviance is **self-injury**—cutting, burning, branding, scratching, picking at skin or reopening wounds, biting, hair pulling, and bone breaking. Adler and Adler (2007) found that most self-injurers never seek help from mental health professionals and that most of the self-incurred wounds do not need medical attention, thus the majority of self-injurers remain hidden within society. Why would anyone purposely hurt themselves? Adler and Adler explain the reasoning behind this:

maladaptive, our subjects overwhelmingly
. They claim that their behaviors provide
, depersonalization, racing thoughts, and
nse of control, reconfirms the presence of
e emotional pain into manageable physical

currently being "demedicalized"—shifted out of
deviance, characterized by the voluntary choice
licalization—or demedicalization—of deviance
hapter 11.
v viewed as a form of personal expression was
a small, liberal arts women's college. Kokaliari
ts in their survey—more than 50% of responding scratching themselves, cutting, burning,
l interviews with 10 of the college women and
cient, independent, and in control. Emotions
women described their use of self-injury as a
d allow them to continue being productive in

viance, body modification is the last example
oing, like Mr. Leppard from the opening story
inked leopard spots. It also includes piercings,
The reasons for body modification vary, but
Modification and view their physical changes
body, mind, and soul.
but the choice may not be respected by the
an girl, Ariana Iocono, was suspended from
school for wearing a small stud in her nose and thus violating the school's dress code, which forbids
piercings. The girl and her mother were members of the Church of Body Modification and claimed that
the nose ring was a religious symbol, but school administrators were unsympathetic, arguing that
Ariana had not met the criteria for a religious exemption (Netter, 2010).

DEVIANCE IN POPULAR CULTURE

A wide variety of deviance can be examined by paying careful attention to popular culture. Below are
a number of documentary films and television shows that offer concrete examples of specific cultural
norms, different types of deviant behavior, and how individuals cope with stigma. What messages about
norms and acceptable behavior are portrayed in each of these examples? What is the deviant behavior
in each film/episode? What does the reaction to the deviant behavior tell you about the larger culture?

(Continued)

(Continued)

Films

Devil's Playground—a documentary following four Amish teenagers through the experience of Rumspringa, during which they are given freedom to experience the outside world before deciding whether or not to commit to a lifetime in the Amish community.

Enron: The Smartest Guys in the Room—a documentary investigating white-collar crime and the greed that toppled what was once the seventh-largest corporate entity in the United States and left 20,000 employees without jobs.

Deliver Us From Evil—a documentary investigating sexual abuse within the Catholic Church. The focus is on Father Oliver O'Grady, a pedophile who sexually assaulted dozens of children.

Dark Days—a documentary featuring people living in the tunnels under the subway system in New York City; filmed in black and white, it shows how one segment of the homeless population built homes and a community under the city.

Television

Reality television and the TLC channel, particularly, feature a number of programs offering an inside view of people perceived as deviant or different in some way and showing how these people deal with stigma from various sources:

Little People, Big World—this program offers an inside view of the life of the Roloff family. The parents, Matt and Amy, are little people standing only four feet tall, and they are raising four children on a 34-acre farm.

Hoarders—an A&E series focusing on individuals whose hoarding of belongings has led them to the verge of personal disasters, including eviction, loss of their children, divorce, jail time, or demolition of their homes.

In paying attention to popular culture and how different subcultures and characteristics are portrayed, we can easily see that deviance is all around us.

◈ Relationships and Deviance

Sexually unconventional behavior is another central topic of discussion when it comes to deviance. As a society, we are generally intrigued with others' intimate relationships and sexual practices. Goode (2005, p. 230) asks, why are there so many norms about sexual behavior? And why are the punishments for violating sexual norms so severe? Concerning the first question, Goode rightly claims the ways that we violate mainstream society's norms by engaging in variant sexual acts are almost infinite. The realm of sexual deviance may include exotic dancers, strippers, sex tourism, anonymous sex in public restrooms, bisexuality, online sexual predators, prostitutes, premarital chastity, and many others. As with virtually every kind of deviance, sexual deviance is largely determined by the community, culture, and context.

Even within the United States, there is considerable disagreement about what sexual activities should and should not be allowed. The issue of gay marriage is one current example where community values are being tested and defined on political ballots across the country. Another example where context matters is prostitution. While considered a crime in most of the country, prostitution is legal in many areas of Nevada. Certain counties in Nevada are allowed to regulate and license brothels, a multimillion-dollar industry based on legalized prostitution.

While societal norms shape our conceptions of appropriate sexual behavior, those boundaries are regularly tested by new fads and businesses and by many different **subcultures** making up their own rules as they go along. The Ashley Madison Agency, for example, bills itself as the world's premiere discreet dating service; it is marketed to those who are married and wish to have affairs. The agency's slogan captures the intent succinctly: "Life is short. Have an affair." The Ashley Madison Agency courts publicity, advertising widely on billboards, in magazines, and on television commercials. Interested adults can go on the Web site and purchase the "Affair Guarantee" package; if they do not find a suitable partner within 3 months, they can get a refund. With over 7 million anonymous members, it is clear that there is widespread interest in relationships outside of marriage. The need for anonymity and discretion also suggests that there is still enough stigma attached to such relationships that it is preferable to shop for a partner before identifying oneself.

Polygamy is another frequently discredited form of relationship. In the United States, monogamy is the legal norm, yet some religions and subcultures still allow and encourage men to take multiple wives. The conflict between a subculture's values and the larger societal norms came vividly into play in 2008 when the state of Texas conducted a military-style raid on the Yearning for Zion Ranch, a polygamous religious sect of the Fundamental Church of Jesus Christ of Latter-day Saints.

Warren S. Jeffs, the leader of the Fundamental Church of Jesus Christ of Latter-day Saints, had been convicted a year earlier on felony charges as an accomplice to rape for his role in coercing the marriage of a 14-year-old girl to her 19-year-old cousin. When the raid on the Yearning for Zion Ranch took place, Jeffs was in the early phases of a 10-year-to-life sentence while awaiting trial on other sex charges in Arizona.

On the basis of an accusation of sexual abuse from an anonymous 16-year-old girl, SWAT teams raided the Yearning for Zion Ranch and forcibly removed more than 400 children from their homes and families. Texas child welfare officials believed that the children were in danger; they suspected young girls were being made into child brides, among other physical and sexual abuse occurring within the polygamous community.

This clash of cultures and values played out dramatically in the media. After being removed from their homes and the insular community in which they were raised, the children of the ranch were suddenly exposed to many strangers, different foods, varied styles of dress, and a new set of norms. When some of their mothers voluntarily left the ranch to be with the children, they were visibly out of their element in their prairie dresses and old-fashioned hairstyles, forced to move to the suburbs and shop at Walmart rather than tend to their gardens and livestock on the ranch.

▲ **Photo 2.2** Community members from the Yearning for Zion Ranch react after the state of Texas forcibly removed more than 400 children from their homes and families.

Source: ©Deseret Morning News/Getty Images.

In the end, the telephone calls that set the raid in motion may have been a hoax or a setup, but the damage was irreparably done. The children of the Yearning for Zion Ranch were returned to their parents approximately 2 months later, but the trauma inflicted on the families from such a forced separation could not be taken back. While this was clearly a difficult situation for everyone involved, it presents sociologically interesting questions about what is deviant and who gets to decide this. Those living at the Yearning for Zion Ranch were nearly self-sufficient and seemed to live quietly by their own rules and norms within its bounds. At what point do you think it would be appropriate for the state of Texas to step in and take the children away from their families? Who should ultimately decide? Who are the deviants in this case—the polygamous families or the state of Texas for breaking up those families and traumatizing a whole community? These are interesting and complex questions without easy answers, which is part of what makes deviance such a fascinating—and ever-changing—field of study.

◈ Deviance in Cyberspace: Making Up the Norms as We Go

One way to clearly see that our ideas about deviance and deviant behavior change over time is to consider the creation of whole new categories of deviant behavior. As new technology has developed, brand-new forms of deviance have also taken shape. Cyberdeviance, for example, is a relatively new phenomenon, but it already has many different forms, including the online pedophile subculture, cyberbullying, online misbehavior of college students, "sexting," and the illegal downloading of music, movies, and readings.

If such behavior is prevalent, particularly among younger people and hidden populations, should it still be considered deviant? That question is difficult to answer; norms and laws are being created and modified all the time, even as technology improves and offers new possibilities for deviant behavior.

RECENT STUDY IN DEVIANCE

Examining the Virtual Subculture of Johns

By Kristi R. Blevins and Thomas J. Holt, 2009, in *Journal of Contemporary Ethnography, 38,* 619–648.

An example of a deviant subculture that crosses the boundaries between cyberdeviance and criminal deviance is the online subculture of "johns," or male heterosexual clients of sex workers. In their qualitative study, Blevins and Holt (2009) explored Web forums in a number of U.S. cities in an attempt to identify the norms and values in the mostly hidden world of the client side of sex work. The authors analyzed Web forums where heterosexual johns shared questions and information while seeking to minimize exposure to law enforcement.

Blevins and Holt (2009) particularly focus on the "argot" or specialized language of the virtual subculture of johns, and they use extensive quotes to illustrate their points. Three themes related to argot emerged from their analysis. The first theme was "experience," which, among other things, categorized the johns across a hierarchy of novices or "newbies" to the more experienced "mongers, trollers, or hobbyists" (note that the derogatory term *john* was not used in the argot of the subculture). The second theme was "commodification"—the notion that the prostitutes themselves and the acts the johns wanted were a commodity that came with a cost. This issue raised a great deal of discussion over how much different prostitutes or different sexual acts were worth or likely to cost. Finally, a related theme of "sexuality," or the various sexual acts desired or experienced, was examined, along with the unique argot for a host of sexual activities. The language and subject matter are crude but offer a glimpse at the subcultural norms and values of these online communities or subcultures of johns.

◈ Subcultural Deviance

The virtual subculture of johns is just one example of many subcultures that might be considered deviant by at least some segment of the population. While the johns are generally a hidden population, as you can see from the earlier example of the Yearning for Zion Ranch, some subcultures are easily identifiable and can be singled out for holding different norms and values than the larger society. That case is particularly dramatic as children were taken from their parents and homes, but many other subcultures also draw strong reactions from the outside community.

Research on subcultures has been wide-ranging. Hamm (2004) studied terrorist subcultures, examining the "complex ways in which music, literature, symbolism and style are used to construct terrorism" (p. 328). Others have written about "fat admirers," men who have a strong, erotic desire for obese women (Goode, 2008b); radical environmentalist organizations (Scarce, 2008); and the subculture of UFO contactees and abductees (Bader, 2008).

The Amish are another example of a subculture, but the question of deviance becomes quite complicated—particularly during the time when Amish youth are encouraged to go outside of the community and explore the "English" way of life. In this case, some types of deviant behavior are sanctioned for a short time before the teenagers choose their adult path and decide whether to be baptized and become an Amish adult in good standing or basically be ostracized from their parents and communities.

Reiling (2002) conducted a study on Amish youths' response to culturally prescribed deviance that presents a number of complex questions. Old Order Amish believe in non-assimilation with the dominant culture, in-group conformity, and a very disciplined lifestyle. Yet Amish teenagers are expected to engage in deviant behavior in the rite of passage known as the "simmie" period when they explore the "English" lifestyle before choosing to either commit to their Amish culture or leave it forever. Reiling found that youth generally stayed in this decision-making period for 2 to 3 years, with 20 to 25% of youth in the settlement choosing to defect from the Amish, at which point they are excommunicated, cut off from their families, and ostracized. Even though Old Order Amish youth are encouraged to dabble in deviance, they are generally not able to do so openly. They must live between rules, and the question of what is deviant—and to whom—takes on a whole new meaning during this timeframe and in this context. Reiling reports that

> virtually every participant reported that they experienced social isolation during this time, which generated a high level of depression and anxiety. Amish youth are caught in a double bind because even though they are culturally mandated to explore their identity, they are granted very little room to do so openly. First, it is believed to be necessary to emotionally distance themselves from their parents to fully explore English identity. Second, the youth are forced to quit school when they turn 16. These conditions create the ironic consequence of Amish youth's becoming socially isolated from English youth and emotionally isolated from their Amish parents at a time when they are deliberating which of those two identities they will adopt. (pp. 155–156)

◈ Elite Deviance, Corporate Deviance, and Workplace Misconduct

Elite deviance is an important topic, but one that does not generally receive as much attention as the potentially more dramatic violent acts and property crimes ("street" crimes) that affect individuals on a personal level. While individuals tend to actively fear being victimized by street crimes, they probably do not realize the enormous impact elite deviance may have on their everyday lives. Mantsios (2010) offers a strong statement/indictment on how the corporate elite gain and maintain their status:

> Corporate America is a world made up of ruthless bosses, massive layoffs, favoritism and nepotism, health and safety violations, pension plan losses, union busting, tax evasions, unfair competition, and price gouging, as well as fast buck deals, financial speculation, and corporate wheeling and dealing that serve the interests of the corporate elite, but are generally wasteful and destructive to workers and the economy in general.
>
> It is no wonder Americans cannot think straight about class. The mass media is neither objective, balanced, independent, nor neutral. Those who own and direct the mass media are themselves part of the upper class. (pp. 240–241)

Elite deviance has been defined as "criminal and deviant acts by the largest corporations and the most powerful political organizations" (Simon, 2008, p. xi). In the introduction to his book on the topic, D. R. Simon (2008) explains that elite deviance refers to acts by elites or organizations that result in harm; he distinguishes between three different types of harm: physical harms, including death or physical injury; financial harms, including robbery, fraud, and various scams; and moral harms, which are harder to define but encourage distrust and alienation among members of the lower and middle classes (p. 35). Simon further breaks the topic of elite deviance down into three types of acts: economic domination, government and governmental control, and denial of basic human rights.

Bandura, Caprara, and Zsolnai (2000) explored corporate transgressions—the exercise and abuse of power closely linked to the legitimate conduct of business—through moral disengagement. Their study offers an interesting analysis of how corporations may adopt institutional practices that violate laws and harm the public. The authors briefly highlight four famous cases: an industrial disaster in Bhopal, India; the Ford Pintos that burst into flame on impact; Nestlé's selling of infant formula to developing countries—a practice that led to the malnutrition of babies in Third World countries; and the Three Mile Island case, the most severe accident in U.S. commercial nuclear power plant history. Unlike most elite deviance, these cases garnered widespread public attention and brought notice—at least temporarily—to harmful corporate practices. Bandura et al. identified a number of disengagement mechanisms that led to these tragic cases, including moral justification, euphemistic labeling, displacement of responsibility, diffusion of responsibility, disregarding consequences, dehumanization of those affected, and attribution of blame to others or circumstances outside of themselves. Bandura et al. (2000) concluded that

> what is informative in these cases is that the moral collusion can end in justifying actions whose outcomes continue to be disapproved. The belief system of the corporation may remain unaffected for a long time by practices that are detrimental to it as well as to the general public. Selective disengagement mechanisms are deployed to mask such a contradiction and to perpetuate harmful corporate practices. (p. 63)

A much more common and smaller-scale form of deviance is workplace deviance. Employee misconduct undoubtedly leads to business failures and higher consumer costs; studies estimate that as many as two-thirds of workers are involved in employee theft or other forms of employee deviance. Table 2.2 documents the percentage of employees taking part in the "invisible social problem" of workplace misconduct (Huiras, Uggen, & McMorris, 2000).

Table 2.2   Employee Deviance in the Previous Year

	Percentage Reporting Act
Got to work late without a good reason	51.0
Called in sick when not sick	47.9
Gave away goods or services	32.7
Claimed to have worked more hours than really did	9.7
Took things from employer or coworker	9.1
Been drunk or high at work	7.2
Lied to get or keep job	5.8
Misused or took money	2.5
Purposely damaged property	2.1

Source: Huiras, Uggen, and McMorris (2000).

◈ Positive Deviance

Even within sociology, there is some debate as to whether such a thing as positive deviance exists. Goode (1991), for example, believes that positive deviance is a contradiction in terms, or an oxymoron. Jones (1998) and others disagree. We encourage you to try the exercise on random acts of kindness in the "Now You . . ." box at the end of the chapter and compare your results with your classmates. In conducting your own small research project, you are addressing a research question (Does positive deviance exist?), collecting data (observing your own feelings and the reactions of others), and drawing conclusions. As a social scientist, what are your thoughts on positive deviance? Which side do you land on in the debate?

While the exercise on random acts of kindness gives you a chance to think about positive deviance on an individual level, scholars have recently been studying the idea of positive deviance at the organizational or corporate level. Spreitzer and Sonenshein (2004) define positive deviance as "intentional behaviors that significantly depart from the norms of a referent group in honorable ways" (p. 841). An example from Spreitzer and Sonenshein's article helps to clarify the concept:

> In 1978, Merck&Co., one of the world's largest pharmaceutical companies, inadvertently discovered a potential cure for river blindness, a disease that inflicts tremendous pain, disfigurement, and blindness on its victims. The medication was first discovered as a veterinarian antibiotic, but it quickly created a major dilemma for Merck when its scientists realized the medication could be adapted to become a cure for river blindness. Because river blindness was indigenous to the developing world, Merck knew that it would never recover its research or distribution expenses for the drug. In addition, the company risked bad publicity for any unexpected side effects of the drug that in turn could damage the drug's reputation as a veterinary antibiotic (Business Enterprise Trust, 1991). Departing from norms in the pharmaceutical industry, Merck decided to manufacture and distribute the drug for free to the developing world, costing the company millions of dollars. Consequently, Merck helped eradicate river blindness, at its own expense. (pp. 834–835)

Spreitzer and Sonenshein (2004) argue that Merck's action in this case is an excellent example of positive deviance. The organization faced great cost and risk to develop, manufacture, and distribute the drug, yet Merck chose to depart from corporate norms prioritizing profit and gains and, in doing so, prevented further suffering from river blindness.

Sometimes the line between positive deviance and crime is extremely hard to define. Edward Snowden, for example, is an individual who went against all corporate and government norms to expose thousands of top-secret government documents. His leaking of these documents was viewed by a former Central Intelligence Agency (CIA) deputy director as "the most serious compromise of classified information in the history of the U.S. intelligence community" (Reitman, 2013). Snowden was a reportedly brilliant high school dropout who began working as a computer technician with the CIA and became increasingly disturbed by "a continuing litany of lies from senior officials to Congress—and therefore the American people" (Reitman, 2013). Snowden eventually downloaded more than 50,000 documents and intelligence reports; he chose to become a whistleblower and outlaw when he leaked those documents to the press. Just two days after the first stories were printed, President Barack Obama admitted that the National Security Agency (NSA) was collecting enormous amounts of intelligence on ordinary citizens; two weeks later, the Obama administration brought criminal charges against Edward Snowden under the Espionage Act, and a number of U.S. officials labeled Snowden a traitor (Reitman, 2013). Snowden was granted temporary asylum in Russia, where he went into hiding. While demonized by the U.S. government, others consider Snowden a hero who risked his life to get the public vital information. History will ultimately be the judge of whether Snowden is remembered as an individual bravely practicing positive deviance for the greater good or a traitor committing crimes against his country.

▲ Photo 2.3   Would you consider the "Free Hugs" movement a form of positive deviance? Why or why not?

Source: http://www.flickr.com/photos/eelssej_/.

The idea of positive deviance is growing at the individual, organizational, and community levels, and new research continues to stretch the concept and add to our understanding of how this "oxymoron" may play out in everyday life. Tufts University even hosts its own Positive Deviance Initiative; the initiative takes the following as its starting point:

> Positive Deviance is based on the observation that in every community there are certain individuals or groups whose uncommon behaviors and strategies enable them to find better solutions to problems than their peers, while having access to the same resources and facing similar or worse challenges. (http://www.positivedeviance.org/)

◈ Explaining Deviance in the Streets and Deviance in the Suites: The Cases of Addiction, Prostitution, and Graffiti

When deciding whether an act or a characteristic is deviant, the social class and status of the actor(s) can make all the difference. Already in this book we have covered examples of elite deviance and what is colloquially referred to as "street" crime and deviance. Above, we considered corporate deviance versus workplace misconduct. A few other examples of street versus elite deviance—and the very different reactions they may receive—follow.

Addiction

Amy Winehouse famously sang about how "they tried to make me go to rehab," but she was one celebrity who declined treatment (saying "no, no, no"), and she tragically died at age 27, cutting short an incredibly promising musical career. Recently, it seems, more and more celebrities are choosing to go to rehab, checking themselves into treatment facilities for a variety of ailments, including addictions to prescription pills, alcohol, and cocaine. It is frequently reported that stars have checked into hospitals or treatment centers for personal and health reasons, with the details left to the imagination. The act of celebrities checking themselves into treatment has lost much of its stigma. While some stars, such as Lindsay Lohan, are sent to inpatient rehabilitation as part of a court order, celebrities who voluntarily choose inpatient treatment are often applauded for attempting to take control of their lives and work through their particular issues. They are fortunate that they have the resources to go to expensive facilities where their privacy and care is closely guarded. Poor and working-class addicts face a much different reality. Many local rehab centers work with community drug courts and jail and prison diversion programs, receiving clients that are sent to them through force rather than choice. A recent study focusing on rehab facilities with strong ties to drug courts, probation, and parole calls such institutions "strong-arm rehab" and identifies "a particular type of court-mandated rehabilitation emphasizing long residential stays, high structure, mutual surveillance, and an intense process of character reform. Strong-arm rehab also tends to be a highly racialized form, consistently linked to poor African American drug offenders" (Gowan & Whetstone, 2012, p. 70). There is nothing glamorous about these facilities; if the clients do not follow the treatment program, their lack of cooperation can lead to criminal sanctions. The treatment received by these addicts is very different than the treatment and response afforded to their celebrity counterparts.

Prostitution

Media images of prostitution range from the hardened streetwalker working the corner to the expensive and exclusive call girls working to satisfy their wealthy clients. While legal in some states, prostitution is generally a criminal act that draws both workers and clients from across the entire spectrum of social classes and cultures. The demand is high, and prostitutes and johns—or call girls and their clients, as the more upscale agencies may refer to them—can meet in many different ways, including through the use of a wide array of Web sites. One such Web site, SeekingArrangement.com, recently advertised a "college tuition sugar daddy," enticing heavily indebted college students to consider setting up profiles as "sugar babies" to arrange for them to have sex with older men to pay their bills. The founder of Seeking Arrangement estimates that 35% of his 800,000 members are students. The nearly 180,000 college sugar babies attend universities that include New York University, Harvard, UCLA, and University of Southern California (Fairbanks, 2012). Seeking Tuition (seekingtuition.com) is another Web site that specifically targets young women who are considering selling themselves to pay for their education; it promotes itself as "providing mutually beneficial arrangements to college girls and wealthy benefactors." Even as they trade sex for money, the college women looking for sugar daddies and using these Web sites generally resist the label and do not consider themselves prostitutes. They often lead two lives—keeping secret their identities as sugar babies for fear of being labeled and stigmatized as they continue their college educations and conforming careers. One young woman involved in a sugar daddy relationship explained her thoughts on her boundaries and her framing of her own identity:

> I'm not a whore. Whores are paid by the hour, can have a high volume of clients in a given day, and it's based on money, not on who the individual actually is. There's no feeling involved and the entire interaction revolves around a sexual act. . . . I don't engage with a high volume of people, instead choosing one or two men I actually like spending time with and have decided to develop a friendship with them. And while sex is involved, the focus is on providing friendship. It's not only about getting paid. (Fairbanks, 2012)

Graffiti

Why is defacing public property sometimes considered vandalism and sometimes considered art? Some graffiti writers set out to offend people in the community, viewing their practice as a key aspect of a rebel lifestyle and describing graffiti "as the space that allowed them to be the assholes they wanted to be" (Monto, Machalek, & Anderson, 2013, p. 273). Illegal graffiti can be viewed as a subcultural activity, offering risk and thrills to the graffiti writers. These writers often lead double lives, hiding their conventional identities behind their chosen graffiti tags (Campos, 2012). "Graffiti elders" such as Andrew "Zephyr" Witten continue wielding the spray paint can into middle age, balancing parenthood and conforming careers with the illicit thrills of "train-bombing," or illegally painting trains or other people's property (Ghosh, 2012). Yet some murals by graffiti writers have been heralded as public art, and British artist Banksy—described in *Smithsonian* magazine as "graffiti master, painter, activist, film-maker and all-purpose *provocateur*"—was named to *Time* magazine's list of the world's most influential people in 2010. The *Smithsonian* article describes Banksy's remarkable success as an "upward trajectory from the outlaw spraying—or, as the argot has it, 'bombing'— walls in Bristol, England, during the 1990s to the artist whose work commands hundreds of thousands of dollars in the auction houses of Britain and America" (Ellsworth-Jones, 2013). Even as his fame and fortune has grown, Banksy has worked hard to remain anonymous, continuing to create memorable street art both in public spaces and in formal art exhibits around the world. When should we consider graffiti a criminal act and a public nuisance and when should we think of it as art? Is Banksy deserving of his success? Will any of today's young graffiti writers have the same kind of artistic success? At what point does the transition from vandal to celebrated artist occur?

▲ **Photo 2.4** Why is graffiti sometimes considered art and sometimes considered vandalism? Which would you consider this piece by Banksy to be? Why?

Source: © jvdwolf/istockphoto.

◈ Ideas in Action: Guerrilla Gardening in Low-Income Areas

Ron Finley has gained fame for his crusade to plant edible gardens in urban areas, allowing those living in low-income communities access to fresh vegetables and produce. He helped to found LA Green Grounds (http://lagreengrounds.org/), a nonprofit volunteer group with the tagline, "Growing, working, teaching: changing turf into edible gardens in South Los Angeles."

Finley's work began when he planted a community garden in the narrow strip of land between the sidewalk and the curb in front of his house in Crenshaw, California. As his organic tomatoes, onions, peppers, and eggplants grew, he garnered attention from both neighbors and the city. The strip of land in front of his house is known as a "parkway"; parkways are managed by the city, and Finley's garden was in violation of city regulations. Finley chose to challenge the rules, and he mobilized the community and the media to support his cause. Los Angeles officials backed off and opened the door to the growth of urban farming.

Finley gave a dynamic, challenging, and inspiring TED talk in 2013 that quickly gained over 1.5 million views (http://www.ted.com/talks/ron_finley_a_guerilla_gardener_in_south_central_la.html). In it, he paints a vivid picture of living in a food desert, an area where there are plenty of liquor stores, fast food restaurants, and vacant lots, but little access to healthy foods. He claims that Los Angeles owns 26 square miles of vacant lots, which he suggests is enough space to plant 700 million tomato plants.

▲ **Photo 2.5**   Ron Finley has challenged people to be "gangster gardeners" and to grow edible gardens in urban areas.

Source: © youngvet/istockphoto.

"It's like my gospel: I'm telling people, grow your own food. Growing your own food is like printing your own money."

Finley calls on audience members to become "ecolutionaries, renegades, gangsters, gangster gardeners," to pick up shovels. Finley sees gardens as a tool for transformation. He asserts that gardening is "the most therapeutic and defiant act you can do—especially in the inner cities." He believes young people want to work, and that kids can be taken off the streets and trained to "take over their communities and have a sustainable life." He wants to "flip the script on what a gangster is . . . if you ain't a gardener, you ain't gangster. Get gangster with your shovel and let that be your weapon of choice."

A 2013 *New York Times* story allowed Finley to share his vision for the future: "I want to plant entire blocks of vegetable beds. . . . I want to turn shipping containers into healthy cafes where customers can pick their salad and juice off the trees. I want our inner-city churches to become ministries of health instead of places that serve up fried, fattening foods. I want to clean up my yard, my street and my 'hood."

Finley and his LA Green Grounds organization are another example of positive deviance—they are acting altruistically and outside of the norms. They have challenged city regulations about the use of parkways and vacant lots. and they are literally transforming low-income areas of Los Angeles from the ground up, providing healthy activities and organic food for community members.

Sources: Gunther, A. (2011, October 3). Hochman, D. (2013, May 3).

NOW YOU . . . TRY AN EXPERIMENT IN POSITIVE DEVIANCE!

One way to explore the idea of positive deviance is to conduct your own small-scale experiment and then decide whether you think positive deviance exists. For this exercise, your task is to go out and commit random acts of kindness—arguably a form of positive deviance.

Many introductory sociology classes ask students to conduct a breaching experiment by breaking a norm and then observing the reactions of those around them. In this case, the goal is to perform a face-to-face act of kindness for a *stranger* and to take note of the reaction to your behavior.

Think about the following questions in completing your act(s) of kindness (you may find it helpful, necessary, or interesting to repeat the act more than once):

1. Why did you choose to do this particular act of kindness?

2. How did you feel while doing the random act of kindness and why do you think you felt this way?

3. How did the recipient—and any others who witnessed the kindness—react? Speculate as to why they reacted the way they did. If the situation was reversed, do you think you would have reacted differently?

Be safe and smart in your choice of kindnesses—be careful not to inflict trauma on yourself or the recipient and be certain that you do not put yourself in a dangerous position. After conducting your experiment, reflect on how you felt and what the reactions to your act of kindness were. Did you take age or gender into consideration in choosing your "target"? Did you feel the need to explain that your act was an experiment or assignment for class? Based on this data, do you think positive deviance exists? Why or why not?

Source: Adapted from Jones (1998).

◈ Question: So Who Are the Deviants? Answer: It Depends on Who You Ask

We cannot emphasize enough how much context matters in any discussion or explanation of deviant behavior. You simply can't discuss forms of deviance without some reference to culture, context, and historical period. What some people regard as deviant, others regard as virtuous. What some might praise, others condemn. To say that deviance exists does not specify which acts are considered deviant by which groups in what situations and at any given time.

◈ Conclusion

We hope that after reading this chapter—and delving further into this book—your ideas about deviant behavior and social control will have greatly expanded. The more commonly studied types of deviant behavior, such as criminal deviance (including street crime) and elite deviance (including corporate and white-collar crimes), are explored further throughout the book. Our goal in this chapter is simply to help broaden your understanding of what constitutes deviance and to realize the question, "What is deviance?" must be followed by the qualifier, "According to whom?" We realize that this chapter and this book will not resolve these issues for you and may very well raise more questions than answers. Still, our goal is to broaden your understanding of deviance and its many forms.

With that goal in mind, we provide a few extra exercises and discussion questions in this chapter to help you explore boundaries, conduct your own experiments, form your own analyses, and begin to think about deviance and social control very broadly. Chapter 3 delves much more specifically into the art and science of researching deviance—you'll soon see that deviance is a very interesting topic to study and research. For now, we hope you will take a close look at the norms and behavior of your community and the larger society; we think you will soon discover an enormous amount of diversity in the deviance that is all around you.

EXERCISES AND DISCUSSION QUESTIONS

1. Look again at Table 2.1, compiled by Simmons in 1965. Give several friends or family members the same instruction that Simmons used, "List those things or types of persons whom you regard as deviant," and compile the responses. Do any of the categories from your small study overlap with those that Simmons found? Do any of the categories from 1965 disappear entirely? How would you explain this?

2. Pay attention over the next 24 hours and see what kinds of deviant behavior you notice. It can be behavior you witness, you commit (hopefully nothing that will get you in trouble!), or you hear about on the news or media. What did you notice? How many different types of deviance were you exposed to in one day?

3. To explore the idea of stigma and how a physical trait can deeply affect an individual's life, you might try imagining a day with a disability. This exercise will begin with a diary entry: Record a typical day (e.g., what you did, the interactions you had, etc.), and then assign yourself a visible attribute typically associated with deviance (e.g., being blind, obese, missing a limb). Rewrite your diary entry to reflect what you imagine would be different that day given your stigma. What obstacles would you face? Would people treat you differently? What did you learn about deviance, social norms, stigma, and coping by completing this exercise?

4. In a recent example of a polygamous lifestyle, the reality television show *Sister Wives* portrays a polygamist family and begins at the point where the husband is courting his fourth wife. His motto is, "Love should be multiplied, not divided." Do you think this kind of polygamy—where the relationships are consensual and the brides are all adults—is deviant? Why or why not?

KEY TERMS

Body modification

Elite deviance

Physical deviance

Polygamy

Positive deviance

Self-injury

Sexual deviance

Stigma

Subcultures

CHAPTER 3

Researching Deviance

THREE RESEARCH-RELATED STORIES FROM THE AUTHORS

Story 1

I was working as an interviewer on a longitudinal research project to evaluate a treatment program for people with cocaine-related problems. This was a relatively small, experimentally designed project, and there were only two interviewers (me male, the other female). The participants were paid to complete the interviews, and the treatment was free. The interview instruments were somewhat complex, and certain items had to be carefully worded and the responses carefully recorded. So, periodically, the interviewers would work in conjunction to assess reliability. I had already interviewed one male program participant at several time points when the other interviewer and I decided to do the interview together. The female interviewer was quite attractive and seemed to elicit far more positive responses (e.g., "Yes, I have used cocaine in the past month") than did I in our previous encounters. There are many possible explanations, but one obvious interpretation is that the participant realized he could get through the interview quicker with me and get paid his nominal fee by responding "no" to certain items (i.e., if he answered "yes," then a slew of questions followed). Getting the interview over with quickly didn't seem to be an issue when my attractive female colleague was asking the questions.

Story 2

I am currently working on a project in which my colleague and I are examining the effect of policing practices on individuals and the community. Specifically, we are interested in finding out how civil gang injunctions affect alleged gang members, their families and friends, and the community in which the injunction is enacted. Before we are allowed to start interviewing participants, we must submit and be approved by our university **institutional review board** (IRB; **human subjects** review).

(Continued)

(Continued)

Given our population—alleged gang members and their families and friends—the IRB process has raised many questions. The IRB is designed to make sure that participants are not harmed (psychologically, emotionally, or physically) by participating in a research study. While our study is not designed to ask questions about deviant or criminal behavior, given our potential **sample**, the IRB committee is very focused on the likelihood that our subjects might discuss their criminal behavior. What are the safeguards we have in place to protect the subjects? What are the safeguards we have in place to protect the community? What are we obligated to report should our subjects discuss deviant behavior?

Story 3

Ethnographers necessarily have a special relationship with data—we're immersed in it and interact continually with the people and places that we study. I have chosen to do most of my research in prisons and juvenile correctional facilities; this kind of work is certainly not as dangerous as researching crack dealers or gang members on the streets, but it does present its own challenges. You have to follow all of the rules of the institution, of course, always remembering that security is the first priority for staff members and administrators. You have to build trust with inmates, which can take time, patience, and an open mind. And you have to set clear boundaries for yourself and your research. Getting too close may compromise the research and your access to the institution. The hardest and most important lesson that I have learned in doing this kind of research is to find a way to keep emotional distance between myself and the people in the institution. There are people in prisons and juvenile facilities that have worked hard for second chances that they may never get. I get to know some very likable people who will never have the opportunity for a better life. These are difficult truths to accept, but as my wise advisor reminded me, as a researcher, I'm not where the action is in their lives, nor should I be. I can witness the process, share their stories, and analyze the system, but I probably can't make things substantially better or drastically change the life chances of any one individual. Once I was able to accept this painful reality, it got easier to take a step back and do my job as a researcher and a sociologist—giving others on the outside a chance to learn about and understand prison culture.

◈ Introduction

On one hand, studying deviant behavior is exciting, intellectually and practically rewarding, and often quite fun. On the other hand, studying deviance can be stressful, heart wrenching, and plagued with difficulties that are extremely challenging to grapple with. Serious researchers must be armed with numerous tools necessary to help deal with problems encountered in the study of behaviors that are often shielded from public purview and/or forced underground by mainstream society. Researchers must also be cognizant of the ethical issues that plague the investigation of deviance. First, researchers must be aware that their influence on individuals through, for example, an experiment can have purely unintended consequences. Second, simply studying the attitudes and beliefs of people can be problematic because holding deviant attitudes and beliefs can be costly to individuals even if they never act on them. Indeed, we all probably hold certain attitudes and beliefs we would not like other people to know about. In this chapter, we discuss various issues that confront researchers of deviance and strategies to overcome those difficulties. Not all hurdles surrounding a full understanding of issues related to deviance can be overcome, but we argue that through persistence and the use of multiple methods, almost invariably a better understanding of deviance can be achieved.

The stories provided above by each of the authors of this book offer insights into several problems associated with researching deviance. The first story brings up issues of measurement and how different interviewers may elicit different responses from subjects. Research has shown that when conducting interviews, good interviewers can get almost anyone to discuss their deviant behavior, attitudes, and beliefs if they can get the subject to feel comfortable. However, a number of factors—most of which are unknown—will affect how good the information is that is collected. For example, in the first story related earlier, we suggested that the "attractive" woman was better able to get the respondent to talk, truthfully or not. However, it could have been that the respondent had simply recently relapsed and felt the need to talk about it. The male interviewer might have elicited the same or very similar responses. The story also relates to the utility and potential problems of paying respondents for their interview time. Although paying respondents for their time is relatively commonplace today, there are many who have advocated against the practice (e.g., Fleisher, 1995).

The second story introduces the existence of human subjects institutional review boards (IRBs), which are a part of virtually all universities and research organizations. IRBs are developed in an effort to protect human subjects, researchers, and the university or organization. Working with an IRB can be a painful process, and they can literally squelch research; alternatively, they can be very helpful in thinking through the research process, and their questions and recommendations can actually make a research project better. We discuss human subjects and the IRB process in detail toward the end of the chapter.

The third story makes us critically aware that studying those who may be considered deviants—be they criminals, "street" people, or persons with severe illnesses such as AIDS—can be tremendously disturbing emotionally. Recognizing that there is often very little we can do to help deserving people is not easy. Furthermore, becoming emotionally involved with those we study, while not necessarily a bad thing, may be a slippery slope: it can lead to a loss of objectivity and potentially damage relationships with institutions or gatekeepers to the research. Although we may not be able to make drastic changes in a person's life, sometimes talking about one's life can be a rewarding experience, especially for those isolated from society. We return to these types of issues when we discuss field research (in particular, qualitative fieldwork) later in this chapter.

Methodological Approaches to Studying Deviance

Experiments in the Study of Deviance

Experiments have been called the "gold standard" for determining causal relationships in the social sciences. In a true experimental design, subjects are randomly assigned to one of two or more conditions that are thought to affect some outcome, usually a behavior. Random assignment ensures that any differences following the intervention or "experimental" stimulus must have been caused by the intervention.

▲ **Photo 3.1** Experiments are the gold standard for determining causal relationships, but are often difficult in the study of deviance.

Source: ©alexey_ds/istockphoto.

For example, Maass, Cadinu, Guarnieri, and Grasselli (2003) were interested in whether men exposed to an identity threat (e.g., exposure to a fictitious feminist versus traditional female interaction) might be more influenced to engage in sexual harassment as measured by sending pornography to a fictitious female through the computer when instigated by another fictitious male (he was supposedly sending porn and encouraging the subject to do so as well). So, in this case, participating males were randomly assigned to one of two conditions. The experimental subjects were presented with an interaction shown to act as an identity threat in previous studies (interaction with a female with a strong feminist stance) and then were encouraged by a confederate to send pornography to a fictitious female. The males in the control group were presented with an innocuous stimulus (interaction with a female with "traditional" gender values) and then encouraged to send porn to the traditional female confederate. The results of the experiment were consistent with the notion that threatening males' identity can lead to a heightened risk of engaging in a particular form of deviance—sexual harassment.

Studies such as the one described earlier are praised because of the high level of internal validity. That is, the subjects are randomly assigned, and the only difference between conditions is planned, controlled, and carried out consistently by the researcher. Hence, no other factor should explain the higher levels of sexual harassment in the experimental condition. Alternatively, such studies are often criticized because of concerns with external validity—that is, to what extent the results can be applied to other contexts, particularly "the real world." So, for example, in the sexual harassment study, the experimental subjects were encouraged by a fictitious confederate who was also sexually harassing the supposed/hypothetical victim. The results suggest that identity threats may increase sexual harassment but only in conditions where the potential victim is anonymous (no face-to-face or verbal contact) and there is considerable pressure from peers to engage in the deviant activity. Given the availability of pornography on the Internet, the situation is obviously possible, but the experiment was clearly contrived and may not be likely to occur in natural settings.

DEVIANCE IN POPULAR CULTURE

The documentary *Quiet Rage: The Stanford Prison Experiment* depicts one of the most famous and disturbing experiments in the history of psychology, deviant behavior, and social control. In 1971, Professor Philip Zimbardo set out to answer the question, "What happens when you put good people in an evil place?"

In an elaborate setup, Zimbardo and colleagues converted part of the basement of the Stanford psychology department into a simulated jail, complete with cells, solitary confinement ("the hole"), and standardized uniforms for both the prisoners and guards.

Zimbardo and colleagues recruited psychologically healthy male college students to participate in the study; individuals were randomly assigned to be either a guard or a prisoner. The experiment was planned to run for 2 weeks but was ended after only 6 days amid grave concerns about the psychological damage incurred by both prisoners and guards.

Watch the film and consider the following questions:

1. What are the ethical considerations that emerged from the Stanford Prison Experiment? What are the potential problems with doing a study like this? The young men agreed to participate in the study and were compensated as agreed upon—what other responsibilities do researchers have to their subjects?

2. Do you think it would be possible to have learned the information garnered from the study in any other way? Why or why not?

3. Do you think the same patterns found in the Stanford Prison Experiment exist in real prison settings? Why do you think as you do?

Problems with true experimental designs have led to a host of "not quite experimental designs" referred to as quasi-experiments (Campbell & Stanley, 1963). The breadth of these designs precludes a thorough discussion in this chapter. Suffice it to say that quasi-experimental designs, in general, lose points in terms of internal validity; the requirement of true random assignment is often relaxed. Alternatively, in many cases, external validity is enhanced—that is, oftentimes, quasi-experiments move to less contrived environments that may have more validity.

For example, suppose you are interested in examining the effectiveness of a school-based drug prevention program. You find two junior high schools that are interested, but you realize that you cannot randomly assign students in the schools to receive the intervention because the nature of the intervention needs to be in a particular type of class (e.g., health education), and it would be impossible to move students between the two schools. Furthermore, you suspect that even if you could move students around, they may come back to their home school and share what they had learned with control students, thus contaminating the manipulation. So the only real way to do this is to assign one school to the intervention and let the other be the control (you may even offer the control school to have the intervention a year or so later if they will participate in the research). The problem, of course, is that the schools may be quite different in terms of faculty and resources, and the student body may be quite different in terms of demographics, exposure to risk factors for drug use, and actual proclivity to use drugs. Still, you may have a relatively large sample from each school to compare. In addition, you can do pretests in both schools to assess those differences and statistically adjust for those differences.[1] While still problematic, this may be a useful starting point and is actually a fairly common problem/solution in the prevention literature.

Another form of quasi-experiment useful in the study of crime and deviance takes advantage of "naturally occurring" events. For example, researchers might compare rates of "deviance" before and after a major event such as a natural disaster (e.g., Hurricane Katrina) or some other social or legal change (e.g., the implementation of a new law or policy). These types of studies can inform both theory and policy. For example, recently Chamlin (2009) theoretically considered the impact of a 2001 race riot in Cincinnati as a potential event to examine consensus or functionalist perspectives versus conflict theory explanations (see Chapter 9). The race riot emerged following the shooting and killing of Timothy Thomas, a 19-year-old black man who was wanted for several nonserious, nonviolent crimes, such as loitering and not wearing a seat belt (Chamlin, 2009, p. 545). In the prior 6 years, 15 other black males had been killed by the Cincinnati police—no whites had been killed by police during this time. Subsequently, and as a direct result of the shooting, 3 days of riots ensued. Chamlin thought that, from a conflict perspective (see Chapter 9), the riots might result in a heightened crackdown on robbery, which is a crime particularly more highly interracial than most crimes. Through a sophisticated statistical analysis, he showed that the riots (a challenge to authority) resulted in significantly higher levels of arrests for robbery. Although there are numerous challenges to Chamlin's interpretation, he supplemented his analyses in a variety of ways and provided unique insights into conflict and consensus perspectives.

Although policy recommendations might be gained from Chamlin's research, his focus was primarily theoretical. In contrast, in a recent article published in *Criminology and Public Policy*, Kovandzic, Vieraitis, and Boots (2009) analyzed state-level data from 1977 to 2006 to examine the impact of changes in death penalty policy, as well as actual executions, on rates of homicide. The objective was to assess the deterrent effect of having the potential of the death penalty, as well as the use of the death penalty, on homicide. The researchers used data from all U.S. states that remained stable in regard to the death penalty and from those that changed their policies at different times and executed offenders at different rates at different times, creating a very persuasive test for or against the deterrent effect of the death penalty. Employing advanced statistical models, the authors concluded that there is no deterrent effect of the death penalty and that while policymakers can still support the practice based on retribution or other philosophical justifications, they should not justify killing offenders on the basis of a deterrent effect. As the reader can imagine, this is controversial research, and in the same issue of the journal, responses from other highly regarded researchers in the field are provided. The point is, however, that quasi-experimental designs can be quite rigorous and useful, especially when true experimental manipulation is impossible, illegal, or unethical, as in the case of much research on deviance.

In conclusion, although experimental and quasi-experimental designs have a long history in the sociological study of deviance, they are fairly rare compared to other research designs. Alternatively, there appear to be more and more experimental and quasi-experimental designs being conducted in criminology and criminal justice—hence the new publication of the *Journal of Experimental Criminology*, which began in 2005. Not all but much of this research focuses on prevention, early intervention, or treatment programs for criminals, juvenile delinquents, or at-risk youth rather than on the etiology of deviance. Research on deviance is often descriptive or correlational, focused on factors associated with how deviance is distributed across different groups or factors thought to be causes or consequences of deviance. We now turn to other research designs more common among studies of deviance.

Large-Scale Survey Research

If experimental designs are the "gold standard" for determining causality, then survey research might be considered a "gold mine" of information for the student of deviance. Ever since Kinsey and his colleagues' work in the 1930s and 1940s on human sexuality (something many believed one couldn't or shouldn't ask about), literally thousands of studies have used survey research techniques to better understand deviant behavior and its correlates—that is, how deviance is distributed across individual, social, and environmental conditions.

We assume that most readers are familiar with various forms of survey research. In fact, we are all literally bombarded with surveys, be they via phone, mail, or the Internet. We are queried by political scientists about who we will vote for; by sociologists about our family and household characteristics; by economists regarding our employment, income, and expenditures; and, of course, by businesses, which are interested in what we are attracted to buying. So we will briefly discuss a few things that scientific surveys attempt to do and how, and then we examine the role that surveys have played in a better understanding of deviance, as well as some of the limitations of survey research.

In general, for students of deviance, survey research involves asking a *sample* of a *target population* questions about their behaviors, attitudes, values, and beliefs. The two italicized words in the previous sentence bear some consideration. A target population is all units in some universe. The target population could be almost anything—for example, all adult residents of the United States in 2012, all fifth-grade students in a particular school district in a particular academic year, or all homeless families staying in homeless shelters between 9 P.M. and 8 A.M. in New York City on December 25, 2012. A sample simply refers to a subset of the target population. When dealing with people, it is usually quite difficult (if not impossible), time-consuming, and expensive to survey an entire target population. Unless one wished to define the target population, for example, as students who show up on time to an Introduction to Sociology class on Wednesday at 1:30 P.M., October 5, 2012, things tend to get tricky, and generally we are more interested in generalizing to larger populations. Generally, when people survey students in courses, we refer to the outcome as a convenience sample—indicating, perhaps, that the class is composed of many different kinds of students since most students take "intro soc" and "may reflect" the population of undergraduates, or at least freshmen and sophomores. Of course, in reality, we wish that the sample reflected an even larger population (e.g., the United States), but that is not very likely. Note that this is not a problem solely of survey research. Many experimental studies, especially in psychology, are studies of how manipulations affect college students because they are a convenient population but very different in many ways from the general population.

Survey researchers usually want a representative sample of the target population so that the sample provides a smaller but accurate description of the population and the researchers can use statistical procedures to generalize to the larger population. There are many ways of obtaining a representative sample, but the simplest in some ways is a random sample. Unfortunately, garnering a random sample generally requires having data on the entire population so that a sample can be drawn from that population. That is, everyone in the population has an equal chance of being surveyed, although only a subset is actually drawn. Thus, for the social scientist, *random* has a very specific meaning that doesn't sound very "random" to the layperson who might think "randomly approaching potential respondents in a mall" to be collecting a random sample. Such an approach produces *anything but* a random sample to the social scientist.

Suffice it to say that there are many strategies for surveying samples of large populations, but it is still an expensive process and usually conducted by large research agencies with considerable funding. Even well-funded projects have problems drawing adequate samples that are representative of the target population and often have to oversample certain populations that are hard to access. For example, most phone surveys of adults we have been involved in result in an older, more female sample and sometimes samples that over-reflect certain racial groups. It is likely that these groups are more likely to have adults at home, to have a home phone, and to be willing to answer a call and respond to the survey.

Hence, a major concern for social scientists is the response rate and how that might affect the results of a survey. If the response rate is low, the sample may still reflect the population, but this is highly unlikely and would occur only if the various demographic groups were equally likely to respond and those who responded versus those who did not respond were similar in all respects related to the study. Of course, this is highly unlikely, especially in the study of deviant behavior, where some may be less willing to provide information, especially to certain types of investigators (see Pruitt, 2008).

A somewhat related concern involves the appropriate sample size. To address many questions, relatively small samples (e.g., 100–200 cases and sometimes even much smaller) may be more than sufficient, and, of course, much qualitative research will use only a few subjects. Garnering enough cases to obtain a nationally representative sample of registered voters' attitudes toward a presidential candidate, or even their opinion on "deviant issues" such as abortion, pornography, or fear of being a victim of crime, may take a thousand or more cases. Indeed, the General Social Survey of the United States, which has been conducted since 1972, includes about 1,500 cases at each time point. Using a sample like this, we would feel quite confident in describing how the American population stands on various issues and how these attitudes and beliefs vary across groups and with other social variables. This is because the issues that surveys address are generally fairly common, and a significant proportion of the population is willing to express attitudes and beliefs about the subject. Alternatively, when events are very rare, much larger samples are required to garner enough respondents to accurately describe the population and how its members vary across subgroups. For example, contrary to popular belief, serious victimization (e.g., rape, robbery, aggravated assault) is fairly rare, and so the National Crime Victimization survey requires approximately 12,000 respondents at each sampling. Similarly, studies such as the Monitor the Future project, which focuses on involvement in serious drug use, including cocaine, heroin, and methamphetamine use among children and young adults, now includes approximately 50,000 respondents annually.

Field Research: Pure Observer to Full Participant

Field research, too, can be a gold mine for investigating various forms of deviance and especially deviant groups and subcultures. *Field research* is a term that brings to mind the anthropologist immersing himself or herself into some foreign, perhaps indigenous, society and learning the language, customs, beliefs, and behaviors of its members. Or the researcher of a religious cult who feigns being a believer and observes others, always under the dangerous possibility that his or her identity will be revealed and he or she will, at best, be alienated from the study site or, worse, physically harmed or even killed. These are of course examples of real cases of fieldwork, but in our perspective, *fieldwork* is a more generic term, with several dimensions and polar extremes. True, the term clearly delineates fieldwork practices from the large-scale mail, phone, or Internet surveys that are indicative of much social survey research. Alternatively, at one polar end, we might include as field research going into a school district or a neighborhood and systematically surveying students/residents, even with short, close-ended survey questions about deviance. On the other extreme, taking a job as a stripper to better understand—indeed, truly empathize with—what the lives of these women (and men) are like and the social structures and relations that dictate a major part of their lives is more likely to be viewed as field research. So to some extent, unless one is studying the deviance of college students actually in the classroom, field research more generally means getting outside the "ivory tower"—getting one's hands dirty, so to speak—to better understand some form of deviance, be it behavior, attitudes, or beliefs.

Excluding our more structured example of handing out surveys to students, two types of field-work are sometimes viewed as two points on a continuum between pure observation and participant observation. Before distinguishing the two, it is important to recognize that both strategies typically involve extensive observation and recording of those observations. Historically, this has been done primarily in written form, although audio recording in various formats has been around for a long time.

Let's start with pure observations, which would theoretically entail observing people not only with them not knowing the researcher is observing them but also with them not observing the researcher whatsoever. Of course, this can be done; one can look through a peephole, through a one-way mirror, or down at a place of social interaction, such as observing a park from a higher building. A study at one of the author's universities involved simply sitting at various intersections and documenting the running of red lights (Porter & England, 2000) and various characteristics of drivers and automobiles associated with the transgressions. Another study at one our universities studied hand-washing behavior (or lack thereof) in public restrooms. This was about as close as it comes to pure observation, although usually it was clear that someone was in the stall doing something (Monk-Turner et al., 2005).

A recent study by McCleary and Tewksbury (2010) used an almost pure observation strategy to study female patrons of sexually oriented book-video-novelty stores in three major counties in California over a 2-year period. Trained researchers observed 33 stores and the customers who entered them, with a total of 271 observation periods spanning 162 hours. The researchers were trained to remain as unobtrusive as possible. McCleary and Tewksbury wrote that

> working from a common protocol, researchers observed customers from at least 250 feet away for 30 consecutive minutes. Researchers were allowed to break the 30-minute rule if necessary. Observation ended before 30 minutes in approximately 20 percent of the trials and lasted longer than 30 minutes in 60 percent of the trials. In every instance, researchers cited the need to remain unobtrusive as the rationale for breaking the 30-minute rule. (p. 212)

The authors found that women were much more likely than men to come to sexually oriented businesses with other females (46%), in mixed-sex groups (22%), or as a male–female couple (15%). In contrast, men were most likely to come alone (76%) or in same-sex groups (18%). Women also preferred "safer"-appearing stores with security guards, more employees, and more business traffic. They avoided stores with "viewing booths," which the authors argued are often viewed as places for male–male encounters. Interestingly, across all observations, approximately half of the store employees were female, but women were significantly less likely to patronize stores with a larger number of women employees.

As shown in this example, researchers often study various forms of deviance with no or very little interaction with the persons they are observing. The benefit of this approach is that the presence of the researcher is very unlikely to affect the behavior of the research subjects. This is similar to what medical researchers do in a double-blind study; in these studies, the medical researchers have very little potential to affect the results of the experiment because they don't know if they are administering a new drug or a placebo.

Let's move to the other extreme of the spectrum and examine the strategies of researchers who actively interact with and participate in the activities of the deviants they study. This method is called participant observation. In contrast to the "objective" pure observer, for other social scientists, active participation is the only way to truly understand the attitudes, beliefs, and behaviors of deviant actors and the factors that shape and affect deviance. Researchers have "become" nudists (Weinberg, 1966), panhandlers (Lankenau, 1999), erotic dancers (Ronai & Ellis, 1989), and "lookouts" for men engaging in homosexual acts in public restrooms (Humphreys, 1970), among many others. A classic study of high-level drug dealing and smuggling was conducted by Patricia Adler (1993). Although Adler was not a drug dealer herself, she revealed that she used marijuana and cocaine; she serendipitously came to know a major dealer, and deals were done in her presence and even in her home. Through this contact, she met many drug dealers and smugglers covertly (they assumed she was in the business) and overtly when she asked to interview them. Her research with drug dealers and smugglers continued for 6 years and resulted in a classic book in the field, *Wheeling and Dealing: An Ethnography of an Upper-Level Drug Dealing and Smuggling Community*. This research was dangerous as many of the dealers obviously did not want others to know about their illegal enterprises. It also raised important ethical considerations. The author obviously knew about illegal behavior and did not report it. Of course, the research could not have been conducted if she reported the behavior, and indeed reporting it would have harmed her subjects—something as researchers we should strive very hard not to do. Indeed, it is unlikely that this research would be approved by most university human subjects committees.

Mark Fleisher (1995) also gained entry into a community of street hustlers, drug addicts, and alcoholics in the Seattle area. Over the course of 3 years (1988–1990), Fleisher completed in-depth interviews of nearly 200 ($n = 194$) deviant street people of various ages, races, ethnicities, and genders. Unlike Patricia Adler, who clearly befriended her primary source and other dealers, Fleisher was skeptical of the responses of street hustlers, especially those based on short interviews on issues that could not be supported with other information.

> I distrust data gathered in a few interviews with informants whom I don't know well or for whom I can't verify the facts with reliable documents. Hustlers', inmates', and former inmates' self-reports are, until proven otherwise, just "folklore," simply informants' comments, opinions, and explanations often engineered to sound legitimate. After all, these informants have been shown to be untrustworthy, manipulative, and disingenuous. Why should they be otherwise with me? (p. 21)

This is not to say that there were not interviewees that he came to like and even felt concern for—indeed, he tried to assist several to get the help they needed. However, his overall commentary on the street hustlers was not pretty or very sympathetic. Ultimately, Fleisher uses his field research to inform both theory and policy. In regard to theory, his work seems most consistent with Gottfredson and Hirschi's (1990) theory of low self-control (see Chapter 7) and the role certain parents play in not socializing their children appropriately. In fact, he argues that the hustlers' lives are largely shaped by abusive, drug- and alcohol-abusing parents. In terms of policy, his conclusions are conservative and emphasize incarceration and making offenders work. Overall, Fleisher's ethnography provides very powerful insights into the lives of "beggars and thieves" in the streets of Seattle and elsewhere.

Participatory observation, be it covert or overt observation, can be dangerous, emotionally and physically draining, and—quite simply—very hard work. It can also be intellectually and emotionally rewarding. Hands-on research of this type brings one much closer to the lives of the deviant and therefore enables a greater sense of empathy and a much closer sense of the experiences of those people shunned by society. Some have argued that this participant observation is the best if not the only approach to truly study deviance (Ferrell & Hamm, 1998). We would disagree and argue that yes, participant observation is a powerful methodology with many benefits, but, like all methodologies, it has many limitations.

RECENT STUDY IN DEVIANCE

How Close Is Too Close?

By Shana L. Maier and Bryan A. Monahan, 2010, in *Deviant Behavior, 31,* 1–32.

One of the trickiest parts of conducting research in the area of deviance is making and maintaining contact with the deviant group being studied. Especially in qualitative research, an important component of collecting data is developing rapport and establishing trust with those you are studying. How might we ever understand the experiences of heroin addicts unless we are allowed to study their daily lives? Why would heroin addicts invite us into their lives if they are worried we might betray their trust? However, while researchers need to establish a trusting bond with their interviewees, the question becomes, what are the issues that might arise as researchers establish a bond with their research participants? How might a researcher balance the relationship between an interviewee and himself or herself? While a major concern of qualitative research used to be that the researcher might get too close, this concern has really shifted to one that the researcher may not get close enough to get authentic, useful data.

Maier and Monahan interviewed 29 researchers to examine their experiences as researchers of deviance and crime. They found that "a researcher's efforts to balance closeness and detachment were often complicated by three common elements of qualitative research" (p. 23). The first of these elements is the amount of time that researchers spend with their research participants to establish a trusting bond—given there are no clear-cut rules about what is appropriate. In addition to time, Maier and Monahan also found researchers invest a significant amount of emotion into the researcher–participant bond. And finally, researchers often feel compelled to "give something back" to research participants, which makes balancing closeness and detachment difficult. These elements mean that researchers sometimes find themselves in situations that have no clear-cut boundaries or rules. From these interviews, Maier and Monahan also found that it was evident that "researchers need to find a balance between closeness and detachment that is right for them" (p. 23).

Content Analysis

Content analysis may be a term less familiar to undergraduate students in general or students of deviance in particular. This research strategy, however, has a long history in the study of deviance and deviant behavior. Content analysis involves reviewing records of communication and systematically searching, recording, and analyzing themes and trends in those records. Sources of communication are virtually unlimited and often free or quite cheap, making content analysis another gold mine of opportunity, especially for the undergraduate student of deviance.

Sources of communication used for studying deviance include transcribed interviews or open-ended responses to surveys, historical documents, legal codes, newspapers, advertisements from many sources, song lyrics, movies, TV shows, books and magazines, and Web sites and chat rooms, among myriad others. Indeed, all of these have been the source of content analyses in the study of deviance. Keys to a successful content analysis include (1) a solid research question, (2) a reasonably good understanding of the population of the materials/sources of interest, (3) a strategy for sampling records of communication, and (4) a systematic approach to extracting and coding themes or looking for trends.

A solid research question is probably the best starting place, and it can come from many directions and levels. The most interesting questions tend to emerge from theory, previous research, debates and conflicts, or suspected myths that one may want to empirically examine to support or debunk. The research question(s) may be very exploratory, especially at first or when there is little or conflicting theoretical or empirical guidance. For example, Pruitt and Krull (2011) recognized that there was actually little systematic research on why males seek female prostitutes and exactly what they want; what little research was available was based on non-representative samples. They argued that a content analysis of female escort Internet advertisements might provide information on what men want from prostitutes, assuming that the escorts are accurate in their perceptions of what males want and therefore choose to advertise these options. Analyzing 237 female escort advertisements, Pruitt and Krull found that ads focused on "girlfriend experiences, unrushed encounters, and escort-type services" were far more common than those focused on specific sex acts.

▲ **Photo 3.2** Measurement is critical to every scientific discipline but is especially interesting and important in the study of deviance.

Source: ©Brand X Pictures/Thinkstock.

Alternatively, Tuggle and Holmes (1997) were interested in the politics surrounding a smoking ban in California and especially in Shasta County, where the debate included 105 letters to the editor, which the authors analyzed. It was no surprise, and even expected, that pro-ban supporters tended to be nonsmokers and anti-ban supporters smokers. The logic of the arguments might also have been expected, with the former focusing on health risks (especially the risks associated with secondhand smoke) and the latter focusing on individuals' right to smoke. What might not have been predicted was that the power, measured by personal property, held by the pro-ban moral crusaders was much greater than that of the smokers arguing for the status quo. Given the large disparity in power, the fact that the ban was successful was not terribly surprising.

As discussed earlier, developing a reasoned understanding of the population of interest and then crafting a strategy for sampling cases to study is not an easy task. If one is interested in the prevalence of "derogatory depictions of women" in pornography, are we talking about magazines, movies, Internet sites, and so on? Once this question has been answered and refined, the sampling process should most likely be determined by a systematic process that fits into one's time and budget constraints.

The final issue, developing a systematic approach to extracting and coding themes or looking for trends, is another important consideration in a quality content analysis. Sticking with the example above, consider how different people are in their perceptions of what is derogatory and what is innocuous or simply entertaining. Developing an operationalization of "derogatory depictions" that can be selected and categorized consistently and replicated by others can be a very difficult issue to grapple with.

Content analysis is an exciting research avenue for those interested in studying deviant behavior and reactions to deviance. As mentioned, because records of communication are often available for free or are accessible quite cheaply, this is an excellent research design for undergraduate students interested in conducting a class research project. Since the topic areas are largely unbounded, we simply offer a few recent examples to stir up interest and possibilities.

Secondary Data Sources

Very important data have already been collected and are readily available for the study of crimes and other forms of deviance. These sources all have limitations but can still be extremely useful for conducting research. In addition, sometimes different sources can be used in conjunction with each other to better understand the causes and consequences of various deviant phenomena. Here we discuss just four general sources of secondary data; thus, we do not cover the entire spectrum of secondary sources but rather highlight just a few of the more useful ones for undergraduate students interested in deviant behavior.

The Uniform Crime Report (UCR) and the
National Incident-Based Reporting System (NIBRS)

The Uniform Crime Report was developed by the Federal Bureau of Investigation (FBI) in the 1930s. Data from nearly 17,000 police agencies are compiled by the bureau and presented online and in many published documents. Data is included on violent crimes (murder, forcible rape, robbery, and aggravated assault) and property crimes (burglary, larceny theft, and motor vehicle theft) known by the police. Data are generally provided in terms of numbers and rates and can be organized by region, state, and city and for longitudinal comparisons. With very little skill, figures such as the following can be created online. Figure 3.1 shows that, in contrast to popular opinion, the rate of violent crime dropped precipitously between 1992 and 2011 (this figure was created by the authors from data available from the FBI Web site at http://www.fbi.gov/about-us/cjis/ucr/crime-in-the-u.s/2011/crime-in-the-u.s.-2011/tables/table-1). The National Incident-Based Reporting System (NIBRS) was also developed by the FBI to provide more detailed information across jurisdictions. Focusing on the "crime incident," the NIBRS includes information on more crime types, weapon involvement, injuries that may have taken place, location of the event, property damage, and characteristics of victims and offenders.

A number of problems are associated with these data. For example, we don't know much about crimes known to police other than the type of offense and where it was detected or reported. For example, the gender, race, and age of the offender are often not known or not provided. However, data are also provided on arrests where we do have demographic information on the accused. Limitations of these data are fairly obvious. First, although they are important crimes, only certain offenses are

Figure 3.1   Violent Crime Rate (1992–2011)

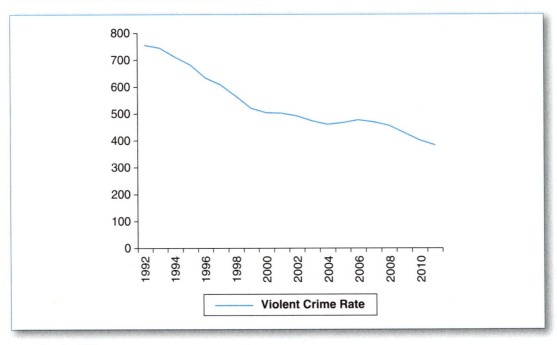

Source: Data from FBI.gov.

recorded and others are ignored, including both street crimes and white-collar offenses. Second, demographic data often used from arrest statistics may reflect not only crime but also activities of the police. That is, arrest statistics may provide a better picture of what the police do as opposed to what criminals do. Finally, there is what has come to be referred to as the "dark figure" of crime and deviance, which reminds us that these data do not take into account all of the crimes that the police never become aware of—and that figure would appear to be huge. Consider all the rapes, assaults, burglaries, and thefts that are never reported to the police or every joint or crack pipe smoked or every shoplifted item that was just listed as missing inventory. In fact, it is common knowledge among criminologists that the best statistics are probably for murder and motor vehicle theft because there is usually a body for the former, and insurance requires a police report for stolen vehicles. Still, these statistics can be very useful and are at the heart of a great deal of criminological research.

Substance Abuse and Mental Health Services Administration

The Substance Abuse and Mental Health Services Administration (SAMHSA) is an agency of the U.S. Department of Health and Human Services. This agency provides critical information on drug use and mental health, making it an excellent source for the student of deviance. In particular, it supports a public health surveillance system, the Drug Abuse Warning Network (DAWN). This system provides information from emergency rooms and medical examiner reports. It records "emergency room episodes" that involve one or more drugs, including overdoses, hallucinations, and suicide attempts, as well as incidents of people requesting help with drug addiction. It also collects data from medical examiners who report on drug-related causes of death through their autopsies. Medical examiners tabulate data for a variety of comparisons, particularly longitudinal analyses that allow us to evaluate trends in the types of drugs causing the most problems in terms of death and emergency room visits.

SAMHSA also supports and provides statistics from the National Survey on Drug Use and Health, which collects self-report data on alcohol and other drug use that better reflect general deviance not resulting in such serious consequences as emergency room episodes or death. The research is equally important, however, for many questions raised by the student of deviance. These statistics also can provide trend-level data and state-level comparisons, and maps of various indicators of drug use can be obtained. The following figure was obtained at www.oas.samhsa.gov/2k7State/Ch2.htm#Fig2–5 on May 22, 2010, and shows the past year self-reported prevalence of marijuana use among persons 12 years or older across states in the mid-2000s. With a few exceptions, it appears that marijuana use is highest in northern states—or at least people are more willing to report it there.

Figure 3.2   Marijuana Use in Past Year Among Persons Aged 12 or Older, by State: Percentages, Annual Averages Based on 2006 and 2007 National Survey on Drug Use and Health

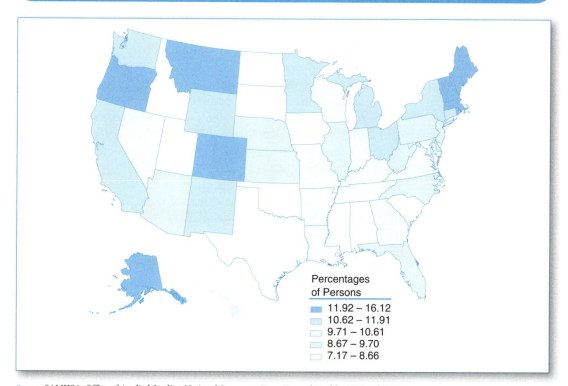

Percentages of Persons

- 11.92 – 16.12
- 10.62 – 11.91
- 9.71 – 10.61
- 8.67 – 9.70
- 7.17 – 8.66

Source: SAMHSA, Office of Applied Studies, National Survey on Drug Use and Health, 2006 and 2007.

SAMSHA also provides a wealth of data on mental health. For example, the Community Mental Health Services' (CMHS) Uniform Reporting System Output Tables provide demographic data (age, race, gender) on people receiving mental health services by state. Various comparisons can be made between states or between a particular set of states and national estimates. These data can be easily found at http://mentalhealth.samhsa.gov/cmhs/MentalHealthStatistics/URS2002.asp.

Monitoring the Future

Although related to SAMHSA, Monitoring the Future (MTF) is such a major, large-scale, longitudinal project that we discuss it separately. Using funding from the National Institutes of Health and the National Institute on Drug Abuse, MTF projects involve surveying students about their attitudes, behaviors, and beliefs concerning legal and illegal drug use (alcohol, tobacco, and other illegal drugs, such as marijuana, cocaine, and heroin). When it began in 1975, the project involved data collected from approximately 16,000 twelfth graders in 133 high schools. In 1991, the study was expanded to include approximately 18,000 eighth graders in 150 schools and 17,000 tenth graders in 140 schools. So, in all, there are approximately 50,000 students in 420 schools surveyed in their classrooms annually. Behaviors can also be linked to large social contexts (e.g., school characteristics) for very interesting analyses. Some of the data are easily downloaded for analysis, and online mechanisms are available to analyze the data.

Archived Data: Inter-University Consortium for Political and Social Science Research

People who have been gathering data for a while sometimes are willing to share that data with other researchers for further analyses. The Inter-University Consortium for Political and Social Science Research (ICPSR) houses a great many data sets. While the majority of these data sets are not relevant to students of deviance, much data are available on crime and the criminal justice system, as well as softer forms of deviance. Students working on class projects or senior theses are encouraged to see if their college or university is a member of the ICPSR and explore the many offerings the ICPSR provides (www .icpsr.umich.edu/icpsrweb/ICPSR/). Below we discuss just a few of the data sets that might be of interest to students of deviance.

Elaine Sharpe provided a data set on how 10 city governments in the United States responded to morality issues in the 1990s. The focus was on how municipalities reacted to deviant issues such as "gay rights, abortion rights, abortion clinic protests, needle exchange programs for drug users, hate speech, hate groups, gambling policies and regulations, animal rights, and regulations pertaining to the sex industry, which included pornography, prostitution, and adult entertainment" (http://www.icpsr .umich.edu/icpsrweb/ICPSR/studies/3735?author%5B0%5D=Sharp%2C+Elaine+B.&paging.star-tRow=1). Martin Monto was the principal investigator on a project that examined characteristics of arrested clients of street prostitutes in four western cities (Portland, Oregon; San Francisco and Santa Clara, California; and Las Vegas, Nevada) between 1996 and 1999. Men arrested for soliciting prostitutes ("johns") were court-referred to client intervention workshops where they were anonymously surveyed. In addition to basic demographic information, clients were questioned extensively about various sexual behaviors and encounters (with prostitutes as well as other sexual relations), attitudes regarding women in general and prostitutes in particular, and beliefs about violence against women and the legality of prostitution. Estes and Weiner provided ICPSR data for the Commercial Sexual Exploitation of Children in the United States (1997–2000). This project attempted to collect systematic data on "the nature, extent, and seriousness of child sexual exploitation (CSE) in the United States" (http://www.icpsr.umich.edu/icpsrweb/ICPSR/studies/2859?author%5B%5D=Monto%2C+Martin+A.&paging.startRow=1). The researchers surveyed staff in nongovernment and government organizations that were tasked with dealing with the transnational trafficking of children for sexual purposes. These are just three data sets focused on deviant behavior and social control.

◈ Ethical Considerations in Studying Deviance

As has been hinted at earlier in this chapter, there are serious ethical considerations in the study of deviance. Many experiments conducted not so long ago would no longer be allowed on college campuses or elsewhere. In the 1960s, Milgram created a study where subjects were told to shock other participants when they provided an incorrect response to a question. The shocks supposedly got more intense with each wrong answer. What made this experiment potentially unethical was not causing pain to humans as no one actually received the shocks. Rather, it was that people quite often continued to "shock" the confederate until it resembled torture, and it was quite likely that subjects experienced guilt and remorse over what they had just done.

Experimental studies are not the only methodology where ethical concerns are raised. The Tearoom Trade, a classic study (Humphreys, 1970) of male homosexual encounters in public bathrooms, is often cited as unethical research. Laud Humphreys acted as a "lookout" in these venues. He did not disclose to the subjects that he was studying them, and, more importantly, he collected license plate numbers and through a police officer contact obtained addresses to do "market research." He then interviewed these men under the guise that he was doing a social health survey. So, several issues of ethics in research are raised. Observing behavior that is public, even if attempts are made to hide the behavior, is probably relatively innocuous, although some might question the ethics of acting as a "lookout" for cops and "straights." He lied to a police officer to access addresses, which certainly fractures the call for honesty and may even be illegal. Finally, he lied to the respondents when he interviewed them, not disclosing that he was actually interested in their homosexual acts.

Today there are structured committees associated with universities and other research organizations that are set up to protect human subjects. These committees are referred to as institutional review boards (IRBs) and are generally composed of persons from different fields (e.g., scientists and nonscientists), an outside person from the community, and a legal representative, among others. These boards meet and review applications to conduct research. Many researchers have come to hold a dim and jaded view of IRBs. IRBs are often seen as gatekeepers prohibiting the researcher from engaging in important work that poses little to no risk to the human subjects involved, and the researchers' own exposure to risk is often seen as being their business, not that of "big brother." Indeed, some see IRBs as being "more concerned about preventing their parent institution from being sued than the rights of human subjects" (Goode, 2008a, p. 121). Furthermore, because of the bureaucratic nature of the beast, IRBs often seem more concerned that the appropriate boxes are checked than with any possible harm the research might present to human subjects. While these views may be accurate of IRBs in some institutions, many individuals on these committees are researchers themselves, and even those not directly involved in research generally have no interest in stifling the pursuit of knowledge.

There are several general concerns when considering the protection of human subjects. The first comes from the medical adage, "First, do no harm." This is an especially problematic issue in experimental studies where subjects are asked to do things they wouldn't normally do. If there are risks, the subjects need to be aware of those risks and how the risks will be minimized. Even an anonymous survey that asks sensitive questions may invoke unpleasant emotions, especially among certain populations (e.g., victims of crimes or other abuses). These risks might be reduced by making the survey voluntary and letting respondents know they can stop at any time or ignore any question. If it is an especially vulnerable population, a referral might be provided to a common service provider. Research must be voluntary, which brings up how subjects are recruited, how they are asked to participate, and what sorts of incentives might be offered for their participation (which should not be coercive).

This gives rise to an interesting issue regarding informed consent. Subjects should be provided with sufficient information to make the decision to participate in various forms of research (e.g., surveys, interviews, experiments) if at all possible. We think, however, that often formal consent forms, especially signed ones, can be off-putting to potential subjects and sometimes result in increased risk. Consider a 5-minute survey; do you really need to have respondents read a two- to three-page consent form? In most cases, probably not. In fact, a long consent form may thwart otherwise interested respondents from participating. Generally, a paragraph that requests participation and states that the research is voluntary and how the respondent's identity will be protected is plenty. Second, consider studies of many deviant populations where others simply finding out that respondents are among a deviant population may put the employment and/or social relations of the respondents at risk, or even lead to their arrest. If we required signed consent to study persons with AIDS, those who use drugs, or those who have been arrested for soliciting prostitution, we may find it very hard to get persons to agree to the research. More important, their signature on the form puts them at risk as it is basically a legal document with their signature saying that they have AIDS, use drugs, or have recently solicited prostitution. Thus, anonymity rather than confidentiality is often far safer for the individuals studied, and a consent form may be totally inappropriate.

◈ Explaining Deviance in the Streets and Deviance in the Suites: In-Depth Research of Street Gangs and NASA

There is no "right way" to study deviance in the streets or in the suites, and most research strategies can be used to study deviance in either domain. That is, in-depth interviews can be just as useful for studying elite deviance as they are for studying street crime. Similarly, analyzing historical documents, surveying various populations, or using official records are all useful for studying deviance at every level of a society's economic and/or social hierarchy. Therefore, we have chosen just two illustrative examples where researchers have studied deviance in the streets and in the suites that we hope you find interesting.

While much social science research is done using surveys and large data sets, some of the most intriguing work uses in-depth qualitative research to give an up-close look into the inner workings of organizations that are often a mystery to outsiders. Sudhir Venkatesh (2008) provides an example of this kind of research into street deviance in his popular book *Gang Leader for a Day*. A self-described "rogue sociologist," Venkatesh went to graduate school in Chicago and befriended a gang leader named J. T. in the city. Under J. T.'s protection and tutelage, he was able to spend years documenting the gang's efforts at selling crack cocaine and evading the law. Venkatesh (2008) explains his relationship with J. T. and J. T.'s view of his illegal industry:

> J. T. seemed to appreciate having the ear of an outsider who would listen for hours to his tales of bravado and managerial prowess. He often expressed how hard it was to oversee the gang, to keep the drug economy running smoothly, and to deal with the law abiding tenants who saw him as an adversary. Sometimes he spoke of his job with dispassion, as if he were the CEO of some widget manufacturer—an attitude that I found not only jarring but, given the violence and destruction his enterprise caused, irresponsible.
>
> He fancied himself a philanthropist as much as a leader. He spoke proudly of quitting his mainstream sales job in downtown Chicago to return to the projects and use his drug profits to "help others." How did he help? He mandated that all his gang members get a high-school diploma and stay off drugs. He gave money to some local youth centers for sports equipment and computers. He willingly loaned out his gang members to Robert Taylor tenant leaders, who deployed them on such tasks as escorting the elderly on errands or beating up a domestic abuser. (pp. 114–115)

Venkatesh's research provides a provocative look at the lives of gang members and the drug trade in Chicago in the 1990s and provides a unique example and study of deviance in the streets. One must wonder how generalizable his research is—and how useful—now that the homes in the Robert Taylor area have largely been torn down by the city. One should also consider the ethical issues raised in this book; Venkatesh certainly knew a great deal about illegal activities operating in the city that he did nothing to stop.

Diane Vaughan took a much different approach in trying to understand the culture of NASA (National Aeronautical and Space Administration) that helped lead to the 1986 space shuttle *Challenger* disaster. A technical failure caused the *Challenger* to explode mere moments after takeoff. The presidential commission appointed to investigate the disaster found that there had been technical issues on previous shuttle missions and that engineers had objected to the launch the night before it took place. Information was suppressed and "NASA managers, experiencing extraordinary schedule pressures, knowingly took a chance, moving forward with a launch they were warned was risky, willfully violating internal rules in the process, in order to launch on time" (Vaughan, 2004, p. 316).

Vaughan conducted an historical ethnography of NASA and the *Challenger* launch decision, relying on documentary records—including 122,000 pages of NASA documents—to reconstruct history. Based on her own research, Vaughan concluded that the accident resulted from a mistake rather than misconduct (p. 316) and that standards of "acceptable risk" were commonplace at NASA and ruled all shuttle launches (p. 324). She argues that there was a normalization of deviance in the culture at NASA and that it was conformity to this organizational culture rather than deviance that caused the disaster. Vaughan (2004) explains:

> This case was not an example of misconduct as I originally thought: rules were not violated. Still, harm was done. Moreover, NASA's actions were deviant in the eyes of outsiders, and, after the accident, also in the eyes of those who made decisions. (p. 341)

The two studies described above are in some ways night and day. The former focuses on gang activity in the streets and relies purely on informal interviews and the researcher's observations and experiences with gang members. The latter involves a researcher's laborious efforts to review 100,000 pages of NASA documents to uncover the cause of a major catastrophe. However, it is interesting to note that in both cases deviance was an important issue for the deviants themselves. In the first case, J. T. (the gang leader), while clearly engaging in illegal activities, insisted that his gang members get an education and stay off drugs. In the second case, while no illegal behavior was technically uncovered, those involved came to recognize their behavior as "deviant." In both cases, much deviant behavior was conformity to the particular organizational culture.

◈ Ideas in Action: Evaluating Programs and Policy

There are some types of deviance that society wishes to control or eliminate, and policies are put into place or programs are developed to help deal with these "social problems." Social scientists are often interested in evaluating these programs and policies. Indeed, phrases such as "evidence-based decision making," "evidence-based practice," "research-based programs," and "cost–benefit analysis of programs and policy" have become quite popular across disciplines in recent years. Funding agencies now often require that the programs they subsidize must be "proven" or at least "promising" based on solid scientific research. And while government officials and other policymakers are often accused of making or changing policy based on whim, political pressure, or popular opinion, we suspect that many are actually trying to "do good"—or at least they are not trying to make things worse. The only proven way to assess the effectiveness of programs and policies to address deviance is with solid research invoking the tools we discussed earlier. Let us acquaint you with several programs and policies and how they have been evaluated.

In the mid-1930s, a juvenile delinquency prevention program known as the Cambridge-Somerville Youth Study was developed. This was a treatment program for boys aged 5–13 and their families. A variety of organizations (e.g., churches) and agencies (e.g., social welfare agencies) and the police recommended boys identified as "average" or "difficult" to the program. Beginning in 1939, boys were randomly assigned to the treatment program or to a control condition that only provided information to the study. The treatment included academic tutoring, medical and psychiatric treatment, counselors who visited the families to discuss problems, and involvement in various activities (e.g., Boy Scouts, YMCA, summer camps). In a thirty-year follow-up study of the intervention, McCord (1978) examined a great deal of information obtained on the boys over their life spans, including but not limited to court, mental health, and alcohol treatment records. Given the large amount of "help" offered the families, one might expect far more positive outcomes among the treated subjects. Actually, very few differences were found in terms of juvenile delinquency and adult criminal activity. Furthermore, there were at least seven negative "side effects." The treated men were more likely to have (1) committed a second offense, (2) showed greater signs of alcoholism, (3) showed greater evidence of mental illness, (4) died younger, (5) suffered from more stress-related diseases (e.g., high blood pressure), (6) held jobs with a lower occupational prestige scores, and (7) reported less satisfaction with their jobs (McCord, 1978). Why were the outcomes of the treated men so poor compared to the outcomes of the control group? Unpacking that relationship is virtually impossible; the lesson to be learned, however, is that bad things can happen when we try to "do good" and, more importantly, when we assume we "do good."

More recently, the Drug Awareness Resistance Education (DARE) program has become very popular. Began in 1983, DARE involves police officers teaching a standardized drug prevention curriculum in classrooms from kindergarten through high school (depending on the school/jurisdiction). While a few early studies suggested that the program may be effective (e.g., DeJong, 1987), larger, more rigorous studies have failed to find significant differences in drug-use behaviors between those who experience the program and those that do not (e.g., Rosenbaum et al., 1998). Subsequently, numerous studies have examined the effectiveness of DARE, and these studies have been reviewed in two comprehensive meta-analyses (Ennet et al., 1994; West & O'Neil, 2004). A meta-analysis is a systematic and statistical review of the literature on a particular issue and is comprised mostly of experiments and often program evaluations. Both meta-analyses concluded that DARE programs were not reducing substance use among youth. Indeed, the bulk of evidence influenced one social scientist to borrow the now classic slogan "Just Say No to Drugs!" and modify it to read "Just Say No to DARE!" (Rosenbaum, 2007).

The point of these two examples is not that "nothing works," but rather that we often don't know *what* works and we promote at great costs programs that are ineffective—or worse, that are negatively affecting participants. In the case of DARE, at one point public funding for the program amounted to $200 million a year (Rosenbaum, 2007). This is a great societal cost for an ineffective program.

So are there programs that have been shown to be effective? The Office of Juvenile Justice and Delinquency Prevention (OJJDP) offers a Web site describing programs that are rated by experts to be either "effective" (solid studies show the program to be effective) or "promising" (studies suggest that the program may be effective, but stronger research designs are needed to confirm this) or to have "no effect," meaning at least to date the program has not been shown to be effective. Each program is rated by more than one expert, and any differences in scoring are reconciled. The Web site also includes programs on a number of social issues, including bullying, drug and alcohol use and abuse, and gang prevention, among others. The site also includes a list of useful program types, including family-based services, school-based and other academic programs, early intervention programs, and programs for courts and corrections.

NOW YOU . . . CONDUCT THE RESEARCH

The Southern Poverty Law Center documented 932 hate groups in the United States in 2010. The following is a map showing the number of hate groups in each state. As a deviance researcher, you are interested in studying *white supremacy* groups, and you need to establish your research question, define your population, and determine your sample. Do you want to conduct macro-level research on trends and characteristics of these hate groups in the United States? Or would you prefer to engage in micro-level research that examines participants in these groups? How will you conduct this research? How will you collect your data? What may some of the challenges be with a study on this topic?

(Continued)

(Continued)

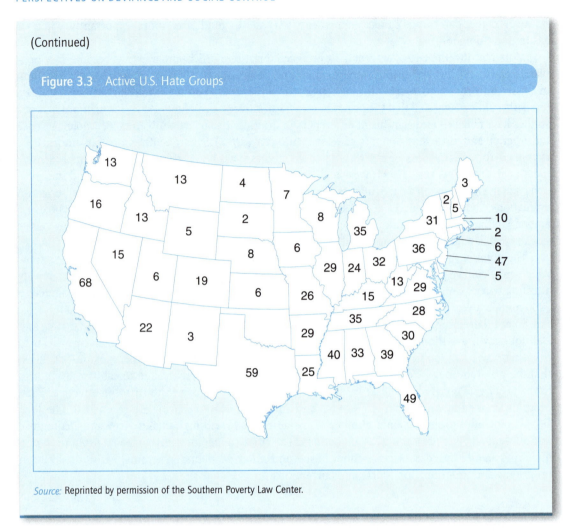

Figure 3.3   Active U.S. Hate Groups

Source: Reprinted by permission of the Southern Poverty Law Center.

◇ Conclusion

In this chapter, we have presented the reader with several strategies to investigate and answer questions regarding deviance. We have not favored any particular approach, resting on the belief that the appropriate methodology comes after the research questions have been decided upon and the population of interest specified, as well as the resources and skills of the researcher or research team spelled out. In fact, it would seem much more profitable to think about how different methodologies might work in concert to better understand the phenomenon at hand than immediately relegating the phenomenon to a specific methodology. A few in-depth interviews might "snowball" into a larger sample, or a survey might be developed based on the interviews to give to a larger, more representative sample. Alternatively, results of a large-scale survey may suggest a subpopulation of which more detailed investigation is warranted, or unexpected results might lead to a qualitative study. Given that these methodologies are not very conducive to tests of causal relationships, an experiment or quasi-experiment might be designed to aid in our knowledge of what factors affect some deviant attitude, belief, or behavior. In conclusion, we find that combining or triangulating research methods may be the only way to truly understand issues involving deviance.

ENDNOTE

1. While beyond the scope of this chapter, there are several ways of matching students across schools or to make statistical adjustments so that more reasonable comparisons can be made.

EXERCISE AND DISCUSSION QUESTIONS

1. Compare the similarities and differences between experimental and quasi-experimental designs. Give an example of one subject that might be best studied using each design.

2. Discuss survey research. What is the importance of sampling and response rates for a good representative sample?

3. What is the difference between being a "pure observer" versus a "full participant" of social events?

4. What are official data? What are the strengths and weaknesses of official data?

5. Discuss the ethical concerns that come with studying deviance. In your opinion, how might we balance these ethical concerns with research on deviant behavior?

KEY TERMS

Content analysis

Covert observation

Ethics in research

Ethnography

Experiments

Field research

Human subjects

Institutional review board

Operationalization

Overt observation

Participant observation

Pure observation (nonparticipant)

Quasi-experimental designs

Response rate

Sample

Secondary data

Survey

CHAPTER 4

Anomie/Strain Theory

In April 1992, a young man from a well-to-do East Coast family hitchhiked to Alaska and walked alone into the wilderness north of Mt. McKinley. Four months later his decomposed body was found by a party of moose hunters. . . .

His name turned out to be Christopher Johnson McCandless. He'd grown up, I learned, in an affluent suburb of Washington, D.C., where he'd excelled academically and had been an elite athlete.

Immediately after graduation, with honors, from Emory University in the summer of 1990, McCandless dropped out of sight. He changed his name, gave the entire balance of a twenty-four-thousand-dollar savings account to charity, abandoned his car and most of his possessions, burned all the cash in his wallet. And then he invented a new life for himself, taking up residence at the ragged margin of society, wandering across North America in search of raw, transcendent experience. His family had no idea where he was or what had become of him until his remains turned up in Alaska.

Jon Krakauer (1996), *Into the Wild,* Author's Note. Copyright ©1996 by Jon Krakauer. Published by Anchor Books, a division of Random House, Inc.

Introduction

Christopher McCandless grew up in a conforming, upper-middle-class family and seemed to be on the fast track to success. He graduated from Emory University with a 3.72 grade point average, and he spoke of going to law school. Instead, he turned his back on his family, adopted the new name of Alexander Supertramp, and set out to make his way alone in the wilderness. How might we explain this drastic turnaround and McCandless's blatant rejection of societal norms and expectations?

Anomie/strain theories are among the first truly sociological explanations of the causes of deviant behavior. These theories seek to understand deviance by focusing on social structures and patterns that emerge as individuals and groups react to conditions they have little control over. The question these theories address is, how exactly does the structure of society constrain behavior and cause deviance?

Strain theories are generally macro-level theories, and they share several core assumptions: first, the idea that social order is the product of a generally cohesive set of norms; second, that those norms are widely shared by community members; and third, that deviance and community reactions to deviance are essential to maintaining order.

◈ Development of Anomie/Strain Theory

Émile Durkheim and Anomie

Émile Durkheim's classic statement of anomie set the stage for one of the most important theoretical traditions in criminology. In one of his major works, Durkheim—often considered the father of sociology—studied suicide in 19th-century Europe. While suicide is generally viewed as a very individualistic and personal act, Durkheim effectively argued that characteristics of communities influence suicide rates, independent of the particular individuals living in those communities. He found that some countries had consistently high rates of suicide over several decades, while other countries had consistently low rates. How can we explain these macro-level differences?

In brief, Durkheim argued that suicide was related to the amount of regulation in a society and the degree of group unity. For Durkheim, social integration and social change are key factors in deviant behavior. As a society undergoes rapid change, norms will be unclear and a state of anomie will result. Anomie is a state of normlessness where society fails to effectively regulate the expectations or behaviors of its members; it occurs when aspirations are allowed to develop beyond the possibility of fulfillment. In better-functioning societies, ambitions are restrained and human needs and desires are regulated by the collective order.

Durkheim argued that "no living being can be happy or even exist unless his needs are sufficiently proportioned to his means" (Durkheim, 1897/1951, p. 246). In Durkheim's understanding, society alone held the moral power over the individual to moderate expectations and limit passions. Durkheim suggested that a state of anomie, or normlessness, results from a breakdown in the regulation of goals; with such lack of regulation, individuals' aspirations become unlimited and deviance may result. Durkheim argued that in a stable society, individuals are generally content with their positions or, as later scholars interpreted, they "aspire to achieve only what is realistically possible for them to achieve" (Cloward & Ohlin, 1960, p. 78).

A macro-level example may clarify the concept of anomie: Think back to what you know about the 1960s in the United States. What was happening nationally at that time? The country was undergoing enormous changes as the civil rights movement took hold, women became more liberated and fought for equal rights, and America sent its young men to war in Vietnam. There was rapid and significant social change. Imagine what it would have been like to be a college student in the 1960s—whole new worlds of opportunities and challenges were opening for women and minorities. What should young people expect? How high could they aspire to go? The answers simply were not clear; the old norms no longer applied. With norms and expectations unclear for a large segment of the society, anomie theory would lead us to expect higher rates of deviance.

Anomie might also be applied to the normative expectations for physical attractiveness. Think for a moment about the standard for female beauty in the United States. Is there one ideal type? Or are there common characteristics we can identify? One trait that has been idealized for decades is that female beauties are nearly always thin, sometimes dangerously thin. Fashion models in magazines and walking the runway are very tall and extremely thin. They spend hours being tended to by professional hair and makeup artists, being photographed by the best photographers in the world, and, even so, their photos are often airbrushed and Photoshopped to make the already beautiful absolutely perfect.

This vision of ideal beauty is pervasive in the media. Young women (and increasingly young men) are exposed to unrealistic expectations of how they should aspire to look. For a time, network television shows glorified improving one's looks through plastic surgery with "reality" shows like *The Swan* and *I Want a Famous Face.* To frame this in terms of the theory, society has failed to regulate the expectations of its members when it comes to physical attractiveness, and we see deviance in the form of eating disorders and extensive elective plastic surgery resulting.

◇ Robert Merton and Adaptations to Anomie/Strain

Informed by Durkheim's writing on anomie, Robert K. Merton narrowed the focus and extended the theory to the United States in his 1938 article "Social Structure and Anomie." Merton argued that anomie does not result simply from unregulated goals but rather from a faulty relationship between cultural goals and the legitimate means to access them. While we are all socialized to desire success, we do not all have the same opportunities to become successful; thus, Merton defined several adaptations to anomie and strain.

Merton was born Meyer Schkolnick, the son of Eastern European Jewish immigrants. He grew up in poverty in a "benign slum" in south Philadelphia. He legally changed to the "Americanized" name of Robert King Merton after he earned a scholarship to Temple University and entered college; he went to Harvard for his PhD and became a professor at Columbia University and one of the most famous sociologists in the world. His own story seems to capture a piece of the "American Dream." Growing up in the pre-Depression era, there was, according to Merton, a sense of "limitless possibilities." As Cullen and Messner (2007) suggest, this sense of limitless possibilities is illuminating. It relates to Merton's view not simply that Americans were urged to pursue some rigidly defined goal of success but rather that there also was a broad cultural message that everyone—even those in Merton's impoverished circumstances—could seek social mobility and expect to enjoy a measure of success (p. 14).

Given this biographical background, Merton's ideas begin to come to life. In "Social Structure and Anomie" (1938), Merton focused on the needs, desires, and processes of cultural socialization. He argued that in the United States, we are all socialized to believe in the sense of limitless possibilities and to desire success on a large scale. These cultural goals are widespread; the problem, however, is that the social structure "restricts or completely eliminates access to approved modes of acquiring these symbols for *a considerable part of the same population*" (p. 680). In other words, structural impediments or obstacles exist for whole classes of people who wish to attain wealth using legitimate means. For those in the lower classes who share the cultural goals for success but have limited means to attain them, lack of education and job opportunities create a strain toward anomie, which may translate into deviance.

Merton argued that there are five general adaptations to anomie. The key to each is whether there is an acceptance or rejection of the cultural goal of success (or, to adopt a concept that is easier to measure, wealth attainment) and whether or not the choice is to strive for the goal via legitimate or conforming means.

Merton's Adaptations to Anomie

Conformity is the most common adaptation. Conformists have accepted the cultural goal of success or wealth attainment, and they are trying to achieve it via legitimate means. Most college students might be considered conformists as they work hard to earn degrees to get better jobs and have more success after graduation. For Merton, conformity was the only nondeviant adaptation to strain and anomie.

Innovation is the adaptation for those who have accepted the cultural goal of success/wealth attainment but are trying to achieve it via illegitimate means. Any crime for profit would be an example of innovation. Robbers, thieves, drug dealers, embezzlers, and high-priced call girls all would be classified as innovators in Merton's adaptations.

Ritualism is the category for those who have abandoned the cultural goal of success/wealth attainment but continue to use legitimate means to make their living. The dedicated workers who will never advance to management might be considered ritualists in Merton's typology.

Retreatism is the adaptation of those who have rejected the cultural goal of success/wealth attainment and have also rejected the legitimate means. Merton describes people who adapt in this way as "in the society but not of it. Sociologically, these constitute the true aliens" (Merton, 1957, p. 153). The chronically homeless and serious drug addicts might be considered retreatists in this model. Christopher McCandless, from this chapter's opening story, is a vivid individual example of a retreatist. He clearly rejected the conforming goals and lifestyle of his parents and the larger society; he chose instead to exist in the margins, occasionally working low-level jobs, hitching rides, and ultimately attempting to live off the land in Alaska.

Rebellion is the category for political deviants—those who don't play by the rules but work to change the system to their own liking. Rebels reject the cultural goal of success/wealth attainment and replace it with another primary goal; they may use either legitimate or illegitimate means to achieve this goal—one way to think about it is that rebels will use whatever means necessary to reach their chosen goal. Perhaps the clearest example of rebellion would be terrorist groups, who often use violence in an attempt to achieve political goals.

Merton's 1938 article "Social Structure and Anomie" (SS&A) remains one of the most influential and referenced works in all of criminology and sociology. Reflecting on his seminal ideas in an interview five decades later, Merton observed that

▲ **Photo 4.1**   This photo might represent either conformity or ritualism in Merton's adaptations. Which concept do you think it best illustrates? Why do you think so?

Source: ©Steve Cole/iStockphoto.

it holds up those goals of success, especially economic, as a legitimate expectation for everybody. You do not have statements anywhere in the history of American aspirations that say: "You the poor, and you the ethnically subordinate—you can have no hopes or legitimate expectation of upward

Figure 4.1   Robert K. Merton's Deviance Typology

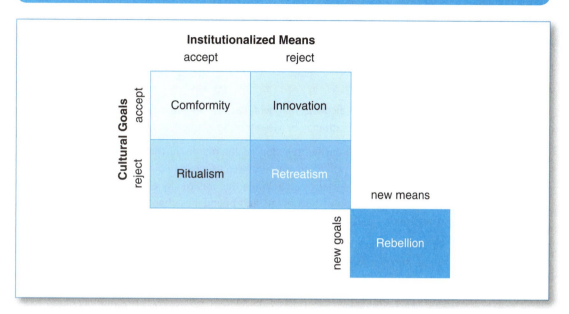

social mobility." You have never heard that said . . . call it rhetoric, call it ideology, call it myth, call it what you will, call it the American Dream. . . . Now that is not typical of other cultural structures and other historical times and places. So it is a very powerful, if you will, theoretically sensitized observation. . . . SS&A '38 was saying what is universal for all is the legitimacy of striving to better yourself, to rise upward and onward. . . . That's the universal thing and that differs from other cultures . . . in which you say: "Of course, you have no right; you are a servant class and you know your place." . . . Now that's the dynamic new component of the cultural structure, and that is what is being said—what is common to all. (Cullen & Messner, 2007, p. 24)

DEVIANCE IN POPULAR CULTURE

Robert Merton's ideas on strain theory and particularly the adaptation of innovation can be easily seen in many movies dealing with the drug trade, audacious heists, kidnappers holding victims for ransom, or virtually any other crime for profit. Many examples are available, including the following:

Blow—a movie based on the true story of George Jung, a working-class kid who built an illegal empire and attained the cultural goal of wealth attainment, making a fortune via illegitimate means first by dealing marijuana and then importing cocaine.

(Continued)

(Continued)

Set It Off—a fictional story of four young African American women struggling to survive in Los Angeles. As their personal troubles mount, they begin robbing banks to solve their money woes.

Merton's other adaptations are less common in film, as they often make for less dramatic stories, but they are represented in popular culture:

Leaving Las Vegas—this story of an alcoholic man who has lost his wife and family and goes to Las Vegas to literally drink himself to death may be viewed as an example of Merton's retreatism.

Murder in Mississippi—a film based on the true story of the murder of three civil rights workers in Mississippi in 1964. The civil rights workers might be viewed as rebels in Merton's typology: They are working and risking their lives for social change. While this was clearly considered deviant in the South, it is another good illustration of how norms and boundaries change over time, perhaps in response to positive deviance and collective action.

As you watch films over the next few weeks and months, try to keep the sociological theories of deviance in mind. It may surprise you how many can easily be applied to the stories and perspectives on the screen.

Richard Cloward and Lloyd Ohlin, Differential Opportunity

Richard Cloward was a student of Merton's and undoubtedly knew his work well. Cloward added an important dimension to anomie/strain theory by extending our focus to include the idea of illegitimate means. Cloward (1959) argued that just as not everyone has equal access to the legitimate means of attaining wealth, we cannot assume that everyone has access to illegitimate means either. This is a key point—imagine that you wanted to become a successful drug dealer. Where would you begin? Would you know where to purchase your product? Would you know where to access customers and how to gain their trust and their business? Would you be able to keep your illicit business going without getting caught and punished? Cloward's point makes perfect sense in this context: Just because you might wish to gain wealth and success via illegitimate means does not mean that you will have the skills and connections to do so.

Cloward teamed up with Lloyd Ohlin in 1960 to write the book *Delinquency and Opportunity*. Just as Cloward was a student of Merton's, Ohlin was a student of Edwin Sutherland's, and he was well versed in the ideas of differential association and the importance of social learning (see Chapter 6 for more details on Sutherland and differential association). They found a research puzzle to be explored in Merton's work: While Merton may generally be accurate in describing pressures and motivations that lead to deviant behavior, the particular type of deviant behavior is unexplained. Cloward and Ohlin argued that we need to understand not just the motivations of individuals to commit deviant behavior but also the availability of opportunities to learn about and participate in illegal or deviant acts.

Cloward and Ohlin incorporated Sutherland's ideas into their theory and argued that criminal and deviant behavior is learned like any other behavior and, importantly, that not everyone has the same opportunities to learn criminal skills and have criminal careers. Their particular focus was on delinquent gangs and the circumstances under which different types of gangs emerged. They focused on neighborhood conditions (still a macro-level theory) and the opportunities available to learn and practice legitimate or illegitimate skills. Ultimately, Cloward and Ohlin suggested that only neighborhoods in which crime flourishes as a stable institution are fertile criminal learning environments for the young.

To further clarify their ideas, Cloward and Ohlin argued that the different kinds of illegitimate opportunities available in poor urban neighborhoods lead to three types of criminal subcultures: criminal, conflict, and retreatist. Because the focus is on disadvantaged neighborhoods, the assumption is that most young people growing up in these conditions will have poor and limited legitimate opportunities for attaining wealth and success. Thus, the availability of illegitimate opportunities becomes extremely important in shaping the deviance that takes place in these neighborhoods and the types of adolescent gangs that develop.

Criminal subcultures develop among lower-class adolescent boys in neighborhoods with open illegitimate opportunity structures. These neighborhoods are characterized by systematic, organized crime, and they provide an outlet in illegal employment for youths to attain wealth and "get paid" via illegitimate means. Successful criminals populate the neighborhood and become visible, serving as distinctive role models for children growing up in the community. For those young people who aspire to emulate these illegitimate role models, there is generally an age-graded criminal structure in place where young males may do low-level jobs and learn from the older criminals in the neighborhood. In this way, social learning takes place, and the young acquire the skills and norms to fully take advantage of the illegitimate opportunities available to them. Compared to alternative poor neighborhoods, those with criminal subcultures are very structured and are relatively safe places to grow up and live. There is an absence of violence in these neighborhoods because violence—and the attention it draws—would be considered disruptive to both criminal and conventional activities.

Conflict subcultures develop in disorganized communities where illegitimate opportunities are largely absent and those that exist are closed to adolescents (see Chapter 5 for more information on social disorganization). Such neighborhoods are characterized by social instability, and youth growing up in these conditions are deprived of both conventional (legitimate) and criminal (illegitimate) opportunities. As Cloward and Ohlin (1960) explained it, "The disorganized slum . . . contains the outcasts of the criminal world . . . what crime there is tends to be individualistic, unorganized, petty, poorly paid, and unprotected" (pp. 173–174). With no real access to legitimate or illegitimate opportunities, adolescents growing up in disorganized neighborhoods suffer acute frustration and turn to violence to prove their personal worth. Social controls are weak in these areas, and violence for violence's sake is valued. With few role models and little chance at success, young men work to earn the toughest reputation and, through their physical prowess, to command some level of respect and deference from those around them.

Retreatist subcultures are associated with drug use and the drug culture among some lower-class adolescents. Cloward and Ohlin characterized adolescents in retreatist subcultures as "double failures" who cannot find a place for themselves in either criminal or conflict subcultures. While this is closely related to Merton's concept of retreatists, Cloward and Ohlin directed attention to the social environment and the conditions that help to explain the formation of each type of deviant subculture. The "double fail-ures" in poor neighborhoods may withdraw from the larger society and retreat into drug use and rela-tive isolation.

It is important to remember that Cloward and Ohlin are still explaining deviance at the macro level. Criminal, conflict, and retreatist subcultures develop primarily because communities are organized differently and offer varying legitimate and illegitimate opportunities.

◈ Albert Cohen, Delinquent Boys

Similar to Cloward and Ohlin, Albert K. Cohen was an undergraduate student of Merton's and a gradu-ate student of Sutherland's, so he, too, combined elements of Merton's anomie theory and Sutherland's ideas on social learning in his work. In his book *Delinquent Boys,* Cohen (1955) introduced the idea of delinquent subcultures. Cohen argued that a lower-class or working-class boy may find himself at the bottom of the status hierarchy in middle-class schools and the larger middle-class world, and

> to the degree to which he values middle-class status, either because he values the good opinion of middle-class persons or because he has to some degree internalized middle-class standards himself, he faces a problem of adjustment and is in the market for a "solution." (Cohen, 1955, p. 119)

Cohen argues that this **status frustration** or strain may lead to the collective solution of forming a delinquent subculture in which middle-class norms and values are replaced with their antithesis—their very opposite. Cohen suggests that the delinquent subculture can be described as non-utilitarian—for example, stealing just "for the hell of it" and not because the boys need or even want what they steal; malicious, or being "just plain mean" and destructive; and negativistic, or taking the norms of the larger culture and turning them upside down. The delinquent subculture forms and is sustained because it offers alternative criteria that working-class boys can meet and excel at; attributes that are disvalued by the larger culture become status giving assets within the subculture.

◈ Robert Agnew, General Strain Theory

Anomie and strain theories have a long history in sociology and criminology and have surged and waned in popularity over the years. Classic strain theories dominated criminological research in the 1950s and 1960s, and their relevance was marked in public policy of the time, particularly in strain theory's impact on the War on Poverty during the 1960s (Cullen & Agnew, 2006). Strain theory came under attack in the 1970s as relativist theorists shifted the focus to conflict and labeling theories (see Chapters 8 and 9), offering a new perspective on societal influences on both crime and punishment.

Robert Agnew (1992) breathed new life into the tradition with his **general strain theory (GST).** Strain theory focuses on what circumstances lead individuals and groups within a society to engage in deviant behavior. Agnew suggests that they are "pressured into crime." Along with the failure to achieve valued goals, Agnew argues that strain may also result from negative relationships. Agnew specifies three major types of negative relations where others

1. prevent or threaten to prevent the achievement of positively valued goals (for example, preventing monetary success or popularity with peers),

2. remove or threaten to remove positive stimuli (for example, the death of a parent or the breakup of a romantic relationship),

3. present or threaten to present negative stimuli (for example, physical assaults, failing grades, public insults).

Such negative relations will likely lead to anger and frustration, which may then lead to deviant behavior, such as physical violence, running away from home, illicit drug use, or self-harming behavior.

Agnew (2006) argues that some types of strain are more likely to cause crime and deviance than others. He identifies the following characteristics as most likely to cause crime: The strain is high in magnitude, the strain is seen as unjust, the strain is associated with low self-control, and/or the strain creates some pressure or incentive for criminal coping. More specifically, examples of strains that are likely to cause crime include parental rejection, erratic or excessively harsh discipline, child abuse and neglect, negative school experiences, abusive peer relationships, chronic unemployment, marital problems, criminal victimization, residence in economically deprived neighborhoods, and discrimination based on characteristics such as race/ethnicity and gender.

Agnew is careful to point out that not all individuals respond to strains with crime and deviance, and, in fact, most people cope in legal and conforming ways. There are many possible coping strategies, including behavioral coping, cognitive coping, and emotional coping (Agnew, 2006). The resources and social support available to the individuals are important: Do they have conforming friends and family they can turn to for help? Do they associate with criminal others? What is their level of self-control? Is the cost of criminal coping high or low? For some individuals, there is low risk in criminal or deviant coping because they have little to lose—they may not have jobs or close relationships that would be put at risk with criminal or deviant acts. While it is difficult to tease out the exact impact of each of these factors, Agnew argues that whether by personality traits, socialization, or learned attitudes and behavior, some individuals are simply more disposed to crime than are others.

Messner and Rosenfeld, Crime and the American Dream—Institutional Anomie Theory

Messner and Rosenfeld (2007) turn attention to the American Dream and how it contributes to crime and deviance:

> The essence of our argument is that the distinctive patterns and levels of crime in the United States are produced by the cultural and structural organization of American society. A strong emphasis on the goal of monetary success and a weak emphasis on the importance of the legitimate means for the pursuit of success characterize American culture. This combination

of strong pressures to succeed monetarily and weak restraints on the selection of means is intrinsic to the dominant cultural ethos: the American Dream. The "American Dream" refers to a cultural commitment to the goal of economic success to be pursued by everyone under conditions of open, individual competition. The American Dream contributes to crime directly by encouraging people to employ illegal means to achieve goals that are culturally approved. (p. x)

▲ **Photo 4.2**   Do you agree with Messner and Rosenfeld that the American Dream fosters an "anything goes" attitude when pursuing monetary success?

Source: ©H-Gall/iStockphoto.

Messner and Rosenfeld argue that the American Dream fosters an "anything goes" mentality when pursuing personal goals. They go on to identify the values underlying the American Dream as follows: achievement, individualism, universalism, and materialism. Achievement is connected to personal worth; Messner and Rosenfeld argue that the cultural pressures to achieve are enormous, and failure to achieve is often perceived as a failure to make any sort of meaningful contribution to society. Individualism encourages everyone to find a way to "make it" on his or her own. Within this framework of intense competition to succeed, others in the society are viewed as competitors and rivals, and, thus, general restraints on behavior are disregarded in the pursuit of personal goals. Universalism echoes Merton's ideas that virtually everyone in American society is encouraged to aspire to success and wealth attainment. Messner and Rosenfeld point out that while everyone may dream about success, "the hazards of failure are also universal" (p. 70). Materialism is the last value that underlies the American Dream. Money has special significance in American culture; it is the preeminent way in which we measure success and achievement.

At the institutional level, Messner and Rosenfeld argue that the major institutions in the United States, including the family, school, and political system, are all dominated by economic institutions. Noneconomic goals and accomplishments are valued much less than economic pursuits and gains, and economic norms have infiltrated and overpowered other important societal institutions.

Messner and Rosenfeld suggest that the American Dream leads to crime and deviance because of its exaggerated emphasis on monetary success and its resistance to restraint or limits on individual pursuit of success. Thus, they extend Merton's idea that the very fabric of American society promotes at least some level of deviance. Even as we all aspire to achieve great things and believe it is possible to realize our dreams, the social structure of American society constrains pathways to success; this, in turn, leads to deviance as some members of society pursue alternative success models by any means necessary.

◆ Application of Anomie and Strain Theories

Today, classic strain theory has renewed support, and it is used to examine group differences in crime rates, inequality, and **relative deprivation**, a perspective that suggests that socioeconomic inequality has a direct effect on community crime rates. At the micro-level, Agnew continues to actively revise and refine his ideas on general strain theory. Many, many studies have tested pieces of Agnew's theory and offer limited support; there are still many hypotheses to be discovered, tested, and explained. While research on general strain theory is quite easy to find in the sociological and criminological literature, in the following we highlight three studies that explore different aspects of anomie and strain.

Anomie and the Abuse at Abu Ghraib

A recent study analyzed the abuse at Abu Ghraib prison in Iraq in terms of Durkheim's concept of ano-mie (Mestrovic & Lorenzo, 2008). You may remember the vivid images of American soldiers torturing and humiliating Iraqi prisoners: Photos were published of soldiers threatening the nude men with snarling dogs, smiling over the bodies of dead Iraqis, forcing the prisoners to walk around and pose nude with hoods and blindfolds blocking their vision, and offering a "thumbs-up" to the cameras as they posed in front of literal piles of prisoners in humiliating positions.

Mestrovic and Lorenzo (2008) argue that there were high levels of social disorganization or anomie at Abu Ghraib and within the social structures of the U.S. Army, other government agencies, civilian contractors, and others who interacted with and had responsibility for the prisoners at Abu Ghraib. The authors argue that the social system at Abu Ghraib was disorga-nized and anomic from the outset and grew progressively worse over time; this confusion produced widespread deviance among prisoners and U.S. personnel alike.

▲ **Photo 4.3**   American soldiers purposely degraded and humiliated Iraqi prisoners at Abu Ghraib. How does Durkheim's theory of anomie help to explain such abuse?

Source: ©Associated Press.

Mestrovic and Lorenzo (2008) identify several sources of confusion that contributed to the anomie and deviance, includ-ing confusion as to who was in charge, insufficient training, lack of social integration within the military units at Abu Ghraib, rapid changes in the social milieu, intense pressure to obtain intelligence, confusion as to which norms to follow, "unhealthy mystique," failure of self-correct-ing mechanisms, and cultural insensitivity. The authors go on to explain,

> The extent of social disorganization, social chaos, dysfunction, lack of coordination, and of a general state of *anomie* was so great at Abu Ghraib that abuse and the breaking of norms that are documented was the *inevitable* outcome and should have been expected. (p. 202)

The American Dream and Incarcerated Young Men

A study by Inderbitzin (2007) focused on boys in a juvenile prison who held deeply to the idea of the American Dream but had few legitimate means to achieve it. The decline of manufacturing jobs and their replacement with low-wage and unskilled work has made it difficult for young men, particularly those with poor educations, to be successful. The ongoing racism experienced by minorities in the labor market imposes an additional barrier to economic success through legitimate means; as such, the loss of viable work for young, poorly educated, minority males seems inextricably linked to their criminal behavior. Committing crimes for profit can help such young men meet their financial needs and counter threats to their self-perception as competent men.

The young men in the study followed the lure of money and status into illegal endeavors that led to confrontations with the law and conforming society. Profit or "getting paid" (Sullivan, 1989) was frequently cited as one of the main motivating factors in their crimes. They were examples of Merton's innovators—"men who hold fast to culturally emphasized goals while abandoning culturally approved ways of seeking them" (Merton, 1964, p. 218). Thus, Merton's ideas remain both useful and relevant some 8 decades after the publication of "Social Structure and Anomie."

Inderbitzin (2007) goes on to argue that staff members in the juvenile facility explicitly encourage the young men in their care to shift their values and aspirations to conforming, less glamorous goals and to adopt new definitions of success and the American Dream. In this way, Durkheim's ideas on anomie are also found in the work that staff members of the juvenile correctional facility or "training school" are doing to resocialize the incarcerated adolescents to more prosocial goals and behavior:

> A latent function of the juvenile prison is to work to normalize the young inmates, re-directing the aspirations of its charges, releasing them back into their communities with more realistic, but essentially deflated goals for their futures. In this way, the institution becomes an important agent of social control in its attempts to combat conditions of anomie and the resulting crime in the larger community. The training school graduates who go on to conforming futures have likely been at least partially normalized and resocialized to expect less from the world outside. (Inderbitzin, 2007, p. 236)

Institutional Anomie Theory and Student Cheating

One attempt to extend and refine Messner and Rosenfeld's (2007) institutional anomie theory took their ideas and applied them to individual student cheating. Muftic (2006) sought to test the idea that the exaggerated emphasis on economic success in the United States has bled into other social institutions, including academia. She surveyed American and international undergraduate students and asked them about their cheating behavior and their economic goals. Results suggested that American students were more oriented to economic goals and were more likely to admit to cheating: "Students with higher adherence to the cultural values of universalism and the fetishism of money had a higher likelihood of cheating. . . . Location of birth (i.e., born in the United States) appeared to have the strongest impact on cheating" (Muftic, 2006, p. 648).

While she found some support for institutional anomie theory, Muftic also points out that adherence to the American Dream is not universal. Even in a fairly homogeneous sample, American students embraced the cultural ideal at varying levels. Muftic concluded her article by suggesting that both micro-level (neighborhood cohesiveness, levels of informal social control) and macro-level (poverty, family disruption, racial heterogeneity, and social mobility) analyses be combined in future studies of institutional anomie theory.

◈ Critiques of Anomie and Strain Theories

Macro-level components of Merton's theory have rarely been tested as it is difficult, if not impossible, to measure how whole societies focus on particular goals and means (Kubrin, Stucky, & Krohn, 2009, p. 127). Messner and Rosenfeld (2007) discuss four primary critiques of Merton's argument and anomie theory. First, Merton assumes that value consensus exists in society and that the goal of monetary success is held above all. As Muftic (2006) pointed out, we should not assume those values are universal; other goals may be equally important, or more important, for many Americans. Second, Merton's theory and many versions of classical strain theory are class biased and have difficulty accounting for deviance among the privileged classes. Third, Merton seems to suggest that providing more equal opportunity offers a realistic solution to crime and deviance in the United States; Messner and Rosenfeld do not believe this to be the case. Finally, Merton never precisely defines anomie.

Messner and Rosenfeld (2007) dispense with the first two critiques as being oversimplified readings of Merton's argument, suggesting that Merton never claimed complete value consensus but that monetary success is a particularly powerful benchmark in the United States. Furthermore, Merton's basic argument can be used to explain deviance and criminal behavior in the middle and upper classes as well, as the definition of success is relative and must still be achieved despite structural constraints.

RECENT STUDY IN DEVIANCE

Stress and Deviance in Policing

By Michael L. Arter, 2008, in *Deviant Behavior, 29*, 43–69.

Policing, as a whole, is one of the most stressful occupations in the United States. But even within policing, certain assignments are considered much more stressful than others. One of these assignments is undercover police work. Arter uses general strain theory to examine these stressful assignments and the reported deviant responses that many police in these assignments report engaging in.

Arter interviewed 32 police officers who were currently in an undercover position, had been in an undercover position in the past, or had never held an undercover position. In addition to discussing the types and levels of stress associated with all of their policing duties, Arter also had the interview participants discuss their perceived deviant behaviors. Arter defined deviance in a couple of ways: (1) as behavior that was considered deviant by the department (i.e., the officer could be sanctioned for it) or a violation of the law and, using a phenomenological approach, (2) as a behavior that the participant defined as deviant, whether or not it was a departmental or a legal violation.

Arter found that individuals in exceptionally stressful policing positions were more likely to report deviant behavior than those in less stressful policing positions. In addition, he found that if stress was reduced through reassignment out of an undercover position, deviant behavior also decreased.

Explaining Deviance in the Streets and Deviance in the Suites: The Occupy Wall Street Movement

The Occupy Wall Street movement in New York in the fall of 2011 focused attention on inequality in the United States and the perceived crumbling of the American Dream. Protesters, embracing the slogan

"We are the 99 percent," took over Zuccotti Park in lower Manhattan, disrupting the work and daily life of wealthy financial traders for weeks and months. The message of the Occupy movement spread quickly, with protests taking root in cities and college campuses across the country. The protests were largely tolerated by local authorities, but law enforcement created headlines when college students protesting on the University of California campus in Davis were pepper sprayed by campus police. The Occupy movement lasted for months; eventually hundreds of Occupy participants were displaced when they were evicted from Zuccotti Park and arrested for violations as simple as disorderly conduct or laying down in public.

Many of the activists of the Occupy movement were young, highly educated adults. Sociologists found that more than a third of the protesters lived in households with annual incomes over $100,000, and more than two-thirds of them held professional jobs (Moynihan, 2013). And yet, their discontent was palpable and spurred them to action.

It seems education is no longer a guaranteed conforming route to a successful, fulfilling, and profitable career. Researchers found that nearly 80% of the Occupy participants had a bachelor's degree, and, of those, about half had a graduate degree, yet a significant portion of the protesters had credit card or student loan debt and were underemployed, working less than 35 hours a week (Moynihan, 2013). Milkman (2012) describes the origin of the Occupy protesters' frustration and activism:

> They followed the prescribed path to prepare themselves for professional jobs or other meaningful careers. But having completed their degrees, they confronted a labor market bleaker than anytime since the 1930s. Adding insult to injury, many were burdened with enormous amounts of student debt.
>
>   In this sense, Occupy might be seen as a classic revolution of rising expectations. But it is not only about blocked economic aspirations: The millennials were also seduced and abandoned *politically.* Their generation enthusiastically supported Barack Obama in 2008; some participated in "Camp Obama," and many were otherwise actively involved in the campaign. But here, too, their expectations were brutally disappointed. (pp. 13–14)

As economic, political, and social expectations are disappointed and new realities created, it might be argued that the United States is again experiencing a time of anomie as Durkheim described it, where society fails to regulate the expectations and behaviors of its members. Young people—who if they had been born into an earlier generation might have found their investment in education paying financial dividends—were so frustrated by the inequality and lack of good opportunities that they literally took to the street in the Occupy movement, banding together and risking arrest in order to make a point and feel heard.

Langman, a sociologist, explains how the Wall Street bailout, in which the federal government committed some $700 billion in taxpayer money to rescue Wall Street banks, showed power differences in the extreme, with wealthy corporations offered enormous financial assistance while middle- and working-class citizens lost their homes, their jobs, and their hope:

> There was an explosion of "subprime" mortgages in which vetting applicants was negligent at best, criminal at worst. Eventually, the bubble burst, the rapidly expanding housing market crashed, the entire financial industry imploded and took the entire economy down. There followed a wave of bankruptcies, layoffs of workers, and subsequent economic stagnation, if not devastation for many in vulnerable positions, who have been dubbed the precariat. But

while surely there was malfeasance, if not criminal behavior, this must be understood as a structural crisis in which the "steering mechanisms" failed.

A vast government bailout pumped trillions of dollars into the insolvent banks and "saved" the banking/financial system. The government rescue halted the plummet, saved the financial system and its elite prospered, yet ordinary people lost jobs, houses were foreclosed, people evicted, and many remain unemployed and/or underemployed. It was soon evident that thanks to "crony capitalism," the casino players won, the banking/finance industries had "recovered," indeed amassed more wealth than ever before. Its elites were well rewarded—thanks to the taxpayers.

Economic crises, implosions, and structural contradictions that threaten survival or the maintenance of living standards, or render social status, dignity and self-esteem problematic, lead to questions and challenges to the legitimacy of the economic system, political leadership, and legitimating ideologies. (Langman, 2013, pp. 511–512)

Even as its members protested extreme inequality in the United States, some controversy arose from within the Occupy movement when chronically homeless people moved into the Occupy camps in areas such as Wall Street, Boston, and Los Angeles. While some Occupy protesters embraced the homeless as epitomizing the very soul of arguments about inequality and the lack of resources of the 99%, others felt like the homeless population took advantage of the comparative luxury and safety of the camps and that their presence brought more stringent scrutiny from authorities and law enforcement.

▲ Photo 4.4 How might the Occupy movement be both an example of Deviance in the Streets and Deviance in the Suites?"

Source: ©CribbVisuals /iStockphoto.

The Occupy Wall Street movement is an interesting example of highly educated individuals literally taking to the streets to protest what they perceive as deviance in the corporate suites. We began this chapter with the example of Christopher McCandless, who after graduating college gave up all of his worldly possessions and struck out to make it on his own in the wilderness far away from the trappings of the larger society. He shared in common with the young people of the Occupy movement a deep frustration with the norms and expectations of American society. In responding to the conditions of anomie and strain, McCandless chose to retreat while the Occupy participants chose to band together and rebel.

◈ Ideas in Action: Defy Ventures—Transforming Innovation Into Legitimate Success

In describing the adaptations to anomie, Robert Merton defined innovation as acceptance of the cultural goal of wealth attainment and the use of illegitimate means to work toward that goal. Thus, crimes committed for money or profit would generally fall under the heading of innovation. While illegal, there are often real skills involved in these illicit business pursuits and individuals may become successful entrepreneurs selling drugs and services.

After visiting Texas prisons in a religious outreach program, Catherine Rohr discovered that many of the skills and talents prisoners developed and used as drug dealers and criminals—street smarts, resourcefulness, money management, risk-taking, and the ability to manage employees—were exactly the traits needed to succeed in more conventional business endeavors. She started the Prisoner Entrepreneurship Program (http://www.prisonentrepreneurship.org/), a nonprofit program that teaches Texas inmates an MBA-level curriculum and encourages them to translate their previous skills and work ethic into new and conforming ventures as they form plans to start their own businesses. The Prison Entrepreneurship Program has proven to be very successful in its first decade; it trains and socializes inmates to prepare them for conforming business opportunities, helps individuals with reentry and job placement upon release, and boasts a recidivism rate of less than 10%.

After a highly publicized scandal involving intimate (but not illegal) relationships with four graduates of her program after they were released from prison, Rohr resigned from her role with the Prison Entrepreneurship Program, but she did not give up on her belief that former prisoners could translate their skills into successful businesses. The following is an excerpt from a 2013 interview with Rohr:

> "America puts these people in the trash pile," Rohr said. "They represent America's most overlooked talent pool: the underdogs." But, she says they are brilliantly equipped to be leaders because of their street-smart and entrepreneurial (albeit illegal) past activities. After going through 1,000 hours of character and business development, the former felons come out as business people ready to face the world. (Menardi, 2013)

Rohr went on to found the New York–based Defy Ventures (http://defyventures.org/), a nonprofit funded and managed by entrepreneurs and venture capitalists who believe that former drug dealers and gang members may share similar skills with top business leaders. A news story checked in with the first class of Defy students, describing the program and the students' evolution and practices:

> These men are the inaugural class of Defy Ventures, a yearlong, M.B.A.-style program that Rohr created to teach former inmates how to start their own companies. For months, they have been meeting here for 14 to 16 hours a week to learn about things such as cash flow, balance sheets, intellectual property, accounting, and taxes. There are workshops on how to behave in professional settings, how to speak in public, and how to be a better parent. These men are also learning how to create business plans. In June, they will compete in a business-plan competition. The winners will split $100,000 in seed funding.
>
> Rohr has an interesting theory about criminals. She says that many of the qualities that made these men good at being bad guys (until they got caught, of course) are the same qualities that make effective entrepreneurs. Some of the men in this class had up to 40 employees under management. Though their merchandise was illegal narcotics and not, say, office supplies, these men developed certain business skills—the ability to motivate a team, identify new markets, manage risk, and inspire loyalty and hard work. Rohr's goal is to help these students apply their abilities to legal endeavors. (Frieswick, 2012)

Graduates of Defy Ventures have started cleaning businesses, concierge services, construction companies, financial planning services, repair businesses, a mobile barbershop, and other startup companies. In their quest to build new lives once they were released from prison, they recognized that Defy Ventures was offering legitimate, conforming opportunities, and they put in the work needed to translate their hard-earned skills and energy into new professional businesses.

NOW YOU . . . USE THE THEORY

The following is a graph of the suicide rates in the United States between 1950 and 2003. Note that the data are broken down by age and gender. Using anomie or general strain theory, explain the following:

The overall trend (all ages, age adjusted) between 1950 and 2003. Start by describing the trend, then choose one of the two theories to explain it.

The trend, over time, for 45- to 64-year-olds between 1950 and 2003. Start by describing the trend, then choose one of the two theories to explain it.

The trend for male suicides and female suicides over time. According to one of the two theories, why might women always be less likely to engage in suicidal behavior than men?

U.S. Suicide Rates, 1950–2003 (per 100,000 population)

	1950	1960	1970	1980	1990	1995	2000	2001	2002	2003
All ages, age adjusted	13.2	13.2	13.2	13.2	12.5	11.8	10.4	10.7	10.9	10.8
5–14 years	0.2	0.3	0.3	0.4	0.8	0.9	0.7	0.7	0.6	0.6
15–24 years	4.5	5.2	8.8	12.3	13.2	13.0	10.2	9.9	9.9	9.7
15–19 years	2.7	3.6	5.9	8.5	11.1	10.3	8.0	7.9	7.4	7.3
20–24 years	6.2	7.1	12.2	16.1	15.1	15.8	12.5	12.0	12.4	12.1
25–44 years	11.6	12.2	15.4	15.6	15.2	15.1	13.4	13.8	14.0	13.8
25–34 years	9.1	10.0	14.1	16.0	15.2	15.0	12.0	12.8	12.6	12.7
35–44 years	14.3	14.2	16.9	15.4	15.3	15.1	14.5	14.7	15.3	14.9
45–64 years	23.5	22.0	20.6	15.9	15.3	13.9	13.5	14.4	14.9	15.0
45–54 years	20.9	20.7	20.0	15.9	14.8	14.4	14.4	15.2	15.7	15.9
55–64 years	26.8	23.7	21.4	15.9	16.0	13.2	12.1	13.1	13.6	13.8
65 years and over	30.0	24.5	20.8	17.6	20.5	17.9	15.2	15.3	15.6	14.6
65–74 years	29.6	23.0	20.8	16.9	17.9	15.7	12.5	13.3	13.5	12.7
75–84 years	31.1	27.9	21.2	19.1	24.9	20.6	17.6	17.4	17.7	16.4
85 years and over	28.8	26.0	19.0	19.2	22.2	21.3	19.6	17.5	18.0	16.9
Male, all ages	21.2	20.0	19.8	19.9	21.5	20.3	17.7	18.2	18.4	18.0
Female, all ages	5.6	5.6	7.4	5.7	4.8	4.3	4.0	4.0	4.2	4.2

Source: Graph from World Health Organization.

Rohr and others working at and supporting Defy Ventures hope to eventually replicate the program in every urban community in the United States. If and when communities come together to support formerly incarcerated people who are trying to change their lives, there will be less strain, less need for innovation, and more opportunities for every member of society to conform and thrive.

◈ Conclusion

Anomie and strain theories have a more clearly developed history than other theoretical traditions. Nearly everyone can agree that these ideas began with Durkheim and Merton and were extended in important ways by Cloward and Ohlin and a handful of other theorists. One recent revision of the theory views strain as a function of relative deprivation. In this model, the reference group is a key element. Your own absolute success or wealth is less important than your position relative to those around you. Comparing yourself to those with more wealth and more material success may lead to strain and deviant behavior. Today, Messner and Rosenfeld's institutional anomie theory might be considered the leading version of anomie theory, and Agnew's general strain theory might be considered the leading version of strain theory (Cullen & Agnew, 2006).

Research continues on both anomie and strain theories. More sophisticated methods are allowing for analyses that bridge both macro-level and micro-level variables, which will offer an ever-increasing understanding of how cultural goals and the social structure affect individuals and lead to deviant behavior.

EXERCISES AND DISCUSSION QUESTIONS

1. Provide another example of a state of anomie. How did it affect rates of deviance?

2. Give a specific example of each of Merton's five adaptations.

3. What are the policy recommendations you might make based on Cloward and Ohlin's ideas? In other words, using Cloward and Ohlin's ideas on delinquency and opportunity, what programs might be put into place to prevent crime and deviance?

4. Institutional anomie theory argues that our economic goals and system have permeated and overrun other social systems/institutions in the United States. Do you think this is true? Can you think of examples from politics, education, and families?

5. Do you think that Agnew is correct that individuals are pressured into crime and deviance? Can you think of an example of a time when you were faced with a negative relationship but did not turn to deviant behavior? How did you react instead?

KEY TERMS

Anomie	Institutional anomie theory	Strain
Conflict subcultures	Relative deprivation	Structural impediments
Criminal subcultures	Retreatist subcultures	
General strain theory (GST)	Status frustration	

CHAPTER 5

Social Disorganization Theory

> To LaJoe, the neighborhood had become a black hole. She could more easily recite what wasn't there than what was there. There were no banks, only currency exchanges, which charged up to $8.00 for every welfare check cashed. There were no public libraries, skating rinks, movie theaters, or bowling alleys to entertain the neighborhood's children. For the infirm there were two neighborhood clinics . . . both of which teetered on bankruptcy and would close by the end of 1989. Yet the death rate of newborn babies exceeded the infant mortality rates in a number of third world countries, including Chili, Costa Rica, Cuba, and Turkey. And there was no rehabilitation center, though drug abuse was rampant.
>
> According to a 1980 profile of Twenty-seventh ward—a political configuration drawn, ironically, in the shape of a gun and including Henry Horner and Rockwell Gardens, a smaller but no less forbidding housing complex—60,110 people lived here, 88 percent of them black, 46 percent of them lived below the poverty level. It was so impoverished that when Mother Teresa visited in 1982, she assigned nuns from her Missionaries of Charity to work at Henry Horner.
>
> *Source:* Kotlowitz (1988, p. 12).

 ## Introduction

Kotlowitz's (1988) description of these Chicago neighborhoods provides an interesting introduction to social disorganization theory, a theory developed to explain patterns of deviance and crime across social locations such as neighborhoods. Unlike many of the micro-level theories discussed in this book, which attempt to explain variation in deviant behavior across individuals, social disorganization theory is a macro-level theory that focuses on larger units of analysis such as neighborhoods, schools, cities, and even states or countries. This is a unique contribution because it is so clear that some places are safer than others and that all sorts of deviances flourish in other places. Rodney Stark (1987) accurately described a major problem in criminology stemming from the advent of self-report surveys:

> This transformation soon led repeatedly to the "discovery" that poverty is unrelated to delinquency. . . . Yet, through it all, social scientists somehow knew better than to stroll the street at night in certain parts of town or even to park there. And despite the fact that countless surveys showed that kids from upper and lower income families scored the same on delinquency batteries, even social scientists know that the parts of town that scared them were not upper-income neighborhoods. (p. 894)

Indeed, violence, drug use, prostitution, mental illness, and other forms of deviance are commonplace in neighborhoods such as Henry Horner and Rockwell Gardens. Other places seem to be able to control crime and deviance (or at least the deviance that does exist is far less visible). Social disorganization theory attempts to explain this variation. Why are certain neighborhoods able to control levels of deviance while others are unable to minimize it or eliminate it entirely? Social disorganization theory assumes that most people do not want to live in unsafe neighborhoods with high levels of delinquency, crime, and deviance. However, because of various structural conditions to be discussed, some people are not able to work together to achieve common goals.

In this chapter, we begin with some history behind the theory of social disorganization, including the creation of a major program in sociology at the University of Chicago toward the end of the 19th century and the social milieu of Chicago at this point in time. We then discuss the development of social disorganization theory and early empirical tests of the theory, which were focused primarily on juvenile delinquency. Historically, the theory was put on the backburner for many years only to come back strong in the 1980s. We discuss this revitalization as well as new advances of the theory. Today, social disorganization theory and variants of it are reasonably popular and are used quite often when investigating deviance at the aggregate level: neighborhoods, schools, cities, even internationally.

◈ Development of Social Disorganization Theory

To provide context for an understanding of the theory of social disorganization, we need to go back to end of the 19th century and the transition to the 20th. Consider Chicago at the turn of the century (perhaps not so different in terms of deviance than it is today—plenty to go around!). Many of the new faculty members at the University of Chicago were from rural and religious backgrounds. They were coming to Chicago, a city where crime and deviance were not hard to find—indeed, they were right in your face. Gambling, prostitution, alcohol consumption, violence, police abuse of power, and many other forms of deviance were common and well known to the citizens of Chicago. The question for these researchers was why these forms of deviance existed and seemed to flourish in certain areas of the city while other areas seemed to be able to control these "social problems."

Alternatively, how did people in general explain deviance at the turn of the century? In other words, what were the popular explanations of crime and deviance? Much like today, the explanations focused on individuals and groups—that is, "types of people" explanations. The criminals and deviants were the "new immigrants." Immigrants who brought their old traditions and who had not been appropriately socialized into the new world were seen as the causes of the social problems of the day. The popular advertisement shown in Photo 5.1 glorifies the prejudice of the day. Irish immigrants need not apply; we do not have work for you. Of course, at different times, different groups felt the brunt of ethnic prejudice and were seen as the cause of various social ills. Italians certainly faced ethnic discrimination and were seen as a source of trouble. Indeed, in 1918, when labor was in high demand and employers were scrounging for workers, advertisements read "Italians and Coloreds" may apply, suggesting an ethnic stratification ranking of Italians as close to African Americans (Luhman, 2002). German Jews immigrating to the United States during the early to mid-1800s because of the repression and discrimination in Germany faced fewer legal restrictions here, but there were still some, including restrictions from "holding public office, becoming lawyers, and serving as officers in state militia" in certain regions (Luhman, 2002, p. 149). Immigration from China beginning around 1850 also brought political and social reaction, leading to Chinese immigrants being viewed as deviant. Hispanics, too, have faced ethnic stereotyping and discrimination. Finally, coming to America as slaves, African Americans have always faced prejudice and discrimination, but as they moved from the South to northern cities, they too became the scapegoat and the "cause" of social problems.

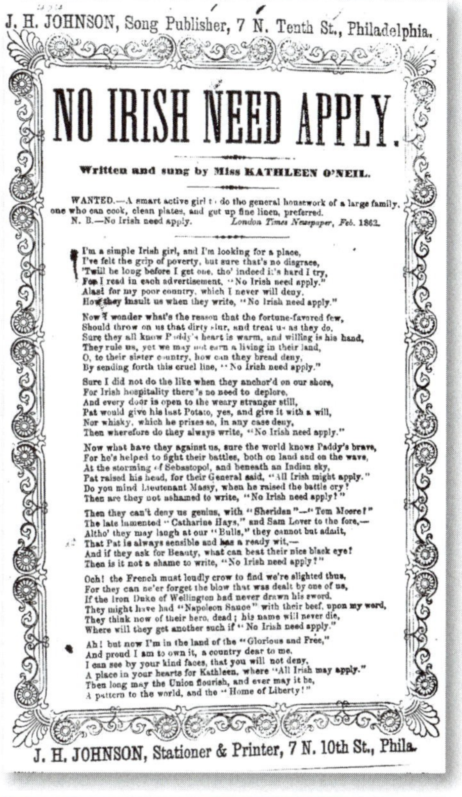

Fortunately, science was also making important discoveries and influencing how we thought about deviance and other social problems. The Chicago school was very familiar with scientific strides being made in plant and animal biology.

▲ **Photo 5.1** Immigrants faced many problems when they arrived in the United States at the turn of the century, including discrimination.

Source: ©Photos.com/Thinkstock.

For example, Darwin's *Origin of Species,* published in 1859, was well known to Chicago sociologists and influenced how they approached the study of human behavior. In contrast to the classical school of criminology, which focused on free will and the role of the government in controlling free will, the Chicago perspective did not ask whether plants "willed" themselves to do better in certain environments than others or whether animals "willed" themselves to reproduce and thrive in certain areas versus others. Rather, its proponents believed that environmental factors affected whether certain plants would grow in certain areas and certain animals would flourish in others. The early Chicago researchers believed that they could find the causes of crime in the structure of the environment. Much like today, thanks to the explosion of information and analysis provided by geographic information systems such as Mapquest or Google Earth, the principle of the Chicago school was that if you want to understand something—Map It! Through this process of mapping social deviance, researchers were able to demonstrate that "types of people" explanations were often limited if not downright wrong. Indeed, certain types of deviance seemed to flourish in some areas over time, even though the "types of people" (racial and ethnic groups) who lived there changed dramatically.

DEVIANCE IN POPULAR CULTURE

When people are asked what causes crime, they tend to think in terms of individualistic causes of deviance. That is, they are looking to answer why certain individuals engage in crime and deviant behavior and others do not. The social disorganization perspective asks a different question: Why is there more crime in certain areas than in others? *What community-level characteristics influence the rate of crime/ deviance in any given area?*

The documentary film *Hoop Dreams* follows two young boys from inner-city Chicago as they are recruited into a private high school and different colleges in pursuit of their goal of basketball stardom. Watch the first 45 minutes of *Hoop Dreams* (freshman and sophomore years of high school), paying careful attention to the different environments that are captured on tape.

- What did you notice about the neighborhoods that Arthur and William grew up and lived in? What did the neighborhoods look like? What kinds of things went on there? What did people say about these areas?
- Now think about the neighborhood in which the high school, St. Joe's, is located. What did it look like? What did people say about it?
- Which neighborhood do you think had higher crime rates? Why do you think so? What are the important characteristics to consider?
- Think about the neighborhood that you grew up in. What was it like? What factors do you think contributed to the crime rates (high or low) in your neighborhood?
- If you were trying to lower crime/deviance rates in a given neighborhood, where would you start? What specifically would you target and try to improve?

Documentary films can sometimes tell us a great deal about deviance and social control, even if that is not the expressed intent of the story. The Chicago neighborhoods shown in *Hoop Dreams* have very different levels of social organization, which affects levels of crime and deviance and the life chances of individuals such as Arthur and William and their family members. Considering the neighborhood you grew up in as an additional case study can help to illustrate how social disorganization affects communities—and how it may have affected you and your friends, even though you may not have realized it at the time. Applying the theories to real examples helps to remind us that these are more than big ideas—deviance is all around us, and sociological theories can help us make sense of our own social worlds.

Shaw and McKay Study of Juvenile Delinquency and Urban Areas

Based on Park and Burgess's human ecology approach, the origin of social disorganization theory is generally attributed to Clifford Shaw and Henry McKay's (1942/1969) seminal work, *Juvenile Delinquency and Urban Areas,* in which they plotted on maps the home addresses of (1) boys brought to court for an alleged delinquent activity, (2) boys committed by the court to a correctional facility, and (3) "boys dealt with by the police probation officers with or without court appearance"

(p. 44). Data on court cases and commitments were available for 1900, 1920, and 1930, while police contacts centered around 1930. As the authors noted, "The distribution of delinquents at different periods of time afford the basis for comparison and for analysis of long-term trends and processes that could not be made for a single period" (Shaw & McKay, 1942/1969, p. 45). Their maps clearly show three things. First, delinquency did not appear to be distributed randomly across the neighborhoods of Chicago. Second, rates of delinquency appeared to cluster in certain neighborhoods and appeared highest close to the central business district (CBD). Shaw and McKay noted that in addition to the high rates of delinquency near the CBD, delinquency was highest in neighborhoods in or around business and industrial areas, often referred to as mixed land use. Third, delinquency, by and large, tended to decline as you move away from the CBD. Indeed, their analyses clearly showed that rates of delinquency as measured by juvenile commitments across five concentric zones around 1900, 1920, and 1930 fell precipitously as one moved away from the CBD.

Shaw and McKay (1942/1969) examined these zones and characterized Zone II, the one closest to the CBD, as a zone in transition. Here resided the most recent immigrants to the city, the poorest and least educated citizens, and those who needed to live close to the CBD for work—

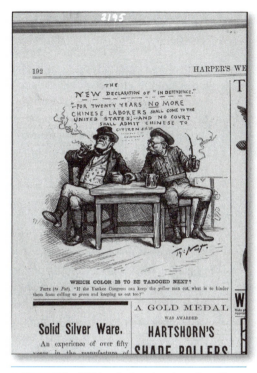

▲ Photo 5.2   Which color is to be tabooed next?

Source: ©Thomas Nast/Library of Congress.

when they could find it. Shaw and McKay found that as you moved away from the zones in transition, you would find residents from earlier waves of immigrants. These were people who had learned English, had received more education, had better jobs, and could afford to get out of the impoverished inner city where only those who had no other choice lived. What was most interesting was that the people who lived in the zone in transition changed—indeed, no one really wanted to live there, and immigrants quickly left the high crime rate and deviant areas for safer neighborhoods as soon as they could afford to, only to be replaced by another group of immigrants who were forced to live in the zone in transition.

To better understand why crime rates declined as one moved out from the inner city, Shaw and McKay (1942/1969) looked to other social factors that characterized these areas. So, other than high rates of delinquency, what characterized these neighborhoods? Shaw and McKay highlighted three factors that characterized neighborhoods with high rates of delinquency: poverty, population turnover, and racial/ethnic heterogeneity. Shaw and McKay did not emphasize a direct link between poverty and delinquency (Bursik, 1988); rather, they found that poor neighborhoods were characterized by population turnover and racial and ethnic heterogeneity. Bursik argues that "in its purest formulation, social disorganization refers to the inability of local communities to realize the common values of their residents or solve commonly experienced problems" (p. 521). When the primary goal of the residents is to move out of the neighborhood, there is little incentive to try to make it a better place. These people were poor and did not own their own residences, and the landlords ("slum lords") had little interest in making these neighborhoods better places to live. In fact, it was in their best interest to invest as little as possible in their apartment buildings and other structures because, as the city expanded, they would be bought out and their buildings torn down and replaced with industrial structures. Similarly, because the populations were changing and composed of people with different ethnic and/or racial backgrounds, further barriers existed, such as limited motivation to work together to reduce the crime and other deviance that characterized the area. These structural factors (poverty, population turnover, and racial/ethnic heterogeneity) consistently characterized high delinquency areas even though the specific "types of people" changed over the decades studied.

◈ Critiques of Social Disorganization Theory

Shaw and McKay's (1942/1969) pioneering work in social disorganization theory was sharply criticized on a number of grounds and then waned in popularity and importance for several reasons as described in a review by Bursik (1988). First, the field of criminology shifted and became far more focused on individuals as opposed to groups, and macro-level theories such as social disorganization rarely have anything to say about individuals, only groups and places. Second, **longitudinal data** (data collected over time) are expensive and sometimes impossible to collect, and later studies typically were restricted to **cross-sectional designs** (data collected at only one point in time). Cross-sectional designs are problematic in the study of deviance, especially studies of a theory based on longitudinal data, because they typically assume a static view of urban life that seems inconsistent with history. Finally, there was considerable confusion about what social disorganization actually was and how it should be measured. In particular, there seemed to be some confusion in distinguishing social disorganization from delinquency itself, resulting in criticisms that the theory was tautological—that is, true by definition, circular, and therefore not testable. However, a number of important works in the late 1970s and 1980s gave social disorganization theory a rebirth.

◈ Rebirth of Social Disorganization Theory

In her classic work, *Social Sources of Delinquency,* Ruth Kornhauser (1978) divided the classic theories of juvenile delinquency into three basic types: cultural deviance (e.g., differential association and social learning; see Chapter 6), strain (see Chapter 4), and social disorganization. She clearly puts social disorganization as a macro-level control theory whereby residents of certain neighborhoods are able to control and minimize unwanted deviance, while residents in some neighborhoods, characterized by poverty, population turnover, and racial/ethnic heterogeneity, cannot control their environments and achieve common goals. Although Shaw and McKay (1942/1969) discussed the subculture found in socially disorganized neighborhoods, Kornhauser and others who followed tended to focus solely on the structural aspects of the theory. Following this important work, a number of scholars began reflecting on and promoting the potential of the theory. Stark (1987), for example, used social disorganization theory along with 100 years' worth of theorizing and empirical research on social ecology to develop 30 propositions linking neighborhood characteristics to high rates of deviance, including "(1) density; (2) poverty; (3) mixed [land] use; (4) transience; and (5) dilapidation" (p. 895).

In turn, Bursik (1988) documented the reasons for the decline in the popularity of the social disorganization theory and suggested several lines for pursuing the theory, including (1) thinking about the neighborhood as a social context for individual behavior, (2) focusing on measures of deviance such as self-reported behavior and victimization surveys that are not the result of official responses by law enforcement, and (3) considering the possible feedback effects of crime and delinquency on social disorganization (the ability to control the environment). Finally, several studies were conducted that empirically tested the validity of the theory.

◈ Application of Social Disorganization Theory

One of the first innovations and empirical tests of the social disorganization theory involved consideration of the mediating factors hypothesized between the social structural variables identified by Shaw and McKay (1942/1969) and crime and delinquency. Sampson and Groves (1989) argued that sparse friendship networks, unsupervised teen peer groups, and low organizational participation should largely explain the relationship between poverty, ethnic heterogeneity, population turnover, family disruption, and urbanization. That is, neighborhoods characterized by these factors would be less able to control certain forms of deviance because residents were not communicating with one another and allowed teens to roam the streets unsupervised. The model is described in Figure 5.1.

Figure 5.1   Sampson and Groves' Model of Social Disorganization

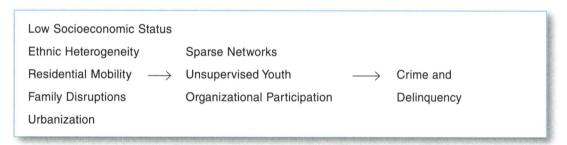

Low Socioeconomic Status

Ethnic Heterogeneity   Sparse Networks

Residential Mobility ⟶ Unsupervised Youth ⟶ Crime and

Family Disruptions   Organizational Participation   Delinquency

Urbanization

Sampson and Groves (1989) analyzed data from the 1982 British Crime Survey (BCS), which included data on more than 10,000 respondents across 238 localities in England and Wales, and then they replicated the analyses using data from a slightly larger number of individuals residing in 300 British communities. They found that neighborhoods with sparse friendship networks, unsupervised teenage peer groups, and low organizational participation were associated with higher rates of victimization and self-reported offending (violence and property crimes) and that these variables explained much of the effect of the standard structural variables generally used to test social disorganization theory.

About a decade later, Veysey and Messner (1999) replicated these analyses using slightly more sophisticated statistical modeling techniques. They were more cautious in their interpretation of the results of their analyses in terms of the theory. They found that the mediating social disorganization variables (sparse friendships, unsupervised teens, and organizational participation) only partially explained the effects of the structural variables and argued that the results were partially consistent with social disorganization theory but were also consistent with theories focused on peer affiliation, such as differential association theory (see Chapter 6). Again using the British Crime Survey, but this time with data from 1994 (more than a decade later), Lowenkamp, Cullen, and Pratt (2003) replicated Sampson and Groves' (1989) model using similar measures. The results were largely consistent, and the authors argued that the consistency of the findings suggests that Sampson and Groves' model was not an idiosyncratic result of the timing of the original study but that the theoretical model is generalizable across time.

Classic social disorganization theory has continued to be tested in other environments. For example, given that Shaw and McKay and many others have focused on urban environments, some have questioned whether the theory is applicable to nonurban areas. Osgood and Chambers (2000) examined the structural correlates of homicide, rape, weapon offenses, and simple assault arrest rates across 264 nonmetropolitan counties in Florida, Georgia, South Carolina, and Nebraska. They found that population turnover, family disruption, and ethnic heterogeneity were all related to these arrest statistics. Jobes, Barclay, and Weinand (2004) found support for social disorganization in 123 rural government areas in New South Wales, Australia.

A criticism raised against Shaw and McKay's (1942/1969) original analyses and many other analyses is the focus on official measures of crime. However, Sampson and Groves' (1989) classic analysis, as well as replications (Lowencamp et al., 2003; Veysey & Messner, 1999) with self-reported offending and victimization with the British Crime Survey, clearly shows the generalizability of the theory. In an interesting approach, Warner and Pierce (1993) used calls to police rather than reactions by the police (e.g., arrests) across 60 Boston neighborhoods in 1980 and found support for social disorganization theory. Finally, while most studies have focused on juvenile delinquency and street crimes, Benson, Wooldredge, and Thistlethwaite (2004) found that neighborhood factors associated with social disorganization theory affect both black and white rates of domestic violence.

As the reader might surmise, the theory of social disorganization has largely focused on delinquency and street crimes, especially violent street crimes, rather than on other forms of deviance, especially what might be seen as "soft deviance." This is not entirely the case, however, as even early researchers were interested in how social disorganization theory might help us understand the geographic concentration of mental illness, prostitution, gambling, alcoholism, and drug use. Some recent research continues in this tradition.

Eric **Silver** (2000) examined the structural correlates of violence, but his focus was on the mentally ill, whereas most research had previously only examined individual-level variables such as gender, race, and socioeconomic status. He obtained data on 270 psychiatric patients discharged from the Western Psychiatric Institute and Clinic in Pittsburgh, Pennsylvania. The patients had been treated for a variety of mental disorders, including schizophrenia, depression, mania, and alcohol or drug dependence, among others. Violence was measured via self-report, "collateral" reports (i.e., reports from someone who knew the respondent well and had frequent interactions), and official records. Neighborhood-level variables included a composite measure of socioeconomic disadvantage and population turnover. Although population turnover was unrelated to violence, socioeconomic disadvantage was related to violence in bivariate analyses as well as in multivariate models controlling for a host of individual-level characteristics.

Another study by Hayes-Smith and Whaley (2009) focused on social disorganization and methamphetamine use. While the Silver study above focused on individuals and the neighborhoods around their homes, Hayes-Smith and Whaley studied school districts in Michigan. Self-reported data collected via an anonymous survey of eighth-, tenth- and twelfth-grade students, about a third from each grade, were aggregated to the school district ($n = 202$). District characteristics included low socioeconomic status, residential instability, racial composition, and family disruption, among others. Findings showed that—consistent with social disorganization theory—methamphetamine use was consistently and positively related to low socioeconomic status and population instability. Interestingly, in contrast to social disorganization theory, racial/ethnic heterogeneity was negatively related to methamphetamine use whereas the percent white was positively related to it, suggesting that meth-amphetamine use may be more common among whites than racial minorities. The suburban, urban, and rural variables were significant in some models but not others. When significant, the results seemed to suggest that methamphetamine use may be higher in suburban and rural areas. Overall, the data largely support social disorganization theory, and this study adds to the literature by focusing on a relatively new and disturbing form of substance use across urban and rural school districts.

RECENT STUDY IN DEVIANCE

Gender, Social Disorganization Theory, and the Location of Sexually Oriented Business

By Michelle Edwards, 2010, in *Deviant Behavior, 31*(2), 135–158.

Edwards examined the neighborhood characteristics of three types of sexually oriented businesses: adult sexuality boutiques, adult entertainment clubs, and adult bookstores. Using social disorganization theory, she critiqued the placement of these different businesses and the impact of race, class, and gender on their placement.

Examining four urban counties in Texas, Edwards determined the existence of the three types of sexually oriented businesses using a generally agreed-upon definition of each type of business. Adult sexuality boutiques are usually stores in which sexually explicit materials such as lingerie, sex toys, fetish paraphernalia, and bachelorette party supplies are sold. These businesses are more likely to be run by women and often emphasize female sexual health. Adult entertainment clubs are usually clubs that specialize in nude or topless dancing by females. These clubs usually cater to men. Finally, adult bookstores also sell sexual paraphernalia like adult sexuality boutiques, but these stores usually specialize in the sale or rental of pornographic videos and magazines and cater to male clientele.

Edwards found that adult sexuality boutiques (which are predominately visited by women) are more likely to be in socially organized and cohesive neighborhoods, while adult entertainment clubs and bookstores (which are predominately visited by men) are more likely to be in socially disorganized neighborhoods. While white men are the predominant clientele of both adult entertainment clubs and adult bookstores, the disorganized neighborhoods the businesses are in are more likely to be lower-income neighborhoods with higher rates of minority residents. This suggests that "certain groups are able to keep their neighborhoods separated from [certain] sexually oriented businesses, while also maintaining anonymity if they choose to visit these businesses" (p. 155).

◈ More Theoretical and Empirical Advances and Divergences: Social and Physical Disorder

Minor misbehavior (e.g., prostitution, public rowdiness or drunkenness) and signs of physical disorder (e.g., litter, graffiti, broken windows) and their relationship to crime has been a concern at least since the 1800s. About 30 years ago, Wilson and Kelling (1982) published an essay titled "Broken Windows: The Police and Neighborhood Safety" in the *Atlantic Monthly* that brought these issues back into the public limelight as well as to the attention of scholars interested in crime and deviance. Basically, the authors argued that disorder leads to greater disorder and attracts and promotes more serious forms of deviance. The notion is simple to the young man living in an area characterized by graffiti and broken windows: Why not break another window—it is fun and what's the harm? Signs of disorder lead to further disorder. This led to the policy implication that police (and other agents of social control) attack crime at its roots and target minor forms of social disorder deviance that seem to be critical causes of the escalation of crime and further deviance. In other words, focus on less serious forms of deviance, and you may deter more serious forms of crime.

Although the two are clearly unique (see Kubrin, 2008), the parallels between the disorder theory and social disorganization theory are fairly obvious. The key to social disorganization theory is the ability of residents to control delinquency and crime, things that most everyone would like to minimize. Similarly, there are areas where residents are able to minimize social and physical disorder (e.g., adults drinking, unsupervised youth, trash, graffiti) and other areas where residents have difficulty minimizing disorder. Physical and social disorder are presumably things that most people would like to avoid if they had the ability to control them or could afford to live in "better" neighborhoods.

▲ **Photo 5.3** Can broken windows actually encourage crime and other forms of deviance?

Source: ©rusm/istockphoto.

Considerable research links physical and social disorder with more serious street crimes. Skogan's (1990) *Disorder and Decline: Crime and the Spiral of Decay in American Neighborhoods,* for example, provides a compelling argument and data detailing that disorder is a major root cause of urban crime. Alternatively, Harcourt (2001) is critical and argues that not enough empirical attention has been given to the causal link between disorder and crime, and he claims the policies (e.g., zero-tolerance policies) drawn from the "theory" are often inappropriate and/or ineffective. Furthermore, Sampson and Raudenbush (2004) provided a very unique test of the relationship between disorder and crime and found that while the two are correlated, factors including poverty and the concentration of minority groups are even stronger predictors. Because it is simple and appealing to the public and public officials, Wilson and Kelling's (1982) broken windows theory will likely remain active and persuasive in terms of policies and practices. Why not focus on problems residents are concerned with, even if they don't have a causal link to more serious crime? In fact, social disorder may really simply be "less serious" crime and deviance.

Collective Efficacy

Another advance in social disorganization theory came from Robert Sampson and his colleagues (Sampson, Raudenbush, & Earls, 1997), who drew an analogy between individual efficacy (i.e., an individual's ability to accomplish a task) and neighborhood or collective efficacy (i.e., a neighborhood's ability to recognize common goals of a safe environment that is largely free from crime and deviance). They defined collective efficacy as "social cohesion among neighbors combined with their willingness to intervene on the behalf of the common good" (p. 918). Social cohesion and trust between neighbors are seen as necessary conditions for residents to be willing to intervene for the common good. Basically, the authors made the argument that collective efficacy is an important mediating effect between structural factors associated with social disorganization and deviant behavior, particularly violent behavior.

Sampson et al. (1997) examined data from the Project on Human Development in Chicago Neighborhoods. Government-defined census tracts are often used as the unit of analysis to characterize neighborhoods. This is a reasonable strategy but nowhere near perfect as they often have arbitrary borders that do not reflect what residents perceive to be as "their neighborhood." To get a better measure of neighborhoods, the researchers combined 847 Chicago census tracts into 343 neighborhood clusters in an attempt to create a unit of analysis that made meaningful sense in terms of composition and geographic boundaries (e.g., roads, waterways). They interviewed 8,782 residents across all neighborhood clusters in the residents' homes. They measured "informal social control" by asking respondents how likely their neighbors could be counted on to intervene in various ways if

- children were skipping school and hanging out on a street corner,
- children were spray-painting a building,
- children were showing disrespect to an adult,
- a fight broke out in front of their house, or
- the fire station closest to the house was threatened with budget cuts.

Cohesion and trust were measured by asking respondents how strongly they agreed with the following:

- People around here are willing to help their neighbors.
- This is a close-knit neighborhood.
- People in this neighborhood can be trusted.
- People in this neighborhood generally don't get along with each other.
- People in this neighborhood do not share the same values.

The two scales were so highly correlated at the neighborhood level that they were combined into a single composite scale termed *collective efficacy*.

Structural variables related to social disorganization theory included concentrated disadvantage, immigrant concentration, and a lack of residential stability. The dependent measures of violence included perceived violence in the neighborhood and violent victimization from the neighborhood survey and the homicide rate from official records. Sampson et al. (1997) were able to assess the influence of structural variables on collective efficacy and the mediating effect of collective efficacy on violence. The results were consistent and robust. The structural variables were clearly related to collective efficacy, and collective efficacy in turn affected each measure of violence. The results strongly supported this modified version of social disorganization theory.

Subsequent to this publication, numerous studies have examined the role that collective efficacy plays on violence and other forms of deviance as well as reactions to deviance (e.g., residents' fear of crime). For example, Bernasco and Block (2009) found that collective efficacy keeps robbers out of certain census tracts in Chicago, while D. Martin (2002) found that social capital (politically active citizens) and collective efficacy (active community organizations) were negatively related to burglary across Detroit neighborhoods in the mid-1990s. Browning (2002) showed that the effects of collective efficacy extend beyond violence and street crime to affect intimate partner violence, and Cancino (2005) showed that collective efficacy not only is important in inner cities but applies to nonmetropolitan areas as well.

Wright and Cullen (2001) developed the analogous concept of **parental efficacy**, which is focused on parents' ability to control their children's behavior through parent–child attachment, rules, supervision, and also social support. Rankin and Quane (2002) linked these ideas directly to the community and examined how collective efficacy leads to greater parental efficacy, which leads to greater social competency and lower levels of problem behavior among children. More recently, Simons and his colleagues (Simons, Simons, Burt, Brody, & Cutrona, 2005) showed that collective efficacy promoted positive parenting strategies and that both were related to lower levels of deviant peer association and delinquency involvement. More interestingly, they found that authoritative parenting had pronounced effects in communities with higher levels of collective efficacy, suggesting that both factors are important in themselves but that in conjunction, the effects are even stronger.

In a more recent study, Berg and Rengifo (2009) focused on robbery and the role of informal social control in the presence of illicit drug markets. They too moved beyond a sole focus on structural characteristics emphasized in social disorganization theory and actually included measures of informal social control, very close to measures of collective efficacy, as critical mediating factors between structural variables and robbery. They argue that the structural factors discussed above negatively affect residents' ability to regulate behavior, keep out drug market activity, and control serious violent crimes such as robbery.

Berg and Rengifo's study focused on 66 block groups purposively selected to obtain variation in drug activity in the Kentucky cities of Louisville and Lexington. Block groups are aggregations of several blocks and are smaller units than census tracts. In fact, census tract are usually aggregations of two or more block groups. In some cities, block groups are even more accurate depictions of "neighborhoods" than census tracts, but this is not always the case. Survey data were collected from just over 2,300 residents of these neighborhoods to measure informal social control and perceptions of drug market activity. Perceptions of drug market activity was measured by two items that asked how often people bought or sold drugs in the neighborhood and how often people used drugs in the neighborhood. Informal social control was measured with a scale consisting of items similar to the intervention variables described above in Sampson and his colleagues' work (1997). These variables were aggregated to the block group level.

Structural variables came from the census and included residential instability (percentage of renters and the percentage of the population residing somewhere else five years earlier); concentrated disadvantage (e.g., percentage living in poverty, unemployment, female-headed households); and population age structure (percentage aged 15–29, a high-risk age group for criminal activity). Robbery data came from crimes known to the local city police agencies. The purposive sampling led to significant variation in neighborhood characteristics. For example, the percentage reporting that drug market activity occurred frequently ranged from 0 to 88%, and robbery rates ranged from 0 to 60 per 1,000 residents. Further, unemployment ranged from 0 to 57%, and population turnover (instability) ranged from 12 to 86%.

Structural equation modeling that allowed the researchers to tease out direct and indirect effects of structural characteristics, informal social control, and drug market activity on rates of robbery were employed. The analyses began with bivariate correlations and, as expected, concentrated disadvantage and residential instability were negatively related to informal social control and positively related to drug market activity and robbery rates. Age structure was not related to either drug market activity or rates of robbery, but remember, this variable has never been seen as one stemming from social disorganization theory. More complex models suggest that the effect of concentrated disadvantage is indirect, working by negatively affecting informal social control and positively affecting the presence of drug market activity, which directly affects rates of robbery. Residential instability also appears to lower informal social controls, in turn affecting drug market activity, which has the strongest direct effect on rates of robbery.

Clearly, collective efficacy has proven to be an important concept that has extended and promoted thought on social disorganization theory and on factors that affect neighborhood deviance. For the most part, research in this area has been largely restricted to violence and other forms of crime, and little attention has been given to collective efficacy's potential implication for other forms of deviance. More research in this direction is clearly warranted.

◈ Explaining Deviance in the Streets and Deviance in the Suites With Social Disorganization Theory

The emphasis of economic deprivation, which encourages population turnover, can lead to racial and ethnic heterogeneity, and ultimately affects the ability to work together toward common community goals such as crime and delinquency, is clearly evoked in virtually all versions of social disorganization theory. Indeed, the vast majority of research testing social disorganization theory has emphasized "crime in the streets." But can social disorganization be utilized to explain "deviance in the suites," or elite deviance? It would appear so.

In 1940 Edwin Sutherland published the article "White-Collar Criminality," and while in it he primarily emphasized his theory of differential association (see Chapter 6), he also alluded to social disorganization. Just as in socially disorganized, lower-class neighborhoods, conflicting pressures exist in the business community. Sutherland argued that "a second general process is social disorganization in the community" (p. 11), which allows for differential association. He further argued that white-collar offenders can operate because the business community cannot confront the powerful business leaders, and the agencies that are commissioned to handle white-collar crime typically focus on lower-level crimes (e.g., "street crime"), ignoring those at their own level.

More recently, Rothe and her colleagues (see Rothe & Kauzlarich, 2010; Rothe & Mullins, 2009) have incorporated social disorganization theory into various frameworks for understanding state crime. Rothe and Kauzlarich (2010) argue that

> essentially, when strong, functioning social institutions are not present, this creates both motivation and opportunity for organized criminal activity. . . . Weak institutions produce a vacuum of formal and informal social control. A nation unable to adequately police or subdue

paramilitary force in its hinterlands creates a gap of institutional control that provides motivation and opportunity for the aris[ing] of organized criminal activity. (p. 169)

Their emphasis on social institutions such as the family, education, and religion and on the ability or inability to control behavior at the state level is clearly in line with the social disorganization tradition. Can you think of other forms of elite deviance that might be enabled by the presence of weak institutions and a lack of informal social controls?

◈ Ideas in Action: Programs and Policy From Social Disorganization and Broken Windows Perspectives

A number of programs and policies have come out of social disorganization theory and variations on it, especially Wilson and Kelling's broken windows theory. Regarding the former, probably the largest program that has become institutionalized is the Chicago Area Project (CAP), which began in the 1930s. Based directly on social disorganization theory and led by sociologist and major contributor to social disorganization theory Clifford Shaw, the CAP sought:

1. The development of youth welfare organizations among residents of delinquency areas,

2. Employment of so-called indigenous workers wherever possible, and

3. The fostering and preservation of the independence of these groups (Kobrin, 1959, p. 24).

The CAP emphasized the individual delinquent in the social context that created the delinquency. In contrast to psychological and psychiatric approaches, the CAP was sociological in nature and emphasized the social milieu that encouraged (or at least did not *dis*courage) delinquency in certain parts of the city. It also emphasized the lack of social organizations (i.e., organized sports with adult supervision) in certain areas of the city that were readily available to "middle-class" adolescents. Although solid statistical evidence of the effectiveness of the CAP to reduce delinquency remains evasive (see Schlossman & Sedlak, 1983, for a detailed discussion of these issues), most researchers agree that there were many benefits of the intervention. Kobrin (1959) makes three important points in this regard. First, the project showed that youth welfare organizations could be developed even in the most impoverished areas of the city with the highest rates of delinquency. Second, the project showed that citizens in high-crime areas could be made aware of the common problems shared by residents and mobilized to take action to confront delinquency and other social problems. Additionally, many of the neighborhood programs created remained stable and active over time. Third, it has been argued that

in all probability, the Area Project was the first organized program in the United States to use workers to establish direct and personal contact with "unreached" boys to help them find their way back to acceptable norms of conduct. The adoption of this pattern in many cities during recent years may be regarded as in part, at least, a contribution of the Area Project. (Kobrin, 1959, p. 25)

Other programs that are somewhat consistent with social disorganization theory are community policing and neighborhood watch programs. Community policing policies and programs attempt to bring law enforcement into the community to work directly with residents to help solve problems and prevent crime and other forms of deviance. The shift from a "paramilitary-bureaucratic" organizational structure to a "friendlier" community-based model of crime prevention has been uneven at best. Chappell and Lanza-Kaduce (2010) argue that even though police academies often espouse community ideals, the training and socialization that takes place in them actually emphasizes and reinforces the paramilitary ideals advocated in earlier decades.

Neighborhood watch programs, often associated with civic leagues, attempt to bring residents together to solve problems themselves. They link often dissimilar residents (based, for example, on race, ethnicity, and/or social class) who might not normally interact together to work to solve common problems such as crime and other forms of deviance. Bennett and his colleagues (2006) conducted a meta-analysis and concluded that 15 of the 18 studies they reviewed showed at least some evidence of these programs' effectiveness. They did raise several questions about the quality of the studies, however, and recommend that more rigorous evaluations be conducted.

Finally, policies and programs related to broken windows theory generally focus on stopping low-level criminal activity before it escalates. This might involve enforcement of city code violations related to broken or abandoned vehicles, litter, graffiti, loud music, and the consumption of alcohol in public. Often there is an emphasis on zero-tolerance police policies. O'Shea (2006) offers a unique and important analysis of Wilson and Kelling's broken windows argument. He argues that the relationships between physical deterioration, disorder, and crime are not straightforward or additive. Rather, physical deterioration interacts with social disorder to affect levels of crime. Another way of thinking about this is that the effect of disorder on crime is dependent on levels of physical disorder (or vice versa). O'Shea finds statistical support for this hypothesis that leads him to be skeptical of simple zero-tolerance policies. He argues that "simple arrests of the disorderly (however broadly defined) and citation of negligent property owners . . . may not be the most efficient use of those scarce law enforcement resources" (p. 185).

NOW YOU . . . USE THE THEORY

The map below is of Norfolk, Virginia. The dots represent prostitution arrests, and the shaded areas represent different levels of social disorganization as measured by a scale based on the level of racial heterogeneity, number of female-headed households, level of unemployment, and level of poverty in a certain area. The top of the map represents the section of the city next to the bay. This section was very popular many years ago but fell into disrepute. Since it is on the water, there has been some gentrification recently, and wealthier individuals and business owners have moved back and reclaimed the space as a desirable area. The southern end of the map is where the central business district is located.

(Continued)

(Continued)

Using social disorganization theory, explain the location of prostitution arrests in Norfolk. Can you use the theory to help explain how these arrests are clustered in the city? Why might these arrests be clustered on the edge of the most disorganized areas of the city?

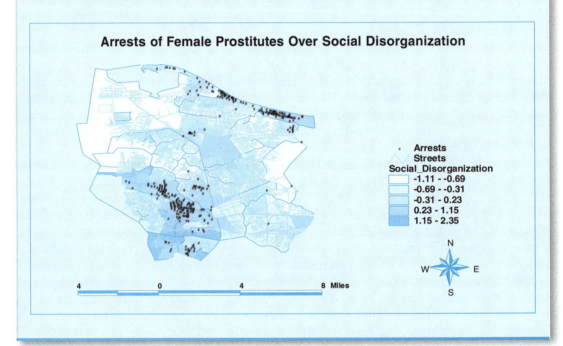

◈ Conclusion

The original work of Shaw and McKay (1942/1969) was clearly groundbreaking in its day and continues to influence the study of deviance. The major contribution of the original work was showing how crime, deviance, and other social problems cannot be understood, at least at the aggregate level, by using "types of people" explanations. Shaw and McKay found that crime and deviance were consistently located in particular parts of Chicago, even though the types of people who resided there changed across several decades. New versions of the theory continue to help us understand the factors that limit social control in certain neighborhoods.

Places such as Henry Horner in Alex Kotlowitz's (1988) *There Are No Children Here* continue to have high rates of crime and deviance (1) because the residents there do not have the resources (political or economic) to control these activities; (2) there is high residential instability or population turnover, resulting in limited social networking, which might lead to decreased social control; and (3) there is very little collective efficacy in that residents lack the willingness and ability to intervene when problems confront them. Most people residing in truly disadvantaged neighborhoods do not engage in a great deal of crime and deviance, and most would love to live in less dangerous places where they could raise their children safely without the opportunities and pressures to deviate. They stay because their opportunities are strictly limited.

EXERCISES AND DISCUSSION QUESTIONS

1. Explain how Shaw and McKay's theory moved us away from "types of people" explanations.

2. Why do you think we are so focused on individual-level explanations rather than on characteristics of social contexts?

3. How does the work of Sampson and his colleagues expand our understanding of social disorganization theory?

4. How does Wilson and Kelling's broken windows theory relate to social disorganization?

5. Consider the city you live in and where the safe areas are, as well as where one might likely go to buy drugs or find a prostitute. What other factors characterize those areas of the city?

6. Go to www.youtube.com/watch?v=niJ3IiURCnE for a presentation of Chicago's deadliest neighborhoods and write a personal reaction to the video.

KEY TERMS

Broken windows theory

Central business district

Collective efficacy

Concentric zones

Cross-sectional designs

Individual efficacy

Longitudinal data

Parental efficacy

Physical disorder

Poverty

Racial/ethnic heterogeneity

Social cohesion

Social disorder

Social disorganization theory

Zone in transition

CHAPTER 6

Differential Association and Social Learning Theory

The Internet is a hotbed of deviant information. Indeed, within a couple of minutes, we found various sites that encouraged a wide variety of deviant behavior and others that provided step-by-step guides offering the basic techniques to learn how to engage in deviance. You can learn how to grow the best marijuana indoors and out, or you can learn how to make crack cocaine or find peyote (a hallucinogenic drug found on San Pedro cacti). For the person considering bulimia, there are "Pro Bulimia Tips and Tricks." There are tips on building a bomb with typical household items. The would-be burglar can get instructions on how to pick locks. And amid all of the porn, there are now Web sites helping married men and women to have affairs. The World Wide Web is clearly a source for virtually any form of deviance.

◈ Introduction

The discussion of Web sites above suggests something that many sociologists of deviance believe today and study—the notion that much deviance, if not all deviant behavior, needs to be learned and that instruction is often required. All of these sites offer encouragement to engage in deviance as well as information to help people learn the techniques necessary to do so. It might not take much to learn to smoke pot or crack, but the drug needs to be made available, and—given its illegal status and the "war on drugs"—for many it would require a certain amount of encouragement.

Of course, the Web is not the only way we learn about deviance. We learn it from family, friends, other media sources, and so on. In this chapter, we discuss two prominent sociological theories that emphasize the importance of learning in the development of deviance. The first, developed by Edwin Sutherland in the 1930s and still prominent today, is differential association theory. The second modifies and builds on differential association theory; it is widely known as social learning theory and is primarily associated with Ronald Akers. We also provide a brief description of a related theory focused on culture and subcultures—cultural deviance theory. Following a general overview and evaluation of the theories, we discuss how they have been useful in understanding a wide range of deviant behaviors from a sociological perspective.

◈ Development of Differential Association Theory

Edwin Sutherland (1883–1950) was a pioneer in sociological criminology who responded to and attacked many of the mainstream criminological ideas of his time and provided a solid sociological approach to understanding crime. While his focus was clearly on crime, his work has obvious implications for other noncriminal forms of deviant behavior. He was a prolific scholar who produced numerous scientific publications, was the president of the American Sociological Association, and was a mentor to many students who continued to advance the field of criminology and the study of deviance. Two of his books are of particular importance for this chapter: *White Collar Crime* (1949b) and a textbook in 1924 later titled *Principles of Criminology* (1934).

Sutherland titled his presidential address to the American Sociological Association "Is White Collar Crime, Crime?" challenging mainstream criminologists who focused almost exclusively (and to some extent still overly focus) on street crime. Here Sutherland set the stage for his classic work, *White Collar Crime,* published 4 years later. Although white-collar crime has become an important area of inquiry and students today are generally familiar with highly exposed cases of white-collar crime, what is important here is what Sutherland brought to the proverbial table, that "conventional generalizations about crime and criminality are invalid because they explain only the crime of the lower classes" (Sutherland, 1949b, p. 217). He viewed crime as ubiquitous, occurring across dimensions of social class, race, gender, and other social conditions. This important work drew attention to crimes of the middle and upper classes whose perpetrators were obviously not suffering from poverty or biological predispositions.

Across editions, Sutherland modified and advanced *Principles of Criminology* to finally include in 1947 his full-fledged theory of differential association, including his nine propositions of the theory. Sutherland's text continued to be updated even after his death in 1950, with Donald Cressey and later David Luckenbill as coauthors. But neither Sutherland nor his collaborators changed the wording or modified in any way the nine propositions. Given the history of the propositions, we list them as originally written in Table 6.1, but in our summary and examples, we use the term *deviance* and use noncriminological examples to better fit this text.

We will focus on the first seven propositions as the latter two are not terribly relevant for our discussion and were later discounted in subsequent formulations (see Akers, 1985; Burgess & Akers, 1966). The first proposition suggests that deviant behavior is learned and not inherited or the result of some biological trait. Today, even those interested in biological predictors of crime and deviance do not argue that *behavior* is inherited, but rather they say that there may be predispositions that make some folks more likely to engage in behavior (see, e.g., Rowe, 2002; Walsh, 2000). The fact remains that the behavioral repertoire of babies is pretty limited. They hold few if any deviant (or nondeviant) thoughts; they don't know how to light a joint or why they would want to; they may have a predisposition for alcoholism, but they don't know why they would want to drink or where to find a bar. This may seem obvious to many, but Sutherland was responding to the early biological and psychological traditions that were fairly deterministic in nature. Even today we speak of "crack babies" as if they are destined to a life of drug use. Furthermore, other schools of thought—in particular, certain social control theorists—still argue that for the most part, the learning necessary for most deviance is trivial and of little theoretical importance (Gottfredson & Hirschi, 1990).

Table 6.1   Sutherland's (1947) Nine Propositions of Differential Association Theory
1. Criminal behavior is learned.
2. Criminal behavior is learned in interaction with other persons in a process of communication.
3. The principal part of the learning of criminal behavior occurs within intimate personal groups.
4. When criminal behavior is learned, the learning includes (a) techniques of committing the crime, which are sometimes very complicated, sometimes very simple, and (b) the specific direction of motives, drives, rationalizations, and attitudes.
5. The specific direction of motives and drives is learned from definitions of the legal code as favorable or unfavorable.
6. A person becomes delinquent because of an excess of definitions favorable to violation of law over definitions unfavorable to violation of the law.
7. Differential associations may vary in frequency, duration, priority, and intensity.
8. The process of learning criminal behavior by association with criminal and anticriminal patterns involves all of the mechanisms that are involved in any other learning.
9. Although criminal behavior is an expression of general needs and values, it is not explained by those general needs and values because noncriminal behavior is an expression of the same needs and values.

From the second and third propositions, we can conclude that deviance is learned from other people, particularly intimate others—one's family and friends. Remember that Sutherland was writing during a time when people were not bombarded with mass media; current researchers have moved beyond intimate others in examining sources of deviance. However, even today much learning takes place between parents and children and between friends and acquaintances. Much research suggests that early deviant behaviors are group activities. Underage drinking, smoking pot or using other drugs, vandalism, bullying, and so on are more often done in groups than in isolation, especially among adolescents and young adults (Warr, 2002).

The fourth proposition suggests that two things need to be learned. First, one must know how to engage in the deviant behavior, and this may be simple or complex. Little technique is needed to vandalize a building by breaking a window. Alternatively, picking locks, hot-wiring cars, and recognizing a drug buying opportunity versus a police sting are more complex. Second, we need to know why people would want to engage in the behavior in the first place. Sutherland believed that people need to learn the motivations, drives, rationalizations, and appropriate attitudes for engaging in deviant behavior. For example, given that smoking is illegal for minors, the massive ad campaigns on the hazards of smoking, and that fact that parents and teachers (even if they are smokers themselves) admonish smoking, why do thousands of youngsters start smoking each year? There must be other sources of "information" that motivate youngsters to start smoking. Hence, the fifth proposition suggests that direction of the motives and drives varies and is learned from exposure to **definitions** (statements, attitudes, beliefs) that are favorable or unfavorable to engaging in particular behaviors.

The sixth proposition is the most important proposition to differential association theory and states that an excess of definitions favorable to deviant behavior over definitions unfavorable to deviant behavior increases the likelihood of committing deviant acts. Going back to the adolescent smoking example, with all of the definitions (laws, warnings of parents and teachers, ad campaigns) unfavorable to smoking, why would one smoke? For Sutherland, the likely answer is that many definitions favorable to smoking (via parents, peers, famous actors and actresses, and other influential people) make smoking appear "cool." Some young people come to hold more definitions favorable to smoking than to not smoking and begin the process of becoming a smoker.

The seventh proposition specifies this further and states that differential associations vary in terms of frequency (how often exposed), duration (length of exposure), priority (how early in life one is exposed), and intensity (the respect or admiration one holds for the person providing the definitions). Again, one can see that even in a society that rebukes smoking (at least symbolically via law, rules, and campaigns), some people are exposed to definitions favorable to smoking: frequently, for long durations of time, from an early age where youth are impressionable, and from people they are expected to respect (e.g., parents, an older sibling, or media figures), making them more likely to engage in the behavior themselves. It is important to note that Sutherland did not emphasize differential association with persons but rather differential exposure to definitions. Although the two variables may be related, they are clearly not the same thing. Smokers (and other deviants) can provide definitions that are favorable ("Smoking makes you look cool; try one") or unfavorable ("Hock, hock, wheeze, wheeze, I wish I could quit these!").

Sutherland's theory of differential association is perhaps the most longstanding and popular theory of deviance in terms of empirical evaluation, and it has made important inroads to policy and programs. It has been instrumental in studying a wide array of criminal and noncriminal deviant behaviors and has found much support. The theory has also been sharply criticized and challenged on a number of grounds (see Kubrin, Stucky, & Krohn, 2009, for a recent overview of the issues). However, it is still cited widely in the social sciences and has been modified and expanded by Ronald Akers and his colleagues.

DEVIANCE IN POPULAR CULTURE

Differential association holds that deviant behavior is learned behavior. Try to think of examples of behaviors that you have learned—deviant or not, the more specific, the better—and the specific processes that you went through to learn those behaviors. Did you learn them from people close to you? Did you learn both attitudes about the behavior and techniques to engage in the behavior?

If you are having a hard time thinking of examples, popular culture offers many films and television shows that illustrate the process of learning deviant attitudes and behaviors:

American History X—a disturbing film that explores the topic of learning hatred and racism; it chronicles the relationship of a neo-Nazi skinhead and his hero-worshipping younger brother.

GoodFellas—based on a true story, this film chronicles the rise to power of gangster Henry Hill. The narration by Henry and his wife offers a perspective on life as part of the mob and how it all came to seem very normal to them.

The television series *Weeds* tells the fictional story of Nancy Botwin, a recently widowed white mother living in an affluent suburb in California. After the death of her husband, Nancy begins a career selling marijuana. As the seasons progress, she builds her customer base, expands her business, and deals with increasing risk to herself and her family.

◈ Development of Akers' Social Learning Theory

An early attempt at a serious reformulation of Sutherland's differential association theory came from Robert Burgess and Ronald Akers' (1966) "A Differential Association Reinforcement Theory of Criminal Behavior," which attempted to introduce the psychological concepts of operant conditioning to the theory. The notion behind operant conditioning is that learning is enhanced by both social and nonsocial **reinforcement**. Their collaboration led to a seven-proposition integration of differential association and operant conditioning concepts. We need not list all seven propositions for the reader to get the gist; therefore, we list the first three (note that Burgess and Akers used the term *criminal behavior* as did Sutherland, but in later work, Akers modified the propositions to reference *deviant behavior*, recognizing the generality of theory—see Akers, 1985):

1. Deviant behavior is learned according to the principles of operant conditioning.

2. Deviant behavior is learned both in nonsocial situations that are reinforcing or discriminating and through that social interaction in which the behavior of other persons is reinforcing or discriminating for such behavior.

3. The principal part of the learning of deviant behavior occurs in those groups that comprise or control the individual's major source of reinforcements.

The attempt at integration was notable and important but never terribly popularized, except that Akers has continued to modify and advance his version of social learning theory (see Akers, 1998). His more recent work focuses on four specific concepts rather than on a larger number of propositions, but he still argues that his is not a new theory but an integration of ideas built around the important contributions of Sutherland. The four concepts are differential association, definitions, **differential reinforcement**, and **imitation**. Note that two of the four concepts come directly from Sutherland.

According to Akers (1998), *definitions* are attitudes, beliefs, and rationalizations that define a behavior as good or bad, right or wrong, appropriate or inappropriate. Definitions can be general or specific. For example, a general definition that might endorse skipping school is the belief that "school rules are arbitrary and discriminatory." Alternately, a more specific definition might be the statement,

"If I can get good grades and miss a few classes, why shouldn't I skip a few classes?" Definitions can also be favorable to a behavior, neutralizing, or reproachful of a behavior. For example:

- Favorable—school is a waste of time and skipping school is cool!
- Neutralizing—skipping school doesn't hurt anyone.
- Reproachful—skipping school not only hurts the offender but other members of the class.

So definitions—these beliefs, orientations, and rationalizations people hold—encourage deviance or neutralize restraints that conventional society might impose. The stronger these definitions favoring or encouraging deviance, the more likely a person is to engage in such behavior.

Definitions are important, but where do they come from? Like Sutherland, Akers argues that definitions are learned from *differential association* with the persons one interacts with. Early on, these contacts are primarily with the family—parents, siblings, and perhaps children of parental friends.

Later, children meet other peers on their own in the neighborhood and in school. Then eventually people get jobs, find romantic relationships, and join new social networks, where new and different sorts of definitions and behaviors are modeled and encouraged (see Capaldi, Kim, & Owen, 2008; Warr, 1993).

Differential reinforcement is clearly a concept that Akers adds to Sutherland's original theory. The concept "refers to the balance of anticipated and actual rewards and punishments that follow or are the consequences of behavior" (Akers, 1998, pp. 66–67). Sutherland wrote a great deal about exposure to definitions but did not say much about how behavioral patterns are actually learned. Akers argues that to the extent it is likely that behaviors will be rewarded or punished (frequently and in terms of quantity), rewards and punishments will reinforce or diminish the behavior, respectively. Therefore, we see differential reinforcement as a factor that should largely predict the continuation or escalation of a behavior rather than initiation.

▲ **Photo 6.1** "It is all in the learning." Practicing smoking with candy cigarettes!

Source: ©Associated Press.

The final concept discussed by Akers (1998) is imitation, which is simply observing modeled behavior. Perhaps you may have seen children imitating cigarette smoking with a stick or straw (at least one of us remembers doing that as a child). Candy cigarettes, too, were once popular with children, allowing them to imitate adult smokers. Whether candy cigarettes promote smoking or whether modeling is a strong predictor of anything is still debated, but the evidence is fairly clear that the tobacco industry has high hopes for both (J. D. Klein & St. Clair, 2000).

◈ Social Structure and Social Learning (SSSL)

The vast majority of Akers' theorizing and research, as well as that of other scholars interested in furthering and evaluating his theory, has focused on the four variables discussed above (definitions, differential association, differential reinforcement, and imitation)—that is, individual-level factors affecting various forms of deviant behavior. More recently, Akers (1998) has expanded his theory to incorporate characteristics of the social structure where the "learning" takes place, and he refers to this modified theory as social structure and social learning theory (SSSL). He argues that characteristics of the social structure provide a context for social learning. Figure 6.1 depicts the causal sequence outlined by Akers and Sellers (2004, p. 97). Note that there are no direct links between the social structural variables and deviant and conforming behavior. This suggests that the social learning processes can fully explain the relationship between social structure and deviant and conforming behaviors.

Figure 6.1   A Depiction of Akers' View of the Causal Effects of Social Structural Variables on Social Learning

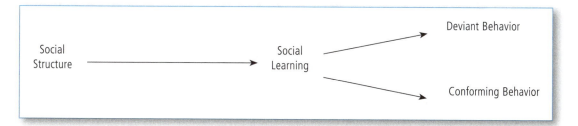

Akers proposes four key characteristics of the social structure that might affect social learning: (1) differential social organization, (2) differential location in the social structure, (3) theoretically defined structural variables, and (4) differential social location in groups. Differential social organization refers to structural correlates of crime—in our case, deviance. These are "ecological, community, or geographic differences across social systems" (Akers, 1998, p. 332). They might include age/gender composition of the community, urban as opposed to rural or suburban communities, or the unemployment rate. Differential location in the social structure refers to social and demographic characteristics of individuals that define or influence one's position or role in the larger social structure. Social class, gender, race/ethnicity, and age are key variables that may influence who one is exposed to as well as the rewards and punishment for behaviors individuals may anticipate or receive. For example, young boys from poor neighborhoods may be differentially exposed to deviant definitions promoting various forms of deviance (gambling, alcohol/drug use, vandalism, graffiti art). Theoretically defined structural variables might include "anomie, class oppression, social disorganization, group conflict, patriarchy," and others (Akers, 1998, p. 333). Socially disorganized communities, for example, because of scarce resources, racial/ethnic heterogeneity, and rapid population turnover, are said to be less able to control crime, delinquency, and other forms of deviance (see Chapter 5). These theoretical variables may also influence the types of people one is exposed to as well as the reinforcing patterns associated with various activities, including deviance. Finally, differential social location in groups refers to membership in various groups such as the family, peer groups in the neighborhood, school or work, and sports or other recreational groups. An obvious example of group membership that might influence social learning is a gang in which various forms of crime and deviant behavior are learned. Alternatively, being the oldest sibling in a family with responsibility for taking care of younger siblings may be a membership that promotes conforming behavior.

The SSSL version of Akers' theory would appear to be a ripe area for sociological theorizing as it clearly attempts to incorporate social variables, both at the macro and micro levels. At the macro level, there is room to think about community characteristics such as social disorganization or the prevalence of prosocial institutions and organizations such as good schools and churches. At the societal level, we might consider linking patriarchy or class oppression to social learning. At a more micro level, we can think about how gender, race, or social class may affect association with deviant or conforming peers, which may affect the learning process. To date, there have been only limited theoretical or empirical advances in this direction, and in a symposium following the publication of *Social Learning and Social Structure* (Akers, 1998), all three reviewers of the book seemed to think the theory was underdeveloped (Krohn, 1999; Morash, 1999; Sampson, 1999). Still, the theory offers fertile ground for thinking about the social structural variables that may affect the social learning of deviant behavior.

◈ Application of Differential Association and Social Learning

Differential association and social learning theories have been among the most thoroughly investigated theories in the study of crime and deviance, and a wide variety of forms of crime and deviance have been investigated. Some have criticized this research because a great deal of it has come from Akers himself and his colleagues and students. For a variety of reasons, smoking has been a theme of this chapter, so we will start there. Smoking is clearly a deviant behavior as defined by at least three criteria: (1) It is illegal for certain segments of our society (those younger than age 18 in most, if not all, states) and in certain places (restaurants and bars in certain states and/or cities); (2) it is clearly a social/health harm in itself and is related to other forms of substance use; and (3) it is likely to bring negative reactions from at least certain segments of society. Akers himself was involved in a longitudinal study of teenage smoking in Iowa (see Akers, 1998). Each of the four key measures of Akers' standard social learning theory was included, and each of the learning variables contributed to the likelihood that teens would smoke cigarettes. Others have also tested the ability of social learning theory to explain smoking behavior among youth. For example, in a large nationwide study of 3,460 youth ages 11–19, Monroe (2004) found unique independent effects of measures of differential association, differential reinforcement, definitions, and imitation on having ever been a smoker.

Other types of substance use have also been studied via social learning theory. Akers and several of his colleagues (see Akers, 1998) were also involved in a large-scale study of drug and alcohol use. A novel aspect of this project was that it not only focused on use versus abstinence but also examined separately the effects of social learning variables on the onset, persistence/escalation, and desistance/cessation of the use of drugs and alcohol. The study involved a self-report study of just over 3,000 students in grades 7–12 in the Midwest. The results showed that social learning variables were predictive of alcohol and marijuana use as well as problems associated with drug and alcohol use (Akers, 1998). In addition, Akers and Cochran (1985) were able to show that social learning variables were more powerful predictors of marijuana use than either social control theory (see Chapter 7) or strain theory (see Chapter 4).

Other researchers have shown that differential association and social learning variables are predictive of substance use. In a study of more than 4,846 male and 576 female juveniles committed to the Virginia Department of Juvenile Justice (1998–2003), peer substance use was one of the strongest factors affecting substance use for both males and females (Neff & Waite, 2007). In a study at four universities in Florida, Kentucky, Tennessee, and Virginia, Higgins and his colleagues (Higgins, Tewksbury, & Mustaine, 2007) found that peer associations were among the strongest factors affecting binge drinking at college sporting events. Finally, Reed and Rountree (1997) found that direct peer pressure exerted little influence on substance use but that differential association and definitions favorable to substance use were important factors affecting substance use. Social learning would appear to be an important theory predictive of both substance use and abuse.

A large number of studies have focused on general or overall delinquency, so our review here focuses on some interesting and more recent findings. For example, Hochstetler, Copes, and DeLisi (2002) analyzed data from the National Survey of Youth (NYS), a longitudinal data set, and showed that variables derived from differential association theory (e.g., friends' attitudes and beliefs) were moderately to strongly related to delinquent behavior and, more importantly, that these effects were not contingent on the presence of co-offenders. This provides support for both differential association and social learning theories and suggests that it is not just peer pressure but the socialization of deviant definitions and differential social reinforcement that leads to delinquent behavior. In another analysis of the NYS, Ploeger (1997) explored the often unanticipated positive correlation between employment and delinquent behavior among youth. He found that the positive correlation between employment and delinquency was largely explained by the deviant peers one encountered in the workplace.

In perhaps the most direct test of Sutherland's differential association theory, Dana Haynie (2002) provided a detailed examination of adolescent peer networks ($n = 2,606$) via the National Longitudinal Adolescent Health Survey (1995–1996). She found that peer networks were very heterogeneous, with a majority of youth having networks with both deviant and conforming associations. She found that "delinquent behavior is influenced by the ratio of definitions favorable to those unfavorable to law violation" and that the percentage of delinquent friends was the strongest factor affecting delinquent behavior (Haynie, 2002, p. 99).

Differential association and social learning theories have been criticized because they have largely focused on juvenile delinquency and other relatively minor forms of deviance (smoking, drinking, and less serious forms of drug use). However, the theories do have relevance for other, more serious forms of deviance. Akers himself, for example, has given a great deal of thought to the applicability of social learning theory on rape and sexual aggression (Akers, 1985). Boeringer, Shehan, and Akers (1991) asked a sample of male undergraduates about proclivities to engage in rape and sexual aggression (e.g., "If you could be assured that you could in no way be punished for engaging in the following acts, how likely, if at all, would you be to force a female to do something sexual she didn't want to do?"). Social learning variables were important factors affecting self-reported proclivity to use force or commit rape. A second study of male undergraduate students was conducted with basically the same dependent variables, but there was the addition of another form of nonphysical technique of sexual aggression, "plying a woman with alcohol or drugs with the intent of making her so intoxicated that she will be physically or mentally unable to refuse sexual intercourse" (Akers, 1998, p. 270). Again, social learning variables were important predictors of these forms of sexual deviance.

RECENT STUDY IN DEVIANCE

Are You Kynd? Conformity and Deviance Within the Jamband Subculture

By Pamela M. Hunt, 2010, in *Deviant* Behavior, *31*, 521–551.

One of the many areas of deviance research is the study of subcultures. This article, by Pamela Hunt (2010), is the study of the jamband subculture. The jamband subculture is an extension of the Deadhead subculture that used to follow the Grateful Dead from venue to venue around the country to their concerts. Jambands follow such bands as Phish and the Dave Matthews Band, much the way the Deadheads followed the Grateful Dead. Jambands promote a counterculture philosophy of "kynd" behavior, which involves the sharing of resources; transitory, communal living; and an aversion to status and authority.

Hunt uses differential association theory to examine whether these counterculture behaviors (albeit considered prosocial) are learned the way other deviant behaviors are learned. In this manner, she is extending the use of differential association theory by examining within-group differences in prosocial and antisocial behavior. In other words, many might want to compare the jamband subculture to larger society—asking why members might opt to follow a particular band across country—but Hunt, instead, examines why some jamband members espouse a stronger "kynd" philosophy than others in the subculture.

Hunt administered 379 surveys to participants in jamband concerts in the Midwest, Southeast, and Northeast. Her participants reported participating in between 1 and 150 jamband-related events per year—with an average of 18 events. Hunt found that those who attend more jamband events and are more emotionally connected to others in the subculture are more likely to believe in and promote "kynd" behaviors. In addition, those who became part of the jamband subculture at a younger age are also more likely to have a strong, positive belief in its philosophy. Those who might follow the subculture but not as closely or who came later in life to the subculture do not have a strong, positive belief in the philosophy.

We have reviewed several empirical studies focusing on or at least including measures derived from differential association and social learning theories—often studies conducted by Akers himself and his colleagues. There are many studies beyond what is included here, but this review should provide the reader with evidence that the theories are quite versatile and large in terms of scope and are able to explain a wide variety of deviant behaviors. In addition, differential/association theories are likely to explain what Goode (2008a, p. 270) has come to refer to as "cognitive or intellectual deviance." He argues, for example, that in U.S. culture, being an atheist and not believing in God is a cognitive deviance. Indeed, a large number of political, religious, and social beliefs are considered deviant by mainstream society, and as the Web sites in the introductory story would indicate, there are thousands of sites where one can learn about various deviant beliefs. Our review of differential association and social learning theories has been quite favorable, but we do recognize that there are limitations to them. The next section provides a short critique of these theories.

 ## Critiques of Differential Association and Social Learning Theories

We have argued that differential association and social learning theories are general theories that can explain a wide variety of deviant behaviors. In this regard, the theories can be described as wide in scope. There are, however, various forms of deviance that social learning theory would have a hard time explaining. Although today we are bombarded by images of serial killers in the popular media, historically it would be difficult to argue that serial killers learn the techniques and motivations to kill through communication with intimate others (but see Castle & Hensley, 2002). Similarly, while there is good evidence to suggest that social factors have a great deal to do with how mentally ill patients are treated (see Krohn & Akers, 1977), the best evidence seems to suggest that the mentally ill are indeed mentally ill (Gove, 1975). All in all, however, differential association and social learning theories would appear to be robust in terms of the scope.

Perhaps one of the greatest debates over differential association concerns the theoretical and empirical role of differential association, often measured as deviant behavior of one's peers. Some have argued that this measure is really a measure of one's own behavior, especially given that much criminal and delinquent behavior is done with peers. Control theorists in particular have charged that birds of a feather flock together and that there is no feathering necessary to understanding deviant behavior (Glueck & Glueck, 1950; Hirschi, 1969). There is probably something to this line of argument, and the correlations found between certain measures of differential association and deviance, especially in cross-sectional studies, are likely somewhat inflated. Alternatively, some good evidence from studies with careful measurement and with longitudinal designs seem to indicate that some of the learning (both motivation and techniques) does come from differential association with deviant others where behavioral patterns are reinforced with rewards and punishments (see Capaldi et al., 2008; Haynie, 2002; Heimer & Matsueda, 1994) and that differential association affects not only group behavior but solo offending as well (Hochstetler et al., 2002). For example, in a longitudinal study of youth, Elliot and Menard (1996) found delinquent peer associations more often than not temporally precede—or come before—delinquent behavior. Furthermore, Thornberry and his colleagues (Thornberry, Lizotte, Krohn, Farnworth, & Sung Joon, 1994) hypothesized and found that association with delinquent peers leads to delinquency, which leads to exposure to other delinquent peers, which again encourages more delinquency. Warr (2002) has argued persuasively that criminologists have been misguided by a black/white or dichotomous conception of the role of peer influence versus selection (i.e., birds of a feather flock together) and that there is no reason why both can't be true (see also Akers, 1998).

 ## Cultural Deviance Theory and Subcultural Explanations of Deviance

Cultural deviance theories, in general, emphasize the values, beliefs, rituals, and practices of societies that promote certain deviant behaviors. Subcultural explanations then emphasize the values, beliefs, rituals, and practices of subgroups in society that distinguish those subcultures from the larger society. To answer the question, "Why do some groups appear to behave in ways so different from mainstream society?" the cultural deviance theorist looks to the unique aspects of the culture or subculture to assess how people learn to tolerate, justify, and approve of deviant activities, at least in certain situations.

Cultural deviance, particularly subcultural explanations, has been very influential in the study of all kinds of deviance, and there is an interesting yet somewhat intractable debate over the relationship between cultural deviance theories and differential association/social learning theories. Thumbing through numerous databases, articles, and abstracts, you will often see cultural deviance theory linked to differential association or social learning theories as if they were one and the same. Similarly, numerous theorists (especially control theorists) link differential association and social learning theories under a cultural deviance label (see Hirschi, 1969; Kornhauser, 1978). Alternatively, Akers (1996) rejects the subcultural label for both Sutherland's differential association and his own social learning theory. He does, however, recognize that culture plays an important role in differential association theory and can play a role in social learning theory. The commonality, of course, is socialization and what one is exposed to and has reinforced in a given culture or subculture.

The linkages between cultural deviance theory and differential association/social learning theory are quite apparent, and this would appear to be an appropriate place for a brief discussion of the important role that theory has played in the study of deviance. The southern subculture of violence thesis (Gastil, 1971; Hackney, 1969) was an early subcultural explanation of deviance focused on the high rates of violence (especially lethal violence) in the South. The authors characterized the history and cultural tolerance of violence and the acceptance and availability of firearms as contributing factors to the high rates of violence in the South. Wolfgang and Ferrcuti (1967) also focused on subcultures of violence but shifted the focus to the high rates of homicide among young, minority males in inner cities. They formulated a subcultural theory that is clearly linked to differential association and social learning theory, as can be seen in their sixth proposition, which states that "the development of favorable attitudes toward, and the use of violence in a subculture usually involve learned behavior and the process of differential learning, association, or identification" (Wolfgang & Ferrcuti, 1967, p. 161).

Extending this line most recently, Anderson (1999) contrasts "decent" and "street" families, terms recognized and used by the residents he studied in a poor, inner-city, largely African American community. He argues that the child-rearing practices vary tremendously between the two groups—"decent" families are strict and focused on the values of mainstream society, and "street" families socialize their children to deal with problems aggressively and with violence that fits the environment of the "code of the streets." However, Anderson argues that the "code of the streets" subculture exists and promotes violent responses to signs of disrespect among inner-city African American youth regardless of whether they come from a "decent" or "street" family.

Subcultural explanations have been useful far outside the study of violence. Indeed, such explanations have historically been used to understand virtually any form of deviance. Recently, subcultural explanations have been used to understand, for example, computer hacking (Holt & Copes, 2010); online gaming (Downing, 2009); ecstasy use in a drug-using subculture (Gourley, 2004); corporate crime (Robinson & Murphy, 2009); excessive thinness and starvation among athletes (Atkinson, 2011; Atkinson & Young, 2008); bondage, discipline, and sadomasochism (Stiles & Clark, 2011); and Internet "johns" seeking prostitutes (Blevins & Holt, 2009), among many others.

Explaining Deviance in the Streets and Deviance in the Suites: Teen Alcohol and Drug Use

There have been relatively few empirical tests of Akers' full social structure and social learning theory of deviance. Whaley, Smith, and Hayes-Smith (2011), however, provided such a test using a very large sample (~85,000 students) across 202 school districts. They focused on teen drug and alcohol use—specifically marijuana use, ecstasy use, methamphetamine use, and what they referred to as binge drinking (recent experience of having five or more drinks in a row). They were able to simultaneously examine the effects of both individual characteristics, including measures of differential association (peer approval of the use of each drug), and several other control variables as well as contextual-level (school district) variables, including a measure of low socioeconomic status of the areas. So, while this was not a "street-level" study per se, one might argue that it is even better because it allowed the researchers to compare rates of drug use in wealthy and poorer areas and to see if the effect of differential associations varied across levels of socioeconomic status. Using relatively sophisticated statistical models, they found that socioeconomic status of the area predicted the use of alcohol and methamphetamines but not marijuana and ecstasy. More importantly, however, differential association was related to each form of drug use and actually mediated the effects of socioeconomic status of the areas, thus providing pretty solid support for Akers' SSSL theory.

Sticking with substance use and Akers' SSSL theory, we now focus on college students. Again, perhaps not the most elite group but, on average, still far above much of the population. In a cleverly titled article, "Liquor Is Quicker: Gender and Social Learning Among College Students," Lanza-Kaduce, Capece, and Alden (2006) examine the use of alcohol prior to sexual activity among male and female college students, some in sororities and fraternities, as well as others. They use secondary data, which leads to the relatively weak test of the theory as they could not design the questionnaire and thus relied on two measures of Akers' concepts. Students were asked about positive (e.g., "Alcohol makes me sexier") and negative (risks associated with drinking and sexual activity) aspects of combining alcohol and sex. These can be seen as definitions favorable and unfavorable to combining alcohol and sex.

Basically, Akers argues that social learning variables subsume other structural variables—that is, structural variables work through social learning variables to affect deviant behavior. Alternatively, feminist theories would disagree, suggesting that some measures should not work entirely through the socialization process. Lanza-Kaduce and his colleagues' basic goal then is to compare and contrast a feminist perspective with social learning theory. Some support for Akers' theory is found; for example, the effect of gender was mediated by the risk and rewards measures. Alternatively, the limited number of social learning variables did not mediate the "Greek effect" (the effect of fraternities), supporting the feminist perspective. In this regard, we are left with a quandary where we can either stick with a feminist perspective or argue that we simply need more and better measures of social learning theory. As usual, we are left hoping for future research to help resolve these issues.

 ## Ideas in Action: Programs and Policy From a Social Learning Perspective

Differential association and social learning have long histories in terms of treatment and prevention programs and in policy, if policy includes the funding and/or implementation of particular programs (e.g., the large government funding of DARE, discussed in Chapter 3). The earliest programs based implicitly or explicitly on differential association focused on the treatment of juvenile delinquents. The key component, of course, was "differential association" of the delinquent with non-delinquent adults or other adolescents who would expose the delinquent to definitions unfavorable to deviance and favorable to prosocial behavior. In the early 1950s, the Highfield Project, for example, offered delinquent boys the opportunity to leave their residential treatment facility during the day to go to work or school and then return to what was referred to as Guided Group Interaction (see Weeks, 1958). The group sessions were led by trained staff, and the boys could discuss problems they were experiencing with their families, in school, or in their jobs. The staff would offer solutions or strategies, but mostly they emphasized non-delinquent attitudes and behaviors. Heavy emphasis was placed on interactions between the youth. Although there were some methodological limitations with the evaluation of the program, most scholars appear to view the program as at least partially successful.

In the 1960s, two experimental treatment programs known as the Silver Lake Experiment were developed and tested first in Provo, Utah, and next in Los Angeles, California. The programs were based directly on differential association and borrowed from the Guided Group Interaction approach. They again emphasized interactions between the youth. A classic quote from one participant began as follows:

> Boys know more about themselves than grownups do. The first couple of months [in this program] don't do any good. Then you find out that the meetin' knows you better than you know yourself. They can tell when you're lyin'. They can tell things about yourself an' find out what your problems are. . . . I jus' don't like listening to adults lecturing . . . it is just boring as hell. All the help I got, I got from the other guys in the meetin'. (Empey & Erickson, 1972, 58)

Again the programs seemed to meet with at least partial success, but mostly only while the youth were involved in them. Once they left the programs, their rates of delinquency were comparable to other boys originally assigned to standard probation or periods of incarceration (Empey & Erickson, 1972; Empey & Lubeck, 1971).

Much has been learned since the 1950s and 1960s, and the programs based on social learning theories continue and often add in principles from other theories, such as social control/bonding theory. Still, the group counseling approach has met with only marginal success at best. Newer programs have moved to cognitive behavioral and social learning approaches that focus on risk and protective factors (Arthur et al., 2007). Some of the most successful programs that clearly emphasize principles of social learning theory come from the Oregon Social Learning Center. Researchers at the center apply the principles of social learning to the context of family, peers, and school. They contend that how children behave and interact with each other is learned in the family and that this transcends into other arenas of life, such as interaction with peers and teachers (Patterson et al., 1984).

The center's Adolescent Transition Program targets at-risk youth and their parents and focuses on family management/disciplinary issues and how parents socialize their children. Parents in the program are trained in family management practices that emphasize skills to teach their children prosocial definitions and how to model and reinforce positive behaviors. Similarly, at-risk youth are provided training intended to promote positive peer associations and attitudes favorable to law abiding/healthy behaviors (Dishion et al., 1992). The program is promising, showing some improvement in family management skills among parents and less deviant behavior among youth.

The group extended its work to move beyond simply at-risk youth and focus on serious delinquents. Its researchers conducted an experiment that tested the effect of a program based on social learning principles for youth offenders who had already been adjudicated by the court as serious delinquents (see Eddy & Chamberlain, 2000). Offenders were randomly assigned to either standard group-based foster home care or to foster home parents that had been trained by staff at the Oregon Social Learning Center. The treated group showed significantly lower rates of both self-reported and officially recorded delinquency over an extended period.

Most recently, the center has extended its work on foster care training and, again using social learning principles, has been evaluating the Multidimensional Treatment Foster Care program for girls in the United States and England (Roades et al., 2013). In both cases, the focus of the studies were young females 12–17 who were referred to foster care due to chronic delinquency. The intervention showed improvements in violence, risky sexual behaviors, and school outcomes in both countries.

NOW YOU . . . USE THE THEORY

Texting has been declared one of the most dangerous activities to do while driving because it involves all three types of distraction—visual, manual, and cognitive. According to Madden and Lenhart (2009):

> 75% of all American teens ages 12–17 own a cell phone, and 66% use their phones to send or receive text messages. Older teens are more likely than younger teens to have cell phones and use text messaging; 82% of teens ages 16–17 have a cell phone and 76% of that cohort are cell texters. One in three (34%) texting teens ages 16–17 say they have texted while driving. That translates into 26% of all American teens ages 16–17. Half (52%) of cell-owning teens ages 16–17 say they have talked on a cell phone while driving. That translates into 43% of all American teens ages 16–17. 48% of all teens ages 12–17 say they have been in a car when the driver was texting. And, 40% say they have been in a car when the driver used a cell phone in a way that put themselves or others in danger. (p. 2)

When asked about their experiences with texting while driving, one teen reported that "I don't really get worried because everyone does it. . . .And when my mother is texting and driving I don't really make a big deal because we joke around with her about it " (Madden & Lenhart, 2009, p. 7). Another stated, "[My dad] drives like he's drunk. His phone is just like sitting right in front of his face, and he puts his knees on the bottom of the steering wheel and tries to text" (Madden & Lenhart, 2009, p. 7).

Using social learning theory, explain the above statistics and quotes concerning texting while driving. Even though it has been declared one of the most dangerous behaviors to engage in while driving, why might teens continue to engage in this behavior in such alarmingly large numbers?

Excerpt is reprinted with permission from Madden, M., and Lenhart, A. (2009). *Teens and Distracted Driving: Texting, Talking and Other Uses of the Cell Phone Behind the Wheel.* Pew Internet and American Life Project, Washington, D.C. Reprinted with permission of Pew Internet & American Life Project.

The Oregon Social Learning Center has many programs, most showing at least moderate success, to thoroughly review here. Furthermore, a number of other programs based at least in part on social learning principles have been found to be successful as well. Suffice it to say that social learning theory clearly has the potential for working with at-risk youth to address a variety of deviant behaviors.

◈ Conclusion

In our reviews of differential association and social learning theories, we have emphasized studies that examine social learning through communication with intimate others, or at least persons known to the deviant. We have shied away from other sources of learning, such as music, movies, TV, video games, and the Internet. We did this for two reasons. First, both differential association and social learning theories have historically focused on learning from intimate others. Second, the research on the effects of the media on various behaviors is complex and far from conclusive.

Alternatively, we began this chapter with a list of Web sites from which people could learn both the techniques necessary to engage in a variety of deviances and the motivations and definitions favorable for doing so. It is clear that the Internet has changed our world and has become a viable source for those wishing to know more about almost any form of deviance and a source of support for those involved in various forms of deviant behavior. Indeed, the Internet is a place where one can be involved in a vast array of deviant activities, including such behaviors as online gambling, cyberporn and cybersex, political protests, and hate crimes, among many others. Many technologies provide us with mechanisms to learn deviant techniques, attitudes, and beliefs and to explore deviant (and nondeviant) relationships. Warr (2002) writes,

> There is no evidence as yet that such virtual peer groups have replaced or supplanted real ones, but no one who visits the United States can fail to be struck by the remarkable similarity among adolescents who live thousands of miles apart in highly disparate communities and climates, or by teenagers who seem to include fictional characters in their real-life reference groups. (p. 87)

Clearly, physically present intimate others are no longer a necessary component of deviant learning.

EXERCISES AND DISCUSSION QUESTIONS

1. Explain the process of differential association. How might one learn to dump toxic waste according to this theory?

2. Explain the difference between favorable, neutralizing, and reproachful definitions of behavior.

3. What are the four key characteristics of the social structure that might affect social learning?

4. Discuss how prosocial behavior can be explained using social learning theory.

5. What are the similarities and differences between differential association and social learning theory?

6. As you continue on to read about social control theory (Chapter 7), think about the differences between how social control theory and differential association theory explain deviant behavior. Which explanation are you most convinced by?

KEY TERMS

Cultural deviance theory

Definitions

Differential association

Differential location in the social structure

Differential reinforcement

Differential social location in groups

Differential social organization

Imitation

Reinforcement

Social structure

Theoretically defined structural variables

CHAPTER 7

Social Control Theories of Deviance

Jamila Pleas and Rashod Bethany are siblings who grew up in Chicago in the 1980s and 1990s. Jamila remembers growing up close to her grandparents, who lived in a two-story house. She knew all of her neighbors, walked to school, and played in the nearby park. However, in the mid-1980s, the neighborhood began to change. Unemployment increased significantly in the area, drug sales increased, and homes were boarded up. Rashod, who was born four years after Jamila, came of age as the neighborhood began to deteriorate and opportunities began to dry up. Their mother became a drug addict. By the time Rashod was seven, he was required to bag marijuana as punishment when he got in trouble. Jamila and Rashod's grandparents permanently stepped in as guardians, but they died within a year of each other when the kids were 11 and 15 years old.

Without their grandparents' guidance, Jamila started to skip school and eventually dropped out. Rashod became more deeply involved in the drug trade and at age 12 was shot in the back.

A long-time family friend and the mother of Jamila's "childhood sweetheart" became aware of Jamila and her struggles and demanded that Jamila come to live with her family, saying that she had promised Jamila's grandmother that Jamila would go to college one day. The family didn't take Rashod in.

Jamila went to live with the family. She went to a new school, buckled down, made up her missed lessons, and applied to colleges. Rashod continued to live in the old neighborhood, getting his guidance from the drug dealers who took over his grandparents' house as a base of operations. After Rashod was shot, a social worker at the hospital noted he had "fallen through the cracks at several agencies" (Meisner, 2013, p. 2). By the time Rashod was in his late teens, he had risen in the ranks of the drug world and was known as "The Man," running two round-the-clock crack houses and cornering the area's drug racket.

(Continued)

(Continued)

Jamila finished college, became a nurse, and lives in a high-rise in Hyde Park; her brother Rashod was recently sentenced to 25 years in prison on drug charges. Jamila's memories of her old neighborhood have faded but continue to influence her, especially when she is dealing with young mothers-to-be caught in tough situations. As for her brother, Jamila still remembers him as intelligent and industrious, the kid who at 6 would sneak down to the store and offer to push shopping carts or load grocery bags for change. "Sometimes I wonder if Rashod had been given another path, what he might have become," she said (Meisner, 2013, p. 3).

Adapted from Meisner, J. (April 14, 2013). Sister escaped "Trigger Town," but bleak fate snared brother. Retrieved from http://articles.chicagotribune.com/2013-04-14/news/ct-met-brother-sister-trigger-town-20130414_1_grammar-school-drugs-family-friend

◈ Introduction

Jamila's and Rashod's stories are not unusual. And, frankly, more than one theory could be used to explain their experiences and life trajectories. This chapter presents the perspective of several social control theories and will explain the behavior of Jamila and Rashod using these theories.

Social control theories of deviance got their start from the early classical theories usually associated with Beccaria. Both the classical school and the neoclassical school have as a basis a belief in the free will and rationalistic hedonism of the individual (Bernard, Snipes, & Gerould, 2009). Beccaria, writing in the 18th century, viewed the individual as a rational actor (the popular belief of the time) and sought under this belief system to reform the system of punishment (Bernard et al., 2009). Most important for modern control theories is Beccaria's overall support for the notion that being free actors, individuals need controls in their lives to keep them from hedonistic action (if that action was harmful to society).

Control theorists assert that human beings are basically antisocial and assume that deviance is part of the natural order in society; individuals are attracted to the idea of norm violation and thus motivated to deviate. This leads control theorists to assert that concern for deviant motivation alone does not account for the forces leading people to deviate—all people are capable of feeling a certain motivation to deviate. "The important question is not 'why do men not obey the rules of society,' but rather 'why do men obey the rules of society'" (Traub & Little, 1985, p. 241).

◈ Development of Social Control Theory

Our first theorist is important for two reasons. The first is that he is one of the earliest theorists to formulate the assumptions of the classical school into a sociological theory of deviance and social control. But more importantly, he is one of the first to articulate a distinction between *internal* and *external* social control. While later theorists do not always explicate their theories in the same dichotomy of internal and external, most accept the notion of internal social control (or a conversation with oneself—in other words, through thoughtful introspection, one decides not to engage in deviance) and **external control** (society places formal controls on the individual to keep him or her from engaging in crime).

Nye

F. Ivan Nye's (1958) position is that most deviant behavior is the result of insufficient social control. He offered four clusters of social control.

The first cluster is internalized control exercised from within through our conscience. Nye argues that every society tries to instill its rules and norms in the conscience of its children. This cluster is the most powerful; in fact, Nye states that if internal controls were entirely effective, then there would be no need for the other three clusters of social control. Unfortunately, internal controls, for a variety of reasons, are never completely effective. He argues that one reason for a variance in effectiveness is that the rules and norms of society are not always agreed upon at a level that allows for perfect socialization. Nye also argues that strong internal control can only be accomplished when the child completely accepts the parent—to the extent that the parent–child relationship is not a perfect one, internal control may not be as effective as necessary.

The second cluster Nye refers to as parents and indirect control. Nye argues that while parents are important to the internalizing of controls, they can also place indirect controls on juveniles. Nye sees these indirect controls as the disapproval the parent might show should the juvenile engage in deviant behavior. To the extent that the juvenile cares about the parent's disapproval, he or she will not engage in deviant behavior, thus being indirectly controlled through the parent's opinion of his or her behavior.

The third cluster is direct control imposed from without by means of restriction and punishment. Nye argues that no society relies solely on the individual to regulate his or her own behavior. Additional controls in the form of punishment, disapproval, ridicule, ostracism, or banishment are used by informal groups or society as a whole to control deviant behavior. These controls are often imposed by the police or other officials.

The final cluster is needed to give individuals reason not to engage in deviant behavior. Nye believes that alternative means to need satisfaction (goals and values) are necessary so that individuals do not have to engage in deviant behavior to get what they want. A readily available set of alternatives will mean that the above three clusters of social control will have a stronger influence on the likelihood of preventing deviant behavior.

Since all variations of social control theory assume that individuals *want* to engage in deviance and therefore the abnormal (or not expected) outcome is *not* engaging in deviance, we use social control theory to explain those instances when Jamila and Rashod are not engaging in deviance.

Given that Jamila never engaged in much deviance of a serious nature (she skipped school and dropped out, but did not engage in the drug trade like her brother did), Nye might argue that while not perfect, Jamila's internalized controls are fairly strong, but her indirect or direct controls were weakened when she lost her grandparents. Rashod, on the other hand, did not benefit from the stability of the family friend's household and lived under the unpredictability of his drug-addicted mother during a more influential time in his life.

Hirschi

The person most associated with control theories is Travis Hirschi. Hirschi's (1969) version of social control theory is often referred to as social bonding theory. This theory concentrates on indirect controls of behavior. Hirschi's social control theory suggests that deviance is not a response to learned behavior or stimuli or the strains surrounding an individual (like differential association theory or strain theory suggests); instead, social control theory assumes that deviant activity is a given and that it is the absence of deviance that needs to be explained. In fact, not only are we capable of it, but we are also willing creators and participants in it. The reason we do not engage in deviance or crime is because we have social bonds to conformity that keep us from engaging in socially unacceptable activities. This social bond comprises four parts: **attachment**, **commitment**, **involvement**, and **belief**.

Attachment is the "emotional" component of the bond. This component suggests that we do not engage in deviance because we care about what conforming others think about us. Hirschi argued that if we are strongly attached to others, we will contemplate what their reaction to our behavior will be before we engage in it. In other words, we will not engage in deviance if we think those we are attached to will be disappointed in us. This is the element of the social bond that may have us saying, "What would Mom think?" or "Mom would be mad if she found out." Hirschi believed that our most important attachment is probably to our parents (and, by extension, other family members), but he also thought that attachments to friends (even if they were not always conforming themselves) and teachers would also keep us from deviating.

Commitment is the "rational" component of the bond. This component suggests that individuals will be less likely to engage in deviance when they have a strong commitment to conventional society. This commitment will cause them to weigh the costs and benefits of deviant behavior. Those who have more to lose will be less likely to misbehave. Hirschi believed that conventional activities were most likely one's education and other school activities for juveniles and, for those who had successfully completed high school, work and occupational attainment. Hirschi actually believed that juveniles who entered adulthood too soon (for example, became young parents or worked while in high school) were more likely to become deviant, not less likely (Kubrin et al., 2009).

Involvement is the component of the bond that suggests the more time spent engaged in conforming activities, the less time available to deviate. Hirschi (1969) characterized this bond as "idle hands are the devil's workshop" (p. 187). In other words, Hirschi argued that juveniles who spend their time in conventional activities, such as sports, homework, or band practice, have, literally, less time for deviant activities. The difference between commitment and involvement (since we have mentioned school and after-school activities when discussing both) is that commitment is the bond that focuses on not wanting to lose the benefits of the conventional activity one is engaging in (you don't want to be benched on the football team because you were caught drinking). Involvement, however, refers specifically to the time you engage in a conventional activity (if you are at football practice, you cannot also be shoplifting at the same time).

Finally, belief is the component of the bond that suggests the stronger the awareness, understanding, and agreement with the rules and norms of society, the less likely one will be to deviate. Given that social control is a normative theory (it assumes that there is societal agreement and understanding about the norms and rules of society), an individual with weakened norms is not thought to be completely unaware of the norms and rules—however, he or she is less accepting of the "moral validity of the law" (Kubrin et al., 2009, p. 172).

Hirschi would argue that Jamila benefitted from changing neighborhoods, schools, and families and increased her

▲ **Photo 7.1**   In Hirschi's theory of social control, finding alternative activities for kids, such as music programs, may keep them from engaging in deviant behavior.

Source: ©Dylan Ellis/Photodisc/Getty Images.

bonds to conformity, while Rashod continued to live in an area that weakened his bonds to conformity because "conventional others" were in short supply.

◈ Techniques of Neutralization

Sykes and Matza (1957) offer an explanation for why individuals might engage in deviance even though they understand it is wrong. Asking, "Why would we violate the norms and laws in which we believe?" they suggest that we employ techniques of neutralization to rationalize away our understanding of the rules. They argue that society is organized for these sorts of rationalizations because much of our understanding of the rules comes with a certain flexibility already. In other words, they point out, while we understand the normative system, we also understand that under certain circumstances, those norms do not apply. For example, while killing someone is generally wrong, we know that during times of war or in self-defense, it is not. Under criminal law, an individual can avoid being guilty because of "non-age, necessity, insanity, drunkenness, compulsion, self-defense, and so on" (p. 666), in other words, if the individual can prove she or he did not *intend* to do harm. Sykes and Matza stated that

> it is our argument that much of delinquency is based on what is essentially an unrecognized extension of defenses to crimes, in the form of justifications for deviance that are seen as valid by the delinquent but not by the legal system or society at large. (p. 666)

Sykes and Matza (1957) argue that we can silence our internalized norms (what Nye refers to as our internalized controls) and external norms by using these techniques of neutralization. They suggest there are five such techniques:

1. The Denial of Responsibility

   The first technique is used by individuals to argue that they are not responsible for their behavior. While some of this might be an argument that their behavior was a mistake or accident, Sykes and Matza (1957) argue that denial of responsibility goes well beyond just the claim that "it was an accident." This technique essentially is used to suggest that the individual is somehow compelled by forces beyond his or her control. The individual is "helplessly propelled" into bad behavior by unloving parents, a bad teacher, a boss, or a neighborhood.

2. The Denial of Injury

   This technique focuses on whether the deviance is perceived to cause injury or harm to anyone. It might be symbolized by the statement "but no one was hurt by it." It is probable that this technique is used frequently in the justification for deviant behavior since much behavior defined as deviant is not defined as harmful enough to be against the law. In these instances when the behavior may go against understood societal norms but not be very harmful to others, it is easy for individuals to argue that their behavior should be allowed and is not really all that bad because it isn't hurting anyone.

3. The Denial of Victim

   An extension of the denial of injury is the rationalization that while a victim might exist, that person deserved the harm or "brought it on themselves." This technique of neutralization focuses on the fact that the victim deserves to be harmed because it is retaliation or punishment for some slight the victim has perpetrated on the deviant. The behavior becomes justified just as Robin Hood's behavior of stealing from the rich to give to the poor was justified. It may be against the rules to steal, but the rich brought it upon themselves by stealing from the poor first.

4. The Condemnation of the Condemners

   This technique shifts the focus or blame to the individuals who are pointing the finger at the deviant's behavior. It is a diversionary tactic used to point out that others' behavior is also deviant, and therefore, those "condemners" have no right to call into question the behavior of the deviant individual. As with all diversionary tactics, the goal of this one is not to have a meaningful conversation about anyone's deviance but to deflect attention from the original assertion and help the deviant slip from view.

5. The Appeal to Higher Loyalties

   The final technique of neutralization is one in which the wishes of the larger group (society) lose out to the wishes of a smaller, more intimate group. In other words, when an individual sees himself or herself as loyal to a group that demands behavior that violates the rules of society, he or she may argue that that loyalty requires breaking the rules for the good of the smaller group. In this instance, the individual may see himself or herself caught between the two groups. For example, a young man may know he should not fight another boy but may do it to protect his younger brother or because his friends demand he show loyalty to their group.

   Sykes and Matza (1957) offer five phrases to sum up the five techniques of neutralization: "I didn't mean it, I didn't really hurt anybody, they had it coming to them, everybody's picking on me, and I didn't do it for myself" (p. 669). With these phrases come the ability to rationalize away an individual's understanding of the normative behavior expected of him or her and an allowance for deviant behavior.

DEVIANCE IN POPULAR CULTURE

The ideas of social control theory can easily be applied to novels and films in popular culture. We offer two examples here but encourage you to think about the storylines of other books and films and see if you can apply the ideas of the theory to the different characters to explain their deviance and/or conformity.

   The Outsiders is a book written by a 16-year-old girl, S. E. Hinton, in 1967 and made into a film in 1983 by Francis Ford Coppola. Hinton examines the experiences of two groups of juvenile delinquents divided by social class—the Greasers and the Socs. *The Outsiders* is narrated by 14-year-old Ponyboy Curtis, a greaser, who lives with his two brothers, Darry and Sodapop, and considers the rest of the "gang"—Johnny, Dally, and Two-bit—his family.

   The Outsiders depicts a world without significant adults; the boys are accountable to each other more than anyone else. Johnny's parents are abusive, the Curtis brothers' parents were killed in a car accident, and the other boys' parents are rarely mentioned. Ponyboy is the only boy in his gang who is interested in school; Sodapop and Darry work full-time and try to stay out of trouble, attempting to hold their small family together after the death of their parents.

Social control theory can help to explain the relative conformity and deviance of each character. As an example, compare the social bonds of Ponyboy and Dally and see if the theory fits the outcome at the end of the novel/film.

For another example from a quite different era and setting, you might apply the ideas of social control theory to the film *Boyz N the Hood*. Set in South Central Los Angeles, the film focuses on the challenges of growing up in an extremely violent setting. The three main characters—Tre, Ricky, and Doughboy—are African American teenage boys with different backgrounds and opportunities.

Using Hirschi's theory, compare and contrast the social bonds of Tre, Ricky, and Doughboy. Do you think the relative strength of attachment, commitment, involvement, and belief explains their different levels of deviant behavior? Why or why not?

Contemporary Additions to Social Control Theory

Power-Control Theory

Developed by Hagan, Gillis, and Simpson (Hagan, 1989; Hagan, Gillis, & Simpson, 1985, 1990; Hagan, Simpson, & Gillis, 1987), power-control theory combines class and control theories of deviance to explain the effects of familial control on gender differences in crime. Hagan et al. (1987) argue that parental positions in the workforce affect patriarchal attitudes in the household. Patriarchal attitudes, in turn, result in different levels of control placed on boys and girls in these households. Finally, differing levels of control affect the likelihood of the children taking risks and ultimately engaging in deviance. In other words, because of the greater levels of control placed on girls in patriarchal households, there are greater gender differences in delinquency in such households, with boys being more delinquent than girls.

Power-control theory begins with the assumption that mothers constitute the primary agents of socialization in the family. In households in which the mother and father have relatively similar levels of power at work—so-called balanced households—mothers will be less likely to differentially exert control upon their daughters. Thus, in balanced households, both sons and daughters will have similar levels of control placed upon them, leading them to develop similar attitudes regarding the risks and benefits of engaging in deviant behavior. This line of reasoning suggests that balanced households will experience fewer gender differences in deviant behavior. Power-control theorists further assume that households in which mothers and fathers have dissimilar levels of power in the workplace—so-called unbalanced households—are more patriarchal in their attitudes regarding gender roles. In such households, parents will place greater levels of control upon daughters than sons. Therefore, daughters will develop attitudes unfavorable toward deviance—higher levels of perceived risk and fewer perceived benefits for engaging in deviant acts. Thus, in unbalanced households, the theory predicts significant gender differences in deviant behavior, with male children being more likely than females to engage in deviant acts.

Initial tests of power-control theory suggested that these gender differences in crime come about because girls are differentially controlled in the household. In other words, female delinquency increases or decreases depending on the level of patriarchy and, thus, control in the household. Later tests of the theory (McCarthy, Hagan, & Woodward, 1999) suggest that gender differences in deviance and crime probably decrease because *both* male and female deviants are affected. Most importantly, McCarthy et al. (1999) demonstrate that in less patriarchal households, sons have more controls placed on them, decreasing their level of deviance.

Theory of Self-Control

Gottfredson and Hirschi introduced their general theory of crime in 1990, situating the theory in the classical school of criminology. Of all the theories discussed in this chapter (and, perhaps, in this book), this theory may be, arguably, the one best positioned to predict deviant behavior. This is because this theory was designed to be able to predict *all* behavior, not just criminal or delinquent behavior.

According to Gottfredson and Hirschi, crime and deviance are just like any other behaviors and should not be set apart as somehow different than, say, brushing one's teeth or listening to music. Using concepts from the classical school (Bentham, 1789/1970), they argue that people engage in all behavior to maximize pleasure and minimize pain. As rational creatures, humans will make choices in their lives that help them increase pleasure and avoid pain whenever they can. In this conception, deviance, then, is just like any other behavior—individuals freely choose to engage in that behavior when it is pleasurable to them.

Gottfredson and Hirschi (1990) define crime (and deviance) as "acts of force or fraud undertaken in pursuit of self-interest" (p. 15). Using the Uniform Crime Reports to illustrate the nature of crime, they argue that there is no difference between trivial and serious crime, between expressive and instrumental crime, between status offenses and delinquency, between victim and victimless crimes—the difference lies not in the behaviors but, to some extent, in the individual. While a strict classical theory would argue that all individuals are likely to make the decision to engage in deviance if it brings with it a reward for the individual and that the likelihood to not engage in deviance is based on that individual's social bond to society, Gottfredson and Hirschi argue that there may be a difference in individuals and their behavior that cannot be explained by the social bond: "What classical theory lacks is an explicit idea of self-control, the idea that people also differ in the extent to which they are vulnerable in the temptations of the moment" (p. 87).

Gottfredson and Hirschi (1990) argue that self-control is a stable construct that develops early in the socialization process (or lack thereof) of an individual. Most likely, **low self-control** develops from an "absence of nurturance, discipline, or training" (p. 95). In other words, the major cause of low self-control is bad parenting or ineffective childrearing. But Gottfredson and Hirschi are emphatic in their assertion that low self-control is not actively created; it is what happens in the absence of socialization, not in the presence of socialization. In other words, Gottfredson and Hirschi believe that since deviant behavior "undermines harmonious group relations and the ability to achieve collective ends" (p. 96), no one would actively teach, learn, or promote deviant behavior.

Six elements make up the construct of low self-control, according to Gottfredson and Hirschi (1990):

1. Criminal acts provide *immediate gratification* of desires. A major characteristic of people with low self-control is therefore a tendency to respond to tangible stimuli in the immediate

environment, to have concrete "here and now" orientation. People with high self-control, in contrast, tend to defer gratification.

2. Criminal acts provide *easy or simple* gratification of desires. They provide money without work, sex without courtship, revenge without court delays. People lacking self-control also tend to lack diligence, tenacity, or persistence in a course of action.

3. Criminal acts are *exciting, risky, or thrilling.* They involve stealth, danger, speed, agility, deception, or power. People lacking self-control therefore tend to be adventuresome, active, and physical. Those with high levels of self-control tend to be cautious, cognitive, and verbal.

4. Crimes provide *few or meager long-term benefits.* They are not equivalent to a job or a career. On the contrary, crimes interfere with long-term commitments to jobs, marriages, family, or friends. People with low self-control thus tend to have unstable marriages, friendships, and job profiles. They tend to be little interested in and unprepared for long-term occupational pursuits.

5. Crimes require *little skill or planning.* The cognitive requirements for most crimes are minimal. It follows that people lacking self-control need not possess or value cognitive or academic skills. The manual skills required for most crimes are minimal. It follows that people lacking self-control need not possess manual skills that require training or apprenticeship.

6. Crimes often result in *pain or discomfort for the victim.* Property is lost, bodies are injured, privacy is violated, trust is broken. It follows that people with low self-control tend to be self-centered, indifferent, or insensitive to the suffering and needs of others. It does not follow, however, that people with low self-control are routinely unkind or antisocial. On the contrary, they may discover the immediate and easy rewards of charm and generosity. (pp. 89–90)

Gottfredson and Hirschi argue that these traits are stable in individuals. In other words, they do not vary over time—once a person with low self-control, always a person with low self-control. What Gottfredson and Hirschi say may vary is the ability or opportunity for individuals to engage in deviance. So while individuals with low self-control might always be inclined to make an easy score, that easy score has to come along first.

Gottfredson and Hirschi would argue that Jamila and Rashod are an excellent contrast in self-control. While Jamila's formative years (according to the general theory, childhood until about age eight) were characterized by a safe, close-knit neighborhood; the strong influence of her grandparents; and the stability of working parents, by the time Rashod was eight, the neighborhood was crime-ridden, his mother was an addict, and he was being used in the drug trade. Gottfredson and Hirschi would argue that these differing experiences affected each child's level of self-control, which in turn meant that Jamila could delay gratification to focus on finishing high school and attend and finish college, while Rashod leaned toward more risky, self-centered pursuits (although critics of the notion of low self-control might point out that Rashod rose in the ranks of the drug trade at a very early age to run two crack houses and corner the drug market in the neighborhood, which some might argue takes quite a bit of organization).

Life Course Theory

While traditional social control or social bonding theory focuses attention on the social bonds that juveniles and young adults maintain—attachment to parents and teachers, commitment to school, involvement in activities such as sports or band—life course theory extends this examination of social bonds from adolescents to adulthood (Sampson & Laub, 1993, 1995). Hirschi (1969) argued that bonds may be weak or broken (or may vary over time), but he never really explored the nature of that variance, while Gottfredson and Hirschi (1990) argue that life events (as they are related to social bonding) do not have an effect on deviant behavior because levels of self-control are set at an early age. Sampson and Laub (1993) argue that over the course of one's life, individuals are likely to go through stages that present them with social bonding opportunities and that, while we may be able to see trajectories toward crime throughout the life course, these trajectories can change with changes in life events.

According to Sampson and Laub (1993), a **trajectory** is a "pathway or line of development over a life span . . . [that] refer[s] to long-term patterns of behavior and [is] marked by a sequence of transitions" (p. 8). A **transition**, then, is a shorter or specific life event that is embedded in a trajectory. For example, your life could be said to be on a working-class trajectory—born in a working-poor neighborhood to parents who had stable but low-paying employment, you received no schooling past high school and ended up working in the service sector. Then you married and got an entry-level position in your in-laws' furniture business (same pay as your other job but with significant room for advancement). It could be said you were on a trajectory for a working-poor lifestyle—barely making ends meet, most likely always working in the service sector, always worrying about the likelihood you might lose your job—but then your marriage (the transition) offered a sudden change from that earlier trajectory.

Sampson and Laub focus on an age-graded theory of informal social control. They argue that there are social bonds between (1) members of society and (2) wider social institutions, such as family, school, and work. As an age-graded theory, they argue that life events may have an effect on the likelihood to persist or desist with deviance (although it is the quality of these life events, not just the existence of them, that is important). They offer three components to their theory. The first is that during childhood and adolescence, social bonds to family and school are important for explaining the likelihood to engage in deviance. Those who hold strong bonds to family and school are less likely to engage in deviance than those with weak or broken bonds. The second component is the argument that there is a certain level of stability to the likelihood to engage in deviance. In other words, those who don't engage in deviance as adolescents are more likely to abstain from deviance as adults, and those who do engage in deviance as adolescents are more likely to engage in deviance as adults. Sampson and Laub argue this is so for two reasons: First, there are stable individual differences in the likelihood to engage in deviance (some people are just more likely to engage in deviance), but, second, there is also a dynamic process by which the adolescent deviant behavior has an effect on later adolescent and adult social bonds (for example, an individual who has been incarcerated or labeled a deviant may have less desirable job prospects).

Finally, the third component, which is where Sampson and Laub spend a significant amount of explanatory time, is that important life events in adulthood have the likelihood of changing a trajectory. "In other words, we contend that trajectories of crime are subject to modification by key institutions of social control in the transition to adulthood" (Sampson & Laub, 1995, p. 146). These are likely to be such transitions as attachment to labor force participation or a particularly cohesive marriage. Sampson and Laub argue that it is not enough for these transitions to just happen; they must be quality transitions (in other words, just getting married or committing to a partner is not enough; it must be a cohesive commitment).

Moffitt (1993, 2003, 2006) makes an extended life course argument, claiming that there are two offender groups. The first is considered a life course persistent group whose deviance stems from neurodevelopmental processes; these individuals are predicted to be fairly consistent in their deviant behavior. In other words, over their life, they are more likely to engage in crime. Moffitt considers this to be a fairly small group. The second group is called adolescence limited. This group is much larger—its deviance stems from social processes, and over time, it is likely that most of its members will stop engaging in deviant behavior (Piquero, Daigle, Gibson, Leeper Piquero, & Tibbetts, 2007).

These variations on the life course theory are often used to explain the **age-crime curve**. The relationship between age and crime is so strong at the aggregate level that many believe it is invariant (meaning that it does not change over era or type of crime, for example), and while this is probably not the case (for two discussions on this, see Farrington, 1986; Piquero et al., 2007), it is a very strong relationship—we see, in general, that the likelihood for crime rises sharply as one ages into the teenage and late teenage/early adult years and then not quite as swiftly drops off (see Figure 7.1). Steffensmeier, Allan, Harer, and Streifel (1989) found that the age-crime relationship was extremely strong but varied for type of crime (for example, while the relationship between age and property crimes might peak at about 17, the relationship between age and violent crime peaks a bit later).

Figure 7.1   Age-Specific Arrest Rates: Robbery and Burglary in 1985

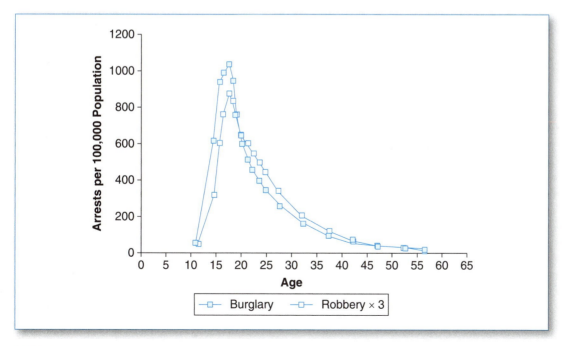

Source: Blumstein (1995).

Theorists who use the life course theory argue that this age-crime relationship exists because as people age, they go through stages that allow them to be more or less deviant. For example, as adolescents become teenagers, they are more likely to pull away from their parents' control, perhaps becoming less attached to their parents and more attached to their peers. Then, as individuals become even older, they enter new stages of their life in which deviant behavior may be less rewarding or available, and thus they begin to engage in less and less deviance and more and more conformity—we call this "aging out of crime and deviance."

◈ Application of Social Control Theories

As you can tell, most versions of social control theory, both the classical and contemporary additions, have explanations for deviance that rely heavily on the socializing capacity of the family. In other words, social control theory, in all of its forms, points to the family as the primary controlling agent of deviance. While the family can be found as a component of many theories of deviance, it plays a central role in empirical works examining the predictive abilities of social control theory. Below is an example of the research examining the socializing abilities of the family.

Instead of an intricate look at the structural characteristics of the single-parent family, some researchers have suggested that family process or family quality should also be a serious focus of examination (Patterson & Dishion, 1985; Rutter & Giller, 1984; Vazsonyi & Klanjsek, 2008) because structure may mask other processes or events in the juvenile's life (Haas, Farrington, Killias, & Sattar, 2004). Studies that have simultaneously examined family structure and family process have generally found that family structure is not a significant predictor of delinquency once family process has been added (Cernkovich & Giordano, 1987; Van Voorhis, Cullen, Mathers, & Garner, 1988) and that family structure at most had an indirect effect on delinquency through measures of family process (Laub & Sampson, 1988; Petts, 2009; Sampson & Laub, 1993).

Family process and/or family quality studies have been less systematic. Many of the studies examine the relationship between attachment and juvenile delinquency. However, the concept, attachment, has been measured in a variety of ways—love or affection, interest or concern, support and help, caring and trust, encouragement, lack of rejection, parental conflict, and control and **supervision** (Rankin & Kern, 1994; see also Rankin & Wells, 1990). These measures of attachment could also be measures of other theoretical components.

In addition to attachment, other family quality measures include overall home quality, discipline, supervision, and level of conflict. For the most part, family process variables, no matter what they are called or how they are

▲ **Photo 7.2**   All of the theories connected to social control suggest that family relationships are an important factor in controlling deviant behavior.

Source: ©Jack Hollingsworth/Thinkstock.

operationalized, are significant predictors of juvenile delinquency. Researchers have found that over-all home quality (Van Voorhis et al., 1988), level of supervision (Cernkovich & Giordano, 1987), attachment to parents (Hirschi, 1969; Johnson, 1986; Warr, 1993), and type of discipline (Laub & Sampson, 1988; Sampson & Laub, 1993) are strong predictors of juvenile delinquency.

Levels of attachment in the family have long been linked to juvenile delinquency (Hirschi, 1969; Rankin & Kern, 1994). While much of this research has examined the direct effect of attachment on delinquency, some has taken a more extensive look at family processes, including such variables as family involvement, family conflict, and supervision (Sampson & Laub, 1993, 1994), and some have examined the effect that racial and ethnic diversity might have on the effect of attachment (Smith & Krohn, 1995; Weber et al., 1995), finding that there does seem to be a relationship between ethnicity and the effect of attachment. Levels of attachment in conjunction with structure have also been examined with various findings. Some studies have shown that attachment is a better predictor of delinquency than structure (Sokol-Katz et al., 1997), while others have found a relationship between attachment and structure (Rankin & Kern, 1994).

Supervision is a second extensively researched process within the family that is said to affect the likelihood of delinquency (Broidy, 1995; Jang & Smith, 1997; Junger & Marshall, 1997). Most of these studies show a relationship between levels of supervision and delinquency (Greenwood, 1992), although this relationship does depend on how family supervision is measured (Broidy, 1995; Wells & Rankin, 1988).

RECENT STUDY IN DEVIANCE

Relationships With Children and AIDS–Risk Behaviors Among Female IDUs

By Susan F. Sharp, 1998, in *Deviant Behavior, 19,* 3–28.

Sharp (1998) examined the effect of social bonds on the likelihood of female intravenous drug users (IDUs) to engage in AIDS-risk behaviors (specifically, sharing drug needles and engaging in unprotected sex). Two factors make this research especially important. First, it was conducted on individuals who were already engaged in risky behavior (IDU) and examined the likelihood that individuals varied in their liability to engage in secondary risky behavior. Second, most research of this nature had been conducted on men and found that careers and marriage are important predictors of risk behaviors—men who are married and have careers that are important to them are less likely to engage in risky behavior. However, research has already found that women are less likely to have meaningful careers than men, and marriage is less likely to keep them from risky behavior.

Sharp conducted in-depth interviews with 18 female IDUs and 2 former IDUs. The interviewees were recruited using a snowball sample (interviewees were asked to refer other IDUs to be interviewed). Each participant received $15 for her time. The participants were between the ages of 20 and 53.

(Continued)

(Continued)

This research found that weakening or rupturing of existing bonds with children—most importantly, if a child had been removed from the custody of the mother (formally or informally)—led to an increase in risky behaviors in the form of unprotected sex and needle sharing. Women who had not lost custody/contact with their children were less likely to report sharing needles or engaging in unprotected sex (even though they were already intravenous drug users).

As Casey, an interviewee, summed up her experience:

Casey: yeah, they convinced DHS that I was putting them in danger and all so they took them and gave them to him and his mom.

S: How did that affect you?

Casey: How the hell do you think? My kids were everything and they were all I had left. I went crazy. I threatened to kill James and his mother. That's when they got the injunction where I couldn't see my kids. I was sick—and I just quit caring anymore. I stayed totally loaded all the time and did whatever it took to get high so I didn't have to think or go home to an empty house. I turned tricks at truck stops for dope money—whatever. (p. 13)

◈ Critiques of Social Control Theory

The earliest versions of social control theory were criticized for having underdeveloped constructs that could not be easily tested. This changed with Hirschi's version of social control theory. Not only did Hirschi present a test of his theory with his initial book (1969) but the theory may be one of the most tested in criminology today (Kubrin et al., 2009). Numerous researchers have found support for the theory using cross-sectional studies, although longitudinal studies show less support (Kubrin et al., 2009).

However, some theorists and researchers argue that traditional social control theory (specifically Hirschi's form of social bonding theory) is better at predicting minor forms of deviance and crime than more serious forms (Krohn & Massey, 1980) and that the four bonds do not really predict future deviance with any success at all (Agnew, 1985).

Contemporary versions of control theory have actually been critiqued by other control theorists—most notably, there is a robust exchange between Hirschi and Gottfredson (1995) and Sampson and Laub (1995) on the merits of the theory of self-control and life course theory. One of their central debates is whether control varies throughout a person's life or whether that control is set by a certain (young) age. Specifically, critics of self-control theory argue that self-control may be something that changes over time in one's life (as opposed to being set in someone by the time they are seven or eight).

Perhaps one of the most common and general critiques about all the theories that fall under the general heading of social control theory is that there is a background assumption that individuals are both rational and have the capacity to perceive the consequences of their behavior. These theories assume that people will weigh the costs and benefits of their behavior, and, in instances where they do not want to give up the connections they have made to society (attachment to their parents, benefits in school, a good job, a good marriage, the esteem of their friends and colleagues), they will be less likely to deviate. However, as we know, when we engage in deviant behavior, often we do not take those things into consideration. For example, we know when we sit down with a pint of ice cream in the middle of the night to watch Spike TV's *The Ultimate Fighter* that this behavior is not good for us, but the consequences of these actions are far off (if perceived at all), while the benefits (a mindless night of chocolate chip mint ice cream and violent TV) are immediate.

 ## Explaining Deviance in the Streets and Deviance in the Suites: The Case of Teenage Runaways/Homelessness and Medical Deviance by Doctors

Teenage Runaways/Throwaways

There is no clear-cut way to estimate how many teenagers run away in a given year or how many teenagers are homeless at any given time. By definition, these are acts that are relatively invisible. Therefore, tracking and counting runaways is more of an art form than a science. When we talk about runaways, are we talking about youth who run away to become homeless? Or who just leave the house they are in for another, friendlier, dwelling? Do we include youth who are forced to leave the family home because the parents demand it (these youth are known as "throwaway kids")? For the purposes of our discussion, we will assume runaway/throwaway means the child ends up on the streets. We only have estimates of the number of youth who run away or are thrown away, and those estimates often vary. Greene, Ringwalt, Kelley, Iachan, and Cohen (1995) reported that in 1992, approximately 2.8 million youth between the ages of 12 and 17 ran away from home. In 1999, the estimate was that approximately 1.7 million youth between the ages of 7 and 17 had had a runaway or throwaway experience (Hammer, Finkelhor, & Sedlak, 2002) (see Table 7.1). And in 2002, the National Survey on Drug Use estimated that about 1.6 million youth between the ages of 12 and 17 had slept in the street in the previous year because they had run away from home (Office of Applied Studies, Substance Abuse and Mental Health Services Administration, 2004). It is unlikely that the estimates vary so much from year to year because the incidence of running away varies that much—this is much more likely an illustration of exactly how hard it is to get an accurate account of youth who run away and sleep on the street.

While there are many reasons why youth run away from home, the most likely reason is family difficulties—most prevalently, child abuse and sexual abuse (Jencks, 1994; Tyler, Hoyt, Whitbeck, & Cauce, 2001). While both sexual and other abuse are strongly related to running away (Kaufman & Widom, 1999; Kempf-Leonard & Johansson, 2007), girls who have run away are more likely to report sexual abuse than runaway boys (Janus, Burgess, & McCormack, 1987; McCormack, Janus, & Burgess, 1986).

Chesney-Lind (1988, 1997) argues that this connection between the likelihood to be sexually abused and running away for girls is a gendered pathway to delinquency and continued victimization both on the streets and by the juvenile justice and adult justice systems. Calling this phenomenon "*the criminalization of girls' survival strategies*" (1989, p. 11), Chesney-Lind argues that the juvenile justice system heaps added problems onto the shoulders of girls just trying to escape their abuse by arresting them for running away after they have left home.

Beside the fact that runaway girls are more likely to report sexual abuse than runaway boys, why does this issue become a gendered one? A quick answer here is that studies tell us that the response to running away from society in general and the justice system in particular is a gendered one. While estimates suggest that both boys and girls are equally likely to run away (Kaufman & Widom, 1999),

Table 7.1 Characteristics of Runaway/Throwaway Youth

Characteristic	Estimate	Percentage (*n* = 1,682,900)	Percentage of U.S. Child Population Aged 7–17* (*n* = 43,372,500)
Age (years)			
7–11	70,100	4	46
12–14	463,200	28	27
15–17	1,149,400	68	27
No information	200+	<1[†]	—
Gender			
Male	841,300	50	51
Female	841,600	50	49
Race/ethnicity			
White, non-Hispanic	963,500	57	66
Black, non-Hispanic	283,300	17	15
Hispanic	244,300	15	14
Other	188,900	11	5
No information	3,000+	<1[†]	—

Source: Hammer, H., Finkelhor, D., and Sedlak, A. J. (2002). Runaway/thrownaway children: National estimates and characteristics. National Incidence Studies of Missing, Abducted, Runaway, and Thrownaway Children. Office of Juvenile Justice and Delinquency Prevention: U.S. Department of Justice.

Note: Because all estimates have been rounded to the nearest 100, percentages may not sum to 100.

* Age, gender, and race for the U.S. population were based on the average monthly estimates of the population aged 7–17 years for 1999 (U.S. Census Bureau, 2000).

[†] Estimate is based on too few sample cases to be reliable.

girls are more likely to be arrested and punished for doing so (Chesney-Lind & Shelden, 1998; Kempf-Leonard & Johansson, 2007). This means that girls who are merely looking to end their abuse are treated as delinquents, and running away becomes the first step in a long path through the juvenile and adult justice systems.

Teenage Runaways/Throwaways and Social Control Theory

Given that one of the strongest predictors of running away or becoming a throwaway is the presence of conflict—and often abuse—in the home, Hirschi's version of social control theory might be useful in explaining why a juvenile might run away and end up engaging in behaviors such as drug use that he or she wouldn't have under normal circumstances. Hirschi argues that if the bonds to conformity are weakened, individuals will engage in deviant behavior. If the attachment bond to parents or other caregivers becomes weakened (even with a caregiver that is not engaging in abuse but that the youth sees as not helping to protect him or her), the youth may see running away as an acceptable alternative. Once homeless with no daily commitment to a conventional lifestyle (the commitment bond) or to the usual conventional activities that the youth may have engaged in (the involvement bond), the youth may be more likely to engage in other deviant behaviors, such as drug use, that he or she would not have engaged in had he or she not run away or been thrown away. Homeless youth are reported to engage in many survival behaviors that extend from their homeless circumstances. Such behaviors include prostitution and pimping, stealing and selling stolen goods, dealing and using drugs, and conning others for goods (Greene, Ennett, & Ringwalt, 1999; Halcon & Lifson, 2004; Kipke, Unger, O'Connor, Palmer, & LaFrance, 1997). Many of these behaviors are engaged in for survival because homeless youth lack parental and other conventional support (Bender, Thompson, McManus, Lantry, & Flynn, 2007). This deviant behavior becomes a vicious circle because it further removes homeless youth from conventional relationships and institutions (Ferguson, Bender, Thompson, Maccio, Xie, & Pollio, 2011).

Medical Deviance by Doctors

Individuals who become doctors learn several ethical codes while studying medicine, the most well-known of which is the Hippocratic Oath. While the Hippocratic Oath has changed over time, at its essence it is a promise by doctors and other medical professionals to practice medicine honestly. But while all doctors go through this training, some still behave in an unethical or criminal manner. There are many ways that doctors can act in a deviant manner while practicing their profession; some of these activities include fraud, unnecessary surgery, providing incompetent care, and over-prescribing medications.

One of the better-documented types of medical deviance is *fraud* because often the victim of that fraud is the government, and the government has established an extensive financial recovery system. Medicaid and Medicare fraud are the most pervasive forms of fraud. In general, fraud accounts for between 3% and 10% of health care spending, which means that each year approximately somewhere between $68 billion and $226 billion is wasted on fraud (National Health Care Anti-Fraud Association, 2010, as cited in Payne, 2013). The following activities are all considered fraud:

- Phantom treatments: billing for services never provided
- Substitute provider: charging for services provided by an unauthorized employee
- Upcoding: billing for more expensive services than provided

- Falsifying records: providers change or lie on medical forms in order to be reimbursed by insurance
- Unbundling: billing separately for services that are considered one procedure
- Ping-ponging: unnecessarily moving patients from one medical provider to the next
- Ganging: billing for services provided to multiple family members when only one was treated

While *unnecessary surgery* is much less prevalent than fraud, the ramifications of this deviance can be much more severe. According to Black (2005), approximately 7.5 million unnecessary surgeries are performed annually (no we didn't mistype that—it works out to about one surgery every 4 or 5 seconds), and approximately 12,000 people in the United States alone are killed each year because of these unnecessary surgeries and procedures. Many of the reasons for these procedures are not deviant themselves. Some of these procedures are done because there are differing opinions about the best course of action for many medical conditions—some doctors may have a more proactive approach, while others "wait and see." However, when it comes to certain types of medical conditions, often patients are uncomfortable with a wait-and-see approach. For example, cancer has such a stigma that patients often think that invasive procedures are the only way to go, even when research suggests otherwise. But although many of these surgeries and procedures are the result of varying opinions, some occur because there is financial gain for doctors in performing surgeries (Black, 2005). In the United States in particular, many of these surgeries are quite expensive (Anderson, Hussey, Frogner, & Waters, 2005; Payne, 2013).

Medical Deviance by Doctors and Techniques of Neutralization

Looking at techniques of neutralization might be an especially fun way to examine how and why medical doctors engage in medical deviance. At first glance, medical doctors are not our first choice for a group that might engage in deviance. As people that we place immense trust in, they are an excellent example of white-collar crime or elite deviance because one of the main elements of their deviance is the violation of that trust. Remember that Sykes and Matza used the techniques of neutralization to explain how an individual can silence his or her internalized norms for conformity. These techniques may especially explain deviance among a group trained first to "do no harm." In many instances, the fraudulent practices are not aimed at doctors' patients but more likely at a third party, such as the government or an insurance company. But there are examples of doctors skirting Medicare limits by contracting separately with the patient for the patient to pay the remaining part of the bill, even though these are not the rules under Medicare. While critics argue that these contracts are coercive because they put patients in a position of having to agree to the arrangement to get the medical care they need, doctors involved justify these contracts and condemn Medicare:

> That is a tyrannical system that forbids wealthy citizens to pay more and that's unfair to doctors and patients....Why should a patient lose the freedom to pay the doctor he wants for service he wants just because he turns 65? (Rosenthal, 1994, n.p.)

This quote can be interpreted as either a denial of injury—by focusing on wealthy patients it seems that no one is getting hurt by the behavior—or a condemnation of the condemners—the system itself is unfair and hurting patients by not letting them choose to pay the doctor an agreed-upon rate for agreed-upon services, thus both the doctor and patient are the true victims of Medicare. A doctor might also appeal to higher loyalties by suggesting that in order to be able to remain in practice at all and treat patients, he or she must overbill Medicare or Medicaid. Thus, the care of the doctor's patients is more important than the rules of Medicare and Medicaid.

◈ Ideas in Action: Homeboy Industries

Homeboy Industries (Homeboy Industries, 2013a) may be one of the best existing examples of the tenets of social control theory in action (although, ironically, this program could be in the critical theories chapter, too, as an example of how when we critique existing policies, think of gang members as human beings instead of deviants, and decide to make changes, the resulting community programs and public policies can have transformative outcomes).

▲ **Photo 7.3**   The Homeboy Industries' motto is "Jobs not Jails," emphasizing both commitment to and involvement in a conventional lifestyle.

Source: http://en.wikipedia.org/wiki/East_Side_Spirit_and_Pride

Homeboy Industries is the largest gang intervention and re-entry program in the country. It was founded by Father Gregory Boyle while he was the pastor of a parish in Boyle Heights (a neighborhood in Los Angeles). The program started in 1988 as Jobs for a Future (JFF), which was a small jobs program focused on decreasing gang violence. Over the years, JFF blossomed into what is known today as Homeboy Industries. Embracing the motto "Jobs Not Jails," Homeboy Industries now offers a variety of services and programs, including (1) tattoo removal; (2) employment services; (3) case management; (4) mental health, substance abuse, and domestic violence services; (5) legal services; (6) educational opportunities; and (7) a solar panel installation training and certification program (Homeboy Industries, 2013b).

In addition to these services and programs, Homeboy Industries has created seven job-training sites that are referred to as "social enterprises." These businesses offer both training and the opportunity for a social experience based on growing a business. These businesses include (1) Homegirl Café & Catering, (2) Homeboy Farmers Markets, (3) Homeboy Bakery, (4) Homeboy Diner, (5) the marketing and sale of Homeboy and Homegirl merchandise, (6) the inclusion of Homeboy grocery items in grocery chains such as Ralphs and Food 4 Less, and (7) Homeboy Silkscreen and Embroidery (Homeboy Industries, 2013b).

It might be argued that Homeboy Industries focuses on all four of Hirschi's social bonds to conformity. As a program that uses the skills and experiences of former gang members to guide new members, the program is emphasizing the importance of attachment and actively building the attachment bond between individuals at various stages of leaving gang life. The central focus on jobs and creating these social enterprises strengthens both the commitment bond and the involvement bond. Not only do jobs and the opportunity to help grow a business increase a commitment to a conventional lifestyle, but the sheer time that one spends on a job strengthens the involvement bond. According to testimonials about Homeboy Industries, "Small, perfect things happen every day at Homeboy. Amazing little happenings, human interactions that touch the soul. These moments are what makes this a place of healing and hope" (Homeboy Industries, 2012).

NOW YOU . . . USE THE THEORY

Below are the copyright infringement statistics for the University of Delaware for the academic year 2009–2010. These statistics and the copyright violation policy are reprinted from the University of Delaware's security Web page (www.udel.edu/security/copyrightstats.html). Using social control theory and its variations, answer the following questions:

1. How might social control theory explain copyright infringement on a college campus?

2. How might social control theory explain the decrease in copyright infringement on the University of Delaware college campus?

3. In addition to the policies below, what might a social control theorist suggest as a policy to decrease copyright infringement on campuses?

Copyright Infringement Statistics Academic Year 2009–2010

This page shows the number of student computers that have been cited for copyright infringement and removed from the university's network in the current academic year. If you are a student, and you violate copyright laws, you:

1. Receive a *Copyright Violation Notice* with infringement specifics in your university e-mail account.

2. Have your network access disabled.

3. Must complete the Copyright Education course in Sakai.

4. Must schedule an appointment to have your computer examined by IT-Client Support & Services. You will be charged a fee for this service.

5. Will have your network access restored upon your completion of the Sakai course **and** examination of your system by IT-Client Support & Services.

Future incidents of alleged copyright infringement will be referred to the Office of Student Conduct.

Copyright Violations by Month

September '09	October '09	November '09	December '09	January '10	February '10	March '10	April '10	May '10	June '10	July '10	August '10
63	60	66	59	23	27	35	40	33	11	9	2

Copyright Violations Academic Year 2009–2010

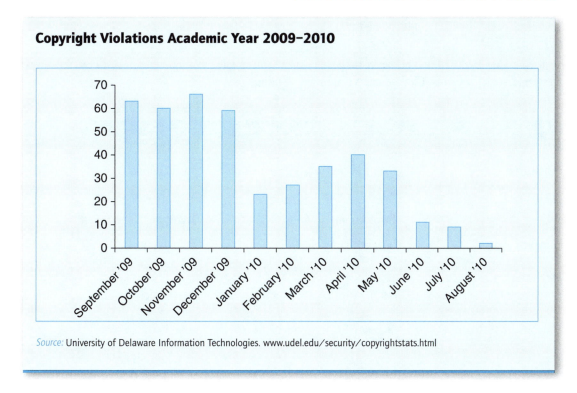

Source: University of Delaware Information Technologies. www.udel.edu/security/copyrightstats.html

◈ Conclusion

After discussing the theories above that traditionally fall under the heading of social control theory, it might be easy to suggest that they do not have much in common. The commonality between these theories, however, is their reliance on background assumptions that are based in the classical tradition of criminology—that is, the belief in a rational mind, an ability to make choices, and a belief that individuals want to maximize their pleasure and minimize their pain and must be restrained from engaging in deviance. And, while many social control theories might engender robust disagreements among those who study deviant behavior, this is what makes this particular type of theory such a dynamic and central explanatory mechanism.

EXERCISES AND DISCUSSION QUESTIONS

1. Explain Sykes and Matza's techniques of neutralization. For each technique, give a real-world example of how that technique is in use today.

2. Watch a political exchange on CNN, MSNBC, or Fox News (preferably one in which two political parties are debating) or follow an exchange from an Internet news source. Can you identify techniques of neutralization in place to justify the behavior of either of the political parties?

3. Compare and contrast the theory of self-control (from *A General Theory of Crime* by Gottfredson and Hirschi, 1990) and the life course theory

(from *Crime in the Making* by Sampson and Laub, 1993).

4. Explain the general difference between internal and external social controls. Choose one version

of social control theory to illustrate the differences.

5. Explain Hirschi's four components of the social bond.

KEY TERMS

Age-crime curve

Attachment

Belief

Commitment

External control

Internal control

Involvement

Low self-control

Social bonds

Supervision

Trajectory

Transition

CHAPTER 8

Labeling Theory

Saturday, March 24, 1984. Shermer High School, Shermer, Illinois. 60062.

Dear Mr. Vernon, we accept the fact that we had to sacrifice a whole Saturday in detention for whatever it was that we did wrong... what we did was wrong, but we think you're crazy to make us write this essay telling you who we think we are. What do you care? You see us as you want to see us... in the simplest terms and the most convenient definitions. You see us as a brain, an athlete, a basket case, a princess and a criminal. Correct? That's the way we saw each other at seven o'clock this morning. We were brainwashed.

From *The Breakfast Club*

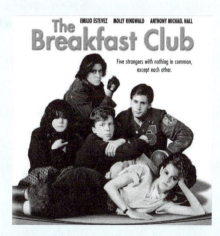

▲ **Photo 8.1** The film *The Breakfast Club* offers a great example of labeling, with each of the main characters representing different high school cliques. Can you recall five distinct student groups from your own high school experience?

Source: http://karlgoestocoimbra.files.wordpress.com/2011/05/025192046186_bluray_ws_2d_clr.jpg

Introduction

The movie *The Breakfast Club* is a classic coming-of-age film that deals squarely with the issue of labeling and how labels can affect the quality of an individual's life. In the film, the group of students represents the popular kids, the jocks, the smart kids, the delinquents, and the outcasts. Think back to your own days in high school . . . can you identify several categories of students and a few specific traits associated with each of those groups? Were those groups treated differently by the school's staff members and the rest of the students? How so? Did that treatment then affect the way the individuals behaved and what was expected of them?

The impact of labeling has been a key idea in literature in works ranging from Hawthorne's Hester Prynne being branded with a scarlet letter for adultery in Puritan Boston to S. E. Hinton's story of the struggles of the teenage Greasers and Socs in 1960s Oklahoma in *The Outsiders*. In real life, as in these works, the way individuals are perceived and labeled can have important and long-lasting consequences for how they are treated by others and the opportunities that are available to them.

The labeling perspective is situated in the larger framework of social psychology and symbolic interactionism in sociology. This is a micro-level, relativist perspective that is focused on individuals and the meanings they attach to objects, people, and interactions around them. Symbolic interactionists advocate direct observation of the social world as it is experienced and understood by the individuals acting in it. Labeling theorists examine the social meaning of deviant labels, how those labels are understood, and how they affect the individuals to whom they are applied.

Labeling theorists argue that, to some extent, deviance is in the eye of the beholder. The reaction to the behavior or the person is the key element in defining deviance. Can you think of an act that is inherently deviant? An act that everyone would agree is and has always been deviant across cultures and across time? Chances are that any act you might initially think of has been accepted behavior in some cultures under some circumstances. For example, we generally consider taking the life of another to be a very serious criminal act; however, in times of war or acts of self-defense, taking a life can be viewed as acceptable and perhaps even laudable behavior. The relativist perspective reminds us that audience reaction is key in defining deviance—no act is thought to be inherently deviant; acts are judged depending on the context and the power of the individuals and groups involved. As Becker (1963/1973) makes clear,

> A major element in every aspect of the drama of deviance is the imposition of definitions— of situations, acts, and people—by those powerful enough or sufficiently legitimated to be able to do so. A full understanding requires the thorough study of those definitions and the processes by which they develop and attain legitimacy and taken-for-grantedness. (p. 207)

According to the labeling perspective, deviance is a status imposed on an individual or a group that may or may not be related to actual rule breaking. The focus is on reactions rather than norm violations; you could be falsely accused but still be labeled deviant and face the repercussions. When there are disagreements over when and whether an actor should be considered deviant, power is a key element through which the status of deviance is imposed. Individuals with power will be better able to both reject a label or to impose a deviant label on another; Matsueda (1992) makes this connection clear:

A hallmark of labeling theory is the proposition that deviant labels are not randomly distributed across the social structure, but are instead more likely to apply to the powerless, the disadvantaged, and the poor. . . . Moreover, the powerless, having fewer cultural and material resources at their disposal, may be more likely to accept deviant labels. Again, the result is a self-fulfilling prophesy: members of disadvantaged groups are labeled delinquent, which alters their self-conceptions and causes them to deviate, thus fulfilling the prophesy of their initial label. (p. 1558)

Development of Labeling Theory

One of the earliest building blocks for the labeling perspective was developed in the work of Franklin Tannenbaum (1938). Tannenbaum suggested that police contact may turn relatively common acts of juvenile delinquency into a "dramatization of evil" that labels the individuals involved in a negative light. This societal reaction may lead to further deviant acts.

In his book *Social Pathology,* Edwin Lemert (1951) made the important distinction between primary and secondary deviation. **Primary deviance** refers to common instances where individuals violate norms without viewing themselves as being involved in a deviant social role. Primary deviance consists of incidental deviant acts—instances in which an individual breaks or violates norms but does not do so chronically. For example, teens may occasionally shoplift while with their friends, but they would not consider themselves delinquent.

With primary deviation, there is no engulfment in a deviant social role, but primary deviance can serve to trigger the labeling process. Individuals can be caught as they engage in deviant acts and they may then be labeled delinquent, criminal, or mentally ill. Once labeled, they may move into secondary deviation. **Secondary deviance** occurs when a person begins to engage in deviant behavior as a means of defense, attack, or adjustment to the problems created by reactions to him or her. In some cases when rules are broken, it elicits a reaction. In defense to the reaction, the individual may commit subsequent deviant acts and begin a more serious deviant career. Labeling someone deviant and treating that person as if he or she is "generally rather than specifically deviant produces a **self-fulfilling prophesy**. It sets in motion several mechanisms which conspire to shape the person in the image people have of him" (Becker, 1963/1973, p. 34).

For Lemert and other labeling theorists, the cause of the initial deviance is left unexplained. Rather than asking why someone commits a deviant act, the question is, who decides what is deviant, who is to be labeled deviant, and under what circumstances should someone be considered deviant? Howard S. Becker's (1963/1973) explanation of this view in his book *Outsiders* has become the classic interactionist or relativist statement of labeling and deviance:

Social groups create deviance by making the rules whose infraction constitutes deviance, and by applying those rules to particular people and labeling them as outsiders. From this point of view, deviance is *not* a quality of the act the person commits, but rather a consequence of the application by others of rules and sanctions to an "offender." The deviant is one to whom that label has successfully been applied; deviant behavior is behavior people so label. (Becker, 1963/1973, p. 9)

How the Labeling Process Works

If diagrammed in its simplest form, the labeling process would look something like this:

Deviance → reaction → role engulfment → secondary deviance

It's not that simple, of course, and the lines would not be so direct. In fact, there would be reciprocal or circular relationships as well, with lines going back and forth between deviance, reaction, secondary deviance, and role engulfment. Imagine that when you were a teenager, you were caught cheating on an exam. If it's your first offense (or the first time you were caught), there may be an informal reaction—a conference with your teacher and parents, a failing grade, and a strict warning. After this event, your teachers and parents may monitor your behavior more closely. You may commit more deviant or criminal acts to push the boundaries or because you are bored or your friends are involved and it looks fun. If you are caught stealing from a store, the case begins to build that you are generally a troublemaker and a "bad kid" likely to cause further trouble. When treated this way and closely monitored, you may start to *feel* like a bad kid. If the reaction is severe enough (for example, being adjudicated delinquent in juvenile court), other parents may not want their children to spend time with you. You may start hanging out with the other "bad" kids (role engulfment) and committing more serious crimes (secondary deviance).

Labeling theory is an interactionist theory and does not suggest that once on the path to deviance, one must continue in that direction. As Becker (1963/1973) explains,

> Obviously, everyone caught in one deviant act and labeled a deviant does not move inevitably toward greater deviance . . . he may decide that he does not want to take the deviant road and turn back. If he makes the right choice, he will be welcomed back into the conventional community; but if he makes the wrong move, he will be rejected and start a cycle of increasing deviance. (pp. 36–37)

Labeling can lead to secondary deviance in three general and overlapping ways: by altering an individual's self-concept, by limiting conforming opportunities, and by encouraging involvement in a deviant subculture (Kubrin et al., 2009, p. 203). Being labeled deviant may also lead to a deviant **master status,** a status that proves to be more important than most others. A deviant master status elicits strong reactions and shapes the perception and behavior of those around you. For example, being labeled a sex offender is often a master status; sex offenders may also be parents, spouses, employees, and friends, but once labeled a sex offender, that identity takes priority in the minds of others.

DEVIANCE IN POPULAR CULTURE

The process of labeling is a powerful theoretical concept and tool in studying deviant behavior. Can the way that others view you and react to you influence how you think of yourself and behave? If you cannot think of examples from your own life or family or friends, popular culture films and television shows portray a wide variety of types of deviance and examples of labeling.

One Flew Over the Cuckoo's Nest—this is a classic film about life in a mental hospital. When R. P. McMurphy is sent to the state mental institution, he is not crazy; he has run afoul of the law and simply believes it will be easier to serve his time in a mental hospital rather than in a corrections facility or work camp. He does not, however, understand the power of the label as it relates to mental illness. Watch this film and pay attention to how McMurphy and the other patients are treated by the hospital staff. How does it make the patients think about themselves? Why is McMurphy's presence so disruptive to the routine of the ward? How is he punished for not playing the expected role?

Girl, Interrupted—this film focuses on the experiences of young women inside a mental institution. Based on Susanna Kaysen's memoir detailing more than a year of voluntary institutionalization, the film is another strong example of labeling and mental illness.

Made—this MTV television show is all about teenagers working to change their labels—the shy boy who wants to become a ladies' man, the tomboy who aspires to be a beauty queen, or the artsy drama girl who wants to make the cheerleading squad. It's difficult to even describe the show without using labels as part of the description. What were some of your labels in high school? How do you think your life would have been different if you had a more positive or a more negative label? Do you think it's possible to re-create yourself—and the way others view you—in a relatively short amount of time as they do on *Made?* Why or why not?

◈ Labeling and Mental Illness

Scheff (1966) laid out a theory of labeling and mental illness that suggests most mental illness begins with a form of primary deviance he calls **residual rule breaking**. Residual rule breaking is essentially deviance for which there exists no clear category—it is not a crime, but it may be behavior that draws attention and makes the societal audience uncomfortable. Inappropriate dress, conversation, or interactions may be perceived as residual rule breaking. Consistent with other labeling theorists' ideas on primary deviance, Scheff is not particularly concerned with why people commit these acts in the first place; he argues that residual rule breaking comes from diverse sources. The acts may stem from biological, psychological, or situational conditions; most residual rule breaking is denied and deemed insignificant, and the individuals get past it and move on with their lives.

Importantly, however, residual rule breaking can activate the labeling process. Say, for example, a college student breaks up with her boyfriend and stays in bed in her pajamas for a week. If she is left alone, this behavior might be written off as painful but temporary heartache and the incident might pass. If, however, her concerned parents take her to a doctor or a hospital, she may be given a diagnosis of clinical depression and labeled as mentally ill. If she is hospitalized for any time at all, her roommates and friends may start treating her as if she is fragile and cannot cope with difficult circumstances.

Scheff (1966) suggests that the symptoms and stereotypes of mental illness are inadvertently reaffirmed in ordinary social interactions. Friends and family may reward those labeled mentally ill for going along with their expectations and playing the stereotyped role. At the same time, labeled deviants may be punished or blocked when attempting to resume their regular activities and return to conventional lives.

While most residual rule breaking can be explained away and deemed insignificant, it can be the starting point for the labeling process. Once labeled, many individuals will have a difficult time continuing or resuming their conventional roles. Thus, Scheff (1966) argues that among residual rule breakers, labeling is a key factor leading to more serious and lengthy deviant careers.

David Rosenhan (1973) conducted a fascinating study of labeling and mental illness when he recruited eight sane citizens to act as "pseudopatients" and simulate symptoms of psychosis; they were admitted to 12 different mental hospitals across the United States over the course of the study. Once hospitalized, the pseudopatients immediately stopped simulating symptoms and began acting "normal" again, yet they had a difficult time proving themselves to be sane. Rosenhan begins his article with a provocative question: "If sanity and insanity exist, how shall we know them?" (p. 250) and he goes on to detail the treatment and medications received by the pseudopatients during their time in the mental hospitals. Real details of the pseudopatients' life histories were interpreted through the lens of their diagnoses; doctors and staff members assigned meaning to behaviors based on the individuals' diagnosis of schizophrenia. Throughout the experiment, the pseudopatients were issued nearly 2,100 pills, but only two of those were actually swallowed. As long as they were not causing trouble, hospital staff did not bother to ensure that the medication was taken as prescribed. The pseudopatients each entered the hospital without knowing when they would be discharged; they would only be released by convincing the staff that they were ready to return to the community. The length of hospitalization ranged from 7 to 53 days, with an average stay of 19 days. Ironically, when the pseudopatients were finally released from the hospital, each was discharged with a diagnosis of schizophrenia "in remission"; none were thought to be sane. Rosenhan concludes, "We now know that we cannot distinguish insanity from insanity . . . psychiatric diagnoses are rarely found to be in error. The label sticks, a mark of inadequacy forever" (1973, p. 257).

A more recent longitudinal study added depth to our understanding of the impact of being labeled mentally ill by exploring the stigma and social rejection experienced by mental patients once they return to the community (Wright, Gronfein, & Owens, 2000). The authors studied a cohort of 88 mental patients in a three-wave survey conducted while the individuals were institutionalized and in the 2 years following their discharge from a state hospital. They found that both institutionalization and community reactions affected the self-concept of former mental patients:

Stigma is a powerful and persistent force in the lives of long-term mental patients . . . even for patients who have had extensive experience in the mental patient role, subsequent experiences of rejection increase and crystalize patients' self-deprecating feelings. . . . Our

▲ **Photo 8.2** From a labeling perspective, being hospitalized in a mental institution can be very damaging to the individual. If you were one of the pseudopatients in Rosenhan's study, how do you think institutionalization would have affected your self-image?

Source: © thepixelchef/iStockphoto.

results demonstrate convincingly that exposure to stigmatizing experiences represents a potentially serious source of chronic or recurrent stress for mental patients who established identities as "mental patients." The fact that these effects persist over time and diminish feelings of mastery provides additional empirical support for modified labeling theory's claims that the impact of stigma on the self has long-term implications for a person's ability to function in society. (E. Wright et al., 2000, pp. 80–82)

◈ Labeling and Delinquency

Juvenile delinquency is another area where the labeling theory has been widely applied and used to create or change policies that affect the lives of young offenders. Although it predates any formal explication of the theory, the juvenile justice system itself was created in part because of a concern over the negative impact being labeled and treated as a criminal would have on a young person. The terminology used in juvenile court reflects this concern: Offenders in the juvenile system are "adjudicated delinquent" rather than convicted of a crime. One result of this gentler language is that delinquents processed through the juvenile system do not need to check the box on job applications that asks if they have been convicted of a felony. Another example that shows concern over labeling juveniles is that in many states, an offender's juvenile record may be sealed or expunged once he or she completes the sentence and stays out of trouble for a specified period of time. In effect, this offers juvenile offenders who pass through troubled times the possibility of a clean slate as adults.

William Chambliss (1973) offered a vivid example of delinquency, social power, and labeling in his article titled "The Saints and the Roughnecks." Chambliss began this research project by simply spending time "hanging out" with two different groups of high school boys—the working-class "Roughnecks" and the upper-middle-class "Saints"—from the same community. While both groups of boys were involved in similar levels and amounts of delinquency, the community reactions were quite different. The Saints were treated as good boys "sowing their wild oats" and were given the benefit of the doubt by teachers, police officers, and other community members. The Saints were never officially arrested for their behavior, and seven of the eight of them graduated from college and went on to lead successful, conforming lives. The Roughnecks, on the other hand, were viewed by the community as bad boys, troublemakers, and delinquents, and they were often in trouble with their teachers and the police. As adults, the Roughnecks had quite different outcomes than the Saints. While two of the Roughnecks went to college on athletic scholarships and later became high school teachers and coaches, two others committed

▲ **Photo 8.3**   Being officially labeled delinquent may decrease the life chances of juvenile offenders; such labeling may lead to secondary deviance and more serious criminal careers.

Source: © Stockbyte/Thinkstock.

murders and were sentenced to lengthy prison terms. One other Roughneck made a career out of illegal gambling and bookmaking.

Chambliss was asked recently what surprised him in studying the Saints and Roughnecks; his response speaks to the impact of labels and how difficult it can be for those with less power to resist them:

> (1) How serious were the crimes of the Saints and how inconsequential were the crimes of the Roughnecks. (2) How readily the boys in each group accepted the labels attached to them even though the labels were incompatible with their actual behavior. (Inderbitzin & Boyd, 2010, p. 205)

Thinking about your own high school and adolescent experiences, you might be surprised at how familiar the story still sounds, long after it was written. Decades later, we see another case of a town's "golden boys" getting the benefit of the doubt even as they are accused of committing a horrific crime. The book, *Our Guys,* by Bernard Lefkowitz (1997), chronicles a case in Glen Ridge, New Jersey, in which a group of well-to-do, popular athletes raped a 17-year-old mentally challenged girl with a baseball bat and a broomstick. When members of the community finally heard about this crime, their reaction was generally sympathy for the boys and concern for "our" guys' reputations—"They'll just be ruined by this." The boys had the power in this setting, and the girl, by virtue of her gender and her mental impairment, was easily labeled as the deviant. The boys in *Our Guys* are similar in some way to the Saints from Chambliss's study in that the community members did not see or chose to ignore years of the boys' escalating deviant behavior. The young men from Glen Ridge were obviously much more delinquent and destructive toward females in their community than the Saints, but they were able to get away with their bad behavior for a surprisingly long time in part due to their positive label as the town's golden boys. Several of the Glen Ridge boys were charged with the rape; Lefkowitz details the lengthy road to trial and, ultimately, the convictions of four of the boys for taking part in the sexual assault. Lefkowitz (1997) offers this overview of the case:

> A large group of charismatic athletes. A retarded young woman. The silence of the students and adults. The inclination to blame the woman and exonerate the men. These elements seemed to be linked by a familiar theme. . . . I began to frame Glen Ridge as a story of power and powerlessness: the power of young males and the community that venerated them, and the powerlessness of one marginalized young woman. (pp. 4–5)

As Lefkowitz's study in *Our Guys* makes clear, context matters when considering the impact of formal sanctioning and official labels of delinquency. While "our guys" benefitted from their privileged position in Glen Ridge and the larger community, stigma may also be deflected or denied in different ways in disadvantaged communities. Hirschfield (2008) conducted interviews with 20 minority youth from high-poverty urban neighborhoods and concluded that in the macro-level context of severely disadvantaged neighborhoods, being arrested carries little stigma. Delinquent youth in his sample were quite concerned with being informally labeled by their family and friends, but arrest and processing by the justice system were viewed as relatively normal parts of adolescence in their neighborhoods and their experiences. Thus, labeling still matters and affects juvenile offenders in important ways, but researchers can work to better specify how macro-level conditions affect perceptions of the label and community reaction.

◈ Application of Labeling Theory

Braithwaite (1989): *Crime, Shame and Reintegration*

In *Crime, Shame and Reintegration,* John Braithwaite (1989) argues that societies will generally have lower crime rates if they can effectively communicate shame about crime. Importantly, however, Braithwaite makes a critical distinction between reintegrative shaming and stigmatization. With reintegrative shaming, the offender can be viewed as a good person who has done a bad deed; stigmatization, on the other hand, labels the offender a bad person. Put differently, "Stigmatization is unforgiving—the offender is left with the stigma permanently, whereas reintegrative shaming is forgiving" (Braithwaite, 2000, p. 282).

In Braithwaite's conceptualization of reintegrative shaming, an accused individual is expected to admit his or her offense, essentially accepting responsibility for the act and labeling the act as deviant, but then he or she is provided with an opportunity for reintegration back into society. In reintegration ceremonies, Braithwaite and Mugford (1994) argue that "disapproval of a bad act is communicated while sustaining the identity of the actor as good. Shame is transmitted within a continuum of respect for the wrongdoer. Repair work is directed at ensuring that a deviant identity (one of the actor's multiple identities) does not become a master status trait that overwhelms other identities" (p. 142).

Braithwaite's work offers an alternative to simply labeling offenders deviant and creating new and harmful master statuses. The idea of reintegrative shaming has not been tested on a large scale in the United States as of yet, but it offers one promising alternative to punitive criminal justice policies that may engender serious deviant careers. According to Braithwaite's theory, while labeling makes things worse when it is stigmatizing, when done respectfully and focused on the act rather than the individual, labeling may actually reduce crime (Braithwaite, 2000, p. 288).

Matsueda (1992): "Reflected Appraisals, Parental Labeling, and Delinquency"

Building on the work of George Herbert Mead, Ross Matsueda (1992) developed an interactionist theory of the self and delinquency. In his study, Matsueda focused on informal labels made by an adolescent's parents and whether those parental appraisals affected delinquency by affecting the adolescent's own reflected appraisals (Matsueda, 1992, p. 1590). In essence, the idea is that labeling and the reflected appraisals of others can create a delinquent "self" that may lead the adolescent further into deviant behavior. Matsueda found that youths' reflected appraisals of themselves were strongly influenced by their parents' appraisals of them. As an example, if a boy perceives that his parents view him as a troublemaker, he may start to perceive himself that way, too, and may be more likely to act the part.

In a later study, Heimer and Matsueda (1994) explain secondary deviance as a "chain of events operating through labeling" (p. 381). According to them,

> Youth who are older, nonblack, urban residents, and from nonintact homes commit more initial delinquent acts than others, which increases the chances that their parents will see them as rule-violators. In turn, labeling by parents increases the likelihood that these youth will affiliate with delinquent peers and see themselves as rule-violators from the standpoint of others, which ultimately increases the likelihood of future delinquent behavior. (pp. 381–382)

Rosenfield (1997): "Labeling Mental Illness"

A prominent study on labeling and mental illness centered on the concept and meaning of *stigma* (Rosenfield, 1997). Rosenfield (1997) suggests that stigma is an important point of disagreement for labeling theorists and their critics. For labeling theorists, the stigma attached to mental illness is a serious problem; in Goffman's words, "By definition, of course, we believe the person with a stigma is not quite human. On this assumption, we exercise varieties of discrimination, through which we effectively, if often unthinkingly, reduce his life chances" (Goffman, 1963, p. 5). Critics of labeling theory, on the other hand, suggest that stigma may be of little consequence to the mentally ill. Rosenfield designed a research project to compare the receipt of treatment and services versus the perception of stigma on the quality of life for people with chronic mental illness.

Rosenfield's (1997) research was conducted at a clubhouse-model program for people with chronic mental illness residing in the community. The club took an "empowerment approach" and offered a range of services, including psychiatric treatment, supervision, life skills, and vocational rehabilitation. Rosenfield found that "stigma is a problem for most people with chronic mental illness, and perceptions of stigma have a significant negative relationship with patients' quality of life. By contrast, services have a strong positive association with quality of life" (p. 669). As might be expected, then, Rosenfield concludes, "Life satisfaction is highest for those who experience little stigma and gain access to high quality services. Life satisfaction is lowest among those perceiving high levels of stigma and lacking such services" (p. 670).

Davies and Tanner (2003): "The Long Arm of the Law: Effects of Labeling on Employment"

A recent study on formal labeling by schools and the justice system suggests that labeling has long-term impacts on opportunities and employment. Davies and Tanner (2003) used a large, nationally representative sample to examine the effect that formal sanctions ranging from school suspension to incarceration during ages 15 to 23 had on subjects' occupational status, income, and employment 14 years later. While controlling for variables such as social background, prior deviant behavior, and family status, Davies and Tanner found that severe forms of labeling did have strong negative effects: "The indirect effects of early encounters with teachers, police officers, courts, and prison systems upon the transition from adolescence to adult work roles are significant and cumulatively damaging" (p. 399). School-based sanctioning, such as being suspended or expelled, had a negative impact on later job outcomes for females but not for males. This finding reminds us of the complexity of the social world and how difficult it can be to tease out all of the relevant factors. While the Davies and Tanner study generally supports labeling theory, there is much work still to be done to fully understand all of the variables and interactions that affect the labeling process.

◈ Impact of Labeling Theory

The labeling perspective caught hold in the United States during the 1970s and had a clear impact on public policy in two distinct areas: juvenile justice and the care of mental patients. As research showed the potential negative impact of being labeled delinquent (Chambliss, 1973) and being labeled mentally ill (Rosenhan, 1973), policymakers took notice and began to rethink how to best serve those populations.

RECENT STUDY IN DEVIANCE

Labeling and the Adoption of a Deviant Status

By Terrell A. Hayes, 2010, in *Deviant Behavior, 31,* 274–302.

Hayes interviewed 46 individuals who attended Debtors Anonymous meetings to examine the process by which these individuals assumed the deviant status of "debtor." He examined both the process of social labeling and self-labeling and found that most individuals went through several stages in which they slowly came to see themselves as a person with a problem.

Hayes found that social labeling involved "active cues" and "passive cues" in which the individual was confronted with the problem. The active cues involved informal interactions with close others (friends, spouses, relatives) who identified the individual's behavior as problematic.

(My husband) was saying that I was sick, sick, sick. I stayed in denial for a while saying (to him) you indulge yourself, I'm certainly entitled to indulge myself. . . . But then I began examining that finally agreeing with my husband (and others) that I overspend. (p. 281)

Passive cues, in the form of literature and other materials, can also be part of the self-labeling process.

When things got really tight I would find myself buying groceries on my Amoco gas card. . . . No one came to me and said, "You know? You are out of control. Here you need to get some help." Even my wife didn't. She never confronted me and said, "I think you need to go get some help." One day I was downtown at the library and I was just browsing through the shelves. I caught the title on the spine of the book, *How to Get Out of Debt, Stay Out of Debt, and Live Prosperously.* It seemed to describe me perfectly. (p. 286)

Finally, Hayes found that self-help groups contributed to the labeling process and likelihood that individuals would label themselves as debtors. Interestingly enough, these self-help groups were not limited to Debtors Anonymous (the group that Hayes initially found his participants through). Several of his participants actually identified their time in other self-help groups as being a catalyst for their self-identification as debtors in need of help.

Some change happened organically as individuals working in these systems strove for better and more humane results. Jerome Miller, the commissioner of the Department of Youth Services in Massachusetts, frustrated with the conditions in the juvenile correctional facilities in his agency, closed all of the state's training schools between 1970 and 1972 (Miller, 1998). Miller's original goal was to make the state's reform schools more humane, with more therapy and individualized treatment for incarcerated youth. But, as he tells it,

Whenever I thought we'd made progress, something happened, a beating, a kid in an isolation cell, an offhand remark by a superintendent or cottage supervisor that told me what I envisioned would never be allowed. . . . The decision to close the institutions grew from my frustration at not being able to keep them caring and decent. (p. 18)

Over a 2-year span, Massachusetts closed its secure reform schools and moved to a system of alternative community treatment and placements for youth considered the most dangerous in the state.

Miller's closing of Massachusetts's reform schools can be viewed in the larger context of **deinstitutionalization** that was occurring in the early 1970s. As Miller (1998) explained, "While we were moving a few hundred delinquents back to the community, state departments of mental health across the United States were deinstitutionalizing thousands of mental patients" (p. 20).

Edwin Schur (1973) suggested that a better way for our juvenile justice system to operate was to not institutionalize young offenders in the first place. Schur argued strongly for a policy of radical **nonintervention**—in other words, in dealing with delinquent youth, we should choose to "leave the kids alone wherever possible." Schur advocated a "hands-off" approach to juvenile misbehavior, which would purposely take moral judgment away from juvenile courts.

In 1974, the United States passed the Juvenile Justice Delinquency Prevention (JJDP) Act, which significantly altered the juvenile corrections system. Concerns over the labeling of minor offenders as delinquents and the potential for criminal learning in juvenile institutions led to widespread attempts to deinstitutionalize youth, tolerate minor misbehavior, and use community alternatives for youth who needed intervention. The JJDP Act offered states funding as an incentive to decriminalize status offenses (behavior such as truancy, disobedience, or running away that would not be crimes if committed by adults) and to deinstitutionalize status offenders. Reform schools and secure juvenile institutions became the agency of last resort, reserved for the most serious juvenile offenders.

Times have certainly changed since then, and while the juvenile justice system still exists and attempts to resocialize delinquent youth, the United States now incarcerates more people than in any other period in history. Punitive laws have largely replaced the goal of rehabilitation, and serious juvenile offenders are routinely tried and convicted as adults.

In recent years, scholars such as Braithwaite (2002) have endorsed a move to **restorative justice**. In a system of restorative justice, "The state functions as an arbiter or partner who works with the victim and the offender to reduce the harm associated with the criminal act that has been committed" (Cullen & Agnew, 2006, p. 270). Typically, restorative justice involves bringing the victims, offenders, and community members together in a mediated conference. The goal of these conferences is for the offenders to take responsibility for their actions and to reach consensus on a plan for them to restore the harm they have caused, often through restitution to the victim and service to the community.

◈ Critiques of Labeling Theory

Labeling theory has been widely critiqued as an explanation for why people commit deviant acts or crime. Rather than asking why individuals commit acts against the norms of society, this perspective focuses on how and under what circumstances the individual is judged as deviant and what impact that judgment may have on his or her self-concept, relationships, opportunities, and life chances. Early analyses of labeling did not show empirical support for the tenets of the theory, but those studies may have misinterpreted the claims of the impact of labeling.

Becker (1963/1973) suggested that labeling was never intended to be a full-blown theory of deviance, but instead it offered a perspective that shifted the focus to the process of constructing deviance. Early proponents of the labeling perspective

> wanted to enlarge the area taken into consideration in the study of deviant phenomena by including in it activities of others than the allegedly deviant actor.... [O]ne of the most important contributions of this approach has been to focus attention on the way labeling places the actor in circumstances which make it harder for him or her to continue the normal routines of everyday life and thus provoke him or her to "abnormal" actions (such as when a prison record make it harder to earn a living at a conventional occupation and so disposes its possessor to move into an illegal one). (Becker, 1963/1973, p. 179)

In discussing the development of labeling theory, Cullen and Agnew (2011) conclude that the ideas of labeling are likely helpful additions to the study of crime and deviance if used judiciously:

> Labeling theorists also often pay insufficient attention to how, independent of societal reaction, structural inequality and the concentration of disadvantage in inner-city communities might affect behavior. Nonetheless, scholars working in this tradition have identified a factor—stigmatizing, rejecting, nasty societal reactions—that rarely makes matters better and more often serves only to solidify an offender's commitment to a criminal career. It would be unwise, therefore, for criminologists to assume that "labeling has no effects," and more prudent for them to continue to specify the conditions under which societal reaction pushes offenders into, rather than out of, a life in crime. (Cullen & Agnew, 2011, p. 246)

Explaining Deviance in the Streets and Deviance in the Suites: Considering Drinking—and Not Drinking—on College Campuses

Drinking alcohol is part of many rituals of college life, including fraternity parties and initiations and sporting events where universities allow tailgating and, implicitly, at least seem to encourage alcohol consumption. Young people in college are often away from home for the first time, and part of their college experience is testing boundaries and trying out their new freedoms. Many use alcohol to get over their own sense of shyness or awkwardness in social situations. Binge drinking and episodic drinking, or going beyond a "buzz," are part of the social life of many college students. Vander Ven (2011) argues that taking care of others who have imbibed to the point of illness offers some student drinkers their first real adult responsibility. Approximately 40% of young Americans between the ages of 18 and 25 reported that they had binged on alcohol (had five or more drinks on one occasion) in the last month, and that number has remained relatively constant for at least a generation (Szalavitz, 2012).

Binge drinking in college might be viewed as a form of elite deviance. Vander Ven suggests that heavy drinking emerged in the Ivy League and remains one way of showing status:

> There was a lot of heavy drinking in the big three Ivy League schools. It represented establishment privilege. If I go away to college and I spend most of my time just drinking, and not working hard, that sort of suggests to my audience that I don't need to work hard and that I'm one of the elite. Some of that still happens today. One way to demonstrate to your audience that you have a lot of money and status is to buy a round of drinks. And students today are jacking up their credit card debt by buying a lot of drinks for others and themselves. (Vander Ven, as quoted in Rogers, 2011)

Many college towns bring together middle-class and elite students and working-class locals. Bars and other local establishments profit from and need the students' business, so they put up with a degree of unpleasant drunkenness in order to keep profits flowing. In a recent study of college students' "determined drunkenness" in England, the authors found that social class mattered in how such behavior was perceived:

> There is a long history of ritualized drinking to excess amongst upper-class young men. However, this often takes place in the more secluded spaces of university colleges or private school grounds, and in the event of more public displays of drunken excess, this elite group have the money to buy themselves out of trouble (Ronay, 2008). The upper class as a whole is seldom subject to the same level of horrified moral outrage and disgust that has been directed at the drinking practices of white working-class youth. (Griffin, Bengry-Howell, Hackley, Mistral, & Szmigin, 2009, p. 460)

Among the study participants, binge drinking was viewed as a bonding activity that sometimes got out of control. There was a sense of escape and fun in student narratives about drinking with their friends, even as they told stories of going out, getting drunk, losing consciousness, and sometimes waking up in a hospital (Griffin et al., 2009). In spite of such serious consequences of binge drinking, the students appeared to suffer no long-term ill effects on their health or their status. Their drinking behavior was virtually ignored by their college administrators and local law enforcement, generally garnering no response or sanction.

College students are in a relatively privileged position, and their status likely offers some level of protection against negative labels. Drinking is often the norm on college campuses; in a recent study of nondrinkers on a "wet" campus or "party school," Herman-Kinney and Kinney (2013) found that only about 17% of students self-identified as nondrinkers. The nondrinkers reported that they were viewed as abnormal by their peers and "labeled deviant if you don't drink" (p. 72). Nondrinkers reported being stigmatized, harassed, and ostracized by their classmates. To avoid the negative labels and stigma, nondrinkers developed strategies to appear to be drinking, such as carrying around red plastic cups or nearly empty drinks and pretending to be getting drunk with their peers. Alternatively, they learned to simply stay away from parties and tailgating where heavy drinking was the norm. The authors concluded that

> the drinkers as a group on the Keg State campus, and the social organizations (e.g., Greek, varsity athletics) of which they are a part, are essentially the ones with the power; the words

that they use to stigmatize nondrinkers are fighting words—pussy, weanie, loser. In addition to the verbal warfare, we found instances of behavioral violence (e.g., showering with beer, damaging personal property). . . . [T]he drinkers may come to the realization that the non-drinkers are more likely to be successful adults because they are not spending time getting wasted and nursing hangovers, but focusing on what college is all about, preparing oneself for a successful future. (Herman-Kinney & Kinney, 2013, p. 95)

 ## Ideas in Action: The "I Have a Dream" Foundation—Instilling Positive Labels

In 1981, millionaire businessman Eugene M. Lang went back to give a speech to the graduating sixth graders at the public elementary school he had attended in East Harlem. The future looked grim for many of those youth—Lang was told that three-quarters of the students would likely never finish high school. As Lang took the stage, he made a surprising spur-of-the-moment decision: He promised the entire sixth-grade class that he would pay the college tuition for every student who stayed in high school and graduated. Lang built relationships with his "Dreamers" and made sure that they had the services and support they needed to succeed. He also began talking about the program and sharing his vision in the media. In 1986, Lang started the "I Have a Dream" Foundation in order to launch more "I Have a Dream" programs across the country.

The mission of the foundation is as follows:

The "I Have A Dream" Foundation empowers children in low-income communities to achieve higher education and fulfill their leadership potential by providing them with guaranteed tuition support and equipping them with the skills, knowledge, and habits they need to gain entry to higher education and succeed in college and beyond.

By helping our Dreamers gain access to college, we are putting our Dreamers on a different academic and life trajectory, while having a broader impact on the students' families and the generations that follow. (http://www.ihaveadreamfoundation.org/html/)

There are now more than 200 "I Have a Dream" programs in 27 states, and more than 15,000 children have become Dreamers. The "I Have a Dream" approach is to sponsor a cohort of students in a lower-income school or public housing development. The students are selected in the early years of elementary school and are given support and encouragement all the way through high school. If they decide to go to college, they are guaranteed that their tuition will be paid. While circumstances may vary by location, there are several common characteristics of "I Have a Dream" programs: (1) They are long term. Dreamers are selected in elementary school and followed and cared for until they enroll in college. (2) They are inclusive. Every child who is in a class at the time of sponsorship is given the same opportunity. They do not select the most promising or the most at-risk children to be Dreamers. All children are believed to be capable of succeeding if given the opportunity. (3) The programs are comprehensive. Along with focusing on education, the programs help Dreamers build life skills and cultural capital. The children are often taken on field trips to other parts of the country to expose them to careers and lifestyles they may aspire to. (4) The programs are leveraged. They work with local and national community partners to support their Dreamers and other children and families in similar circumstances.

Research on "I Have a Dream" programs has shown that Dreamers have improved school attendance and grades, have higher aspirations, and have more positive attitudes about the future. The Dreamers are better able to resist peer pressure, and they often graduate high school and attend college at double the rate of their peers.

Eugene Lang and the "I Have a Dream" Foundation have inspired other wealthy sponsors to create their own programs. Businessman Paul Tudor Jones started the Robin Hood Foundation (www.robin-hood.org) to fight poverty in New York; the Robin Hood Foundation's board of directors personally pay for all operating costs, so every dollar that is donated goes directly to fighting poverty. Over the past twenty years, the Robin Hood Foundation has distributed over a billion dollars to the most effective poverty-fighting programs.

The "I Have a Dream" Foundation offers children growing up in poor areas hope for a better future. Being labeled a Dreamer inspires positive deviance in the form of graduating high school and going to college, and it brings about a whole new set of expectations for the children's behavior and future. Children who were demographically at high risk of dropping out of school are given a reason to keep attending, keep working, and to stay out of trouble. The positive label of "Dreamer" has certainly changed and improved the lives of many children. Just as negative labels can lead to stigma and negative responses from the individual, positive labels and opportunities can set youth on a trajectory for success.

NOW YOU . . . USE THE THEORY

In 1983, Edwin Schur published a book titled *Labeling Women Deviant: Gender, Stigma and Social Control*. One of Schur's arguments in the book is that women are more quickly and strongly labeled for their behavior if it steps out of normative boundaries than men are. To highlight this gender imbalance in labeling, an often-used class exercise is one in which students are asked to think up all the derogatory labels that they can for men and women. Inevitably, that list is much longer for women than for men.

What are the normative expectations for women and men in society? Make a list of expected behaviors for each group. After making this list, make a list of positive labels associated with each group. Now make a list of negative labels associated with each group. How are these labels used in society? What is the relationship with power—both the use of power and the loss of power associated with these labels? According to the labels, which normative behaviors are most likely to produce a reaction if violated?

Was Schur right? Are women more likely to be labeled for stepping outside the normative boundaries than men?

◈ Conclusion

Returning for a moment to the film *The Breakfast Club*, the letter that opened this chapter also opened the film. By the end of their day in detention—and the end of the film—the students have started to know each other and have learned to look beyond the labels of their high school cliques. They view and treat each other much differently at the end of the day than they did in the beginning. Each student contributes his or her voice to the final letter left for the principal when they are freed from detention:

> Brian Johnson: Dear Mr. Vernon, we accept the fact that we had to sacrifice a whole Saturday in detention for whatever it was we did wrong . . . but we think you're crazy to make us write an essay telling you who we think we are. You see us as you want to see us . . . in the simplest terms and the most convenient definitions. But what we found out is that each one of us is a brain . . .

> Andrew Clark: . . . and an athlete . . .

> Allison Reynolds: . . . and a basket case . . .

> Claire Standish: . . . a princess . . .

> John Bender: . . . and a criminal.

> Brian Johnson: Does that answer your question? Sincerely yours, the Breakfast Club.

If you pay attention to the world around you, you will see labels everywhere. They offer a convenient shorthand and can be helpful in categorizing complex relationships and interactions. But, as the labeling perspective points out, being labeled deviant can have long-lasting, harmful impacts on an individual's self-concept and life chances. These issues will be further discussed in Chapter 11 (Social Control of Deviance) and Chapter 12 (Deviant Careers and Career Deviance), where we will explore the role of prisons, juvenile facilities, and mental hospitals as agents of social control and examine how they can affect the individual long after the original act and application of the deviant label.

In pointing to the larger ideas of the labeling perspective and to Howard Becker's work, particularly, as offering important sensitizing concepts for sociologists studying deviant behavior, Orcutt (1983) suggests that

> the impact of labeling theory on the field of deviance cannot be measured in strictly scientific terms alone. The work of the labeling theorists not only portrayed the definition and control of deviance as analytically problematic but also as morally and politically problematic. . . . This relativistic conception of labeling as a power game provides the basic ingredient for a political critique of the uses and abuses of social control by certain dominant groups in modern, complex societies. (pp. 241–242)

Certainly the relativist perspective broadened the way we think about deviant behavior and social control. Studies from labeling and conflict theories have highlighted the importance of power and inequality in defining deviance and in the differential enforcement of norms and laws. Chapter 9 will build on these ideas by introducing you to conflict theory, and Chapter 10 will provide an overview of critical theories of deviance.

EXERCISES AND DISCUSSION QUESTIONS

1. Imagine you were officially labeled deviant in junior high school. How do you think this would have affected your life and your opportunities? Would your parents, teachers, and peers have treated you differently? Where do you think you would be now if you had been labeled delinquent?

2. Another surprising finding Chambliss mentioned in studying the Saints and the Roughnecks was "how easily some of them [the two football players] changed their self image, their behavior and their lives" (Inderbitzin & Boyd, 2010). What do you think might have made the difference for those young men? What does that suggest for how we treat delinquents?

3. Why do you think the athletes from Glen Ridge (in *Our Guys*) were so difficult to label deviant? What affected the process? How might the victim's gender and mental challenges have contributed to the situation?

4. Can you imagine volunteering as a pseudopatient if we were going to replicate Rosenhan's study in "On Being Sane in Insane Places"? Why or why not? As a (presumably) sane person, how do you think being labeled as mentally ill and hospitalized would affect your self-concept?

5. Sex offenders have been particularly demonized and feared in the United States. While ostensibly set up to provide important information to community members, sex offender registries have taken public labeling to a whole new level. There is real reason for fear when one's vital statistics, address, and photo are posted online on sex offender registries: Vigilantes killed two sex offenders in Washington state in 2005, and two more were shot to death in Maine in 2006 (Daniel, 2006; J. Martin & O'Hagan, 2005; O'Hagan & Brooks, 2005).

   a. An important issue is that the label "sex offender" is a broad one, encompassing both predatory crimes and statutory ones. Take, for example, the case of Ricky Blackman, convicted as a sex offender for having intercourse with a 13-year-old girl when he was 16. The label and his place on a sex offender registry affected Blackman's life in many ways: He couldn't go to high school, couldn't attend sporting events, and couldn't even go into the public library (Grinberg, 2010).

   b. What do you think of sex offender registries? What are their strengths and weaknesses? How do you think society should deal with cases like Ricky Blackman?

KEY TERMS

Deinstitutionalization	Reintegrative shaming	Self-fulfilling prophesy
Master status	Residual rule breaking	Symbolic interactionism
Nonintervention	Restorative justice	
Primary deviance	Secondary deviance	

CHAPTER 9

Marxist/Conflict Theories of Deviance

Sandy was born in 1941. She realized she was a lesbian in her late teens but did not tell anyone of her feelings for many years. It wasn't easy being gay in the late 1950s–1960s. Gays and lesbians were discriminated against legally and socially. Men and women were driven from their schools and towns if it was suspected they were gay. Government hearings (the McCarthy hearings) persecuted individuals who were suspected of being gay. Police harassed and arrested individuals who were suspected of being gay.

On June 28, 1969, in New York City's Greenwich Village, a riot broke out in response to a police raid on an inn suspected of catering to gays and lesbians. Sandy was 28 at the time and could hardly believe that there were people in New York rioting over these raids. She had lived with the fear that someone might suspect she was a lesbian for a long time and was amazed that other individuals were so open with their feelings. These riots, called the Stonewall riots, became known as the start of the gay rights movement.

Over the years, Sandy slowly came out to her friends and family; some did not understand her feelings and were cruel and judgmental, but many were supportive, and she surrounded herself with a close group of loved ones and built a satisfying life for herself. She met an amazing woman when she was 34 and became more active in the gay rights movement, attending protests and advocating for social acceptance and legal equality.

As the years passed, Sandy saw that for many individuals, homosexuality became an accepted lifestyle. She saw pop culture embrace gays and lesbians in many ways. In many cities, she felt accepted enough to openly acknowledge her relationship with her partner, but this was not the case everywhere in the United States. In addition, while in some circles there was a cultural acceptance of her lifestyle,

(Continued)

(Continued)

legally she was still not protected equally. Only recently had her state acknowledged domestic partnership enough that she and her partner could share health care, and while they had celebrated in a union ceremony 20 years previously, they were still struggling for the right to marry and see that marriage accepted in all 50 states in the United States.

Several states have signed bills that make same-sex marriage legal, but those laws have been challenged in court. The right to marry in California was allowed and then overturned and then spent several years in the court system. In 2013, the Supreme Court declined to uphold the ban on same-sex marriages in California that had been enacted with Proposition 8. On that same day, the Court overturned the federal Defense of Marriage Act (DOMA; enacted in 1996), which declared that marriage is a union between one man and one woman and that the states do not have to acknowledge a same-sex union. (Up until the passage of this act, states were required to acknowledge a marriage legally obtained in any state and offer the rights and privileges of marriage to that couple.) These Court decisions meant that the legality and acceptance of same-sex marriage became a decision for each state to make individually.

Now in her 70s, Sandy wants more than anything to marry her longtime partner. She remembers the challenges she has faced throughout her lifetime—the social and legal discrimination against her. She knows in many ways that her lifestyle is becoming more accepted, but she also sees many ways that she is still made to feel deviant. While same-sex marriages are now accepted in some states, Sandy wonders what the next challenges will be and how long it will take to have a marriage to her partner recognized in all 50 states and whether this would mean the end to the challenges to their lifestyle.

Introduction

Perhaps one of the most striking ways that deviance textbooks have changed over the past 30 years is that many early textbooks on deviance had a chapter discussing homosexuality as a deviant act. Many groups in society still argue that homosexuality is a deviant lifestyle (for the most part, these groups are conservative religious groups), but the days in which the idea that gays and lesbians are deviant are waning. Advocacy groups are increasing, and the gay rights movement has been very successful in the fight for social acceptance and equal rights. A discussion of deviance in a textbook today that focused on gays and lesbians would not focus on the lifestyle as deviant but might instead focus on the discourse, the changing attitudes, and the constantly changing legal rights, as well as the implication of these changes. This study of deviance might ask the following questions: What arguments do opponents of homosexuality make? What arguments do advocates of gays and lesbians make? How do these groups use the law to support their arguments? Under what conditions do these arguments "win" or "lose"? These questions help illustrate the social construction of deviance and the social construction of gays and lesbians from a group uniformly accepted as deviant to a group growing in social acceptance that has strong, vocal advocates.

This chapter presents the perspectives of the Marxist and conflict theories. While the theorists discussed in this chapter do not always agree on all the tenets of their theories, these theories come from the same social constructionist or *relativist* perspective and so are often discussed together. There are two general ways in which these theories differ from each other. The first is their definition of power. Marxists focus on the political economy and the capitalist system in their analyses of power and conflict (Moyer, 2001), while conflict theorists have traditionally expanded their definitions of power beyond a singular focus on the capitalist system. The second difference between the two is the policy implications that stem from the theories. Marxists tend to advocate for a revolutionary overthrow of the capitalist system as the only

▲ Photo 9.1   Marxist and conflict theories examine why certain laws, such as marriage laws, are written and who may or may not benefit from such laws.

Source: ©BananaStock/Thinkstock.

way to solve power differentials and conflict, while conflict theorists are more open to reforms that do not advocate revolution (Bohm, 1982). Both theories operate from a macro perspective, meaning that they focus on structural issues, institutions, and group behaviors, not on individual behavior or experiences. Much of the focus of these theories is on the creation and maintenance of laws that benefit one group over another (Liska & Messner, 1999). For a book on deviance, then, we might say that Marxist and conflict theorists are interested in why and how some groups are defined as deviant and how their behavior, now defined as deviant, gets translated into illegal behavior through application of the law.

At the center of this perspective is the acknowledgment that conflict exists (especially in a capitalist society), and this conflict arises from power differentials in society. These theories focus on two questions: (1) Why are certain groups more likely to be considered deviant? and (2) Why are some actions, which many might consider harmful, not considered deviant or criminal? These questions have implications for what is often studied using the various theories that make up this perspective—as you will see from the discussions in this chapter, a variety of social phenomena, including same-sex marriage, the effects of the abolition of slavery on prison populations, and workplace misconduct, can be evaluated from a Marxist/conflict perspective. The rest of this chapter explores the theories that make up the Marxist/conflict perspective.

Development of Marxist Theory

The best place to start any discussion of Marxist/conflict theories is with Karl Marx (and his colleague Frederick Engels) (Marx, 1867/1992, 1885/1993; Marx & Engels, 1848/1961). Marx was not a criminologist, and he did not study crime or deviance to any extent. In fact, while criminologists claim him as a key theorist in the field, communication studies, economics, political science, and sociology all make formal claims, too. At the core of Marxist theory is a focus on the capitalist system as one that creates conflict, inequality, and power differentials. Some argue that because the capitalist system is central to Marxist thought, such phenomena as the conflict surrounding same-sex marriage cannot be adequately explained by this theory. However, Turk (2002) argues that much capitalist conflict is diversionary in nature, designed to keep the "workers" focused on issues that keep them divided rather than uniting to fight for their rights against capitalists. "To leftists, particularly those inspired by Marxism, class, racial and other forms of discrimination are promoted by the 'ruling class' to keep the workforce divided, thus more easily controlled" (Turk, 2002, p. 312). In other words, an emotional and heated conflict over same-sex marriage could benefit capitalism by diverting attention away from issues those in power do not want to discuss and by dividing the working class on a social issue, thus making it harder for them to come together to fight the powerful when the need arises. As we examine Marxist and conflict theory, think about how this conflict may benefit the capitalist system and/or the ruling class.

Conflict

Marx, writing during the Industrial Revolution in Europe, argued that society could best be understood by its *social relationships* (Meyer, 1963), and given the era he was writing in, Marx argued that the fundamental basis of society was *class conflict*. In other words, he saw capitalism as creating a conflict between the social relationships of the owners of the means of production (the bourgeoisie) and the laborers (the proletariat). This conflict would arise because to maximize profits, the bourgeoisie needed to keep costs down. Since labor is one of the most significant costs in business, owners must maximize their profits by paying the laborer as little as possible. Marx argued that since the laborer was the actual creator of a given product, that laborer was the true owner of the profits from its creation. Therefore, laborers should earn the full price of the product (maximize their earnings). Laborers' maximization of their wages comes in direct conflict with the bourgeoisie's maximization of profit.

Marx went on to argue that a struggle for power—namely, conflict—arises as both groups try to maximize their advantage. In the short run, according to Marx, the bourgeoisie would win because they have the control over the means of production and communication. But in the long run, Marx believed, the proletariat would win. He believed that capitalism had sown the seeds of its own destruction, and, as soon as proletariats understood the exploitive nature of capitalism, they would rise up and overthrow the system.

Dialectical Materialism

Marx based much of his philosophy about social relationships, conflict, and the working of society on the concept of dialectical materialism. In many respects, this concept is the reason that Marxist and conflict theories fall under the heading of relativist theories. Marx believed that reality existed in the *material* world. The material world had a meaning or reality separate from the meaning that individuals gave it (Mayo, 1960)—or, more specifically, the material world is important, separate from ideas, and for our ideas to have importance, we must put them into action. He also believed in the *dialectic,* which in its simplest form means a negotiation of contradictions. He believed that nature (the material world) was full of contradictions (conflict) and that through a process of negotiating those contradictions, we could arrive at a new reality. Mayo (1960) explains this process as the thesis, antithesis, and synthesis of an idea (or reality). Using our legal definitions of the right to marry as an example, we can say that there has been heated debate in this country over the right of gays and lesbians to marry. The thesis of this idea may be "gays and lesbians have the right to marry," the antithesis of this reality may be "gays and lesbians do not have the right to marry," and from these contradictions may come the synthesis "gays and lesbians may have civil unions but may not marry." This synthesis becomes the new thesis, and the process starts all over again.

Marxism and Revolution

Two phenomena needed to occur before revolution could take place. The first was that the number of laborers needed to grow until the capitalist system could not support the masses. Marx believed this would certainly happen as failed entrepreneurs ended up in the laborer class and as the capitalist system became more "efficient" and less laborers were needed to produce the same level of product. The second, and most important phenomena, was that the laborer must throw off her or his **false consciousness** (Lukács, 1920/1971; Mannheim, 1936/1959) and become aware of the exploitation she or he was experiencing at the hands of the bourgeoisie and capitalism. While Marx did not use the term *false consciousness* himself, he believed that the capitalist system created in the laborer class a false sense of upward mobility, meaning that its members could not see the exploitation and oppression they were experiencing because of the belief they could "move up" in the capitalist system.

Marx believed the only reason that the revolutionary end to capitalism had not already happened was that the laborer was still experiencing a false consciousness about her or his exploitation. In other words, capitalism and the bourgeoisie had convinced laborers that they were *not* being used to maximize the profits of the bourgeoisie and that, instead, capitalism benefitted them. Marx believed that as soon as laborers understood their exploitation, they would throw off the shackles of capitalism and would ultimately create a system in which capital did not accumulate unequally to one group.

Marxism and the Creation of Law and Deviance

While Marx was not a criminologist, he spent a fair amount of time writing about the importance of the law. He never gave a specific definition of the law (Cain, 1974), but he did discuss how it was used to maintain the status quo (keep the bourgeoisie in power). Marx saw the law as the instrument used to support the ideology of capitalism. That is to say, he believed that the function of the law in a capitalist society was to maintain capitalism. For Marx, this meant that the law might be used to control the proletariat, but it was also used to settle disputes that might arise among the bourgeoisie because disputes weakened the power of the bourgeoisie and ultimately the power of the capitalist system (Cain, 1974).

The function of the law, according to Marx and Engels, was to obscure real power by offering power, on paper, to everyone equally (Cain, 1974; Marx & Engels, 1957). In other words, Marx believed that by emphasizing the rationality of the law and the recourse for everyone to use the law equally, the fact that in practice everyone does not have the power to use the law equally could be overlooked. In fact, this could not only be overlooked but actively ignored—if everyone has the right to use the law, then it becomes the *individual's responsibility* to use the law. Equality on paper means we can ignore inequality in practice.

At the beginning of the 20th century, William Bonger, a Dutch scholar, built upon Marxist ideas and explicitly related them to the topic of crime in his book *Criminality and Economic Conditions*

(1916). He forwarded the idea that capitalism is a system in which business owners are encouraged to dominate and take advantage of the others in society—the workers and the consumers—in order to make a profit. Bonger claimed that capitalism basically tears apart the social fabric by making people, especially capitalists, inclined to egotism, or selfishness. According to Bonger, crime, especially economic crime, is to be expected in a system that dehumanizes and pits people against one another in the name of profit. In order to minimize criminal activity, he stated that a large step would have to be made—a redistribution of wealth that took all people's needs into account and a shared ownership of the means of production (i.e., a shift to socialism). These proposed measures would be ones that would shift the societal emphasis on domination to one focused on cooperation.

In the 1960s and 1970s, many radical or conflict criminologists picked up on the work of Bonger and his predecessors, as well as the work of labeling theorists, and focused on the role of the economy and class conflict in the production of law and crime (e.g., Beirne, 1979; Chambliss, 1964, 1969, 1975; Chambliss & Seidman, 1971; Hall, Critcher, Jefferson, Clarke, & Roberts, 1978; Platt, 1974; Schwendinger & Schwendinger, 1970; Spitzer, 1975; Taylor, Walton, & Young, 1973; Turk, 1969, 1976, 1977).

Marxism was expanded by Piers Beirne (1979) to more specifically explain the creation of law. **Instrumental Marxism** sees the state (for example, politicians or the police) as an *instrument* of the capitalists. The bourgeoisie use the creation of laws to try to overcome conflict and benefit the ruling class. This is systematically and actively done by creating civil laws that focus on benefits for the ruling class (e.g., laws limiting workers' rights) and criminal laws that focus on street crime and the underclass, thus shifting attention from the crimes of the ruling class. In this iteration of Marxism, much agency is attributed to the ruling class as its members manipulate the state to benefit themselves.

Structural Marxism, on the other hand, does not assume that the law is controlled solely by the ruling class; instead, this theory assumes that law is less about maintaining power and benefits for the ruling class and more about maintaining the interests of the *capitalist system*. For this reason, laws that may benefit the system (such as laws against monopolies) but that do not benefit those in the ruling class are still seen as beneficial. Where instrumental Marxism sees the law as existing to benefit people, structural Marxism sees the law as existing to benefit the system.

Steven Spitzer (1975, 1983) did expand on traditional Marxist thought to develop a theory of deviance. He argued that capitalism was changing to advanced (or monopoly) capitalism. Monopoly capitalism was likely to promote two realities. The first was that as capitalism advanced, it would become more efficient. This efficiency would make it more likely that some capitalists would fail (as monopolies became stronger); these failed capitalists would fall into the laborer class, and this ever-growing class would become less and less useful as fewer laborers became needed to do the same work. The second was that advanced capitalism would promote increased levels of education needed to do the more advanced work of the economy. This education would create a more thoughtful population that was likely to criticize the system. Spitzer called these two populations "problem populations" and argued that capitalists (those in power) would see these two groups as "social junk" (the unneeded laborers) and "social dynamite" (those critical of the system). These problem populations would need to be controlled (most likely through criminalization—creating

▲ **Photo 9.2** Spitzer argues that as monopoly capitalism grows, "problem populations" will develop. One of those problem populations is "social dynamite"—a group willing to protest those in power.

Source © Shutterstock/eyeidea.

laws focused on their status or behaviors) when the populations got too big, too organized, or no longer responded to informal social control (for example, family or school) (Liska & Messner, 1999).

We might argue, then, that one of the ways in which Marxist theory can help explain deviance is in the use of deviance to control certain groups for the benefit of the capitalist system. As Marx said, the power of the capitalists comes from their ability to control both the means of production and *communication*. If laborers live under a false consciousness that does not allow them to understand or acknowledge their oppression and exploitation, then the bourgeoisie can manipulate them by labeling behaviors or groups that are dangerous to capitalism as deviant. Much of this labeling can be communicated through the media. In our example, if same-sex marriage can be labeled as deviant and harmful, then the capitalist system and ruling class may benefit in two ways: (1) The focus is taken off of harmful/deviant behaviors that the ruling class may be engaged in,

▲ **Photo 9.3**   The Occupy Wall Street protests that started in the fall of 2011 are an excellent example of what many might call "the social dynamite" —individuals who are protesting the current status quo and perceived sources of power in the United States (and the world).

Source: ©BananaStock/Thinkstock.

and (2) the workers will be divided over their opinion of same-sex marriage, thus weakening their own connection to other workers. While same-sex marriage may not be harmful to capitalism, promoting it as a deviant behavior benefits capitalism by diverting attention away from harms (deviance) produced by capitalism and keeping individuals or groups who would benefit from banding together to fight the harms of the system divided over a diversionary issue (same-sex marriage).

DEVIANCE IN POPULAR CULTURE

Examples of conflict theory and its focus on power abound in popular culture. Here we offer recommendations for a few films and television segments that you might watch; we think you will find it quite easy to apply general ideas from the conflict perspective to these specific cases.

Documentary films such as Michael Moore's *Capitalism: A Love Story* or *The Corporation* give an inside—and often critical—look at big business in the United States. Moore, in particular, juxtaposes the greed of corporations against the human suffering their actions may cause. Moore's ideas are compatible with a Marxist perspective; for a broader view of issues of power in the United States, you might watch one or more of the following:

Murder on a Sunday Morning—a documentary following the case of a 15-year-old African American male who is arrested for the murder of an elderly woman after an eyewitness places him near the

(Continued)

scene of the crime. This film gives you a chance to question whether race still matters in our criminal justice system and how it might play out.

North Country—a woman goes to work in a Minnesota steel mine and is harassed, verbally abused, and assaulted by her male coworkers. When she decides to file a lawsuit for sexual harassment, she faces resistance from both men and women in the community.

What Would You Do—this series from ABC News offers a number of experimental vignettes in which actors stage scenes about hate crimes or "shopping while black," and cameras watch to see how the people witnessing the interaction will react. Many of the scenarios deal with race and ethnicity, and the reactions of the public can be directly related to the readings in this chapter. In one vivid example, a group of white boys vandalized a car in a neighborhood park as many people passed them by; few reacted or called the police. The producers then switched it up and had a group of black boys vandalize the car in the same park; in this case, there were more calls to the police and more suspicion. Most telling of all, while the white boys vandalized the car, a stranger called 911 not about the vandals but about two African American young men who were sleeping in their car in the parking lot. You can watch these vignettes online at abcnews.go.com; most run less than 15 minutes, and several provide concrete examples of conflict and labeling theories in action.

◈ Development of Conflict Theory

While Marx did not spend much time focusing on crime or deviance, his work has been expanded by a series of criminologists who focused specifically on the law and thus definitions of crime and deviance. We have already discussed Spitzer, who remained fairly true to the Marxian fundamentals of economic structure and the social class; the following theorists focused on what some have called culture conflict. At its most basic, this expansion allows that there may be more groups in conflict than just the bourgeoisie and proletariat.

Gusfield

Gusfield (1967, 1968) examined the legislation of morality—the use of law to control behaviors that did not necessarily create victims (prostitution, drug use, gambling, and homosexuality). He argued that law has two functions: instrumental and symbolic. The instrumental function of law is one in which the behavior of individuals is proscribed; the law tells individuals what actions they can and cannot engage in, and agents of the law enforce those rules by arresting individuals who break the law. This is important but not nearly as important as the symbolic function of the law for our understanding of culture conflict, power differentials, and the imposition of deviance in society.

The symbolic function of law does not rely on enforcement or action but instead "invites consideration" (Gusfield, 1967, 1968) of what is considered moral by a society. "In a pluralistic society these defining and designating acts can become political issues because they support or reject one or another of the competing and conflicting cultural groups in the society" (Gusfield, 1968, p. 57). In other words, a law that supports the cultural beliefs of one group over another suggests that those beliefs are the moral, normative beliefs of society as a whole. The process of creating that law becomes the political process of supporting that group. More so than even the enforcement of that law, the ability of the cultural group to claim that its beliefs are supported by law is what is important.

Applying the symbolic function of law to the continued struggles for and against same-sex marriage shows the importance of these laws in justifying the beliefs of both proponents and opponents of this legislation. Opponents of same-sex marriage are most often socially and religiously conservative. Laws that ban same-sex marriage are seen to support a socially and religiously conservative agenda. Beyond the specific prohibition that two people of the same sex may not marry, these bans give strength to general cultural beliefs in social conservatism, making the whole movement stronger in areas well beyond the issue of same-sex marriage. In contrast, proponents of same-sex marriage are generally more socially and religiously progressive. Laws that support same-sex marriage are evidence of a progressive agenda that advocates for equality under the law for all groups. Laws that support same-sex marriage, then, also further other legal arguments for equality and thus strengthen the cultural beliefs of socially and religiously progressive groups.

Kitsuse and Spector

Kitsuse and Spector (1975) focused on the importance of value judgments in defining deviance and social problems. According to these theorists, value-conflict was the most important predictor of how something became defined as deviant. In other words, value judgments are what lead to definitions of deviance; when values are in conflict, those with the power to define conflicting values as deviant do so, thus "defining" or "creating" a social problem.

For Kitsuse and Spector (1973), then, the definitional process is most in need of study—what is defined as deviant is of little importance compared to *how* it is defined as deviant. They suggest that deviance arises when groups make assertions that some act or issue is deviant. The success of these claims is based on how organized the group is and how strongly its members make their claims. Many assertions of deviance and social problems do not take hold. A group is successful in its claim only if it can successfully maintain that claim. According to Kitsuse and Spector, an act or group is only continually defined as deviant as long as the group making the claim continues to exist.

Vold

George Vold expanded on Marxist/conflict theory by developing a theory of group conflict in his 1958 book *Theoretical Criminology*. Vold describes the process by which individuals become a part of a particular group and how the relationships between various groups develop as they compete for space, resources, and power.

The Creation and Maintenance of "the Group"

Vold (1958) argues that individuals are "group-involved beings" (p. 203) who both influence and are influenced by the groups of which they are a part. Individuals become a part of their groups because of similar interests with other group members. The more similarity between the interests and loyalties of its members, the stronger the group. Groups are created because of the needs of group members; groups that cannot fulfill these needs are disbanded, while groups that can fulfill them flourish and become stronger. Old groups are disbanded when they can no longer further their cause, and new groups form with the onslaught of new interests or needs.

Society, then, is made up of constant interaction between these various groups. Groups jockey for position and power in relation to the other groups and, through the "social process," gain and/or lose status relative to their counterparts. What is most important about this part of Vold's theory is that groups are in a constant state of action as they fight for the interests of their constituents.

Conflict arises between groups when their interests and needs overlap. Groups that do not have overlapping interests and needs are less likely to develop a conflicted relationship with one another. When interests and needs overlap, there is the danger of one group replacing the other (or groups can perceive this danger as their worlds encroach on each other). The goal of all groups, then, becomes to not be replaced, disbanded, or abandoned. In other words, the goal of all groups is to maintain the interests and serve the needs of the group and to flourish in the face of other groups.

Vold argues that when conflicts between groups arise and groups are threatened by the competing interests of other groups, individuals increase loyalty to their group. And the harder one must fight for her or his respective group, the more loyal that person becomes. "Nothing promotes harmony and self-sacrifice within the group quite as effectively as a serious struggle with another group for survival" (Vold, 1958, p. 206).

Vold's ideas about the creation and maintenance of a group can be applied to our example of same-sex marriage. We can argue that both same-sex groups and conservative religious groups are struggling for control of the definition of marriage (the interests and needs of both groups overlap on the issue of marriage). It could easily be argued that both groups have increased their solidarity and group member loyalty as the fight over same-sex marriage has intensified and that this power struggle or conflict has increased the membership of both groups. For example, many people who are not gay or lesbian themselves now identify with the cause of marriage equality and support gay and lesbian groups, counting themselves as members even though, as heterosexuals, they already have the right to marry.

The Use of the Law to Maintain Interests

According to Vold, the law becomes a way for groups to maintain their interests and protect themselves. Sometimes this process is a negotiation between two competing groups in which the political process develops a compromise that both sides can live with. Vold used the example of liquor laws to illustrate this compromise. If we see two groups—those who believe in prohibition as one group and the liquor industry as the other—we can see that the prohibition group would like to see liquor outlawed, while we can imagine that the liquor industry would prefer to have no restrictions on the selling and use of alcohol. Liquor laws, rules about where, when, and how alcohol can be sold, can then be seen as a way to compromise between these groups. (We can also see this as an example of Marx's dialectical materialism, where prohibition may be the thesis, the selling of liquor with no restriction may be the antithesis, and liquor laws may be the synthesis of the competing ideas.)

However, law can also be understood as the tool that more powerful groups can use to maintain their interests and service their needs. Vold argued that those groups that were powerful enough to control the law were also powerful enough to codify their values into law. This control means that certain groups who are in conflict with the values of the most powerful group(s) are more likely to be deemed criminal because they are more likely to have values and engage in behavior that is in conflict with the power group. Vold argued that this is how crime and deviance come about.

Turk

Turk (1969, 1976), like Vold, focused on the use of law as a social controlling agent. He saw law as a resource that groups struggled to control. Groups who had the power to control the law had the power to criminalize (or make deviant) groups who did not have that power. He argued that laws were more likely to be enforced when they represented cultural values or were being enforced on subjects who had very little power (Liska & Messner, 1999).

The Use of the Law as a Socially Controlling Agent

In discussing his belief of "law as power" (1976, p. 279), Turk argued that the resources that groups marshal go beyond just the economic resources that are often focused on in Marxist and conflict theory. Turk conceptualized five types of resource control (or power):

> These are (1) control of the means of direct physical violence, i.e., war or police power; (2) control of the production, allocation, and/or use of material resources, i.e., economic power; (3) control of decision-making processes, i.e., political power; (4) control of definitions of and access to knowledge, beliefs, values, i.e., ideological power; and (5) control of human attention and living-time, i.e., diversionary power. (Turk, 1976, p. 280)

Police power means that if a group controls the law, it is often justified in using force or violence (i.e., the police) when other groups are not. For example, the police may forcefully carry protestors away from a rally or protest, but the individuals protesting may not in any way use force against the police or counter-protestors. Turk was interested in how and to what extent "economic power was enhanced or eroded by the law" (1976, p. 280). For example, he saw the use of tax laws to protect the economic gains of the wealthy as an example of the law protecting and enhancing the resource of economic power for a certain group. Political power means that the law serves the purpose of organizing and supporting the political system. For example, the law supports the two-party system in the United States that benefits the Democrats and Republicans at the expense of those not associated with either party. Ideological power is supported by the law in two important ways. First, given that the law is the central tenet of political order, it legitimates itself (creates an ideological understanding of the importance and rightness of itself) by its very existence. Second, the law is used to both deny the rightness of certain ideas or to legitimate others who justify the overall ideology of groups in power. Finally, diversionary power means that the law can be used to divert the attention of groups and individuals from more pressing concerns. For example, encouraging our preoccupation with street crime is an excellent tactic to divert attention away from other harms that might be more far-reaching. Turk argued that the law is less likely to be used as a consensus-building negotiator of problems and is more likely to be the ultimate purveyor of power and manipulator of resources.

Quinney

While Quinney has written over many decades, spanning many theories, his work with Marxist/conflict theory took place during a similar time as Turk's—1960s and 1970s. Quinney's (1963, 1970, 1991) work has ranged from positivist to relativist (Einstadter & Henry, 1995), with important works theorizing

Marxist, conflict, and finally peacemaking criminologies (which you will read about in the next chapter). In his work *The Social Reality of Crime,* Quinney (1970) puts forth a theory of the law that offers an explanation for the social construction of crime.

Process

While Quinney does not mention dialectical materialism in his discussion of process, it is easy to see the Marxian philosophy in his work. Quinney argues that most work on crime to this point in time has been static (instead of dynamic). This static worldview has a strong impact on how we view deviance and crime. Quinney believes that this static view means that deviance and crime rest in the realm of the pathological (Quinney, 1970). In other words, our definition of deviance and crime is normative—it cannot and does not change with our understanding of the world. He argues that our social relationships and thus our understanding of the world is a *process*. Because it is a process, our understanding of the world changes as the process evolves.

Conflict and Power

Quinney (1970) also believes that conflict is inevitable in society and that "society is held together by force and constraint and is characterized by ubiquitous conflicts that result in continuous change" (pp. 9–10). This view of society links conflict and power very closely because it assumes that coercion is needed to keep society functioning. Namely, coercion is needed for one group to impose its beliefs or values on the society as a whole. Only those groups with sufficient power to coerce the whole will be able to impose their will.

Theory: The Social Reality of Crime

In Quinney's (1970) book, he outlined six propositions describing what he called the "social reality of crime" (p. 3). These propositions are as follows:

> **Proposition 1 (definition of crime):** Crime is a definition of human conduct that is created by authorized agents in a politically organized society. In other words . . . crime is a definition of behavior that is conferred on some persons by others.

> **Proposition 2 (formulation of criminal definition):** Criminal definitions describe behaviors that conflict with the interests of the segments of society that have the power to shape public policy.

> **Proposition 3 (application of criminal definition):** Criminal definitions are applied by the segments of society that have the power to shape the enforcement and administration of criminal law.

> **Proposition 4 (development of behavior patterns in relation to criminal definitions):** Behavior patterns are structured in segmentally organized society in relation to criminal definitions, and within this context persons engage in actions that have relative probabilities of being defined as criminal.

Proposition 5 (construction of criminal conceptions): Conceptions of crime are constructed and diffused in the segments of society by various means of communication.

Proposition 6 (the social reality of crime): The social reality of crime is constructed by formulation and application of criminal definitions, the development of behavior patterns related to criminal definitions, and the construction of criminal conceptions. (pp. 15–23)

Our example of same-sex marriage legislation can be evaluated using several of Quinney's propositions. The same-sex marriage debate has been played out in a very political manner in California, with the right to marry or not marry being decided in several ballot measures over an extended period of time. While various state polls have suggested that a majority of Californians are not opposed to same-sex marriage, a constitutional ban on same-sex marriage was enacted with the passage of Proposition 8 on November 4, 2008. The passage of this constitutional amendment, then, effectively defined same-sex marriage as deviant (or not legally allowed, like heterosexual marriage), thus illustrating the abilities of one group to define another group's actions as deviant and not sanctioned by the law. Then, on June 26, 2013, the Supreme Court ruled that DOMA was unconstitutional and that those supporting Proposition 8 did not have standing to challenge a lower court decision that Proposition 8 was unconstitutional (because the state of California chose not to defend the proposition). These Court decisions meant that the decision of whether same-sex marriage was legal is passed to each state individually (thus ensuring that the argument gets played out over and over again) and that in California, because a lower court had deemed that Proposition 8 was unconstitutional, it was legal.

Chambliss

In his article "Toward a Political Economy of Crime," Chambliss (1975) argues that the question, "Why do some individuals become involved with criminal behavior, while others do not?" (p. 165) is meaningless because, as he puts it, "everyone commits crime" (p. 165). In fact, much of Chambliss's (1964, 1975, 1978, 1999; Chambliss & Seidman, 1971) work focuses on the corrupt behavior and policies of "the state" (police, bureaucrats, politicians). Given that he focuses on the state, many might put his work under Marxist theory (indeed, the following excerpt detailing his paradigm of crime and criminal law is Marxian), and Chambliss does focus significantly on the corruption of the capitalist system. However, his works go beyond an analysis of the owners of the means of production and laborers, and, for this reason, we have chosen to discuss him under conflict theory.

The following propositions highlight the most important implications of a Marxian paradigm of crime and criminal law.

A. On the content and operation of criminal law

   1. Acts are defined as criminal because it is in the interests of the ruling class to so define them.

   2. Members of the ruling class will be able to violate the laws with impunity while members of the subject classes will be punished.

3. As capitalist societies industrialize and the gap between the bourgeoisie and the proletariat widens, penal law will expand in an effort to coerce the proletariat into submission.

B. On the consequences of crime for society

1. Crime reduces surplus labor by creating employment not only for the criminals but for law enforcers, locksmiths, welfare workers, professors of criminology and a horde of people who live off of the fact that crime exists.

2. Crime diverts the lower classes' attention from the exploitation they experience, and directs it toward other members of their own class rather than towards the capitalist class or the economic system.

3. Crime is a reality which exists only as it is created by those in the society whose interests are served by its presence.

C. On the etiology of criminal behavior

1. Criminal and non-criminal behavior stem from people acting rationally in ways that are compatible with their class position. Crime is a reaction to the life conditions of a person's social class.

2. Crime varies from society to society depending on the political and economic structures of society.

3. Socialist societies should have much lower rates of crime because the less intense class struggle should reduce the forces leading to and the functions of crime. (Chambliss, 1975, pp. 152–153)

While our example of same-sex marriage is not about criminalization per se, it does illustrate several of Chambliss's propositions. Opponents to same-sex marriage spent significant amounts of time and money diverting the attention of the general public (*San Diego Union Tribune,* September 18, 2008). Opponents argue that children should only be raised in households where a father and mother (as opposed to father/father or mother/mother) are present and that society in general is threatened by same-sex marriage because if same-sex marriage remains legalized, "our children" will be exposed to its existence in the public schools. As it has been argued that same-sex marriage threatens the hegemonic control of a patriarchal society, then it serves the interests of capitalists in general to oppose same-sex marriage. Same-sex marriage is thus presented as a deviant idea or lifestyle that would harm groups everyone should want to keep safe—families and children.

◈ Applications of Marxist/Conflict Theory

A significant number of studies have used conflict theory to examine racial discrimination in the law and/or justice system (Blalock, 1967; Bridges & Crutchfield, 1988; Chamlin, 2009; Leiber & Stairs, 1999; Percival, 2010). One of the ways these studies have used this theory is by arguing that the perceived threat of minority individuals (in many cases, racial minorities) will increase the likelihood of social control on that group. In other words, as a given minority population increases in size, the perceived threat to the ruling population also increases. Blalock (1967), in his power-threat hypothesis, argued that the relationship between minority threat and social control would be curvilinear (that is to say, as the minority size increases, so would social control *to a certain point,* and then at a tipping point—in his argument, as the minority group reaches 50% of the population—the increase in minority size would actually likely lead to a decrease in formal social control). This curvilinear relationship has been partially supported in more than one study (Greenberg, Kessler, & Loftin, 1985; Jackson & Carroll, 1981), although support depends on both geography and historical time period.

Payne and Welch (2010) studied the discipline practices of 294 public schools and also supported conflict theory through a racial-threat hypothesis. They argued that schools are mirroring the get-tough policies of the criminal justice system even though delinquency is decreasing. They found that while most schools have a range of responses to bad behavior (from punitive to restorative), schools set in disadvantaged, urban locations with a disproportionate student population of color (black and Latino) are more likely to use punitive forms of discipline and less likely to use restorative forms of discipline.

Another contemporary study has used the ideas of conflict theory to predict perceptions of injustice of people of color—in this instance, black and Latino youth (Hagan, Shedd, & Payne, 2005). Many have argued that one of the detrimental effects of increased conflict, and thus increased social control on any minority group (e.g., people of color, women, gays, lesbians), is that this leads to perceptions of injustice and a delegitimization of the justice system (see Cole, 1998). Hagan et al. (2005) argue that there is a comparative nature to exploitation and social control in that disadvantaged social groups can compare their disadvantage with other groups. They find that it is indeed the case that both black and Latino youth compare their disadvantage to one another and to white youth and that this comparative disadvantage does lead to increased perceptions of injustice at the hands of the criminal justice system. Hagan et al. conclude that "it is a possible further irony . . . that efforts to make city schools safer through increased deployment of the police may have the unintended consequence of alienating the students who are ostensibly being protected" (p. 400).

Writing in 1901, the African American scholar W. E. B. Du Bois vividly documented the way blacks and whites were historically dealt with by the criminal justice system in the South. Because slaves were literally property owned by whites prior to the Civil War, they had little to do with the criminal justice system. Misbehavior was generally dealt with by their owners and/or informal groups of whites who worked to keep blacks from associating, and the criminal justice system focused primarily on whites. As Du Bois put it, the system was "lenient in theory and lax in execution" (p. 83). Following the war, owners lost power, but a more formal illegal group, the Ku Klux Klan, emerged. More importantly, however, because whites so believed in the slave system and were convinced that freed slaves would not work as they had before, a new criminal justice system emerged "to restore slavery in everything but in name" (p. 84). New laws were passed, and the courts now became focused on African Americans. The convict-lease system emerged, with the labor of blacks being sold to the highest bidder. The conditions were abysmal. The unintended consequences of the changes were to make the criminal justice system appear less legitimate and therefore ineffective. Du Bois concluded with some statistics documenting the poor governmental support for the criminal justice system in the South—there was little need as the convict-lease system was a "money maker," but it was a deplorable system that remained problematic (Du Bois, 1901).

RECENT STUDY IN DEVIANCE

Threat to Whom? Conflict, Consensus, and Social Control

By Mitchell B. Chamlin, 2009, in *Deviant Behavior, 30,* 539–559.

Conflict theory is often juxtaposed against consensus theories of deviance—the basic question being, do police crackdowns in neighborhoods stem from a perceived threat to elites or a perceived threat to society as a whole? Conflict theory argues that these crackdowns happen when there is a perceived threat to the elites (for example, racial threat theory argues that when a community of color is perceived as a threat to white society, there will be an increase in social control of that community). Consensus theories, on the other hand, argue that crime is a threat to society in general; therefore, any crackdown is for the protection of society as a whole.

Chamlin (2009) studied the Cincinnati race riots of 2001 and also supported conflict theory through a racial-threat hypothesis. What made this study especially important was that Chamlin made the link between perceived threat and social control clearer by going one step further than using minority population size as a proxy for threat. Instead, Chamlin examined robbery arrests before and after the 2001 Cincinnati race riots, arguing that race riots carry much more threatening overtones to the ruling elite than does just population size. He found that controlling for level of robbery, "the April 2001 riot in Cincinnati produced an appreciable and lasting increase in robbery arrests" (p. 555).

◈ Critiques of Marxism and Conflict Theory

There are numerous critiques of both Marxist and conflict theory (for thorough and surprisingly different critiques, see Bohm, 1997; Kubrin et al., 2009; Liska & Messner, 1999). In general, it has been argued that in dismissing social consensus, Marxist and conflict theorists ignore that some laws seem to protect the interests of everyone (e.g., homicide or rape laws) (Liska & Messner, 1999). We might argue, however, that this critique is something of a straw man since so many laws (1) do not seem to protect the interests of everyone or (2) are differentially enforced on certain groups. It has also been argued that both perspectives are just that, perspectives, more than they are theories. In other words, they are hard to test, and theorists have been more focused on the theorizing than the "empirical inquiry" (Kubrin et al., 2009, p. 239). Those who argue this see the empirical inquiry as necessary to move the theory forward—without it, theory cannot be refined. There are those who go further with this critique and argue that these theories not only lack empirical evidence but, in many ways, are not theories but political statements about how the world works and how it should work (Akers & Sellers, 2004; Kubrin et al., 2009; Liska & Messner, 1999).

A critique specific to conflict theory (in which Marxist theory is held up as a "better" theory) is that conflict theory has not identified how power is established (Bohm, 1997). In other words, Marxist theory has very strictly and specifically linked the construction of power and conflict to the capitalist system, the mode of production, exploitation in general, and the creation of a ruling class that exploits a laborer class. Conflict theory, on the other hand, while it has expanded the discussion of power, has not explained where that power comes from. Why do some groups control more power than others? And how is that power conferred? A critique specific to Marxist theory is that the theory has not specified how laborers will lose their false consciousness; while there is general discussion, there are no testable propositions about how laborers come to be aware of their exploitation and then act on this awareness.

What do these and the many other critiques mean for the theories? Well, in many ways, they mean that the theories are robust and still stimulate discussion and use. They also mean that there is much room for continued work, work that focuses attention on the creation and maintenance of deviance, that is empirically testable, and that sharpens the direction of the theories as more data are analyzed. Next we will examine a sample of contemporary studies that spring from Marxist or conflict theory.

 ## Explaining Deviance in the Streets and Deviance in the Suites: The Cases of Shoplifting and Employees Locked in the Workplace

Both discussions below stem from the underlying act of theft. In a capitalist society, one of the behaviors commonly focused on as harmful is the taking of property from individuals or businesses. Our example of deviance in the streets, then, is shoplifting, and one response to the notion of employee shoplifting—physically locking employees in the workplace—is our example of deviance in the suites.

Shoplifting

According to the FBI and the Uniform Crime Reports (UCR), shoplifting, a subcategory of larceny, is "the theft by a person (other than an employee) of goods or merchandise exposed for sale" (Federal Bureau of Investigation, 2004, p. 32). In 2010, there were approximately 6,185,000 larceny-thefts reported in the United States; 17.2% of these (approximately 925,000) were incidences of shoplifting (Federal Bureau of Investigation, 2011) (see Figure 9.1). Between 2009 and 2010, reports of shoplifting decreased 7.1%. These figures, however, are from the UCR, the data of which come from "crimes known to police" or arrest statistics. Both underestimate the amount of crime that exists. According to the National Association for Shoplifting Prevention (NASP; 2013) and the National Epidemiologic Survey on Alcohol and Related Conditions (Shteir, 2011) between 9% and 11% of the U.S. population has shoplifted. It is estimated that, on average, the loss from a single shoplifting event in 2009 was $178, up from $104 in 1990. The NASP estimates that more than $13 billion are lost to shoplifting in a single year.

Shoplifting has been presented in three manifestations: (1) as a crime, (2) as a disease, and (3) as a form of protest (Shteir, 2011). The most popular manifestation of shoplifting is as a crime (as we have seen, it is categorized as a type of larceny). It has contributed to increases in technological surveillance, including closed circuit television, electronic article surveillance, radio-frequency identification, and metal detectors. In addition to technological surveillance, many stores use loss prevention personnel, uniformed guards, and exit inspections. Shoplifting has also been characterized as a disease, much like

Figure 9.1   Larceny–Theft Percentage Distribution, 2010

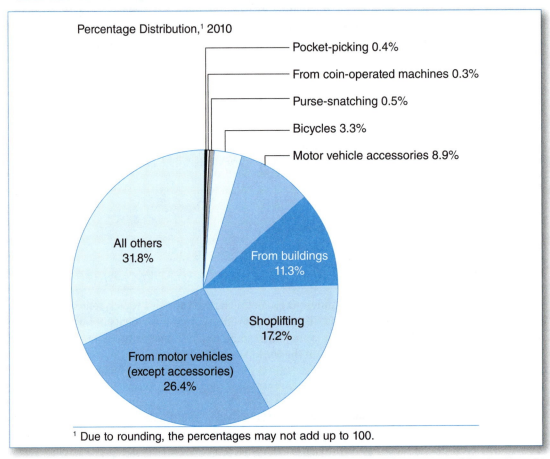

Percentage Distribution,[1] 2010

Pocket-picking 0.4%

From coin-operated machines 0.3%

Purse-snatching 0.5%

Bicycles 3.3%

Motor vehicle accessories 8.9%

All others 31.8%

From buildings 11.3%

Shoplifting 17.2%

From motor vehicles (except accessories) 26.4%

[1] Due to rounding, the percentages may not add up to 100.

Source: Federal Bureau of Investigation. (2011). Crime in the United States, 2010. U.S. Department of Justice. Retrieved from http://www.fbi .gov/about-us/cjis/ucr/crime-in-the-u.s/2010/crime-in-the-u.s.-2010/property-crime/larcenytheftmain

alcoholism. Shoplifting Anonymous groups have been started, and many argue that shoplifting is an addiction that cannot be controlled. Finally, shoplifting has been presented as a form of protest against the establishment, corporations, and capitalism. Abbie Hoffman, an activist of the anti-establishment movement, wrote a book titled *Steal This Book* (1971/2002) in which he advocates for the counterculture movement and for fighting against the government and corporations. The first section of the book focuses on how to acquire things such as food, clothing, transportation, land, entertainment, money, dope, and medical care for free.

Solomon and Ray (1984, p. 1076) identified eight rationalizations (that they referred to as irrational beliefs) of shoplifters: (1) If I am careful and smart, I will not get caught; (2) even if I do get caught, I will not be turned in; (3) even if I am prosecuted, the punishment will not be severe; (4) the merchants deserve what they get; (5) everybody, at some time or another, has shoplifted, therefore it is OK for me to do it; (6) shoplifting is not a major crime; (7) I must have the item I want to shoplift, or if I want it I should have it; and (8) it is OK to shoplift because the merchants expect it.

Shoplifting and Conflict Theory

Conflict theory would not be used to explain why an individual might shoplift; instead it might be used to explain why one group is targeted and accused of shoplifting more than another group. Since the events of September 11, 2001, considerable concern and debate has been raised over racial profiling, especially the profiling of people from the Middle East in airports. In the 1990s, concerns arose (and continue to be discussed) over racial profiling by the police, who in some cases seem to target persons of color in traffic stops. This phenomenon is sometimes referred to as "driving while black" (DWB). Shaun Gabbidon (2003) examined another source of targeting—"shopping while black," or SWB. The concern is with store employees and private security officers who may racially profile black shoppers. Borrowing from conflict theory, Gabbidon argues that the power differential in class and race leads to racial profiling. Using key terms such as false arrest, shoplifting, and racial profiling in the LexisNexis Legal research database, he focused on 29 clear-cut cases of racial profiling in retail settings from 1967 to 2002. Although he used only a relatively small number of cases, they are very interesting ones, and it is likely that the practice is much larger since the vast majority of unpleasant encounters between employees and shoppers probably do not make it to court or even to the attention of the police. This is an excellent example of the transitory nature of the definition of deviance. In most of these cases, these individuals were engaged in the same behaviors as the white shoppers—examining and/or paying for merchandise—yet the organizational policies of the stores, the perceptions of store clerks, and the color of the shoppers' skin meant they were treated as deviants instead of customers.

Employees Locked in Workplace

There have been numerous incidents of fire exits, back doors, or all exits of a workplace being locked during or after business hours so that employees do not have free and clear access to leave. We will discuss two examples of this.

The first example is the Hamlet fire. On September 3, 1991, a fire broke out at Imperial Food Products, a food processing plant Hamlet, North Carolina, that processed chicken for restaurants. The one-story structure, built from bricks and cinder blocks, had housed the processing plant for 11 years (Taylor, 1991). The fire broke out in or near a 25-foot-deep fat-fryer vat around 8:20 a.m. In addition to the fire in the vat, nearby gas lines in the ceiling also ignited (Haygood, 2002). Thick smoke from the oil fire and ignited insulation quickly filled the building. Because the building did not have many interior walls, there were few barriers to the smoke and heat from the fire.

Although the front doors were unlocked, the back doors were kept padlocked and the windows boarded up, allegedly to prevent theft, vandalism, and other crimes. Those closest to the front of the building

▲ **Photo 9.4**   While locking exit doors when employees or the public are present is illegal, businesses have been found to do just that to address theft concerns, with often disastrous results.

Source: © nojustice/istockphoto.

escaped the fire, but heavy smoke and heat kept many of the other workers from being able to get to the front of the plant. Twenty-five people died in the fire—some huddled near the padlocked back door, others trapped in a walk-in freezer where they had taken refuge. In addition to the 25 dead, 54 were injured. Some of the injuries were extremely severe and included burns; blindness; and smoke inhalation that led to respiratory disease and neurological and brain damage (Emergency Response and Research Institute, 1991).

The owner of the plant, Emmett Roe; Roe's son, who was the operations manager; and the plant manager were charged with non-negligent manslaughter. But only Emmett Roe was found guilty after he entered into a plea agreement for 25 counts of involuntary manslaughter. His sentence was 19 years and 11 months, but he served slightly less than 4 years (Haygood, 2002; Riley, 1995).

The second example is the Walmart/Target lock-ins. According to Walmart workers, in some locations the company policy was to lock the doors after hours (Greenhouse, 2004). In 2004, reports surfaced that in many of these lock-in stores there were no keys on site to unlock the doors, effectively holding workers prisoner until management arrived to unlock the doors in the morning. Although the stores all had working fire exits, workers reported that they were told that the fire exits were not to be used unless there was a "real emergency," such as a fire, and even though workers had been hurt and severely ill in some of these lock-in stores, they were told they would lose their jobs if they complained or used the fire exits to leave the store. When asked about this policy, a Walmart spokeswoman said the company told all its employees to use common sense and that if an employee was hurt, "he was clearly capable of walking out a fire door anytime during the night" (Greenhouse, 2004, n.p.).

Walmart confirmed that about 10% of their stores had a policy of locking the doors at night (Greenhouse, 2004) and in 2004 changed the policy to require a manager with a key to be on site during the night shift. Walmart said this policy was in place for stores in high-crime areas in order to keep the stores and employees safe. However, former store managers said that the reason for the lock-ins was to prevent shrinkage (thefts by employees or outsiders) and to increase efficiency by making sure no one went outside to smoke or leave the premises for a long break.

As recently as early 2013, Target has also been accused of locking in their employees overnight (Eidelson, 2013). Complaints were filed with the Occupational Safety and Health Administration (OSHA) on behalf of 25 workers with three janitorial services that contract with Target. In these instances, a Target manager was on the premises with a key, but if a worker needed to leave the building for any reason, the manager had to be tracked down, which was not always a quick task. OSHA requires that employees be "able to open an exit route door from the inside at all times without keys, tools, or special knowledge" (Kennedy, 2013, n.p.). However, there is evidence of these rules being broken by Target and other companies.

Workplace Lock-ins and Conflict Theory

We can use Chambliss's propositions on the content and operation of criminal law to examine workplace lock-ins.

- *Acts are defined as criminal because it is in the interest of the ruling class to so define them.* The mere assumption that workers are thieves means that business owners can treat them as such. In the Walmart and Target cases above, it was not the employees working on any given night that were accused of shoplifting, and even if one or more employees on any given shift *was* stealing from the organization, the locking-in policy was not exercised on just these employees. *All* employees on the shift were locked in. By both suggesting to management that workers cannot be trusted and must be locked in *and* suggesting to the public that the lock-in policies are established to keep employees working in high-crime neighborhoods safe, the company benefits twice from the policy. First, employee power is decreased by stigmatizing them as alleged criminals, and, second, company power (in the form of good press) is increased by suggesting that companies care about the well-being of employees beyond the basic employer–employee relationship.

- *Members of the ruling class will be able to violate the laws with impunity while members of the subject classes will be punished.* While both of these instances of locking in employees are known because the company deviance was uncovered, the punishment that these companies (or management in these companies) experienced was not as severe as the harm they inflicted. For example, while the employees at the chicken processing plant experienced the trauma of a fire, injuries, and, in some cases, death, one of the three owners of the company served 4 years in prison for this tragic event. While Walmart and Target employees have also been locked in (although no one died, there were reports of bodily harm), the companies merely experienced the filing of complaints with OSHA that could end in a civil penalty (most likely a fine) if they were found to have violated OSHA policy. This means that all employees on these night shifts were punished for the suspected behavior of a few (although if there was evidence against any individual employee, that employee would have been fired and arrested for theft), while a majority of owners escape any punishment at all.

◈ Ideas in Action: Racial Impact Statements

Racial impact statements have existed since 2008 when Iowa governor Chet Culver signed legislation requiring that all proposed legislation affecting sentencing, probation, or parole be evaluated for its likelihood to impact racial disparity in the criminal justice system. Other states soon followed with similar legislation. According to Mauer,

> The premise behind racial impact statements is that policies often have unintended consequences that would be best addressed prior to adoption of new initiatives. In this sense they are similar to fiscal and environmental impact statements. Policy makers contemplating new construction projects or social initiatives routinely conduct such assessments, which are now widely viewed as responsible mechanisms of government. . . . Racial impact statements are particularly important for criminal justice policy because it is exceedingly difficult to reverse sentencing policies once they have been adopted. (Mauer, 2009, p. 19)

One of the most obvious public policies that could have benefitted from a racial impact statement is the crack cocaine mandatory sentencing policies that significantly impact black Americans disproportionate to their use of crack cocaine. Even though it is common to critique this policy and acknowledge its unequal application, the policy has not been overturned. Politicians fear appearing soft on crime if they overturn any criminal justice policy. Racial impact statements are intended to stop such disparity-producing legislation before it gets enacted and becomes exceedingly hard to change.

Racial Impact Statements and Conflict Theory

Racial impact statements are a useful example of the type of legislation that extends from the tenets of conflict theory. Given that conflict theorists explore the effects of power differentials on the creation and maintenance of laws, a public policy that is designed to critique proposed legislation and specifically examine it for its effects on groups (people of color) that have traditionally had less power in relation to the criminal justice system extends from these theoretical propositions. A further examination of this legislation from the conflict perspective would explore the success of racial impact statements in changing or limiting policies that would disproportionately affect communities of color.

NOW YOU . . . USE THE THEORY

In April 2010, Arizona enacted SB 1070, the toughest immigration bill in existence, into law. This law requires police officers to detain people they "reasonably suspect" are undocumented and verify their status. It also makes it a misdemeanor to not carry papers proving one's immigration status. Finally, it allows individuals to sue public agencies that they think are not enforcing the law. The law is so controversial that its enactment was postponed while the courts determined its constitutionality. Subsequently, in 2012, the Supreme Court upheld portions of the law and struck down others.

In October 2010, National Public Radio (NPR) uncovered a direct link between SB 1070 and the largest private prison corporation in the nation. The law was written by Russell Pearce, a congressman for Arizona, but it was written with considerable help from a group called the American Legislative Exchange Council (ALEC). ALEC comprises legislators and members of major corporations such as Reynolds Tobacco, ExxonMobil, the National Rifle Association, and the Corrections Corporation of America (CCA). Pearce and the CCA both sit on the board of ALEC.

The CCA, according to company documents, anticipates a significant portion of their future profits will come from supplying private prison services to Immigration and Customs Enforcement.

When asked if both the congressman and the CCA were at the same meeting in which the legislation was crafted, Michael Hough, staff director of ALEC, is quoted as saying, "Yeah. That's the way it's set up. It's a, you know, it's a public-private partnership. And that's how it's set up, so that—we believe both sides, businesses and lawmakers should be at the same table, together" (L. Sullivan, 2010).

There is nothing illegal about what Pearce or the CCA did in co-crafting the legislation. However, the partnership was not made public.

Use Marxist and/or conflict theory to comment on ALEC, the partnership between Pearce and the CCA, SB 1070, and the impact of SB 1070 on legal immigrants, undocumented workers, and the state of immigration policy in the United States.

Source: Facts of this case were taken from NPR.org (L. Sullivan, 2010).

Conclusion

The importance of Marxist/conflict theories in the study of deviance cannot be denied. As some of the first theories to take a relativist (or social constructionist) perspective on deviance, they allow us to question how deviance is defined and used to maintain positions of power in society. While the earliest tenets of these theories focused solely on the impact of the capitalist system on power, group structure, and group conflict, later iterations of the theory have shifted from a sole focus on capitalism to one that examines other power differentials—most notably, power differentials among racial groups and the ways in which legislation and agents of social control (the police) are used to control these groups. While these critical analyses may make some people (and groups) uncomfortable, they are necessary for a better understanding of deviance and society.

EXERCISES AND DISCUSSION QUESTIONS

1. As Reiman and Leighton (2009) wrote, "The rich get richer and the poor get prison." How might a Marxist or conflict theorist explain this sentence? Discuss a specific theorist.

2. Given the global recession that began in 2008, using Marxist/conflict theories, predict the trends we may see in legislation and incarceration in the United States.

3. Using the concept of dialectical materialism, trace the history of marijuana legislation in the United States.

4. Give an example of controlling "problem populations" through the creation and maintenance of deviance. How is deviance used to control this population?

5. This chapter used same-sex marriage legislation as an example of the struggle of competing groups to control the law and avoid deviant labels. Give another example of a group, its interests, and its struggle for power and how legislation is/was used to negate this power.

6. Identify a specific law in your town, city, or state and critique its creation using Marxist or conflict theory. In other words, why was it created, and who does it benefit?

KEY TERMS

Conflict

Dialectical materialism

False consciousness

Instrumental Marxism

Normative

Relativist

Social consensus

Social construction

Structural Marxism

CHAPTER 10

Critical Theories of Deviance

In 2004, Little Rock, Arkansas, was voted the meanest city in United States by the National Coalition for the Homeless. What made Little Rock the meanest city toward the homeless? The city at the time "managed" the homeless population by ordering the police to engage in ongoing raids of the 27 homeless encampments found in the area. Police came into these encampments during the day, while the inhabitants were not there, and demolished the sites, often destroying the few belongings that inhabitants owned. While the mayor of Little Rock at the time (Jim Dailey) admitted that he did not know where the homeless were supposed to go, the police continued the raids, often without warning to the residents. The city justified the raids by calling the homeless panhandlers and petty thieves. While the homeless have been cast as common criminals by the city, there is no evidence this is the case. In fact, the fastest-growing homeless population in the area was single women with children. At the time, only 75 shelter beds were available for homeless women. (Adapted from Rampona, 2004)

◈ Introduction

The story above highlights an all-too-common problem for the homeless in the United States—the criminalization or stigmatization of their homeless plight. While many organizations—national and local, religious and secular—focus on helping the homeless through such means as soup kitchens, shelters, and "10-year plans" to eradicate homelessness, the major governmental response to homelessness in many cities is one of social control and banishment (Beckett & Herbert, 2010).

The deviance theories examined in this chapter are considered critical theories. In other words, they examine issues of deviance and crime from a perspective that questions the normative and status quo. While earlier theories in this book might look at the plight of homelessness and ask how someone becomes homeless or why the homeless are homeless—oftentimes focusing specifically on what many might consider individual flaws or propensities to engage in this "deviance"—these critical theories

▲ **Photo 10.1** How do we address homelessness? The answer depends on the theory we are using to understand it.

Source: ©Rubberball/istockphoto.

instead examine societal responses to homelessness often from the perspective of those with less societal power (people of color or women) or those with nontraditional philosophies (peacemaking). In other words, just like Marxist/conflict theory in Chapter 9, the theories in this chapter will ask, what role does society play in the creation and maintenance of homelessness? Critical theories are wide-ranging and we have chosen three—feminist theory, critical race theory, and peacemaking theory—that represent a variety of those theories. Some argue that critical theories are just an extension of Marxist/conflict theories, and it is certainly the case that these critical theories developed because of the existence of those earlier theories, but each critical theory adds something well-beyond the theories in Chapter 9, and they are different enough to warrant their own chapter. While some of these theories are newer (for example, peacemaking does not have the body of empirical work that feminist theory does), they offer a way of looking at the world that broadens our understanding and discussion of deviance.

◈ Development of Feminist Criminology

Feminist criminology questions the status quo, most specifically the male-centered view that much of criminology takes. Feminist thought has a long, rich history in the United States, feminist criminology emerging in the 1970s with the influential works of Adler (1975), Simon (1975), and Smart (1977). As with many of these critical perspectives, there is no single ideology but rather a diversity of feminist thought with ranging, often competing, viewpoints: liberal feminism; radical feminism; Marxist feminism; socialist feminism; postmodern feminism (Burgess-Proctor, 2006; Daly & Chesney-Lind, 1988; Tong, 1998); black feminism and critical race feminism (Burgess-Proctor, 2006); psychoanalytic feminism; gender feminism; existentialist feminism; global and multicultural feminism; and ecofeminism (Tong, 1998).

While a diverse set of theories falls under the feminist perspective, these theories all stem from the critique that criminological theories and theories of deviance prior to the introduction of feminist thought treated women in one of two ways: either as subsumed under the heading of "men," assuming that general theories of deviance could explain female deviance, or in a sexist manner, assuming that women were somehow "different" or "pathological" in their makeup and their deviance stemmed from this pathology. Until the feminist perspective, none of the theories acknowledged the position of women in a patriarchal society and the structural oppression that women experienced in this society (Smart, 1977).

For the purposes of this overview, this chapter will highlight five branches of feminism that have produced much research on deviance and crime. Liberal feminism focuses on gender role socialization. The roles that women are socialized into are not valued as much as the roles men are socialized—in other words, nurturing roles such as teacher are not valued as much as competitive roles such as CEO. For this reason, liberal feminists focus on equal rights and opportunities, especially in education and the workplace, that would allow women to compete fairly with men. Liberal feminist scholars argue that women engage in deviance less because they are socialized in a manner that provides them fewer opportunities to deviate (Burgess-Proctor, 2006).

Radical feminism focuses on the sexual control of women, seeing their oppression as emerging from a social order dominated by men. Because of their emphasis on sexual control, radical feminists focus much of their theoretical insights on sex, gender, and reproduction (Tong, 1998), as well as in the areas of crime and deviance on domestic violence, rape, sexual harassment, and pornography (Burgess-Proctor, 2006).

Socialist feminism focuses on structural differences, especially those we find in the capitalist modes of production. Social feminists argue that both patriarchy and capitalism are oppressive forces for women and that until the patriarchal system and the class-based system are eradicated, there can be no equality for women (Tong, 1998).

Finally, postmodern feminism may be closest to **peacemaking criminology** in that it questions the idea of a single "truth" or way of knowing and understanding. Postmodern feminists examine the social construction of such "accepted" ideas as crime and deviance (Burgess-Proctor, 2006). Even with their rich diversity, at the center of all of these strands of feminist thought is an emphasis on the oppression of women.

Certainly for a book on deviance and social control, one of the most central forms of oppression to be examined would be the criminal justice system and prison-industrial complex. Many feminist scholars have examined the effect of increasing social controls on the experiences of women. Between 1970 and 2001, the female prison population increased from 5,600 to 161,200 women (a 2,800% increase), even though for much of this time, crime rates were actually decreasing in the United States (Sudbury, 2005). Many have looked at this increase and tried to explain it with individual-level theories that focus on increasing female criminality, but feminist scholars argue that to really understand both the reasons behind such an exponential increase and the effect such an increase has on women and society, we must examine the business of criminalization that has made more behaviors deviant and punishments harsher over the past 30 years.

Feminist theories examine the label of deviant from the perspective of the outsider. Like conflict theory in Chapter 9 and critical race theory later in this chapter, feminist theory argues that the label of deviant is used to control women, especially poor women and women of color (Neve & Pate, 2005; Ogden, 2005). Instead of acknowledging a structural system of oppression that pays women less than men, does not adequately support childcare, and offers far fewer opportunities for women than men, the system criminalizes sexuality, makes the rules for welfare almost impossible to follow and then considers welfare fraud a crime punishable with 5 years in prison (Ogden, 2005), and labels women deviant for many behaviors they engage in as a means of survival (for example, running away and prostitution). Feminist theorists argue that the system itself must be changed instead of a narrow focus on women's behavior.

Feminism and Homelessness

Feminist theorists have devoted themselves to the study of women and their experiences in the social world (Burgess-Proctor, 2006). Much of this research—on domestic violence, the physical and sexual abuse of teenagers, and the position of women in the economic system—can have a significant impact on our understanding of women and homelessness. Feminist theory would ask what is it about women's position in society that might affect their likelihood of becoming homeless and how this position affects them once they are homeless.

For example, patriarchal society normalizes the abuse of women. The fact that victimization of women is considered normal or acceptable means that many women are not helped in any systematic fashion. Women who want to escape abusive situations can quickly find themselves homeless. In addition, women who have no choice but to become homeless when they want to leave an abusive relationship are likely to delay or completely cancel their escape because homelessness presents its own hardships. These women are left with few alternatives.

Extensive research has documented the experience of teenage girls who run away from home (see Chesney-Lind & Shelden, 2003). These girls are often escaping very abusive families and running away becomes a preservation technique, but our public policies for running away do not take into consideration the reasons why girls may be running away. These policies criminalize this behavior and treat the girls as deviants who need to be punished or "reformed" for leaving their families. Feminists have long argued that good public policy would acknowledge the oppressive social structure that exists and not hold young girls accountable for the systems of oppression they are subject to. In other words, public policy should not focus on labeling the girls as deviant for running away and becoming homeless but should instead focus on services and policies that stop physical and sexual abuse in the home and that offer girls who have been abused a safe haven—resources, affordable housing, educational and work opportunities, and counseling to make sense of their experiences.

DEVIANCE IN POPULAR CULTURE

This chapter introduces you to critical theories and peacemaking criminology. As with many theoretical perspectives, the ideas may become more clear and accessible to you if you can apply them to specific examples. Popular culture and films, once again, offer compelling real-life and fictional cases for you to watch and practice using these perspectives:

The Accused—this film is a fictional account of a young woman who is gang raped in a bar. The victim's judgment and character are questioned when she decides to take the case to court. How would feminist theory view this case? From a peacemaking perspective, how might it have been better handled?

Crash—this popular film offers examples of racial prejudice and profiling from several different perspectives. Each character reveals his or her own biases throughout the film; some learn significant lessons as they interact in surprising ways, but every character feels the powerful effect of fear and racial discrimination. Each character eventually questions his or her belief system and the larger society we live in.

The Dhamma Brothers—this documentary explores the power of meditation in a maximum-security prison. The film takes you inside the Donaldson Correctional Facility in Alabama as inmates embark upon an emotionally and physically demanding program of silent meditation lasting 10 days and requiring 100 hours of meditation. Can such a program change these men, and can it change the larger culture of the prison? Is this a desirable outcome?

Redemption—this is a made-for-television movie about the life of Stan "Tookie" Williams, founder of the Crips, who was nominated for the Nobel Peace Prize while on death row. Can a man who was convicted of terrible crimes turn his life around and be a role model for youth in the larger community? From his prison cell, Tookie Williams wrote a number of children's books speaking out against gang violence; you can check out his Web site (www.tookie.com) to get an idea of the work he was trying to do and the population he hoped to reach. Williams was executed by the state of California in 2005; whether redemption was possible in his case is now an academic question, but it is one we would like you to consider.

 # Development of Critical Race Theory

Critical race theory is an extension of critical legal studies that came to prominence through the writings of legal scholars in the 1970s. Scholars of critical race theory were interested in explaining why the civil rights movement of the 1960s had stalled and why the advances in the 1960s and 1970s had come under attack (Crenshaw, Gotanda, Peller, & Thomas, 1995). These scholars offered a counter-story to the dominant, mainstream accounts of the events of the civil rights movement and the use of law as a tool of equality. According to Cornell West (1995), "Critical Race theory . . . compels us to confront critically the most explosive issue in American civilization: the historical centrality and complicity of law in upholding white supremacy" (p. xi).

While the theory first began to coalesce among legal scholars, today it is used in the areas of communication, education, and sociology by an array of race scholars who are unified by two goals:

> The first is to understand how a regime of white supremacy and its subordination of people of color have been created and maintained in America, and, in particular, to examine the relationship between that social structure and professed ideals such as "the rule of law" and "equal protection." The second is a desire not merely to understand the vexed bond between law and racial power but to change it. (Crenshaw et al., 1995, p. xiii)

Challenging this idea of white supremacy and thus the belief that the white experience is the normative standard by which all other experiences are measured, critical race theorists argue that to understand law and racial exclusion, we must understand the experiences of people of color under this legal system. These scholars insist "that the social and experiential context of racial oppression is crucial for understanding racial dynamics, particularly the way that current inequalities are connected to earlier, more overt, practices of racial exclusion" (Taylor, 1998, p. 122). Critical race theory, then, can be used to examine the use of law to negate the experiences of discrimination and victimization of people of color, while heightening the focus on deviance that may or may not exist in communities of color.

Critical legal scholars argue that the law is not "neutral" or "objective" in its creation or application and, instead, has been used, overtly, when possible, and covertly, when necessary, to subordinate people of color (Crenshaw et al., 1995). Even in such arenas as affirmative action, a policy from the civil rights era designed to help people of color, the law has been used, in the end, to mute this effort (Aguirre, 2000; Crenshaw et al., 1995).

At its very foundation, critical race theory offers a unique position in the forum of legal critique by proposing that racism is an intricate and enduring pattern in the fabric of American life, woven into the social structure and social institutions of the modern day (Crenshaw et al., 1995). This is in direct contrast to most liberal legal and social scholars who argue that racism and discrimination, in general, are sociopathic, anomalous acts that not only can be explained by individual, evil behavior but also can be fixed through accepted legal practices (Fan, 1997). As Crenshaw et al. (1995) note,

> From its inception mainstream legal thinking in the U.S. has been characterized by a curiously constricted understanding of race and power. Within this cramped conception of racial domination, the evil of racism exists when—and only when—one can point to specific, discrete acts of racial discrimination, which is in turn narrowly defined as decision-making based on the irrational and irrelevant attribute of race. (p. xx)

One of the most important tenets of critical race theory may be its supposition that racial domination is at the center of much of today's legal and social decision making—and that this domination is so routine, it is accepted as both legally and morally legitimate. Critical race scholars in essence argue that the "white" experience is so established as the "proper" experience that this viewpoint has been institutionalized as normative, and experiences or viewpoints that deviate from this are seen as harmful and therefore deviant.

Critical Race Theory and Homelessness

Critical race theory, then, is used to analyze the use of law and legal processes to maintain the status quo or "protect" a white, middle-class interpretation of the world in the face of poor communities and communities of color. This perspective can be used to examine the experiences of the homeless in general, focusing on how laws are used to socially control the homeless instead of helping them. An excellent, specific example of this can be seen in the experiences of the homeless, migrant populations, and Latino populations during the San Diego fire evacuations of 2007 (see American Civil Liberties Union [ACLU], 2007). According to a report published November 1, 2007, the evacuation process for many San Diegans was subject to extra scrutiny and social control for what appeared to be racially and class-motivated reasons.

On October 21, 2007, fires broke out in San Diego County that required the evacuation of thousands of residents. One of the main evacuation centers was Qualcomm Stadium in the city of San Diego. While the ACLU reports that volunteers at the evacuation center were meticulous in their help of those in need, in more than a few instances, law enforcement seemed to be working at cross-purposes with these volunteers. One such example was that on more than one occasion (and with only evacuees of color), law enforcement detained individuals after they had been given their supplies from volunteers and accused these individuals of looting the supplies or "taking too many supplies" for their needs. In a second example, law enforcement entered the evacuation center during the late evening and woke up evacuees, requesting that they show identification proving they were from official evacuation areas. This was especially harmful for evacuees who were homeless (but living on the streets in evacuated areas) because they had no documentation with an official address given that they were homeless. These evacuees were ordered to leave the evacuation shelter because it was assumed they were not "in need" of the services and were taking advantage of the situation by staying at the shelter. While volunteers repeatedly emphasized that the services were available for anyone who came to the facility, many of the evacuees were assumed to be there under false pretenses. The ACLU (2007) report suggests that most, if not all, of those who were accused of unlawful behavior were the homeless or evacuees of color. In other words, white, middle-class evacuees were seen as deserving of help, while the homeless or evacuees of color were not (by law enforcement, not volunteers).

▲ Photo 10.2   When a firestorm hit San Diego County, some individuals were treated as victims while others were treated as deviants. This treatment was often based on the individual's race/ethnicity.

Source: ©Stockbyte/Thinkstock.

Critical race theory as a theory that emphasizes the importance of capturing individuals' stories and highlighting the experiences of everyone, not just those most visible or "deserving" of storytelling, allows for a more thorough examination of many experiences that usually go unnoticed or unrecorded. Certainly during the firestorms of 2007 in San Diego County, the experiences of the homeless and evacuees of color were overlooked by most who focused on more visible evacuees. Critical race theory gives voice to individuals who may not have their stories told in more traditional settings.

◈ Development of Peacemaking

It is fitting to include peacemaking criminology as one of the theories in this chapter because one of its strongest proponents is Richard Quinney, the critical criminologist whose early work we read about in Chapter 9 under conflict theories. One might say that peacemaking theory (Pepinsky & Quinney, 1991; Quinney, 1995) is the contemporary extension of Quinney's work in conflict theory. Writing and theorizing with Hal Pepinsky, Quinney continued with this theory to critically examine not only our understanding of crime and deviance but also our understanding of how we come to know what we know. In other words, they critically examined criminology *and* criminologists as well.

According to the peacemaking philosophy, most criminology today is "war-like" because at its foundation, it advocates making war on crime. This war on crime is evidenced in two ways in traditional criminology: (1) through the "us versus them" philosophy that suggests that those who engage in crime are somehow different from the rest of society and (2) through the advocating of punishment as the primary means to stop crime (Pepinsky & Quinney, 1991). Pepinsky and Quinney (1991) argue that neither of these viewpoints has reduced criminal activity; in fact, both have increased the suffering of not only victims but offenders alike. According to Pepinsky and Quinney,

There are basically two kinds of criminologists, those who think criminals are different from themselves and those who don't. You cannot separate a criminal's self-understanding from our understanding of the criminal. More than empathy, understanding requires our sympathy— allowing ourselves to feel the offender's pain and committing ourselves to trying to alleviate the pain for us both. (p. 303)

Peacemaking criminology, on the other hand, is focused on a different way of seeing and organizing the world around compassion, sympathy, and understanding. Quinney (1991) defines this way of thinking:

In other words, without inner peace in each of us, without peace of mind and heart, there can be no social peace between people and no peace in societies, nations, and in the world. To be explicitly engaged in this process, of bringing about peace on all levels, of joining ends and means, is to be engaged in peacemaking. (p. 10)

The peacemaking tradition has no single tenet or assumption, and it has many followers in both the academic world and the world of praxis (Pepinsky & Quinney, 1991). In 1991, Pepinsky and Quinney published the first book on the peacemaking perspective. They outline three substantive areas that flourish in the peacemaking tradition: religious, feminist, and critical. Peacemakers coming from a religious perspective focus on a variety of religious traditions, including Christianity, Buddhism, Hinduism, Islam, Judaism, and Native American (Braswell, Fuller, & Lozoff, 2001). They look to these traditions to advocate a way of meeting those who might engage in harm not as enemies but as members of the community who need understanding. "It is rather that when violence happens, they [the Mennonites] choose to try to restore peace rather than to respond in kind. And once again, the method is the way" (Pepinsky & Quinney, 1991, p. 305).

In contrast, the feminist peacemaking tradition is broad and varied and hard to summarize in a short space. However, at its core, those working in this tradition are focused on a humane system of justice that acknowledges that women are placed at a disadvantage in a patriarchal society (Fuller & Wozniak, 2006). This patriarchy and, by definition, gendered power differences create an oppressive, war-like experience for women both within and beyond the criminal justice system. Finally, the critical tradition of peacemaking also includes a robust examination of societal power differences, including, but not limited to, gender, race, and class.

All three of these traditions have in common a belief that a different paradigm must be established for criminal justice—one that focuses on restoration and not retribution. **Restorative justice** as a practical method advocates for the use of restorative practices or mediation between victims and offenders, offering victims a real opportunity to work through their victimization, often by playing a central role in the offender's justice experience. Many restorative justice practices are informed by the concept of **reintegrative shaming** (Braithwaite, 1989), the idea that the shaming of someone who has done wrong that is then followed by reintegration of the wrongdoer into the fabric of his or her family or greater community is a powerful way of influencing the offender's future behavior. This type of shaming is thought to work best in settings in which the people being shamed are generally treated in positive and encouraging ways most of the time and then when they face disapproval about their acts, they are ashamed and feel bad.

The majority of the scholarly literature related to restorative justice addresses the particulars of restorative methods and/or the philosophical and theoretical bases of restorative principles (e.g., Cragg, 1992; Messmer & Otto, 1992; Strang & Braithwaite, 2001; Umbreit, 1994; M. Wright, 1996; Zehr, 1990). Also evident in the literature are the attendant critiques of statements of restorative theory and practice and discussions of the challenges facing restorative justice (e.g., Andersen, 1999; Ashworth, 1993; Hudson, 1998; LaPrairie, 1998; Minor & Morrison, 1996). These critiques echo longstanding concerns about informal justice expressed in the sociolegal literature (Abel, 1982; Merry, 1989)—namely, that the lack of formal authority involved in mediation and community dispute resolution practices may result in greater injustices than the very system it seeks to improve.

Peacemaking and Homelessness

Gregg Barak (1991) offers a peacemaking analysis of homelessness as a deviant status in the United States. At the core of his analysis is an argument that we must approach homelessness from a place of kindness and regard for those who have found themselves homeless. Most debates about homelessness have at their core an individualistic deficits model that suggests that those who are homeless are so because of individual problems or deficits of their character (they are lazy, like being homeless, are drug addicts, etc.). This characterization allows for treatment of the homeless that is war-like and inhumane.

▲ **Photo 10.3** Peacemaking theory suggests that we should help those with a "deviant" status, such as the homeless, instead of criminalizing them.

Source: ©Brand X Pictures/Thinkstock.

For example, if we assume that individuals are homeless because of personal "problems" such as laziness or drug use, it is easy to also characterize the homeless as immoral and more likely to be dangerous. These characterizations lead to public policies that focus on (1) making the homeless invisible and (2) criminalizing the homeless and homelessness.

Public policies that focus on making homelessness invisible use tactics such as banishment (Beckett & Herbert, 2010) and loitering laws that make standing or sitting on public sidewalks against the law. While these policies in the short run may move the homeless to different parts of the city or to different cities altogether, they do nothing to alleviate the problem of homelessness or offer individuals who are homeless any hope of finding permanent affordable housing.

The example at the beginning of this chapter offers an even more war-like law enforcement practice of using sweeps to destroy the encampments of the homeless. In most instances, this means that these individuals lose the

▲ **Photo 10.4** Peacemaking theory argues that we often "make war" on deviant behavior by criminalizing it.

Source: ©Filo/istockphoto.

few possessions they have saved and can mean arrest if they are caught in the encampments during the sweep, although often sweeps are conducted during the day when the homeless are less likely to be on site. This practice does nothing to help those who are homeless find affordable housing. It does, however, exacerbate the feelings of alienation and helplessness that the homeless are likely to feel (Barak, 1991).

Peacemaking practices designed to help homelessness would not focus on an individual deficit model of homelessness but instead would focus on structural conditions that may lead to homelessness (Barak, 1991). For example, young women often run away from home because of physical, emotional, or sexual abuse they are experiencing in the home. Individuals and families often find themselves homeless because of market forces such as the tightening of the low-income housing market, an increasing unemployment rate due to market fluctuations, or the globalization of the economy. Public policies that focus on offering services and places of refuge for young women who are abused or services for workers and families who have been affected by the structural conditions of the economy are more peace-like in nature. However, even these policies can be conducted in a war-like manner if the homeless are not treated as complete human beings and are made to "prove their worth" in order to receive these services.

For example, many social service agencies require that individuals take special classes to earn the "right" to receive their help. Individualized hoops that assume that the homeless are in need of extra education are still within a deficit model that places most of the blame for homelessness on the individual. A true peacemaking approach to homelessness would offer services and empathy without assuming that the homeless are different from those who enjoy stable housing. In other words, the homeless would not need to prove their worth while getting help.

RECENT STUDY IN DEVIANCE

Racial Profiling and Immigration Law Enforcement: Rounding Up the Usual Suspects in the Latino Community

By Mary Romero, 2006, in *Critical Sociology, 32*, 447–473.

A 1975 Supreme Court decision makes stopping persons for no other reason than having a "Mexican appearance" legal under the Fourth Amendment. However, because the Immigration and Naturalization Service (INS) does not keep statistics on incidents of stopping and interrogating legal residents (false positives), there is little information on the extent to which Latino Americans are differentially treated and discriminated against by the agency of the criminal justice system.

In an effort to describe the injustices Latino Americans (both legal citizens and undocumented residents) face, Mary Romero (2006) uses a case study approach and describes a 5-day immigration raid in the late 1990s known as the Chandler roundup that took place in Chandler,

Arizona. More than 400 stops were documented, and she examined data on 91 complaints filed during the 5 days. All of the complainants were Latino or of Mexican descent. Several (14) were stopped more than once during the 5-day period. Nearly half of the complainants (42) were clearly not undocumented immigrants. Only 33 outcomes for the 91 incidences were documented; 23 were detained, and only 3 of those were clear cases of illegal residence. Equally disconcerting is how the "suspects" were treated; some were handcuffed, and others were interrogated in a manner inconsistent with the way "white" people are typically stopped and questioned.

Romero (2006) wrote about two specific instances of Latino Americans being questioned by law enforcement:

All the people shopping at this shopping center appeared to be Hispanic and many were being stopped and questioned by the officers. D and his uncle were conversing in Spanish and leaving the store with a package when they were approached by a Chandler police officer and an INS/Border Patrol agent asked them in Spanish for their papers. The uncle, who had just become a United States citizen, had his citizenship papers with him and showed those to the officer. D had only a social security card and a driver's license.... D took his wallet from his pocket to get his identification; the INS/Border Patrol officer then asked him for the wallet and examined everything in it. D feared that if he did not give the officer his wallet he would be arrested. Neither officer wrote any information down or kept anything from the wallet. No explanation was given for the stop. (Office of Attorney General Wood, 1997, p. 21, as cited in Romero, 2006, pp. 463–464)

C is the highest-ranked left-handed golfer in Arizona. C is a large, dark complected, Hispanic, and native-born Arizonan.... Returning from a golf match in July, he stopped ... for a cold drink and saw Chandler police officers talking to different people of apparent Mexican descent. At the time he was wearing an old tee shirt and a baseball cap. As he tried to exit the market, he was barred exit by a Chandler Police officer who asked if he was a local, if he had papers, and whether he was a citizen. C told the officer that he was a citizen and was leaving and the officer told him "No, you are not." C then walked around the officer and went over to his car, which was a 1997 Acura. The officer followed him but when he saw what car he was driving, permitted him to drive off. (Office of Attorney General Wood 1997, p. 21, as cited in Romero, 2006, p. 465)

Discussion Question:

1. How are the experiences of D and C similar and different? Using critical theories, explain why these experiences might be similar and different.

Critiques of Critical Theories

It may be unfair to lump the critiques of three such different critical theories as peacemaking, feminist theory, and critical race theory into one discussion, but it seems that one of the main critiques of all three theories is that *they do not see the world the way other theories see the world*. In other words, the very features that set these theories apart as unique or special are used to dismiss them. For example, Akers (1998) argued that peacemaking criminology was

> a utopian vision of society that calls for reforming and restructuring to get away from war, crime, and violence. . . . This is a highly laudable philosophy of criminal justice, but it does not offer an explanation of why the system operates as it does or why offenders commit crime. It can be evaluated on other grounds but not on empirical validity. (p. 183)

Moyer (2001) argued that the peacemaking perspective was in its infancy (compared to other crime and deviance theories) and pointed out that Akers offered no empirical evidence himself for his claims. Feminist criminology has often been criticized as reductionist (namely, reducing the discussion of crime to the single variable of gender)—a critique that is ironic given that one of the main reasons for the emergence of feminist criminology in the first place was the androcentric nature of both theory and research in the field of crime and deviance. Similarly, critical race theory is often criticized for "playing the race card" or essentially making race a singularly important predictor of experience in U.S. society (for a discussion of this critique, see Levit, 1999). In all of these criticisms, the common denominator is that the theories are denounced for critically analyzing the status quo.

 ## Explaining Deviance in the Streets and Deviance in the Suites: The Cases of Pornography and Illegal Governmental Surveillance

Both of the discussions of deviance below have the common thread of changing technology running through them. While changing technology has allowed for an explosion of opportunities in the pornography industry, offering exponential growth, it has also made both the surveillance of United States citizens and the exposing of those surveillance programs easier.

Pornography

Pornography is so diverse and its mediums so varied, it would be almost impossible to cover it comprehensively here. In many ways, it is an industry of contradictions. On the one hand, there is little known about it (for example, its true net worth and number of users); on the other hand, general estimates suggest that enough people are familiar with some form of pornography to suggest it is one of the worst-kept secrets on the planet. Adult videos, escort services, magazines, sex clubs, phone sex lines, cable and pay per view channels, Internet sites, and novelties have all been listed under the heading of pornography (although many might argue that this list ranges from the sex/pleasure industry to pornography). Of this list the most revolutionary medium would be the Internet.

The Internet has made pornography "ubiquitous" (Ruvolo, 2011, n.p.). While it is estimated that in 1991 (before the Internet), there were less than 90 U.S. porn magazines, in the late 2000s there were well over 2 million porn sites and over 100 million individuals logging into them (Ogas & Gaddam, 2011, as discussed in Ruvolo, 2011). Pornhub, one of the largest online pornography sites, reported 14.7 billion visits in 2013 (individual users may have returned more than once and would have, then, been counted more than once), and over 63 billion videos were viewed (Pornhub, 2013). In addition to the Internet making pornography much more accessible to the viewer, it has also made it much more accessible to the participant, with numerous sites devoted to "amateur" pornography.

Sidebar: Is Erotica Pornography?

The question of whether literary erotica (sexually explicit romance novels) is pornography is one that the courts have recently weighed in on. The First Appellate District, Division Two, Court of Appeal of the State of California recently ruled on whether erotica violated the obscenity rules of the California prison system:

> [The] San Francisco appeals court has ruled that a werewolf erotica novel must be returned to Andres Martinez, an inmate of Pelican Bay State Prison, after prison guards took it away from him on the grounds that it was pornography. Although the court grants that the novel in question, *The Silver Crown*, by Mathilde Madden, is "less than Shakespearean," it argues that the book nevertheless has literary merit and shouldn't be banned under prison obscenity laws. The court also notes that "the sex appears to be between consenting adults. No minors are involved. No bestiality is portrayed (unless werewolves count)." (Quinn, 2013, n.p.)

The Internet has made pornography so ubiquitous that some argue it has overwhelmed its own prosecution (Ruvolo, 2011). While child pornography has been the focus of federal prosecution for many years, in 2005, Alberto Gonzales, then the attorney general, created the Obscenity Prosecution Task Force to focus on adult pornography because of concerns he had about the prevalence and ease of use of Internet pornography. In 2011, Attorney General Eric Holder disbanded the task force for several reasons, one of which was that there was too much porn to prosecute, but also because the Internet had so blurred the lines between pornography and pop culture (Gerstein, 2011). Instead, all prosecutions of pornography (with that prosecution focused on child pornography) would again be handled through the U.S. attorneys' offices and the Child Exploitation and Obscenity Section of the Department of Justice's Criminal Division.

Pornography and Feminist Theory

There has been a continuing debate within feminist theory as to the advantages or disadvantages of pornography. Anti-porn feminism became popular in the 1970s with the work of Catharine MacKinnon and Andrea Dworkin. Anti-porn feminists argue that pornography subordinates women to men, making women second-class citizens (MacKinnon, 1984). According to MacKinnon (1984), pornography is a form of forced sex:

> Pornography is not harmless fantasy or a corrupt and confused misrepresentation of an otherwise natural and healthy sexuality. With the rape and prostitution in which it participates, pornography institutionalizes the sexuality of male supremacy, which fuses the erotization of dominance and submission with the social construction of male and female. . . . In pornography, women desire dispossession and cruelty. Men, permitted to put words (and other things) in women's mouths, create scenes in which women desperately want to be bound, battered, tortured, humiliated, and killed. Or, merely taken and used. This is erotic to the male point of view. (pp. 325–326)

MacKinnon was referring to pornographic films shown in theaters at the time she wrote this passage in 1984. However, she has since argued that in whatever form pornography exists, it still subjugates women and contributes to gender inequality (Ciclitira, 2004). Feminists who advocate a more pro-pornography viewpoint argue that anti-porn feminists are anti-sex, racist, and classist because they do not acknowledge the context of pornography. Focusing specifically on Internet pornography, these feminists argue that cybersex offers several opportunities: identity-bending, improved access to sex education, opportunities for "safe" sex, increased opportunities for women and minorities to produce and distribute pornography, female access to pornography in the privacy of their homes, and the allowance of exploring differing sexualities. In other words, Internet pornography has increased the level of control and power that women can have over their own bodies, the image of their bodies, and the definition of sexuality, and it offers an opportunity for women to more fully participate in and enjoy pornography, if they so choose (Ciclitira, 2004).

Even those who may not go as far as to say that Internet pornography has all the benefits above argue that it at least allows greater access and more information for women:

> Crucially, pornography has become truly available to women for the first time in history. . . . This central mechanism of sexual subordination, this means of systematizing the definition of women as a sexual class, has now become available to its victims for scrutiny and analysis as an open public system. (as cited in Ruvolo, 2011, n.p.)

Illegal Government Surveillance

The U.S. government has been engaging in electronic surveillance of American citizens both abroad and in the country since at least 2001. Initial reports of electronic surveillance suggested that it was of communications outside the United States (although reports suggested that some of the monitoring was still of American citizens even if the communication may not have occurred in the United States). Later reports suggest that the surveillance did occur inside the United States as well. Both e-mails and phone conversations were monitored. The Bush Administration initiated the first surveillance program, working with AT&T to collect a mass of e-mails and phone logs.

The surveillance program continued into the Obama Administration, with whistleblower Edward Snowden in 2013 reporting the partnership between the National Security Agency (NSA) and Verizon to collect telecommunications data on U.S. citizens in the United States without a warrant. Snowden, who was an employee of both the NSA and Central Intelligence Agency (CIA), handed over top-secret documents detailing the surveillance program to the United Kingdom newspaper the *Guardian*. Many of these documents "confirmed longstanding suspicions that NSA's surveillance in this country is far more intrusive than we knew" (Shane & Somaiya, 2013, n.p.).

The current program, referred to as PRISM, went into effect in 2007 and includes the collection of data from such providers as Microsoft, Google, Yahoo!, Facebook, PalTalk, YouTube, Skype, AOL, and Apple. The depth of data collection is staggering. The *Washington Post* reports the type of data that can be collected includes

> audio and video chats, photographs, e-mails, documents, and connection logs. . . . [Skype] can be monitored for audio when one end of the call is a conventional telephone, and for any combination of "audio, video, chat, and file transfers" when Skype users connect by computer alone. Google's offerings include Gmail, voice and video chat, Google Drive files, photo libraries, and live surveillance of search terms. (Gellman & Poitras, 2013, n.p.)

At issue is the violation of the Fourth Amendment, which stipulates that

> the right of the people to be secure in their persons, houses, papers, and effects, against unreasonable searches and seizures, shall not be violated, and no warrants shall issue, but upon probable cause, supported by oath or affirmation, and particularly describing the place to be searched, and the persons or things to be seized.

This means that, according to the Constitution, the state should not be allowed to collect information without probable cause and a warrant describing what is, specifically, being searched for. There are several general arguments for whether or not the NSA collection of telecommunications data is a violation of the Fourth Amendment. First, some argue that it is not a violation because the Foreign Intelligence Surveillance Act (FISA) allows for electronic surveillance without a warrant when national security is an issue. However, FISA requires that the government get court approval (basically, a warrant) within 7 days. Second, some argue that it is not a violation because the information is being collected by private companies (AT&T and Verizon, for example) and not the government. But these companies are being compelled by the government to give this information over, and FISA has released these companies from liability for providing this information to the government. Finally, some just argue that the violation of the Fourth Amendment is outweighed by the greater good of searching for terrorist activity.

A second issue involving the PRISM program and potential violations of the Fourth Amendment is whether Snowden should be considered a criminal or spy (he has been charged with theft and espionage) or a whistleblower for providing the top-secret documents and exposing the PRISM program. The Whistleblower Protection Program is conducted from the United States Department of Labor and

> enforces the whistleblower provisions of more than twenty whistleblower statutes protecting employees who report violations of various workplace safety, airline, commercial motor carrier, consumer product, environmental, financial reform, food safety, health insurance reform, motor vehicle safety, nuclear, pipeline, public transportation agency, railroad, maritime, and

securities laws. Rights afforded by these whistleblower acts include, but are not limited to, worker participation in safety and health activities, reporting a work related injury, illness or fatality, or reporting a violation of the statutes. (OSHA, 2013)

However, the program does not condone or allow for the breaking of laws in order to bring this information to light, which Snowden did when he provided top-secret documents to the *Guardian* to support his allegations. Some argue that these illegal activities (considered espionage by the U.S. government) were the reason the program was uncovered, and, given that these actions uncovered other illegal activities, Snowden should not be held accountable for these actions:

> In GAP's view, Edward Snowden is a whistleblower. He disclosed information about a secret program that he reasonably believed to be illegal, and his actions alone brought about the long-overdue national debate about the proper balance between privacy and civil liberties, on the one hand, and national security on the other. Charging Snowden with espionage is yet another effort to retaliate against those who criticize the overreach of U.S. intelligence agencies under this administration. The charges send a clear message to potential whistleblowers: this is the treatment they can expect should they speak out about constitutional violations. (Government Accountability Project, 2013)

For his part, Snowden seems to believe that he will be held accountable for his actions, saying, "I understand that I will be made to suffer for my actions," but "I will be satisfied if the federation of secret law, unequal pardon and irresistible executive powers that rule the world that I love are revealed even for an instant" (Greenwald, MacAskill, & Poitras, 2013, n.p.).

Illegal Surveillance and Critical Theories

Both critical race theory/critical legal studies and peacemaking criminology can be used to examine the events surrounding PRISM and Snowden's leaking of information. Remember that critical race theory examines the use of law as a way to increase social control on certain groups—even laws that on the surface are theoretically meant to help those groups. In this instance, we might examine the language used to justify PRISM/NSA spying. On the one hand, it is a clear violation of the Fourth Amendment and introduces a level of social control on U.S. citizens in general that goes far beyond what one would expect. However, its very existence is used as a justification for keeping U.S. citizens safer in the "war on terror." U.S. citizens are asked to give up one form of safety—safety from a government that collects large amounts of information on them—in order to increase their safety from terrorist threats.

Peacemaking criminology can now add to this analysis by examining how the argument for PRISM is framed as an assault on terrorism in which personal privacy is an acceptable casualty. In addition, Peacemaking criminology can be used to examine the government reaction to Snowden. Those advocating a peacemaking perspective would argue that once Snowden uncovered PRISM that the government should have listened to the concerns of the public and at least negotiated, if not disbanded, PRISM outright because of its Fourth Amendment violations. Instead, the government has "made war" on Snowden, labelling him a traitor to the United States and charging him with espionage.

Ideas in Action: Navajo Peacemaking and Domestic Violence

One of the stark differences between critical theories and more traditional theories of deviance and crime is the strong connection between the theoretical tenets of critical theories and advocating for public policy and social change. The Navajo focus on peacemaking is an excellent example of this.

The Navajo Nation, using the philosophy of peacemaking, led an effort during the 1980s and 1990s to reform Navajo law to better support the Navajo people. These changes included the following:

- The Peacemaking Division [was] established by the Navajo Judiciary in 1982
- In the 1990s, the Navajo Supreme Court began a strong effort to promote Peacemaking, receiving a federal grant to fund the payment of Peacemaking personnel
- Eliminating fines and incarceration for over 60 offences, requiring instead that court use Peacemaking, security bonds, and/or community service
- Requiring that judges speak both Navajo and English, and have some knowledge of Navajo culture and tradition
- Navajo women having meaningful access to the political process (Coker, 2006, pp. 71–72)

Coker (2006) examines the use of peacemaking practices in offering alternatives to how battered women receive just outcomes for their abuse. She situates this peacemaking philosophy in a feminist and critical race theory understanding of both battered women's and abusers' experiences. This article offers an example of the intersections of three critical theories by showing how feminist, peacemaking, and critical race theories may come together to better inform our understanding of the experiences of battered women.

Coker (2006) argues that the feminist tradition advocates for safety and empowerment for abused individuals, as well as changes in both cultural and political conditions that support violence toward women. In addition, the critical race perspective advocates for a deeper understanding of the choices that women may make while in an abusive relationship. While conventional wisdom argues that the only way for a woman to make herself safe is to permanently leave an abusive partner, critical race scholars contend that this view does not acknowledge that for some women, the choice is not that simple. Women often resist domestic violence in a more complicated way than just "staying" or "leaving," and often separating from an abusive partner may also mean leaving behind a community and cultural resources that are needed for survival. This focus on separation as the end goal can oftentimes leave the victim worse off than if she had stayed with her abuser. The peacemaking philosophy (also known as restorative justice) can offer alternatives to separation.

The peacemaking philosophy allows battered women to experience "horizontal" justice, which is focused on the process of solving the problem—including allowing a woman (and her family members) to confront her abuser, validate her feelings, and facilitate a solution that best fits her circumstances, rather than a "vertical" justice that focuses on coercion, power, and punishment and most often does not take the wishes of the woman into account.

Coker (2006) found that the peacemaking process was a fruitful avenue for seeking justice for battered women as long as the process made safety of the women a priority and did not make forgiveness of the abuser a condition of the process.

NOW YOU . . . USE THE THEORY

Using feminist, critical race, and peacemaking theories, analyze the account below. According to the theories, what would be considered deviant in the story below? Why?

I am a middle-aged white woman from the East Coast and a town that was 99% white, who now lives in a barrio, an original neighborhood settled by Latino families residing in California for generations. The town incorporated in the early 1960s with a population of 19,000 and grew rapidly to over 80,000 by 2000. As an inland town built around agriculture, it lacks the same degree of good vibrations and laid-back atmosphere of stereotypical Southern California beach communities.

More than 75% of the households in this working-class town make less than $100,000. The Latino population is 47%, up from 38% in 2000. While the particulars of this increase are not clear, what is clear is that a large portion of that 47% live in the barrio area and have brought much to this town in terms of culture, economics, and opportunity.

Life in the barrio is richly textured. Mexican restaurants and corner stores flourish; families and friends gather in parks and yards to grill *carne asada* accompanied by *salsa fresco*. Pedestrians abound, with mothers walking their children to school, youth walking to high school, and people going to stores. There are always men and women waiting for the bus and commuter train. Many people work more than one job to make ends meet in the expensive living environment of California. Being part of this vibrant community and knowing my neighbors has made it clear that their hopes, dreams, and determination include working hard to prosper and to realize the American Dream for themselves and their families. Their hopes and dreams surely mirror immigrants who have come before.

In 2005, things began to erupt between the sheriffs and the community as three young Latino men met their death through the use of lethal force by the police. Shortly after that, in early 2006, the Minute Men descended upon the town to address what they saw as a problem with "illegals." The Minute Men continued their vigilance over the "illegal" problem, shoving cameras in people's faces, waving signs that dehumanized and criminalized immigrants, and winning over the politicians of the city and effectively diminishing the numbers of day laborers in the city.

Since that time period, law enforcement in the barrio has continued. Various strategies are used to enhance routine community patrols. These strategies include directed patrols, saturation patrols, Immigration Control and Enforcement (ICE) raids, speed traps, and sweeps of buses and transit stations. These are conducted primarily in the barrio area, with two checkpoints conducted in the parking lot of the county courthouse. In general, a checkpoint consists of pulling over about 1,000 cars, arresting several people, handing out numerous citations, and towing an average of 30 cars. In the entire year of 2008, for example, checkpoints garnered over 200 citations, 155 cars were impounded, and 15 were arrested for DUI. Unlicensed drivers, including immigrants without documents and cars that are not registered or insured, are impounded for 30 days. This results in approximately $1,500 fees for towing and storage. Unable to pay the impound fees, many people lose their cars.

When there are heavy patrols and checkpoints, the usually active sidewalks and stores of the city are empty. It does not take much to recognize when these are happening as there are always several black and whites in a very small area, about a square mile, for hours. I have had comments from visitors who witness this and ask about it. When I tell them about these activities, they always look in disbelief.

While these activities have become routine, their impact remains disturbing. It is never routine to see people walking away from cars that will be towed, carrying their belongings, groceries, children, and car seats. It is disheartening to see people who are simply living their lives—coming home from work, going to work, going to the doctors, delivering children to school and picking them up. It is difficult to know that parents are deported and their children left with family, friends, or to fend for themselves.

There is a weariness that comes with this much law enforcement and a great sadness to see people criminalized and treated in this manner. It has also created in me a distrust of law enforcement, in those who should be trusted to protect the community. Ultimately, given the increase in the size of the prison-industrial complex of this country, it begs the question of how things will be in the future if law enforcement strategies continue in this trajectory, meaning to target large groups and populations instead of individuals. Living in the barrio has created the realization of the mutuality of freedom—that individual freedom is dependent on and relative to the freedom of all people.

By Mary Jo Poole, January 16, 2011

Conclusion

Much of the deviance research that exists makes fairly traditional assumptions about how we define deviance. From a traditional perspective, these definitions tend to favor whites, men, and the middle and upper classes. In other words, these groups end up defining what is considered acceptable or deviant behavior. The theories presented in this chapter question the status quo and offer a nontraditional definition of acceptable behavior. What this means is that our taken-for-granted assumptions about deviance are questioned and expanded, allowing for more diversity in our understanding of deviant behavior. Not only do these perspectives give voice to individuals who may be considered deviant but they also question the very makeup of society as we know it, suggesting that war-like, patriarchal, racist systems of oppression are what are truly deviant.

EXERCISES AND DISCUSSION QUESTIONS

1. Compare the experience of Muslim Americans after 9/11 with the experience of whites in America after Timothy McVeigh was captured for committing the Oklahoma City bombing in 1995. How would peacemaking criminology and critical race theory explain these different experiences?

2. Choose another structural deviance (such as homelessness) and evaluate it using peacemaking, feminist, and critical race theories. What would each theory offer as a public policy to address this deviance?

KEY TERMS

Critical race theory

Feminist criminology

Liberal feminism

Peacemaking criminology

Postmodern feminism

Radical feminism

Socialist feminism

CHAPTER 11

Social Control of Deviance

I will always be a felon . . . a felon is a term here, obviously it's not a bad term . . . for me to leave here, it will affect my job, it will affect my education . . . custody, it can affect child support, it can affect everywhere—family, friends, housing. . . . People that are convicted of drug crimes can't even get housing anymore. . . . Yes, I did my prison time. How long are you going to punish me as a result of it? And not only on paper, I'm only on paper for ten months when I leave here, that's all the parole I have. But that parole isn't going to be anything. It's the housing, it's the credit re-establishing . . . I mean even to go into the school to work with my child's class—and I'm not even a sex offender—but all I need is one parent who says, "Isn't she a felon? I don't want her with my child." Bingo. And you know that there are people out there like that.

—"Karen," discussing how being labeled a felon will affect virtually every area of her life, from Manza and Uggen, *Locked Out* (2006), p. 152. Copyright ©2006 by Oxford University Press, Inc.

◈ Introduction

The comments above illustrate some of the long-term effects that involvement in deviance can have on individuals, families, and communities. While much of this book so far has focused on different *causes* of deviant behavior, this chapter focuses on societal reactions to deviance and will look in more detail at a few of the varied forms that social control may take. We focused on these ideas a bit in Chapter 8, when looking at labeling theory, but here we offer ideas and examples from different contexts and reiterate the real and lasting consequences of social control.

Philosophers have suggested that human societies are possible because of the social contract; the idea is that individuals give up some personal freedoms and abide by general rules of conduct to live in a community and enjoy the protection and companionship of the group (Rousseau, 1987). If most in the group live by the social contract, what is to be done when an individual breaks the contract? How should the community or larger society react to the breach? Should the individual be punished? Once punished, should members of the community be responsible to help the offender reintegrate back into the community?

There are many different forms of social control. One basic distinction is between formal and informal controls. Formal social controls would include hospitalization in a mental ward or rehabilitation facility, expulsion from school, and all types of processing by the criminal justice system, including probation, parole, imprisonment, and fines. Informal controls are often just as powerful, but they are implemented by those around you—your family members, your church, or your peers. If you have ever been given the silent treatment or felt your parents' disappointment, you have experienced informal social control.

As suggested by the critical theorists in Chapter 10, social control and sanctions for deviant behavior are not meted out equally. Recent studies have made clear that the U.S. criminal justice system and particularly our reliance on mass incarceration disproportionately affect minorities and the poor and have long-lasting impact on the life chances and opportunities available to individuals, families, and whole communities (Haney, 2010; Pager, 2007; Tonry, 2011; Waquant, 2000).

◈ Medicalization of Deviant Behavior

We don't always think of medicine as an institution of social control, but just as legal definitions turn some acts into crimes, medical definitions are important in societal conceptions of what is deemed deviant and how such behavior should be managed. Medicalization is "a process by which nonmedical problems become defined and treated as medical problems, usually in terms of illnesses or disorders" (Conrad, 1992, p. 209). There are many examples of medicalized deviant behavior, including mental illness, hyperactivity in children, alcoholism, eating disorders, compulsive gambling, and addiction. It is important to remember that these are social constructions of deviance, and our definitions can and do change over time and vary across cultures.

Medical diagnoses of deviant behavior can have an enormous impact on individuals and communities. Daphne Scholinski's (1997) memoir, *The Last Time I Wore a Dress,* offers an individual perspective on what it is like to spend one's adolescent years in a series of mental hospitals. As a troubled teenage girl, Scholinski was diagnosed with gender identity disorder, which her doctor believed she had developed around the third grade: "He said what this means is you are not an appropriate female, you don't act the way a female is supposed to act" (p. 16).

Scholinski was 14 years old when she was admitted to her first mental hospital; she was released just after her 18th birthday, when her insurance and ability to pay for the treatment ran out. Looking back on the experience, she writes, "One million dollars my treatment cost. Insurance money, but still. Three years in three mental hospitals for girly lessons" (Scholinski, 1997, p. xi). While she was generally happy to be released from her last institution, she occasionally had doubts about her ability to survive and succeed in the community: "Sometimes I wish I could return to the hospital. It's ridiculous, I know. But it's hard to figure out everything on my own. In the hospitals, I lost my ability to trust myself" (p. 196). The medicalized diagnosis and treatment of her behavior had undermined her sense of self-efficacy.

Medicalization can take many forms; on the extreme end, individuals can be institutionalized in mental hospitals and/or heavily medicated. They can also be compelled to enter counseling or to join self-help groups; once they admit they have a problem, they can begin working toward a "cure."

A recent article in a Florida newspaper (Laforgia, 2011) investigated the heavy doses of powerful drugs administered to children in state-operated jails and residential programs. These children were given a lot of antipsychotic medications, which temporarily control behavior but do little to provide meaningful treatment for incarcerated youth. These drugs can also cause suicidal thoughts and harmful side effects. The reporter writes,

> Overall, in 24 months, the department [Florida's Department of Juvenile Justice] bought 326,081 tablets of Seroquel, Abilify, Risperdal and other antipsychotic drugs for use in state-operated jails and homes for children. . . . That's enough to hand out 446 pills a day, seven days a week, for two years in a row, to kids in jails and programs that can hold no more than 2,300 boys and girls on a given day.

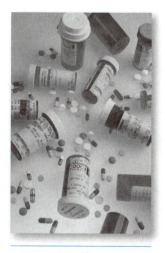

▲ **Photo 11.1** The medicalization of social control can include compelling individuals to take heavy doses of prescription drugs.

Source: ©Comstock/Thinkstock.

The changing definitions of deviance can clearly be seen in the field of medicalization. As Conrad (1992) explains, "A key aspect of medicalization refers to the emergence of medical definitions for previously nonmedical problems" (p. 223). While new categories of deviance emerge through medicalization, the process can also work in the opposite direction: Behaviors previously thought to be deviant can be *demedicalized*. Demedicalization refers to the process where problems or behaviors no longer retain medical definitions. A vivid example of demedicalization is homosexuality; if you read early textbooks on deviant behavior, you will often see homosexuality included as deviant behavior in need of treatment. Our conceptions of homosexuality changed in American society in the 1970s to the point that it is no longer defined as an illness (Conrad, 1992).

We hope that you can see that while it is often less blatant than the social control practiced by criminal justice agencies, the medicalization of deviance has a profound effect on individuals and communities. We now turn to a discussion of social control and surveillance by the criminal justice system.

◈ Policing, Supervision, and the Impact of Incarceration on Disadvantaged Populations and Communities

Two recent studies offer compelling insight into the way that poor and disadvantaged populations and communities are supervised and controlled. In their book *Banished,* Beckett and Herbert (2010) discuss how city laws and ordinances are used to control where and how populations can congregate. Using Seattle as a case study, they describe how individuals—often poor or homeless—may be arrested and then subsequently prohibited from entering or occupying areas associated with drug dealing or prostitution. Beckett and Herbert view banishment as "an emerging and consequential social control practice . . . banishment is consequential, even more so than the civility codes that they increasingly supplant. Not only do these new tools enable banishment, they provide the police greater license to question and to arrest those who occupy public space" (p. 16).

In an ethnographic study of young African American men in Philadelphia, Alice Goffman (2009) shows how police surveillance, outstanding arrest warrants, and the status of being on probation can affect every part of "wanted" young men's lives. Among the vivid descriptions of the impact of such surveillance is the story of a young man who went to the hospital for the birth of his baby and was arrested there on an outstanding warrant. The risk of being captured makes young men such as this afraid to go to hospitals or other social service agencies; it compels them to keep moving and to stay "on the run" rather than find stable housing.

Goffman (2009) explains the different ways these young men find to resist the formal social control of the state, but despite this, the constant threat and surveillance deeply affects their lives. Their partners are often frustrated by the lack of stability but at times also find they can control a particular young man by threatening to call the police on him. She explains why this population faces unique challenges in maintaining conforming relationships:

▲ **Photo 11.2**   Alice Goffman's research offers a look into the lives of "wanted" young men—those who are on probation or have warrants out for their arrest. Resisting the formal social control of the state often keeps them on the run.

Source: ©Can Stock Photo Inc. / oscarcwilliams.

> Young men who are wanted by the police find that activities, relations, and localities that others rely on to maintain a decent and respectable identity are transformed into a system that the authorities make use of to arrest and confine them. The police and the courts become dangerous to interact with, as does showing up to work or going to places like hospitals. Instead of a safe place to sleep, eat, and find acceptance and support, mothers' homes are transformed into a "last known address," one of the first places the police will look for them. Close relatives, friends, and neighbors become potential informants. (Goffman, 2009, p. 353)

Todd Clear (2007) focuses on communities burdened by high incarceration rates, describing certain disadvantaged neighborhoods as "prison places." He explains the impact of unstable, imprisoned populations as they contribute to social disorganization (the theory described in Chapter 5) in the larger communities:

> Incarceration can operate as a kind of "coercive mobility," destabilizing neighborhoods by increasing levels of disorganization, first when a person is removed to go to prison, then later when that person reenters the community. In high-incarceration neighborhoods, the processes of incarceration and reentry create an environment where a significant portion of residents are constantly in flux. (p. 73)

Clear (2007) argues that these prison places suffer distinct disadvantages and that the effect of incarceration is felt far beyond the lives of the individual inmates: "The concentration of imprisonment of young men from disadvantaged places has grown to such a point that it is now a bedrock experience, a force that affects families and children, institutions and businesses, social groups and interpersonal relations" (p. 3).

DEVIANCE IN POPULAR CULTURE

There are many representations of institutions of social control in popular culture. In the chapter on labeling theory, we recommended the films *One Flew Over the Cuckoo's Nest* and *Girl, Interrupted*. While those films are good examples for labeling, they also show the role of mental hospitals as formal institutions for social control. Prisons are another popular setting for films and television documentaries; watch one or more of the following to get an inside glimpse at social control of deviance:

The Shawshank Redemption—a classic prison film that tells the fictional story of how an innocent man survives decades in prison. In the character of Brooks, we see a clear example of how a man can be "institutionalized" after living the majority of his adult life in prison—when he is finally paroled, how will he adapt? If you have not seen *The Shawshank Redemption*, it is definitely worth your time.

Girlhood—a documentary featuring Shanae and Megan, two teenage girls with troubled histories who have committed violent crimes. The filmmaker met them while they were incarcerated in the Waxter Juvenile Facility in Baltimore and follows them both in the facility and when they are released and reunited with their mothers. By focusing on these two young women, this documentary gives human faces to larger issues of abuse, neglect, and social control.

Lockup—an MSNBC series that travels the country to take viewers inside a wide range of prisons, jails, and juvenile facilities. By watching several episodes, you can begin to get a sense of the similarities these total institutions share, as well as the differences in how inmates are treated.

Little Children—this fictional film is about life in the suburbs and includes a plotline about a convicted (and registered) sex offender who has just returned from prison to live with his mother. The community's nearly hysterical reaction to his presence among them provides a memorable example of both informal and formal social control.

Total Institutions

Perhaps the most severe form of social control (other than the death penalty) is institutionalization in a prison, jail, juvenile correctional facility, or mental hospital. Sociologist Erving Goffman (1961) characterized such facilities as total institutions; he explained the defining characteristics of total institutions as follows:

A basic social arrangement in modern society is that the individual tends to sleep, play, and work in different places, with different co-participants, under different authorities, and without an over-all rational plan. The central feature of total institutions can be described as a breakdown of the barriers ordinarily separating these three spheres of life. First, all aspects of life are conducted in the same place and under the same single authority. Second, each phase of the member's daily activity is carried on in the immediate company of a large batch of others, all of whom are treated alike and required to do the same thing together. Third, all phases of the day's activities are tightly scheduled, with one activity leading at a prearranged time into the next, the whole system of activities being imposed from above by a system of explicit formal rulings and a body of officials. Finally, the various enforced activities are brought together into a single, rational plan purportedly designed to fulfill the official aims of the institution. (pp. 5–6)

As described, total institutions include prisons, jails, juvenile correctional facilities, mental hospitals, rehabilitation facilities, nursing homes, boarding schools, army barracks, monasteries, and convents. While some total institutions are entered into voluntarily, others—including prisons and secure hospitals—represent society's strongest reaction or sanction to deviant behavior. If you take the time to watch films such as *One Flew Over the Cuckoo's Nest* or *Girl, Interrupted,* you can get a small sense of what it might feel like to be deemed mentally ill and a threat to yourself and/or the larger society.

Once confined in a total institution, it can be extremely difficult to make the transition back into the community. After spending months and years in the relative isolation of a prison, mental hospital, or other total institution, individuals may become institutionalized (or "prisonized" as Clemmer [1940/1958] so aptly phrased it) to at least some extent. They may become so used to the structure and routine of the facility that they lose the confidence and capability to exist independently in the outside world.

◈ Correctional Facilities and the Purposes of Punishment

While this book is not about the criminal justice system, it is useful to at least briefly examine the different rationales for formal social control and punishment. Criminologists generally differentiate between several philosophies or purposes of punishment; by understanding the purpose, we can often make better sense of why the particular sanctions are used. Hagan (1985, pp. 288–289) offers seven purposes of criminal sanctions: (1) restraint or incapacitation, (2) individual or specific deterrence, (3) general deterrence, (4) reform or rehabilitation, (5) moral affirmation or symbolism, (6) retribution, and (7) restitution or compensation.

Correctional facilities reside near the deep end of social control and are used primarily for incapacitation—to hold offenders in a contained space away from the rest of society. Punishing those individuals who act outside of the accepted range of behavior also serves the function of moral affirmation or symbolism; when an offender is caught and sanctioned, the boundaries of the community are clearly tested, set, and reaffirmed (Erikson, 1966). If individuals find the reality of incapacitation unpleasant enough, they may be prevented from committing further deviant acts; this is the idea behind specific deterrence. If punishing one individual harshly enough keeps others from committing similar crimes, general deterrence has

▲ Photo 11.3 Incarceration in a prison or other correctional facility is one of the most severe forms of social control. How do you think years of living in cells such as these affects the individuals?

Source: ©Getty Images/Thinkstock.

been achieved. Retribution is punishment as a form of payment for the harm done; this view is best represented in the expressions "an eye for an eye" or "a life for a life." Restitution is repayment for damage or harm, and rehabilitation generally involves an effort to treat the offender in order to make him or her more capable of living as a conforming citizen.

Gresham Sykes and the Pains of Imprisonment

In the *Society of Captives,* a classic work on life inside a maximum-security prison, Gresham Sykes (1958) offers a sociological view of prison culture and how time spent in prison affects both inmates and staff. He outlines five central **pains of imprisonment**, highlighting the fact that the costs of confinement are both physical and psychological. The pains of imprisonment are described as follows:

▲ **Photo 11.4**   Gresham Sykes writes about the pains of imprisonment; which do you think would be hardest to adapt to?

Source: ©Louoates/iStockphoto.

Deprivation of liberty—confined to the claustrophobic world of the prison, the isolation cuts deep: "The mere fact that the individual's movements are restricted, however, is far less serious than the fact that imprisonment means that the inmate is cut off from family, relatives, and friends, not in the self-isolation of the hermit or the misanthrope, but in the involuntary seclusion of the out-law . . . what makes this pain of imprisonment bite most deeply is the fact that the confinement of the criminal represents a deliberate, moral rejection of the criminal by the free community" (p. 65).

Deprivation of goods and services—inmates are without most of their personal possessions; "The inmate population defines its present material impoverishment as a painful loss" (p. 68).

Deprivation of heterosexual relationships—in male prisons, the inmate is "figuratively castrated by his involuntary celibacy" (p. 70). Sykes makes clear that living with only members of your own sex can be damaging to inmates' self-image and identity.

Deprivation of autonomy—every significant movement an inmate makes is controlled by others; inmates must abide by others' decisions and submit with enforced respect and deference. Treating adult offenders in this way may make the inmates feel like helpless children.

Deprivation of security—Sykes quotes an inmate: "The worst thing about prison is you have to live with other prisoners" (p. 77). Individual inmates are likely to be tested by other inmates and may have to engage in physical fights for their own safety, sanity, and possessions.

Juvenile Correctional Facilities

Juvenile correctional facilities—often called training schools or reform schools—are quite similar to adult prisons. After committing a crime and being adjudicated delinquent or convicted of the offense, the youth are sentenced to confinement. Incarcerated youth experience the same pains of imprisonment as their adult counterparts, but juvenile institutions generally have more of a focus on rehabilitation so

RECENT STUDY IN DEVIANCE

Values, Rules, and Keeping the Peace:
How Men Describe Order and the Inmate Code in California Prisons

By Rebecca Trammell, 2009, in *Deviant Behavior, 30,* 746–771.

Trammell (2009) interviews former male inmates of California prisons to examine how and why some inmates follow the inmate code. There is some controversy about the existence of an inmate code, with some arguing that it doesn't exist (instead inmates bring their code of the street to their experiences in prison) and others arguing the code is no more than the norms in a prison. However, some argue that a clear-cut code in prison helps to organize the structure and relations of prison life.

To address these various definitions of an inmate code, Trammell (2009) examines how inmates describe the informal rules of the prison and how the inmate code may or may not fit these rules. She interviewed 40 former inmates of California prisons and six correctional officers. Focusing specifically on the connections between the informal rules, underground economy of the prison, and the inmate code, Trammell found that the inmate code may have changed since it was first examined in the 1950s (Trammell was not comparing the two eras but instead notes that early research on the inmate code suggested that inmates used the code to defy the goals of prison staff). She argues that today the code is used to keep the peace, which benefits the underground economies that have emerged over time in the prison system.

Trammell (2009) found that both those within and outside gangs knew of and followed a code while in prison—if the code was followed, inmates reported having an easier time than if they did not follow the code:

> I didn't know shit going into prison. I was totally clueless. I was strung out on drugs, sick and dumb and the brothers tell me right off the bat where to go, what to do. I thought they were joking at first. I knew prison was hard but I never thought I would have to know the rules about who uses the shower first and who sits with who and who the leaders are. I think that's why there are fights, the dumb guys don't know the code going in and they screw up (Mac). (p. 756)

Finally, according to Trammell, the code seems to have changed with the recent mass incarceration—the code is used less to defy prison authority and more to keep peace and the underground economy (mostly the sale of drugs) operating.

there is more emphasis on education and programming (such as therapy groups for anger management, victim empathy, or drug and alcohol issues).

Juvenile correctional facilities are the last stop and are often the last chance in the juvenile justice system for delinquent youth. If a youth commits another offense after being released from a juvenile facility, he or she often faces adult prison, punishment, and a permanent criminal record.

Historically, juvenile facilities were used as a sort of catch-all for troubled youth, housing serious delinquents alongside status offenders (whose acts would not be crimes if they were committed by adults) and dependent and neglected children who needed help in meeting their basic needs. While grouping these children and adolescents all in one place made basic supervision and care possible, it also caused many problems as younger and weaker children were victimized by peers and staff members (Bartollas, Miller, & Dinitz, 1976; Feld, 1977), and all were branded with a delinquent label once they returned to the community.

In the 1970s, the ideas of labeling theory were taken seriously, and states were encouraged to deinstitutionalize status offenders and noncriminal youth. Juvenile correctional facilities now generally house the most serious delinquents in the state. While this once seemed like a harsh placement—particularly when compared to community options such as group homes or foster care—the comparison has now shifted. Youth incarcerated in juvenile facilities may be the lucky ones, especially when compared to youth tried and convicted as adults who will spend a significant portion of their lives in adult prisons.

The push and pull between punishment and treatment can be clearly viewed in juvenile correctional facilities as states struggle with trying to balance public fear and possibilities for rehabilitating wayward youth. The lessons juvenile correctional facilities intend to teach and those that young men and women in confinement actually learn while serving their sentences can be quite different (Inderbitzin, 2006). Knowing that nearly all juvenile offenders will return to the community within months or years, it is worth exploring what they are actually learning while they are incarcerated and thinking about what skills and coping mechanisms we would like them to gain before emerging from the institution.

◈ Reentry—Challenges in Returning to the Community After Time in an Institution

Reentering society after time spent in any total institution is a shock to the system and requires adjustment by the individual, his or her family, and the larger community. As the statement that opened this chapter clearly shows, individuals with a felony record face an especially difficult time in coping with the stigma of their conviction and trying to overcome the numerous obstacles felons must overcome in building new lives.

These problems are shared by an ever-increasing segment of the population. Figure 11.1 shows the growth of adult correctional populations over three decades; the numbers of people in prison and on probation are striking. If state laws and community practices close doors and take away opportunities for the millions of individuals involved with the criminal justice system, what message of social control are we sending? How should we expect these individuals to respond?

Prisoner reentry is a delicate process. While the many challenges faced by former inmates in rebuilding their lives are relatively clear, Maruna (2011) takes a wider view and describes the challenge to the larger society: "Like the commission of a crime, the reintegration of the former outcast back into society represents a challenge to the moral order, a delicate transition fraught with danger and possibility" (p. 3).

For those who have been formally convicted of a crime, the repercussions can last a lifetime. The stigma of a felony conviction may lead to a "closing of doors" (Sampson & Laub, 1993, p. 124), negatively affecting employment opportunities, educational funding, housing, and the ability to vote

Figure 11.1 Adult Correctional Populations, 1980–2009

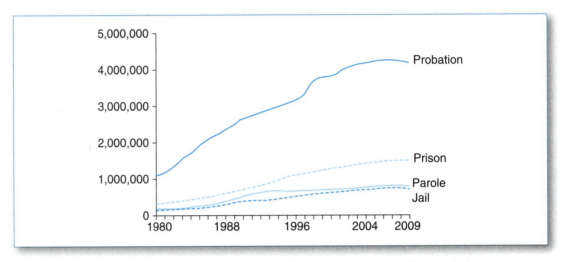

Source: Bureau of Justice Statistics Correctional Surveys. Retrieved from http://bjs.ojp.usdoj.gov/content/glance/corr2.cfm

alongside fellow community members. Marc Mauer (2005) provides a clear illustration of the potential collateral consequences of imprisonment for a felony conviction:

> An 18-year-old with a first-time felony conviction for drug possession now may be barred from receiving welfare for life, prohibited from living in public housing, denied student loans to attend college, permanently excluded from voting, and if not a citizen, be deported. (p. 610)

To better understand how felony convictions interact with race and affect the search for employment, Devah Pager (2007) designed an experimental study in which she sent out young men with matched credentials and fictional criminal records to apply for various entry-level jobs. While employers were generally reluctant to hire any ex-offenders, Pager and Quillian (2005) found that black ex-offenders were much less likely to be offered a job and a second chance than their white counterparts. Pager and Quillian's study is a strong example of using experimental methods to learn more about the obstacles convicted offenders face; the fact that African American males were given significantly fewer opportunities clearly shows how race and a criminal label interact to close doors and diminish individuals' life chances.

Felon Disenfranchisement

As we have illustrated, felony convictions and the stigma of incarceration limit individuals' opportunities for employment and housing. A more formal consequence of a felony conviction is "civil death," or the loss of the right to vote in local and national elections. Felon disenfranchisement varies by state, but most states have at least some limits in place whereby those who have committed felony offenses lose the right to participate in democratic elections. In most states, currently incarcerated felons are not allowed to vote from prison or jail. States are split as to whether parolees and probationers living in the community are allowed to vote, and some states ban ex-felons from ever voting again. For the most updated and comprehensive overview of felon voting rights, check out the Web site of The Sentencing Project (www.sentencingproject.org), which includes an interactive map with information available for every state.

Christopher Uggen and Jeff Manza have spent the past decade studying felon disenfranchisement, estimating the scope and number of individuals affected, as well as the impact on communities and elections. Uggen, Manza, and Thompson (2006, p. 283) further estimate that there now exists a "felon class" of more than 16 million felons and ex-felons in the United States; these individuals represent 7.5% of the adult population, 22.3% of the black adult population, and 33.4% of the black adult male population. In other words, a full one-third of African American men in the United States have serious criminal records and have their rights restricted, even though they have "paid their debt to society." In interviews with incarcerated felons and ex-felons, Manza and Uggen (2006) found that the right to vote did indeed matter to the individuals affected; their interviewees felt the sting of being classified as "less than the average citizen" (p. 155) even as they were still expected to pay taxes and work in the communities that denied them a voice.

Public Fear and Social Control: The Case of Sex Offenders

The social control of sex offenders offers an extreme example of public fear and widespread panic over a particular offense and group. Despite relatively low recidivism rates, sex offenders are arguably the most feared and demonized of all criminals. All 50 states have adopted sex offender registration and notification laws, and more than 20 states allow involuntary civil commitment of sexual predators, whereby sex offenders can be held indefinitely, even after completing their criminal justice sentences (Harris & Lurigio, 2010).

Online registries and mandatory registration make it easy for community members to learn about convicted sex offenders living—or attempting to find housing—in their midst. It opens the possibility for harassment of the offenders and, in extreme cases, murder by overzealous vigilantes. Local residency laws severely restrict where sex offenders may live, stipulating, for example, that they must stay 2,500 feet away from schools, parks, and playgrounds. A story in *Newsweek* highlights the desperate circumstances sex offenders may face under such restrictions:

> The impact on the offenders was severe. Entire cities were suddenly off limits to them. They became pariahs, confined to remote and shrinking slivers of land. The most egregious example is a colony of predators camped out under the Julia Tuttle Causeway, which spans Miami's Biscayne Bay—a place so surreal and outlandish that it has become a lightning rod in the debate over America's treatment of sex offenders. . . .
>
> At the Julia Tuttle camp, the sex offenders begin trickling in around dusk. It is a squalid and dreary place. The air is thick and stifling, reeking of human feces and of cat urine from all the strays that live there. Overhead, the bridge drones and trembles with six lanes of traffic. Makeshift dwellings sprawl out in every direction—tents clinging to concrete pylons, rickety shacks fashioned out of plywood, a camper shell infested with cockroaches. There is

no running water or sewage system; inhabitants relieve themselves in shopping bags and toss the sacks into a pile of refuse that they burn periodically. Some men fish along the shoreline, then gut and fry up the catch for anyone who's hungry. For diversion, there's a nightly dominoes game, or perhaps a bottle of booze sipped in solitude.

The three-year-old settlement now numbers more than 70 people, including an 83-year-old deaf man, a wheelchair-bound fellow, and one woman. Some have lived there so long that their driver's licenses list their addresses as "Julia Tuttle Causeway Bridge." (Skipp, 2009)

Clearly, as a society, we must learn to balance public fear and public safety with individual rights. Have individuals forfeited their rights forever once they are convicted of a crime? Or should those rights (and opportunities) be restored once they have served their mandated sentences? Are redemption and reintegration possible? These are complicated questions that we must continue to grapple with and explore. As Maruna (2011) explains,

Criminal sanctions, for the most part, end very badly. Indeed, by most accounts, they do not end at all. Except for a very fortunate few who have their offenses formally forgiven through pardons or other legal means, individuals with felony records can remain permanently stigmatized, excluded from employment, educational and social opportunities, on the grounds of something they did many years or decades earlier. (p. 5)

◈ Collateral Consequences—Effects on Communities and Families

If prisons affected no one except the criminals on the inside, they would matter less. But, after thirty years of penal population growth, the impact of America's prisons extends far beyond their walls. By zealously punishing lawbreakers—including a large new class of nonviolent drug offenders—the criminal justice system at the end of the 1990s drew into its orbit families and whole communities. These most fragile families and neighborhoods were the least equipped to counter any shocks or additional deprivations. (Western, 2006, p. 11)

Just as police surveillance and supervision is concentrated among poor and dominantly minority neighborhoods, incarceration is concentrated among poor, often minority men and women from disorganized areas. This affects not only the imprisoned individuals but also their family members and the larger community. Todd Clear (2007) explains the impact:

The way these young people cycle through our system of prisons and jails, then back into the community, leaves considerable collateral damage in its wake. Families are disrupted, social networks and other forms of social support are weakened, health is endangered, labor markets are thinned, and—more important than anything else—children are put at risk of the depleted human and social capital that promotes delinquency. After a certain point, the collateral effects of these high rates of incarceration seem to contribute to more crime in these places. (p. 175)

On any given day, approximately 1.5 million children have a parent serving time in a state or federal prison (Mumola, 2000). Mass incarceration in the United States affects literally millions of family members who come into prisons to visit their loved ones even as they deal with depleted resources and troubled surroundings at home.

Meagan Comfort (2003, 2008) describes the "secondary prisonization" women experience in "the tube," or the visitor waiting area at San Quentin. She calculated that approximately 95% of the visitors to the men's prison were women, and, even though they were legally innocent of any crimes, they were subject to marginalization and their own pains of imprisonment due to their extended contact with the correctional facility. Comfort offers a detailed description of the rules and dress code of the prison, the women who arrive hours in advance and then wait patiently or resentfully to be allowed into the visiting room to see their loved ones, and the humiliating treatment these women often receive at the hands of correctional officers processing them into and out of the institution. While inmates experience the pains of imprisonment, Comfort makes clear that their visitors also suffer from the contaminative contact of the prison.

In another article, Comfort (2002) explores how these women work to prevent the institutionalization of their loved ones while they are in the prison. Comfort explains that the visitors move important life and family events into the prison's visiting room so that the fathers/boyfriends/husbands can maintain involvement and strengthen family ties. San Quentin allows family visits where inmates and their guests can spend nearly 2 days together in bungalows on the prison grounds. The women dip into their savings and plan carefully to purchase the approved ingredients to make memorable meals for their partners, who can in that moment escape prison food if not prison supervision.

In addition to intimate visits and special meals and celebrations in the prison visiting room, Comfort also describes weddings held within the prison (2002, 2008), happy days for the brides despite the bleak setting. She suggests that the women involved with inmates essentially fight for the sanity and souls of their men by reminding them of their families and their humanity: "Wives, fiancées, and girlfriends of inmates strive to bridge the distance between the outside world and their loved one: unable to bring him home, they bring home to him through the relocation of intimate activities inside the penitentiary walls" (Comfort, 2002, p. 492).

 Explaining Deviance in the Streets and Deviance in the Suites: Considering How Money Can Matter in Local Jails

In some states and under some circumstances, money can help ease the pain if you are facing a jail sentence. In California, the Fremont detention center near San Francisco acts as a pay-to-stay prison, allowing healthy, nonviolent offenders without gang affiliation to stay in one of Fremont's cells for $155 per night and a one-time $45 fee. The detention center, which is rarely full, can make over $140 per night in profit from such stays (Watson, 2013). Fremont officials claim that it is just a jail with no special treatment or benefits; their residents get the same food, blankets, and amenities as those at other jails. The main advantage is that Fremont it is a smaller, quieter facility and its detainees will not have to interact with the full population of the county jail.

In 2007, the *New York Times* reported on pay-to-stay jails:

For roughly $75 to $127 a day, these convicts—who are known in the self-pay parlance as "clients"—get a small cell behind a regular door, distance of some amplitude from violent offenders and, in some cases, the right to bring an iPod or computer on which to compose a novel, or perhaps a song.

> Many of the overnighters are granted work furlough, enabling them to do most of their time on the job, returning to the jail simply to go to bed (often following a strip search, which granted is not so five-star).
>
> The clients usually share a cell, but otherwise mix little with the ordinary nonpaying inmates, who tend to be people arrested and awaiting arraignment, or federal prisoners on trial or awaiting deportation and simply passing through. (Steinhauer, 2007)

By contrast, today's jails and prisons are also serving as the new asylums for the country's mentally ill who cannot afford treatment, medication, private hospitals, and much-needed psychiatric care (Fields & Phillips, 2013). The National Institute of Health estimates that one in four American adults suffers from a diagnosable mental illness in any given year (www.nimh.nih.gov), but that nearly two-thirds of inmates in local jails were diagnosed or treated for mental health problems. Many mentally ill inmates commit minor crimes that land them in jail for brief sentences. While in the facility they may be diagnosed, treated, and given a small supply of medication upon their release. The medication often runs out before they can get treatment in the community, and many end up back in jail in a continuing cycle. The *Wall Street Journal* illustrated the beginning of this pattern with the story of Steven Dorsey:

> Mr. Dorsey, 48, was a part-time worker at a janitorial supply company, but his hours had dried up in recent months, and he lost his job. Mr. Dorsey, who said he had been diagnosed as bipolar and schizophrenic, had felt lucky to be placed in a group home. He had to leave, though, after Medicaid turned him down for benefits, he said.
>
> He ended up living on the streets, occasionally scrounging in dumpsters for food scraps. . . .
>
> "I didn't have a way of eating or sleeping," says Mr. Dorsey. Voices told him to "steal what you need." He ended up in jail after allegedly lifting a sandwich and a toothbrush from a convenience store. A sheriff's spokesman said he was charged with retail theft under $300. (Fields & Phillips, 2013)

A *Frontline* documentary called "The Released" (http://www.pbs.org/wgbh/pages/frontline/released/) offers a vivid and disturbing look into the lives of men who suffer from serious mental illness and find themselves in and out of jail. In jail, these men are medicated and often get their symptoms under control; they may feel like they are again capable of living in the community. But, once they are released, they have a limited supply of medication and many of them struggle to find housing and stability. Once the medication runs out, they are frequently rearrested and brought to jail for new crimes.

So here we see again how social class and privilege matter in one's treatment in our communities and criminal justice system. If you are fortunate enough to be able to afford psychiatric treatment and proper medication, you are much less likely to end up in jail in the first place. If, however, jail is unavoidable, you may be able to pay your way into a nicer facility and serve your time as pleasantly as possible.

◈ Ideas in Action: College Programs in Prisons

While social control of deviance is often about sanctions and punishment, social control in its many forms can also be focused on prevention of future deviant and criminal acts and the rehabilitation of offenders. College programs in prison are an excellent example of rehabilitative programming in a secure facility. Education has long been shown to be one of the most effective correctional interventions to decrease recidivism. The largest ever meta-analysis of studies of correctional education showed that prisoners who participated in correctional education programs had 43% lower odds of returning to prison than inmates who did not. The study also found that prison education programs are cost effective, suggesting that a $1 investment in prison education can reduce incarceration costs by $4 to $5 during the first three years after release, which is when those leaving prison are most likely to return (Davis, Bozick, Steele, Saunders, & Miles, 2013).

Even when convicted offenders are incarcerated and incapacitated for the duration of their sentences, they may still be able to learn new skills and to find new direction for their lives. College programs operating within correctional facilities generally receive no public funding and are made possible through private grants, individual sponsorship, and hours donated by faculty and volunteers around the country. Below we offer examples of several of the most successful college prison programs operating in the United States.

The *Bard Prison Initiative* (http://bpi.bard.edu/) is a division of Bard College that offers incarcerated men and women the chance to enroll in academic programs and earn degrees from Bard College. The program offers a liberal arts curriculum, and incarcerated students are held to the exact same standards as undergraduates on campus. The BPI Web site explains its success and its goals:

> As the largest program of its kind in the United States, BPI enrolls 250 incarcerated men and women across a full spectrum of academic disciplines, and offers over 60 courses each semester. By 2013, Bard granted nearly 275 degrees to BPI participants and enrolled a total of nearly 550 students. . . . With the help of a significant private grant, the Consortium for the Liberal Arts in Prison was created to support other innovative college-in-prison programs throughout the country. Wesleyan University in Connecticut, Grinnell College in Iowa, Goucher College in Maryland, and the University of Notre Dame and Holy Cross College in Indiana have now established programs, and the Consortium plans to establish programs in as many as ten more states within the next five years. (http://bpi.bard.edu/what-we-do/)

The *Prison University Project* (http://www.prisonuniversityproject.org/about-us) was formed to support the College Program at San Quentin. Currently, more than 20 college courses are offered each semester in San Quentin, and more than 300 students are enrolled. All faculty working in the program are volunteers, and there are more than 100 faculty, teaching assistants, and tutors guiding classes and studies in the prison.

The *Bedford Hills College Program* (http://www.mmm.edu/study/resources/academicachievement/bhcp.html) at Marymount Manhattan College offers courses leading to an Associate of Arts degree in social science and a Bachelor of Arts degree in sociology at the Bedford Hills Correctional Facility, a New York State maximum-security prison for women. In a unique twist, the Bedford Hills College Program is now an extension campus of Marymount Manhattan College; students in both locations take the same core courses for the sociology major as well as a wide variety of electives. The Bedford Hills College Program involves over 175 students per semester, and students who have already earned their bachelor's degrees serve as mentors and tutors. Annually, over 200 women register for college courses. As of 2011, the Bedford Hills College Program has graduated 142 students.

The *Inside-Out Prison Exchange Program* (http://www.insideoutcenter.org/index.html), started by Lori Pompa at Temple University in Philadelphia, brings college students into correctional facilities to share class with prisoners for a full term. "Inside" and "outside" students read the same books, do the same assignments, and work collaboratively on class projects. Throughout the term, students engage in extensive dialogue, helping everyone involved to see beyond labels and to value each individual class member's contributions. Classes cover any number of topics and disciplines, including sociology, criminal justice, literature, philosophy, nursing, and drama; no matter what the specific subject matter, students who participate in the classes are exposed to a deep, transformative learning experience. Inside-Out requires intensive, hands-on training for prospective instructors, and all participants must agree to follow the program's strict rules in order to ensure Inside-Out's continued success and growth. At this point, more than 400 potential instructors have completed the Inside-Out training, and more than 10,000 students have been part of over 300 distinct classes. Inside-Out classes have been held in more than 25 states; the program has begun offering classes in Canada, and the network is rapidly growing.

The *Prison-to-College Pipeline* is one of the newest prison college programs, developed at John Jay College in New York in 2011. The Prison-to-College Pipeline is a small program (only involving about 25 male prisoners by 2013) with big goals:

> The program has three components: 1) offering college credit courses, 2) a re-entry program that works with Osborne Association, an organization that helps parolees gain housing, jobs and continue their education, 3) a learning exchange program where John Jay students volunteer to study with the prisoners. (Stern, 2013)

NOW YOU . . . THINK ABOUT SOCIAL CONTROL

We have explored myriad forms of deviance in this book: police misconduct, drug use, corporate misconduct, prostitution, and making "war" on various behaviors, to name a few. What we can probably conclude by these disparate behaviors, issues, and perspectives is that deviance is often in the eye of the beholder. While one person might define the homeless person as deviant, many others might define a society that does not have enough safety nets for those in need—thus allowing homelessness—as deviant.

In the same vein, social control of "deviants" takes on many faces. Some of this social control is informal, while much of it has been formalized, leading to an explosion in both regulations and prison populations.

Given what you have learned about deviants, deviance, and theory in this book, what should be the relationship between deviance and social control? If we asked you to build a better vision of social control, what would your philosophy be? What behaviors would you focus on? What behaviors would you allow? Would you focus on informal or formal social control? On individuals or groups? On making peace or war? Why?

◈ Conclusion

In this chapter, we have given you a quick glimpse into some specific forms of social control of deviant behavior. Much more could be, and has been, written on the topic, but we chose to keep it simple and highlight some current practices that show the challenges of effectively controlling deviant behavior without creating widespread damage to individuals, families, and communities.

We would like to point out, too, that reactions to deviant behavior and efforts at social control are constantly evolving. For example, as prison populations have soared over the past several decades, states are now looking for more creative—and less expensive—responses to criminal behavior. "Ban the Box" campaigns have sprung up around the country, encouraging states and counties to eliminate the box on employment and housing forms that asks whether the applicant has a criminal conviction or criminal record. In addition, some progress has been made in efforts to restore voting rights to felons, with current research suggesting that the benefits of civic reintegration of ex-offenders far outweigh the potential risks (Uggen & Inderbitzin, 2010). What changes will be next?

In the next chapter, you will read about deviant careers and career deviance. While most theories and books on deviant behavior focus on how individuals enter deviance, we think it is just as interesting and important to examine how the majority of individuals change their life trajectories and sooner or later find a way to exit deviance.

EXERCISES AND DISCUSSION QUESTIONS

1. Do you think deviance and social control are necessary to society? What functions do they serve? Which of the purposes of punishment do you think best fit our current criminal justice system? Why do you think so?

2. Should we be concerned about the institutionalization of inmates? Why or why not? What might be done to prevent institutionalization/prisonization?

3. Felony records disqualify individuals from a number of different types of jobs that are not necessarily related to the type of crime committed. Do you think this is a fair practice? Why or why not? What do you think would be appropriate guidelines in terms of felony convictions and employment?

4. Check out the interactive map on The Sentencing Project's Web site (http://www.sentencingproject.org/map/map.cfm). How does your state compare to others and the national average in terms of corrections populations, corrections expenditures, and felon disenfranchisement? Are you surprised by any of this information?

5. Do you think persons convicted of felony offenses should be able to vote in local and national elections? What restrictions, if any, do you think would be appropriate? What are the laws in your state?

6. Should sex offenders be treated differently than other violent offenders? Does the community have a right to know and perhaps even dictate where they live and work? Do you think civil commitment of sex offenders is appropriate?

KEY TERMS

Civil commitment	Felon disenfranchisement	Prisonization
Collateral consequences of imprisonment	Institutionalization	Social contract
Demedicalization	Medicalization of deviance	Total institutions
	Pains of imprisonment	

CHAPTER 12

Deviant Careers and Career Deviance

I felt a little inferior at first, because I had no knowledge myself of nudist camps. . . . I started to enjoy myself, but I couldn't quite feel comfortable. In the nude. In front of a lot of people. A lack of confidence. By not having complete knowledge. I really didn't know what to expect.

—A soon-to-be nudist's first experience at a nudist camp. (From Weinberg, 1966, p. 20)

A really bad work day is, nobody's calling, [you're] stressed trying to pick from people that you kind of don't want to have over because you don't know them, they might be—they're probably not cops but it's not clear, because they either won't give their work number or they won't do something [else that is part of her screening process]—and trying to [decide] to see them or not to see them, since it's already pledged as a work day and not [a day off]. . . . Just sitting around and waiting is really one of the higher-level bad days, I think.

—A really bad day for an "elite prostitute."
(From Lucas, 2005, p. 524)

I can if somebody says something to me that I don't like you know it doesn't bother me any more . . . it meant (after being saved) that I could literally get ease with myself and not jump up and beat the crap out of somebody or if somebody comes and gets something from me and didn't bring it back you know at a certain time I'd go and beat the crap out of them.

> —An ex-offender previously incarcerated in a state facility describing how being "saved" helped keep him from violence in situations that would have provoked him earlier. (From Giordano, Longmore, Schroeder, & Seffrin, 2008, p. 117)

◈ Introduction

The three stories above seem quite different. The first discusses a novice nudist's first experience at a nudist camp and how she felt as she entered a new deviant context and form of deviant behavior. The second is from an "elite prostitute" whose worst "working day" is where she is ambivalent about what work (i.e., clients) she will take. The final quote is from an ex-offender who believes that his spirituality helps prevent him from violence in situations when he normally would have "beaten the crap out of someone." What links these very different quotes is that they are from persons deemed deviant by much of society, but each of these people is at a different stage of a deviant life course. The first is entering a deviant lifestyle, the second presumably is actively involved in a deviant career, and the last one is desisting from a violent history. These are the themes of this chapter—how deviance changes over time and often has a beginning, a middle, and an end.

As the title of this chapter implies, a distinction can be made between deviant careers and career deviance. The term *deviant careers* implies an actual career: a job, room for possible advancement (or dismissal), "regular" pay, and possibly even taxes. In a deviant career it is clear that there is work for money, a beginning to the career, and an end to the career (retirement, change in jobs, or death). The careers in question, however, are ones that are formally or informally sanctioned (socially, morally, or legally) or are typically disrespected by society—or at least certain segments of society. For simplicity's sake, examples might include dancers in strip clubs, sex workers in pornography, certain prostitutes, drug dealers and smugglers, and professional thieves, among others.

The notion of *career deviance* brings a different connotation. Our view of a career deviant is one who becomes involved in crime or other deviant behavior not so much as a career, per se, but a sequence of deviant events occurs over time with a beginning and an end. The career can be very short, such as that of a rebellious youth who has a few run-ins with the law, or it could be a long-term pattern of sexual encounters with same-sex strangers in public restrooms. The major commonality about deviant careers and career deviance is time.

Many of the theories we have discussed are static in nature and attempt to distinguish deviants from conformists using any number of variables (e.g., social bonds, self-control, strains, association with deviant peers). Thinking about deviance in terms of careers forces us to think longitudinally (over time) and brings up some very interesting questions that are not necessarily intuitive. Thinking longitudinally, we start to recognize that different factors may influence (1) the onset of deviance, (2) continuation or escalation of deviance, (3) and desistance from deviance (be it almost immediate or gradually over time). We also start thinking about whether deviants specialize in particular forms of deviance or are generalists, engaging in many forms of deviance given the opportunities available, and whether specialization or diversification changes over time.

Development of a Deviant Careers and Career Deviance Approach

We raise this distinction between deviant careers and career deviance in part because of a very large debate in criminology, referred to by some as the "great debate" (Soothill, Fitzpatrick, & Brian, 2009, p. 14), that escalated in the 1980s and continues today. The debate is largely between those who believe that longitudinal research is too expensive and not necessary for a thorough understanding of criminal behavior and those who believe longitudinal designs are crucial. The former typically believe that the factors that affect criminal behavior are relatively static and that cross-sectional designs are perfectly appropriate to test theories and develop appropriate programs and policies. The latter believe that different factors may affect the onset/initiation of criminal behavior, its continuation and possible escalation, and the desistance process. This is not a trivial debate, and both sides have made important points. For example, it may seem "obvious" to many that knowing when different types of criminal behaviors begin, how long they persist across the life course, and when different types of offenders age out of crime is useful information. Indeed, several statistical analyses and reviews seem to support the conclusion that there are certain groups of offenders who consistently offend over time that could be incarcerated for long periods of time, thus resulting in significantly lower rates of crime (see Blumstein & Cohen, 1979; Farrington, Gallagher, Morley, Ledger, & West, 1985; Greenberg, 1985). Alternatively, others disagree and argue that similar factors affect criminal behavior whether it is early or late in the game. They seriously challenge the notion that high-risk groups can be identified early on and argue that most offenders age out of crime fairly early in the life course and that the "career criminal" paradigm is basically without merit (Gottfredson & Hirschi, 1986).

We bring this debate regarding career criminals and criminal careers to your attention because we feel that it is important that students have at least heard of the debate. For the student of the sociology of deviance about which this book was written (as opposed to criminal behavior), this is just one small tree in a huge forest. First, there are many forms of deviance that we have no interest in trying to stop, particularly through incarceration. Second, the chronological age that people typically begin to engage in deviance may not be terribly interesting in itself. Alternatively, why some people become interested in a particular form of deviance or the circumstances under which they initiate the behavior is fascinating to most all of us. Why do people begin to use or sell drugs, turn tricks, enter a nudist colony, begin a career in pornography, become a compulsive consumer of porn, or any number of other deviant behaviors? Similarly, estimating the length of a deviant career may be somewhat interesting but probably not as interesting as studying how people live a deviant lifestyle, the challenges they face with conventional society, or the dangers inherent in many deviant careers. Finally and related, what pushes or pulls people out of careers of deviance? Indeed, the process of desistance—getting out of the business or "out of the life"—is one of the most interesting aspects of the sociological study of deviance.

Getting Into Deviance: Onset of a Deviant Career

At a very general level, it doesn't take much to initiate many deviant acts. Sneaking a drink from the parents' liquor cabinet, stealing a cigarette from an unguarded purse, breaking into an unlocked home,

DEVIANCE IN POPULAR CULTURE

The subject of deviant careers and career deviance has gained momentum in recent years as more and more scholars have focused on issues of desistance and community reentry. As you learned in the last chapter, labeling is often an important factor in deviant careers; once labeled, it can be extremely difficult to get a job, rent an apartment, or lead a conforming lifestyle. Here we offer several examples of films that address this issue:

The Released—this PBS Frontline documentary (available to watch online) is about mentally ill inmates being released back into the community with no care or safety net. The filmmakers follow several men over an extended period of time and show their struggles trying to manage mental illness and survive in the community.

Tequila Sunrise—a popular fictional film from the 1980s starring Mel Gibson as a successful drug dealer trying to leave his illegitimate business and start a conforming one. In one memorable scene, Gibson's character tries to explain how difficult it can be to leave the drug dealing scene, detailing a list of people that don't want him to quit, each for his or her own reasons.

The Woodsman—in this dark film starring Kevin Bacon, a convicted sex offender is released after 12 years in prison. The film follows his attempts to build a conforming and quiet life in the community.

Sherrybaby—after 3 years in prison, a drug addict with a troubled history struggles to reconnect with her young daughter. The strong performance by Maggie Gyllenhaal showcases the difficulty of trying to rebuild relationships and become a good mother.

or cheating on a spouse or partner after too much drinking is fairly easy given the opportunity, a little interest or motivation, or especially some encouragement. Becoming a serious underage drinker or smoker, a burglar, or a career cheater will likely take more effort. The entrances to deviant careers vary considerably depending on the behavior in question, so in this section of the book, we discuss several different forms of deviance to provide the reader with some idea of the complexities and tremendous variation in ways individuals get into a career of deviance.

Howard Becker (1953) presented a series of socially interactive stages that he argued one needed to go through to become a user of marijuana. He contended that to become a "marijuana smoker," one must (1) learn to smoke the drug properly, (2) feel the intoxicating "high" associated with smoking marijuana, and (3) come to understand the feeling of intoxication as pleasurable. That is, one needs to learn to take in the smoke and hold the smoke for some time to get enough THC (the active chemical in marijuana) to actually get intoxicated. He argued that even if enough THC is ingested, individuals don't always feel the high of the drug, and, even when they do, they may not find it terribly enjoyable. More recent research supports Becker's theory but suggests that times have changed, at least to some extent. For example, most of Becker's research subjects did not get high their first time, but perhaps that was because of the quality of the marijuana in the 1950s versus the 1980s and 1990s. More recent research (Hallstone, 2002; Hirsch, Conforti, & Graney, 1990) shows that most first timers do feel the effects of smoking pot, and some recall their very first experience as pleasant. However, the first experience is not always pleasurable and may in fact be quite negative physically (dry mouth, coughing, etc.) and emotionally. As one of Hallstone's (2002) respondents reported when asked if he enjoyed getting high the first time,

> Umm . . . (emphatically) nooo! I was scared. I was very scared because not only could I not tell anybody, but um . . . I did not know if I was going to come down, how long it was going to last, and is my mom going to know. (p. 839)

Marijuana is clearly the most popular and widespread illegal drug in this country. A 2010 survey of 8th, 10th, and 12th graders conducted by Monitoring the Future showed lifetime prevalence of marijuana use at 17%, 33%, and 44%, respectively. When asked about the availability of marijuana, 41% of 8th graders, 69% of 10th graders, and 83% of 12th graders said that it would be fairly or very easy to obtain. Given the innocuous or even positive representation of marijuana in the media, few would be surprised that even "good kids" have experimented with the substance. Alternatively, consider what might be required for the initiation of harder, less "popular" drugs, such as heroin, which has been tried by around 1% of people. Or, in line with a true deviant career, what is involved in becoming a drug dealer?

▲ **Photo 12.1**   Marijuana can be experienced in very different ways, especially among novice users.

Source: ©Doug Menuez/Thinkstock.

Adler and Adler (1983) studied a group of upper-level drug dealers and smugglers (of mostly marijuana and cocaine in a county in southwest California). They found three routes to becoming upper-level drug dealers and smugglers: low-level entry, middle-level entry, and smuggling, which was considered the highest level. People who started at the bottom, as it were, were largely heavy drug users who basically had to deal to support their own habits. Most low-level dealers stayed low-level dealers, not having the motivation and/or never developing the skills or the resources to make it into the middle level. The Adlers found that only about 20% of their upper-level dealer sample began as low-level dealers, and most of these dealers came from other parts of the country and had graduated into mid-level dealing before moving into the lucrative California market.

Middle-level entry was more common (about 75%) among their sample of upper-level dealers, and these dealers often came from other professions—some conventional and others on the seedier side. For example, one of the mid-level dealers was involved in a conventional real estate business but was laundering money through the business. Mid-level dealers had money and went in big, but they still had to learn the drug trafficking trade, including "how to establish business connections, organize profitable transactions, avoid arrest, transport illegal goods, and coordinate participants and equipment" (Adler & Adler, 1983, pp. 198–199). These were largely entrepreneurs who wanted to make it to the top and found the social networks needed in the drug subculture to make that happen.

Only a small proportion of the smugglers (about 10%) got into smuggling on their own; even upper-level drug dealers didn't have the knowledge, skills, connections, equipment, and other resources to embark on their own smuggling operation. Rather, "most novice smugglers were recruited and trained by a sponsor with whom they forged an apprentice-mentor relationship" (Adler & Adler, 1983, p. 199). Through this relationship, the recruits learned the techniques, acquired resources, and, most importantly, made contacts, and they eventually branched out or, in some cases, took over the operation when someone retired from the business. This is clearly consistent with the differential association and social learning theories discussed in Chapter 6. It also brings up the notion of stratification within deviant careers. Just as there are hierarchies in conventional business (workers, supervisors and managers, upper administration, presidents and owners), so too is there stratification in the world of deviant careers. Just as in conventional organizations, upward mobility is possible but not always easy.

Other research on entering the business of drug dealing, which examines the dealing of crack and meth, shows that it actually looks somewhat similar to that of these upper-level cocaine and marijuana dealers (see Dunlap, Johnson, & Manwar, 1994; Murphy, Waldorf, & Reinarman, 1990; VanNostrand & Tewksbury, 1997). Most research suggests that the motivations, techniques, and contacts need to be learned over the course of time for a full career to develop.

Truly getting into deviance often requires the acquisition of a deviant identity. As people come to define themselves as drinkers and smokers, they drink and smoke; it is part of their identity. Socially, drinkers are offered alcoholic beverages, and it is understood that when smokers walk outside, they are probably going for a cigarette. But how do deviant identities emerge? Penelope McLorg and Diane Taub (1987) provide an excellent example of how anorexics and bulimics move through a process from very conforming behavior, to primary deviance, to secondary deviance. Specifically, through participant observations of the self-help group BANISH (Bulimics/Anorexics in Self-Help), they conducted qualitative interviews with 15 participants and found that the women and men they studied started out quite conventionally. They had strong attachments to their families, did well in school, and internalized the cultural norm that slim is beautiful. They were rewarded when they lost weight, but, like most dieters, they often were unable to maintain lowered weights, resulting in seemingly extreme behaviors to maintain desired weights. Here the anorexics and bulimics moved into a stage of primary deviance where they did not consider themselves anorexic or bulimic, their deviance was largely unknown to others, and the outcome of their behaviors was both psychologically and socially rewarding—they were slim and therefore more "beautiful." At some point, however, friends and family came to recognize compulsive behaviors surrounding food and exercise among the anorexics and evidence of binging and purging among the bulimics. As with many other forms of deviance, friends and families were resistant to labeling the behaviors problematic, and, among

RECENT STUDY IN DEVIANCE

Club Drug Initiation Among Gay and Bisexual Men

By P. N. Halkitis and J. J. Palamar, 2008, Multivariate modeling of club drug use initiation among gay and bisexual men, in *Substance Use and Misuse, 43*, pp. 871–879.

Researchers have long been interested in factors associated with the initiation of both legal (e.g., alcohol and tobacco) and illegal drugs (e.g., marijuana, cocaine, and heroin). They have theorized (using gateway theory) and studied the sequence in which people generally use these drugs, finding that people usually begin with alcohol or tobacco, then move to marijuana then cocaine, and then a far smaller proportion moves on to heroin and other hard drugs. Few studies have focused on the initiation of "club drugs," or designer drugs associated with all-night dance clubs, raves, and the party scene. In a recent study, Halkitis and Palamer (2008) interviewed and surveyed a sample of gay (n = 385) and bisexual men (n = 52) in the early to mid-2000s over the course of a year about their club drug use. At the initial assessment, the majority of respondents (79%) had used cocaine in the previous 4 months (the time frame for most of the drug-use questions). Similarly, a majority had used ecstasy (75%), methamphetamines (55%), and ketamine (55%). Just under a third (29%) had used GHB. A clear majority (59%) reported that cocaine was the first club drug they initiated, followed by ecstasy at 35%. Rarely was ketamine, methamphetamine, or GHB the first club drug initiated (5% reporting one of them to be the first). Interestingly, the most common second drug initiated was ecstasy, again at 35%. So, if we combine the most common first and second club drug initiated, we get almost equal proportions for cocaine and ecstasy (74% and 75%, respectively).

Using these statistics, the authors developed a model that distinguished first initiation of various drugs compared to cocaine (the most commonly first initiated). They found that those who initiated ecstasy first tended to be older and tended to use more club drugs (i.e., they were polydrug users). Those who initiated ketamine first were also more likely to be polydrug users. Interestingly, those initiating methamphetamines first were indistinguishable from cocaine initiators on every variable available, including age, race/ethnicity, HIV status, sexual orientation, and polydrug use. Gay and bisexual men, like the general population, were more likely to use cocaine first, which is consistent with sequential theories. It is only after these initiating drugs that a difference in type of drug use emerges between this population and the general population.

the anorexics, there was a great deal of denial when called out on their compulsive behaviors. In contrast, bulimics tended to know that binging and purging was abnormal and unhealthy and, when confronted, were more likely to admit that they were bulimic.

By the nature of McLorg and Taub's (1987) study design, all of the anorexics and bulimics were part of a self-help group designed to help those stigmatized as deviant regain a sense of normality. Their disorder, then, became a master status, something that provided a new identity that dramatically affected their lives.

What should be clear from this section is that getting into deviance takes many forms, and various stages of development are required in almost any career in deviance.

Risk and Protective Factors for Onset

Over the past several decades, great concerns have arisen over the onset of certain forms of deviant behavior, including drug and alcohol use, violence, teen pregnancy, high-risk sexual behavior, and other problematic behaviors. Because of societal concern over these issues, a tremendous amount of literature has emerged attempting to find factors that are positively related to deviant involvement (risk factors). Intricately related is a line of research that attempts to find factors that minimize the deleterious effects of risk factors (protective factors). An overview of risk and protective factors for adolescent problem behaviors, developed by the Social Development Group at the University of Washington, is provided in Figure 12.1. Risk factors have been categorized under several domains, including (1) individual and peer factors (e.g., rebelliousness of the child and deviant peers); (2) school (e.g., lack of commitment to school); (3) family (e.g., family conflict and management problems); and (4) the community (e.g., availability of alcohol and drugs and economic deprivation). Protective factors that mitigate the risk factors are also listed by domain. Protective factors are particularly important because they provide insights for developing effective policy and programs based on research evidence. So, at the community level, we might encourage programs that provide opportunities for conventional involvement and rewards for doing good things in the neighborhood. High-risk families might be targeted and offered parent training courses or social supports that help them manage daily life. There are obviously a number of school-based programs that encourage students to feel that they are a part of the institution and structured activities to make them committed to doing well in school. Similarly, we might encourage individual counseling or other programs (be they school or family based) to help young persons become attached to prosocial individuals (e.g., mentors) and institutions (the family or the school).

❖ Getting Out of the Game: Desistance From Career Deviance

If you think about most traditional theories of deviance, they have typically focused on two questions: (1) Why do people begin to engage in deviance, and (2) why does deviance persist (Paternoster & Bushway, 2009). For example, Hirschi's (1969) early social control theory, which we covered in Chapter 7, would say that deviance is fun, easy, and rewarding, and people are drawn toward it. Deviance is initiated because of a lack of the social controls (attachment, commitment, involvement, and beliefs) that usually prevent people from initiating deviance. Unless there is a significant change in social bonds (e.g., a good job, investment in school or marriage), deviance persists because bonds remain weak. His later theory with Gottfredson (Gottfredson & Hirschi, 1990), which focused on self-control, shares a similar perspective and furthermore insists that self-control is stable and that is why deviance persists. Strain theorists (especially Agnew with his individual-level version) introduced in Chapter 4 suggest that initial deviance is a reaction to frustration and anger, and deviance persists because the structure of society means certain people remain in stressful conditions (Agnew, 2006). Finally, differential association and social learning theories, covered in Chapter 6, suggest that deviance emerges when definitions favorable to deviance outweigh definitions unfavorable to deviance. To the extent people are, for example, immersed in a subculture conducive to deviance, the deviance is likely to continue. This is the way these theories have typically been used. However, with the emergence of the criminal career paradigm or the life course perspective introduced earlier in Chapter 7, people started to be much more concerned with the tail end of the deviant career and how and why criminals and other deviants desist.

Surely the theories above might be used to explain desistance. Social controls or bonds can emerge by entering a solid relationship such as marriage or obtaining stable employment (Sampson & Laub, 1993). Or, one might escape situations that produce strain or develop skills to help deal with frustrating conditions (Agnew, 1997). Finally, people sometimes do change their social networks and therefore the definitions they are exposed to, enabling them to exit a deviant career (Akers, 1998). Indeed, social

Figure 12.1   Risk and Protective Factor Framework

The following graph supports a public health model using a theoretical framework of risk reduction and protection enhancement. Developments in prevention and intervention science have shown that there are characteristics of individuals and their families and their environment (i.e., community neighborhood, school) that affect the likelihood of negative outcomes including substance abuse, delinquency, violence, and school dropout. Other characteristics serve to protect or provide a buffer to moderate the influence of the negative characteristics. These characteristics are identified as risk factors and protective factors. (Arthur, Hawkins, et al., 1994, Hawkins, Catalano, Miller, 1992).

Risk Factors	Adolescent Problem Behaviors						Protective Factors	Social Development Model (SDM)
	Substance Abuse	Depression & Anxiety	Delinquency	Teen Pregnancy	School Drop-Out	Violence		
Domains: Risk factors are characteristics of individuals, their family, school, and community environments that are associated with increases in alcohol and other drug use, delinquency, teen pregnancy, school dropout, and violence. The following factors have been identified that increase the likelihood that children and youth may develop such problem behaviors.							Factors associated with reduced potential for drug use are called protective factors. Protective factors encompass family, social, psychological, and behavioral characteristics that can provide a buffer for the children and youth. These factors mitigate the effects of risk factors that are present in the child or youth's environment.	SDM is a synthesis of three existing theories of criminology (control, social learning, and differential association). It incorporates the results of research on risk and protective factors for problem behaviors and a developmental perspective of age, specific problem, and prosocial behavior. It is based on the assumption that children learn behaviors.
Community								
Availability of alcohol/other drugs	✓					✓	Opportunities for prosocial involvement in community	
Availability of Firearms			✓			✓	Recognition for prosocial involvement	
Community laws and norms favorable to drug use, firearms, and crime	✓		✓			✓		Healthy Behaviors
Transitions and mobility	✓	✓	✓		✓			
Low neighborhood attachment and community disorganization	✓		✓			✓		Healthy Beliefs and Clear Standards
Media Portrayals of Violence						✓		
Extreme economic deprivation	✓		✓	✓	✓	✓		
Family								
Family history of the problem behavior	✓	✓	✓	✓	✓	✓	Bonding to family with healthy beliefs and clear standards.	
Family management problems	✓	✓	✓	✓	✓	✓	Attachment to family with healthy beliefs & clear standards	Bonding • Attachment • Commitment
Family conflict	✓	✓	✓	✓	✓	✓	Opportunities for prosocial involvement	
Favorable parental attitudes and involvement in problem behaviors	✓		✓			✓	Recognition for prosocial involvement	
School								
Academic failure beginning in late elementary school	✓	✓	✓	✓	✓	✓	Bonding and Attachment to School	Opportunities Skills Recognition
Lack of commitment to school	✓		✓	✓	✓	✓	Opportunities for prosocial involvement	
							Recognition for prosocial involvement	
Individual / Peer								
Early and persistent antisocial behavior	✓	✓	✓	✓	✓	✓	Bonding to peers with healthy beliefs and clear standards.	
Rebelliousness	✓		✓		✓		Attachment to peers with healthy beliefs & clear standards	Individual Characteristics
Friends who engage in the problem behavior	✓		✓	✓	✓	✓	Opportunities for prosocial involvement	
Favorable attitudes toward the problem behavior (including low perceived risk of harm)	✓		✓	✓	✓		Increase in Social skills	
Early initiation of the problem behavior	✓		✓	✓	✓	✓		
Gang Involvement	✓		✓			✓		
Constitutional factors	✓	✓	✓			✓		

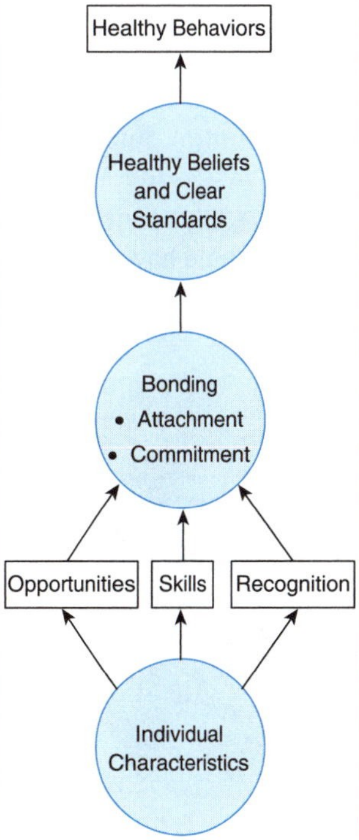

Source: The Substance Abuse and Medical Services Administration, U.S. Department of Health and Human Services. Retrieved from http://sde.state.ok.us/ Schools/SafeHealthy/pdf/RiskProtectFactor.pdf

control, strain, and differential association theories have all been placed within a life course perspective and can be used to help explain the desistance process (Agnew, 2006; Sampson & Laub, 1995; Warr, 2002). Importantly, these theories have also been used to identify key concepts associated with several other theories and relate those ideas to desistance. For example, Peggy Giordano and her colleagues (Giordano, Longmore, Schroeder, & Seffrin, 2008) argue that "spirituality," a key component of many self-help and formal treatment programs as well as prison-based support groups, can be linked to desistance through social control, strain, and differential association theories. Spirituality can be linked to social control theory through the bond of "belief" as well as informal agents of social control that deviants may associate with because of newfound spiritual beliefs. Similarly, because of newfound spirituality, deviants may begin to disassociate with nonbelievers and begin to associate with believers who reinforce nondeviant definitions. Finally, spirituality and association with other believers may provide a source of social support that reduces frustrations and strains that earlier may have led to deviant involvement.

Giordano et al. interviewed incarcerated adolescents (half male and half female) in 1995 and again in 2003. Quantitative analyses of these data lend no support to the idea that spirituality (closeness to God and church attendance) was related to desistance. However, the sample size was fairly small, and it was therefore difficult to detect statistical significance. Indeed, few variables in this model were statistically significant.

Alternatively, in-depth qualitative interviews with 41 of the incarcerated youth seemed to suggest that spirituality was a strong "hook" for some offenders to change their lives and desist from criminal involvement. These qualitative comments were related to the theories discussed earlier. For example, spirituality often brought couples or parents and children together, increasing attachment and social control. Said one respondent, "Without Christ and the church we would never be together, and I mean we already know that. We prayed a lot and we know it's through prayer that we're together and our family's together" (Giordano et al., 2008, p. 119). Another references the bond of involvement: "If you would have told me ten years ago or say the last time I seen you, seven years ago that I would be singing in the choir regularly, going to church regularly I probably would have thought you were crazy" (p. 114). In terms of differential association and social learning, another said, "The things that preacher say from out of the Bible. I love that. He's just teaching you the ways to live. To live like the way God wants you to live right" (p. 114). Finally, referencing social support and ability to reduce strain, one interviewee stated, "I don't worry like I used to before. I know all things are in the Lord's hands and I know he takes care of me" (p. 117).

▲ **Photo 12.2** Can religion "save" people from a career in deviance?

Source: ©Stockbyte/Thinkstock.

Spirituality can be seen as a "hook"—something that some involved in career deviance can grab hold of to help them use their own **human agency** to open doors out of the lifestyle they wish to exit. Spirituality is clearly something that will garner more theoretical and empirical attention as federal money is invested into faith-based approaches to reforming criminals and other deviants. Other "hooks," such as new relationships, occupations, and geographic moves away from "bad influences," are also likely to be carefully studied both quantitatively and qualitatively in the future.

Exiting a deviant career can be difficult. Adler and Adler's (1983) upper-level drug dealers and smugglers had a hard time "phasing out" of their careers because they had become accustomed to the "hedonistic and materialistic satisfactions the drug world provided" (p. 202) and, in fact, had a hard time finding legitimate jobs because they had been out of the lawful labor market for so long they had few legal opportunities. The drug-using lifestyles of alcoholics and drug addicts are also difficult to leave. Recovery requires motivation, social support, and often treatment, and the process is frequently plagued by back-and-forth periods of abstinence and use (Brownell, Marlatt, Lichteustein, & Wilson, 1986).

Recently, Lynda Baker and her colleagues reviewed several general and prostitution-specific models of change, as well as the empirical literature on the specific barriers women face when exiting prostitution (Baker, Dalla, & Williamson, 2010, pp. 588–590). These barriers included the following:

1. Individual factors
   a. Self-destructive behavior and substance abuse
   b. Mental health problems
   c. Effects of trauma from adverse childhood
   d. Psychological trauma/injury from violence
   e. Chronic psychological stress
   f. Self-esteem/shame and guilt
   g. Physical health problems
   h. Lack of knowledge regarding services

2. Relational factors
   a. Limited conventional formal and informal support
   b. Strained family relations
   c. Pimps
   d. Drug dealers
   e. Social isolation

3. Structural factors
   a. Employment, job skills, limited employment options
   b. Basic needs (e.g., housing, poverty, economic self-sufficiency)
   c. Education
   d. Criminal record
   e. Inadequate services

4. Societal factors

  a. Discrimination and stigma

Through an analysis of previous models and the barriers that women face when exiting prostitution, the authors developed an integrated model that is described in Figure 12.2. The model focuses on prostitution but could also be used to understand exiting other deviant careers (drug dealing, drug and alcohol addiction, anorexia/bulimia, etc.). The first stage is immersion, and, technically, this stage is not about change at all but precedes any inkling of leaving the business—that is, the woman is immersed in a lifestyle of prostitution. In the second stage, the woman becomes aware that things are not as they should be. Of course, at either part of this stage, there are the barriers listed above to leaving, and the woman could (and often does) return to the immersion stage. If the woman makes it past this stage, she enters the stage of deliberate planning and preparation. At this stage, attempts are made to contact informal social support (e.g., family and friends) as well as formal agents of social support, such as drug and alcohol treatment centers and homeless shelters. The

Figure 12.2 Baker, Dalla, and Williamson's (2010) Integrated Model of Exiting Prostitution

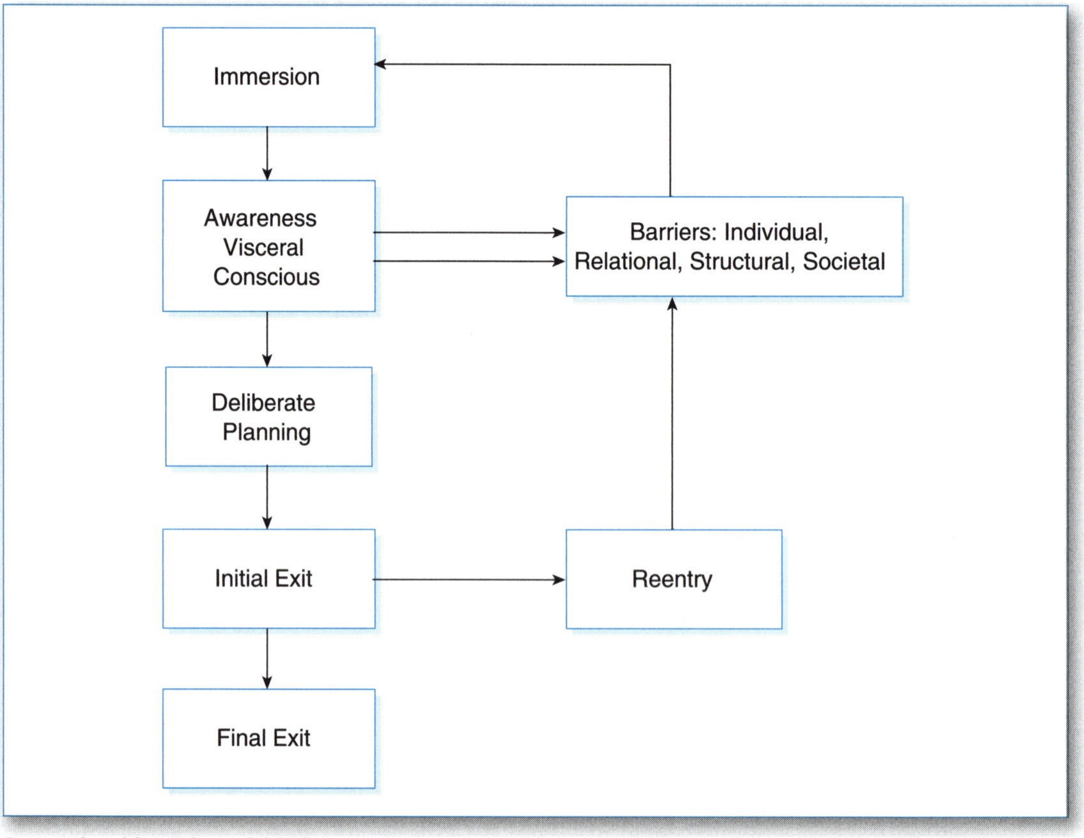

Source: Adapted from Baker et al. (2010).

initial exit period begins when the woman actively and behaviorally works to get out of the lifestyle. She may use informal contacts, such as family and friends, or she may invoke formal measures, such as counseling or drug treatment. Breaking through the barriers is critical at this stage, and human agency becomes especially important. At this point,

> Some women may enter a drug treatment program, actively engaged and ready to change; they may rely on their support system (e.g., sponsors), internalize knowledge gained, and then apply newly acquired skills to their own lives. Others may begin a treatment program, fail to utilize available support or internalize knowledge and, therefore, be unable to make behavioral changes. These women will likely abandon the program prior to completion and eventually return to the sex industry. It is at this stage of the model that a woman's internal desire and motivation to exit are severely tested. (Baker et al., 2010, p. 592)

▲ **Photo 12.3** Sociological research shows the very different lives of elite sex workers and street prostitutes.

Source: ©RapidEye/iStock.

In the former case, the woman may enter the final exit stage or she may not—she may reenter the business. In the latter case, the woman will almost always go back to prostitution, and in either case, there may be what Sanders (2007) termed "yo-yoing," where multiple attempts are made to exit the business and lifestyle. Baker and colleagues (2010) conclude that very often the final exiting stage comes after many attempts to leave a career in prostitution.

◈ Explaining Deviance in the Streets and Deviance in the Suites: Street Prostitutes Versus Elite Prostitutes

Living the life of a deviant can be exciting, challenging, difficult, taxing, demoralizing, frightening, upsetting, and a host of other adjectives depending on the type of deviance and where in the deviant career we look. Consider the upper-level drug dealers discussed by Adler and Adler (1983) earlier. On one side, many dealers were drawn to the business because of the fun and excitement of the party and druggy lifestyle and the potential to make large sums of money. On the other side, dealing and smuggling was real work with many risks, including the dangers of associating with other criminals (some not to be trusted) and getting busted by law enforcement. In this section, we describe two studies concerning the lives of very different types of sex workers: women who exchange sex for drugs and money in the streets and elite prostitutes who exchange sex for large sums of money and expensive material goods. The comparison sheds light on how class and power differentiate the deviant careers of those involved in different levels of prostitution.

Living with deviance on a daily basis can be physically and emotionally draining. A large body of research has developed describing the lives of street prostitutes and the stigma, social rejection, and abuses they face on a day-to-day basis (see Farley & Barkan, 1998; Hunter, 1993; Nixon, Tutty, Downe, Gorkoff, & Ursel, 2002). Recently, Jolanda Sallman (2010) reported on her interviews with 14 women recruited from a program that provided social services ("prostitution-specific services") to women in need. Because these women did not necessarily consider themselves to be "prostitutes" or "sex workers," she began each interview with the following:

> I'm interested in learning as much as possible about what it's like to be a woman who has sex for material goods, such as money, drugs, shelter, or clothing. I'm particularly interested in hearing about your experience. It would be helpful for me if you would begin by describing a situation that stands out for you. (p. 149)

From these interviews, she derived five themes that provide insights into the daily lives of these women. First was living with the labeling and stigma by members of society (including conventional citizens, pimps, and the police), who viewed them as "whores," "dispensable," "garbage," and "less than human." Such devaluation led directly to the second theme that involved comments concerning the day-to-day living with violence. The prostitutes reported being kidnapped, raped, gang raped, beaten, and being cut with knifes by pimps. Responses to these incidents of victimization showed clear evidence of their stigmatized and devalued status. One pimp immediately put a prostitute back on the street after she had been kidnapped and raped at knifepoint by a "john." The police response to rapes was equally demoralizing as law enforcement officers seemed either not to believe a prostitute could be raped or to think that it was a good thing. The third theme involved living with discrimination, especially by the criminal justice system, which often denied the women's victimization or blamed them for it. The fourth theme involved how their experiences had altered their perceptions of themselves even after they had given up prostitution. That is, their own devalued sense of self (self-stigma) remained even after they stopped engaging in sex in exchange for drugs and money. A final and almost positive theme that Sallman (2010) unearthed in her interviews had to do with "resistance." She describes how some of the women refused to accept societal stigma and often lashed out at those who judged them negatively.

The research is clear that violence is prevalent in the working lives of both indoor and street prostitutes (Raphael & Shapiro, 2004), but compare the prior descriptions of street prostitution with the following analysis of the lives of 30 elite prostitutes interviewed by Ann Lucas (2005). The women she interviewed unanimously voiced positive sentiments regarding their profession. They found it lucrative and empowering in terms of interpersonal skills and boundary setting, and they often said it exposed them less to sexual harassment. These women felt very in control of their environments:

> I think that they think, a lot of times, that they've rented me for an hour so I should have to do anything they want to. I think, maybe, it takes them by surprise that I walk in and take charge of the situation, and I'm like, "OK, let's do this" and they can make suggestions but if I don't want to do something I'm not gonna do it. (p. 520)

For some of these women, prostitution was clearly a means to an end in terms of finance and lifestyle. Some "stressed their ability to be independent, to have control over their work and non-work lives, to be able to afford some indulgences, and to vary how much they worked each month" (Lucas, 2004, p. 526). Others stressed the nonsexual nature of their work, which often involved providing conversation and company to lonely men, some of them regulars. This is in contrast to other work that describes prostitutes as "exploitative, man-hating con artists; whether friendly or strictly professional, these women largely appreciated and respected their clients" (Lucas, 2005, p. 536).

The point of this comparison between drug-using street prostitutes and elite sex workers is not to generate debate about the morality and politics of prostitution, although there is plenty there to discuss. Rather, the point is to highlight massive differences in two seemingly similar deviant careers and how social class and power affect the lives of "deviant women" who exchange sex for material goods. This reiterates an emerging theme in this chapter—that just like social stratification in conventional careers, there is also important stratification in deviant careers. In a conventional organization, there are usually clear levels related to pay, power, flexibility, and other benefits. This is also the case in many deviant careers.

Ideas in Action: Programs and Policy From a Career Deviance/Deviant Career Perspective

Although we did not use the term *policy,* we certainly hinted at it in the beginning of this chapter when we discussed the "great debate." Basically, the debate was about policy. On the one hand, some believe that longitudinal research is necessary and important. If we know the characteristics of persistent and serious offenders, we can incarcerate them, making the public feel safer and preventing needlessly lost lives, saving property, and maybe even saving costs to the criminal justice system if these are the primary offenders requiring the most attention from the police and court personnel. We have also briefly, but more directly, discussed policy as it relates to risk and protective factors. Here we would like to continue that discussion, although not by focusing on specific policies or programs that come from a deviant career/career deviance perspective because that would be a daunting task—indeed, one well beyond the scope of this small section. Instead, we will provide some policy-related issues to think about when working from a risk and protective factor approach.

We first recommend thinking about the importance of the issue of concern. This is sometimes, but not always, a quantitative issue (e.g., the extent of the problem), though this argument is often used to push for policy and/or resources for programs. Probably most research proposals begin with some numbers regarding the extent of the problem that they want to research, and students are notorious for starting papers with "The crime (or juvenile delinquency, or social problem X) is worse now than it has ever been," regardless of whether or not that is true. The nice thing about numbers is that they can help make an argument persuasive. Another nice thing about numbers is that they can be checked for accuracy and compared to others: "WOW, there sure is a lot of X going on, and it is very bad, but look how much Y is going on, and it is bad too." These are important general issues to think about when people are proposing programs and policy.

Clearly there are also rare events or behaviors that warrant attention. Medical scientists study some of the rarest diseases, and billions are spent on space exploration, but, compared to all of the problems we experience on earth, at times this may seem questionable. Alternatively, people working at NASA are very smart and persuasive. Closer to home, homicide occurs far less often than marijuana use, but, if given a voice, we may be more eager to put efforts (time, energy, and money) toward reducing one over the other. The point here is that we need to consider the importance of an issue before developing programs and policies.

On a related note, although it is difficult to predict unintended consequences of policies and programs, remember the negative effects of various programs discussed in Chapter 3. It is also easy to think of the unintended consequences of large-scale policies developed in the past. While research does suggest that alcohol consumption probably went down during Prohibition (1919–1933), people who continued to drink became criminals (the crime rate almost by definition went up), organized crime rose to levels that never previously existed in this country, and a great deal of "bad" alcohol was produced and consumed, sometimes with serious health consequences. More recently, changes in drug seizure laws have led to police corruption as departments basically use money taken from citizens to fund their budgets. Furthermore, it is quite clear that these innocent citizens have little or no recourse as they are often threatened with more severe sanctions and/or having their children taken away if they complain. Stillman (2013) reports that

> in general, you needn't be found guilty to have your assets claimed by law enforcement; in some states, suspicion on a par with "probable cause" is sufficient. Nor must you be charged with a crime, or even be accused of one. Unlike criminal forfeiture, which requires that person be convicted of an offense before his or her property is confiscated, civil forfeiture amounts to a lawsuit filed directly against a possession, regardless of the owner's guilt or innocence. (p. 50)

Once a deviant issue has been defined as important and worthy of developing programs or policies for, then we need to think about (1) where in the process we think we should focus, and (2) what are the risk and protective factors that might be important in helping the situation. Regarding the former, we might think that preventing some form of deviance is most important. At that point it is probably best to think about the population that should be the focus of a policy or program. One question that is raised a great deal these days is whether a program or policy should be universal or targeted (Hopkins et al., 2008). That is, should the program be delivered to the entire population or a targeted subset of that population? So, for example, if the issue is drug-abuse prevention, and you believe that the intervention would be best administered in the fifth grade, should the program be delivered to all fifth graders (universally)? Only to males since they are at greater risk of drug use (targeted)? Or only to the students who have shown clear risk factors for drug use, such as feelings of alienation, parental drug use, or poor social skills (targeted)? There may be some subsets of a population where the risk is so small that the intervention would be a true waste of time and scarce resources, while for another group the risk is so high that it makes much more sense to focus on that group. Of course, knowing in advance who is at greater risk is not always clear. Once we move past the prevention stage and focus on persistence/escalation or desistance, we are generally thinking about targeted programs, but where, when, and how we want to focus those programs may make them even more targeted. For example, do we want to focus on treatment for all heroin addicts, only those who have shown an interest in quitting, or those who are incarcerated so you have a captive audience?

Regarding the second issue, we have to ask what risk or protective factors are mostly likely to affect the problem and whether, even if we are sure which factors are most important, we can help to reduce the risk or increase protection. For both of these questions, we recommend relying on science. In terms of risk factors, we may think that A, B, or C is strongly and causally related to Z, but science has often shown that common sense is wrong or overly simplified. Similarly, as we discussed in Chapter 3, doing things that sound good (e.g., the DARE program) may have no effect whatsoever and may actually have negative unintended consequences. In many cases, we do not have the ability or resources we need, or there may be ethical or political constraints so that even if we "know" what would work, there is little or nothing we can do to resolve the problem. We hate to end on such a negative note, but these are important things to consider, and it is better to think them through as thoroughly as possible before making a potentially serious bad move.

NOW YOU . . . THINK ABOUT DEVIANT CAREERS

Individuals labeled as sex offenders are often assumed to be some of the most likely to become career offenders. For this reason, Megan's Law has mandated that sex offenders register with local law enforcement—making their status of sex offender public information. Government registry Web sites list these men and women by name and oftentimes address. However, over the years, the label of sex offender has been applied to a wide array of behaviors beyond those of rapist and child molester. These behaviors include urinating in public, streaking, engaging in a consensual relationship with someone younger than age 18, and having consensual sex in a public place.

A report conducted by Robert Barnoski (2005) of the Washington State Institute for Public Policy tracked the recidivism rate of sex offenders released from Washington state prisons. Below are the rates (by year). Barnoski found that compared to all felony offenders, felony sex offenders had the lowest recidivism rates.

Year	5-Year Rate	Year	5-Year Rate
1986	6%	1993	8%
1987	7.5%	1994	6%
1988	7.5%	1995	4%
1989	6%	1996	3%
1990	7%	1997	2%
1991	8%	1998	3%
1992	6%	1999	3.7%

First, using the figures above, describe the recidivism rate of sex offenders. How do you think it compares to other offenders? (You could actually do the research here to find an answer.) Now, using the understanding of deviant careers you've gained from this chapter, discuss the expected and actual recidivism rates for sex offenders. What does this mean for understanding sex offending as a deviant career? How might the broad set of behaviors defined as sex offenses and the public treatment of sex offenders affect our beliefs about the offenders' deviant careers?

◈ Conclusion

In this chapter, we have discussed deviant careers, meaning one's work is deviant, and career deviance, meaning a period of deviant behavior that has a beginning, a middle that might include escalation or specialization, and an end. We view this period of deviant behavior as a process. In fact, each stage of many deviant careers or career deviances can be viewed as a process. The obvious exception might be a quick, untimely death before one even considers exiting the career. We should note that in this chapter, we have focused on deviant behaviors that are criminal, or at least unhealthy (e.g., smoking, excessive drinking, and eating disorders)—cases where we felt most students would expect or hope to see an end to the behaviors. Many forms of deviance do not fit this model. Homosexuality is still considered deviant by many in our society, but most of us recognize that one's sexual orientation may not and should not change over time. As well, various mental and physical disorders and the behaviors that accompany them may not change greatly over the life course.

Still, the career paradigm does offer some useful insights into the initiation process, a better understanding of how people manage their deviant careers or career deviance, and useful knowledge of the process of desistance for many forms of deviance. A prestigious sociologist, Francis Cullen (2011), in his Sutherland Award address, lamented how the study of deviant careers became less popular with the rise of survey research so easily used in schools to study "delinquency." He described how static, cross-sectional research is now falling to the wayside (or at least that it should) and that we need to take a life course perspective, including longitudinal data collection, if we are to advance the study of crime and deviance. We agree that cross-sectional designs are limited, especially when it comes to studying career deviance and deviant careers, and we hope more longitudinal designs will emerge that are focused on noncriminal forms of deviance. However, it is the reemergence and popularity of the study of life course deviance that excites us, no matter what research design is used to address the issues in question.

EXERCISES AND DISCUSSION QUESTIONS

1. How might different factors influence people to initiate, persist in, and exit a deviant career?

2. Consider any deviant behavior that you have been involved in. What factors motivated you to initiate this behavior? If you persisted, what factors led you to do this? If you didn't persist, what factors motivated you to stop?

3. What deviant behaviors might best be explained from a life course perspective, and which ones probably can be explained from a static perspective?

4. Choose a theory from the list below and describe how it might be particularly useful to employ from a life course perspective. Would any of the theories not work well from a life course perspective? Why?

   a. Differential association/social learning

   b. Social control or bonding

   c. Self-control

   d. Labeling

   e. Conflict

f. Critical theories (feminist, peacemaking, critical race theory)

5. If you had to study just one aspect of deviance in the life course perspective (e.g., onset/initiation, persistence/escalation/specialization, desistance), what would you study and why?

KEY TERMS

Criminal career paradigm

Desistance

Escalation

Human agency

Life course perspective

Onset/initiation

Protective factors

Risk factors

Specialization

CHAPTER 13

Global Perspectives on Deviance and Social Control

A recent *USA Today* featured a short article on weird laws from around the world. While all are truly "weird," some appear to actually have a rational reason for their existence, while others do not. For example, in Rome it is illegal to eat or drink near landmarks, and in Greece it is illegal to wear stiletto heels. While both these laws appear to be rather random, when explored they make perfect sense. The laws are designed to preserve the ancient landmarks found in both places. It is fairly obvious that eating and drinking in historic places could lead to sticky walls or ruined artifacts, but stiletto heels may be just as dangerous. It turns out that the pressure from a thin stiletto heel is roughly equal to the pressure of an elephant walking in the same spot. Thailand and Canada both have laws that dictate how people treat or use their currency. In Thailand, it is illegal to step on the nation's currency. All currency in Thailand carries a picture of the king, and, because the king is so revered, it is a great offense to treat the currency and thus the king disrespectfully. In Canada, it is illegal to use more than 25 pennies in a single transaction. Why? Not quite sure, except there appears to be a strong feeling that the penny is worthless—the government has phased out the coin. Not to be outdone, the United States has its fair share of weird laws, too. In Washington State it is illegal to harass Bigfoot, Sasquatch, or any other undiscovered subspecies. In North Dakota, it is illegal to serve beer and pretzels at the same time at a bar or restaurant. And in Missouri, you can't ride in a car with an uncaged bear.

Sources: Sarkis, C. (2012, December 20). 10 weird laws from around the world. *USA Today*. Retrieved from http://www.usatoday.com/story/travel/destinations/2012/12/19/10-weird-laws-from-around-the-world/1779931/; Dumb Laws. (2013). *The Dumb Network*. Retrieved from http://www.dumblaws.com/law/1917

◈ Introduction

It is fun to sit and ponder the weird laws that exist around the world, but there are two larger points to be made in a chapter on global perspectives on deviance and social control. First, there is no greater example of the relativist nature of deviance than examining the laws of a country or region. While it is unlikely anyone is getting into a car with an uncaged bear anytime soon, it is much more likely that beer and pretzels will be served at the same time, that stiletto heels will be worn, and that someone might mistreat the currency of a country. While some might engage in these acts knowing their behavior will be defined as deviant, it is our bet that a good number will have no clue that their actions are defined as deviant, at least by the laws in that country. Second, the responses to these forms of deviance are also relative. While it is true that the law says you cannot eat or drink near historic landmarks in Rome, it is rarely enforced, and while the authors have not had the pleasure of drinking a beer in North Dakota, we bet we could find at least one restaurant that would serve us a pretzel, too. None of us are willing to test the uncaged bear law. As you will see in this chapter, there is much to be studied about global deviance and social control.

Most of this book is dedicated to how we think about, understand, describe, and explain deviance. In other words, most of this book is dedicated to a sociological and theoretical understanding of deviance. For this reason, this chapter is outside the norm (or, as some might say, deviant) in this book. We have chosen to include it because we believe that an analysis of global perspectives in deviance and social control helps us appreciate an examination of deviance by including perspectives we do not often experience. It also allows us the opportunity to apply those theories we have been discussing in the rest of the book. For this reason, you will see the structure of this chapter mirrors the structure of the book: first we examine researching deviance globally, then we look at empirical tests of theories of deviance globally, and finally we discuss social control in a global context.

◈ Researching Deviance Globally

For the undergraduate student of deviant behavior, and especially those interested in deviance across the globe, research should always start with the work of others. There are a number of journals that purport to publish studies of crime and criminal justice outside the United States or internationally. Others focus on particular forms of deviance and make an effort to include research with an international or interdisciplinary focus. Thumbing through those journals one will find some research outside the United States and some truly international research—that is, research that transcends borders. Alternatively, a great deal of research will be conducted by Americans and focus on American citizens. On its Web site, the journal *Deviant Behavior* purports to be

> the only journal that specifically and exclusively addresses social deviance. International and interdisciplinary in scope; it publishes refereed theoretical, descriptive, methodological, and applied papers. All aspects of deviant behavior are discussed, including: crime, juvenile delinquency, alcohol abuse and narcotic addiction, sexual deviance, societal reaction to handicap and disfigurement, mental illness, and socially inappropriate behavior.

While the journal is open to research from around the world, and perhaps even actively strives to be international and interdisciplinary, a great many of the articles are written by U.S. researchers focused on American citizens. The next section discusses issues surrounding doing research outside of the United States.

Trials and Tribulations Involved in Researching Deviance Across the Globe

Laws and official reporting and recording practices vary significantly across countries (Newman, 2008), thus making comparisons of deviance rates using official statistics problematic. That is, while official statistics may be very useful, they measure as much what officials do as how deviant individuals behave and the correlates of that behavior. This leaves many thinking that self-report measures may provide more valid information regarding deviance in other countries. While this may be true, there are definite problems collecting data regarding deviance in other countries and cultures, and many things must be considered in advance.

As with any scientific research, the research protocol must be approved by an institutional review board (IRB). As discussed in Chapter 3, while most IRBs support research, they have to make sure that certain procedures are followed, and this may become even more complex and problematic when one is proposing to do research outside the United States. First, the IRB will want evidence that the researcher has permission to do research in a foreign country. Some countries legally prohibit research. Indeed, the U.S. Department of Health and Human Services Web site (http://www.hhs.gov/ohrp/international/intlcompilation/intlcompilation.html) provides "a listing of over 1,000 laws, regulations, and guidelines on human subjects' protections in over 100 countries and from several international organizations." IRBs will want documentation from public citizens, schools, or local officials showing that they understand the nature of the research and that they agree to allow the research to take place.

Second, and most generally, an IRB will want to make sure that culturally appropriate procedures are in place to protect participants in the research activity. Although the researcher may (or indeed may not) know a great deal about the culture and local customs outside the United States, it is very likely that some IRB members will not be aware of the norms, customs, and beliefs that may offend research participants or their leaders, and the IRB will probably need to be educated in these regards before it can approve research. It would behoove a researcher, even one with a vast knowledge of a particular culture, to have an endorsement from another expert that the research will not cause offense or concern in the society in question.

A third issue is language. If the research involves in-depth interviews, the researcher or research team must know the language well enough to conduct the interviews. Usually, in-depth interviews do not follow a specific script, and the researcher will begin with only a set of key questions that he or she expects will change as more is learned about the specific issues being studied. This could become a slippery slope in studies of deviance because the research may go down a path that was not approved by an IRB and lead to problems. There is not much an IRB can do about this, but the researcher(s) would be required to let the IRB know if any adverse events occur.

When conducting survey research in a foreign country that speaks a language other than English, it is likely that the survey will need to be translated. Once again, IRB members will not likely speak the other language, and so they may want to have the survey translated, then back-translated, so that they know that what is being included in the translated document is consistent with the original. While this may be time consuming and potentially expensive, it would appear to be the right thing to do and would ultimately make the results of the research more valid.

A fourth issue has to do with protected groups. There are several protected populations where special consideration must be given to the respondents' ability to provide consent to participate in research. For example, prisoners may feel compelled to do research if a guard is supplying the survey or even in the room when the researcher is asking for consent. Children are also an issue as they are not legally eligible to give consent. In the United States, the legal age of consent is 18, but it may be older or younger in other countries. This raises an interesting question. It may seem self-evident that if the legal age of consent in a country is older than 18, the local law should be followed. However, if the local law is younger than 18, do we follow local custom or U.S. regulations? Another issue that arises when studying children is parental consent. In the United States, parental consent is usually required to conduct research on children. But what if parental consent is culturally inappropriate in a particular society—for example, one in which tribal elders or other family members are responsible for the children? In any case, the person who needs to provide the consent, be it a parent or other person, must be provided with a request that is written in the language of the resident at such a level that he or she will understand the protocol (what is being asked of the child). This request should inform the consent giver that he or she does not have to allow the child to participate and/or can stop the research at any point without penalty. If a waiver of active parental permission is granted, a letter informing the parents of the research, written at a literacy level that would be understood by the parents, may be required and should be prepared and sent to them by the most expeditious method possible.

Finally, how the data will be kept anonymous or confidential must be specified. If and how the data will be handled by different individuals or agencies must be laid out. How the data might be transferred physically or electronically and how the information will be protected must be demonstrated. In some cases, it will be important to describe how the data will be analyzed and presented to the public so that concerns about disclosing individual information are minimized.

These are many issues to consider, and they may not seem all that relevant to undergraduate students. However, just because undergraduates may not be conducting their own actual research outside the United States, it does not follow that such issues should not be considered and discussed. Understanding the practical and ethical issues surrounding such research will help us to understand the limitations of other studies we come across, making us both more appreciative and skeptical of what we are reading or hearing about in class or in social media. The next section provides a quick look into a few alternatives available to study deviance in other countries.

DEVIANCE IN POPULAR CULTURE

Because many of us have not had the opportunity to travel around the world—or the misfortune to be held in a foreign prison—much of what we think we know about deviance and social control in global context comes from popular culture. Here we have selected a few films that portray foreign cultures, deviance, crime, and prisons. What messages do you think these films share with their mainstream audiences? How do they shape perceptions of deviance and social control in countries around the world?

Brokedown Palace (1999)—Claire Danes and Kate Beckinsale play American high school friends vacationing in Thailand who, whether they intended to do so or were simply vulnerable victims, are caught smuggling drugs and sentenced to 33 years in a Thai prison. The film shows their adjustment to life in a prison in a foreign land and their attempts to find a way out.

Return to Paradise (1998)—three friends meet on vacation in Malaysia, indulging in alcohol, drugs, and the beach. After two return to their lives in the United States, one is caught with a large amount of their shared hashish. In an interesting plot twist and moral question, if the others will return and accept responsibility and ownership of the drugs, they will all do shorter sentences in the third world prison. Otherwise, the friend who was caught will be sentenced to death because the large amount has branded him a trafficker and earned him a death sentence.

City of God (2002)—a vivid film and story focusing on the City of God housing project, plagued by crushing poverty, violence, and gangs in the slums of Rio de Janeiro. The focus is on two boys growing up surrounded by and immersed in deviance, drugs, and weapons.

Trainspotting (1996)—something of a cult favorite film about a group of heroin addicts in the Edinburgh drug scene, famous for its "Choose life" monologue. The film displays all kinds of deviant behavior, mixing humor with horrifying scenes. The plot details the main character's efforts to kick his habit.

Hunger (2008)—film based on the true story of a 1981 hunger strike in which 10 Irish Republican Army prisoners died. The film focuses on inhumane prison conditions and highlights three different stories: the daily life of a prison guard, the IRA prisoners' refusal to bathe or wear prison clothes, and the hunger strike. The film pays special attention to Bobby Sands, who was the first prisoner to die.

 ## More Reasonable Strategies for Undergraduates to Study Deviance Outside the United States

Most students will not have the resources to directly study (e.g., go to the foreign country and conduct surveys or interviews) deviance outside the United States. There are several existing large-scale data sets for studying deviance across countries. Sometimes the focus is on the criminal justice system or reactions to deviance. For example, Interpol and the United Nations provide data on what crimes are known to the police across a large number of countries and also about how these crimes are handled—for example, the number or rates of arrests, prosecutions, and convictions. Alternatively, a number of data sets exist that use surveys to collect self-reported measures of "crime," "delinquency," or "victimization" across countries. While these titles highlight a criminological emphasis, note that these generic terms include numerous offenses that may or may not come to the attention of the police and softer forms of deviant behavior that even if they came to the attention of authorities might provoke little or no reaction.

For example, the International Self-Reported Delinquency Study of 1992 (Junger-Tas et al., 1994) focused on self-reported misbehavior and victimization among youth aged 12 to 15 in 13 countries. A follow-up of this project resulted in the Second International Self-Reported Delinquency Study (Enzmann & Podana, 2010), now expanded to 31 countries. Self-report items ranged from relatively minor forms of deviance (e.g., "Steal something from a shop or department store") to quite serious ones (e.g., "Intentionally beat someone up, or hurt him with a stick or knife, so bad that they had to see a doctor") (Enzmann & Podana, 2010, p. 183). Vazsonyi and his colleagues (2001) developed the Normative Deviance Scale, which was designed to measure noncriminal forms of lifetime deviance. They collected data from several countries, including the United States, Switzerland, Hungary, and New Zealand.

The following list highlights just a few data sets that are available through the International Consortium of Political and Social Research (see Chapter 3), which your university may be affiliated with. These data sets focus on deviance and social control internationally, or at least outside the United States.

- International Dating Violence Study, 2001–2006 (covering 32 countries)
- International Crime Victimization Survey, 1989–2000 (the 2000 wave covering 47 industrialized and developing countries)
- Correlates of Crime: A Study of 52 Nations, 1960–1984
- United Nations Surveys of Crime Trends and Operations of Criminal Justice Systems Series, Waves 1–10, 1970–2006
- Citizenship, Democracy, and Drug-Related Violence, 2011 (Mexico)
- Center for Research on Social Reality [Spain] Survey, December 1993: Attitudes and Behavior Regarding Alcohol, Tobacco, and Drugs
- Euro-Barometer 32: The Single European Market, Drugs, Alcohol, and Cancer, November 1989

In the following section, we describe how several theories developed in the United States have been tested in other countries.

◈ Empirical Tests of Theories of Deviance Globally

Studying deviance around the world is nothing new. Indeed, much anthropological work might be seen as the study of customs, attitudes, behaviors, and beliefs that modern Western society might find deviant. However, the sociological research focusing on the theories described in this book, most all carried out in the United States or in other developed Western societies, has only recently been empirically investigated outside the United States. This investigative extension might very likely stem from the seemingly audacious claim by Gottfredson and Hirschi (1990) that their general theory of crime could explain not only crime but other analogous behaviors (i.e., deviance) across all cultures and historical times; this claim led others to test Gottfredson and Hirschi's theory, and other theories of deviance as well. In this chapter, we examine empirical evidence as it relates to a variety of theories of deviance and social control.

Empirical Tests of Gottfredson and Hirschi's General Theory of Deviance: Self-Control and Deviance in Other Countries

As discussed in Chapter 7, Gottfredson and Hirschi's (1990) general theory of crime, which focuses on the relationship between low self-control and crime and analogous behaviors (i.e., deviance), has been well researched, especially in the United States. Indeed, in the meta-analysis conducted by Pratt and Cullen (2000), they concluded that "with these caveats stated, the meta-analysis reported here furnishes fairly impressive empirical support for Gottfredson and Hirschi's theory" (p. 951). Interestingly, the meta-analysis, which was conducted nearly 10 years after Gottfredson and Hirschi first published their book, did not include empirical tests conducted outside the United States, presumably because they were not available to be included. Subsequent to the publication of the meta-analysis, there have been a number of important empirical tests of the relationship between self-control and deviant behavior outside the United States.

Cretacci and his colleagues published several studies examining self-control theory based on convenience samples collected in China (Cretacci et al., 2010; Cretacci & Cretacci, 2012). In their most direct test of the theory, which focused on the relationship between self-control and deviance, they collected data from students ($n = 148$) in the law and social work departments at a Beijing university (Cretacci et al., 2010). Interestingly, the survey was administered in English. At least one of the authors, however, had interacted enough with the respondents to be confident that they could complete the relatively simple survey the researchers had designed. Deviance was measured with a 14-item scale asking about various forms of deviance. The study found support for Hirschi's (1969 and 2004) social control construct, which was significantly associated with lower levels of deviance.

Lu and colleagues (2013) provide a more recent analysis using the Second International Self-Report Delinquency Study. The data came from a probability sample of seventh-, eighth-, and ninth-grade students from nine schools in five urban areas in the city of Hanzhou, China (the capital city of the Zhejiang Province). In this study, the self-report instrument was translated and pretested with exchange students at an American university. Two dependent variables measuring deviance were (1) minor "risky behaviors" (e.g., drinking and smoking); and (2) "delinquency" (e.g., fighting, carrying a weapon, vandalism). Self-control was measured with a shorter adaptation of Grasmick's scale, including the dimensions of "impulsivity, risk-seeking, self-centeredness, and temper" (Lu et al., 2013, p. 39). Social control measures included family and school bonding, school commitment, and beliefs. As in most studies conducted in the United States, the results supported the general theory of crime, showing self-control to be a significant and relatively robust predictor of both forms of deviance after controlling for a number of theoretically relevant variables (e.g., measure social control) and standard control variables (e.g., age and sex). Some support was also found for social control theory, especially as family bonding and beliefs appeared significant in at least two models. Given that this was a much more rigorous examination of the relationship between self-control and deviance, we conclude that the Gottfredson and Hirschi's theory of deviance is indeed generalizable to China.

Self-control has been tested in other countries as well, by researchers such as Vazsonyi and his colleagues. One especially interesting study (Vazsonyi et al., 2001) involved a test of self-control theory among youths in America ($n = 2,213$), Switzerland ($n = 889$), Hungary ($n = 4,018$), and the Netherlands ($n = 1,315$). Deviance was measured with a 55-item normative deviance scale, with subscales including vandalism, alcohol and drug use, school misconduct, general deviance, theft, and assault. Self-control was measured with Grasmick's 24-item scale. The researchers found consistent support across countries for the general theory of crime in that self-control explained between 10–16% of the variation in the deviant behavior subscales and over 20% of the variation in the full measure of deviance. In another study using the same measures, Vazsonyi and colleagues (2004) tested the theory among Japanese youth (n = 334), finding comparable outcomes to a U.S. sample of youth. In yet another study using similar measures but with the addition of family process measures related to social control (closeness, support, and monitoring), Vazsonyi and Klanjsek (2008) examined the relationship between self-control, social control, and deviance with over 3,000 Swiss. They found at least some support for both Hirschi's social control theory and Hirschi's general theory of crime.

Özbay and Köksoy (2008, 2009) provided tests of self-control theory in the developing country of Turkey. They focused on predicted general violence and political violence among college students (n = 974) using a modified version of Grasmick's scale. Özbay and Köksoy (2009) found that low self-control was associated with a significantly greater likelihood of both forms of violence after controlling for a host of theoretically relevant variables (e.g., strain, criminal friends) and standard control variables (e.g., age and gender). In another article, Özbay (2008) examines the generalizability of self-control across gender. Using the same data set, the researcher finds that not only is self-control generalizable across males and females, the empirical evidence suggests that the theory is more generalizable than other theories, including bonding and strain theories.

We will conclude this section with a discussion of what is clearly the largest global test of Gottfredson and Hirschi's general theory. In "Self-Control in a Global Perspective," Rebellon, Straus, and Medeiros (2008) tested several aspects of the general theory within and across fully 32 nations spanning "all six humanly habitable continents" (p. 331) and including Western, non-Western, developed, and developing countries. The data came from the International Dating Violence Consortium, which collected it from college students in universities across the 32 countries. Straus and Medeiros developed a six-item scale to measure the six dimensions of self-control described by Gottfredson and Hirschi. These items included the following:

Self-Centered: I don't think about how what I do will affect other people

Risk-Taking: I often do things that other people think are dangerous.

Temper: There is nothing I can do to control my feelings when my partner hassles me.

Preference for Physical: I often get hurt by the things that I do.

Impulsivity: I have trouble following the rules at work or in school.

Long-Term Consequences: I have goals in life that I try to reach.

For each question, respondents were asked to what extent they agreed or disagreed with the statement on a four-point scale (1 = "strongly disagree" to 4 = "strongly agree").

Criminal behavior included both property crime (stolen property worth more than $50 U.S. and stolen money from anyone, including family) and violent crime (physical attack of someone with intention of seriously harming them and hit or threatened to hit a nonfamily member). Each of the four items were conditioned in terms of age, so respondents were asked once if the event happened before they were 15 years old and then asked again if it had occurred after they were 15. Two scales were then created with four items each, measuring property and violent crime, respectively.

Given Gottfredson and Hirschi's emphasis on child rearing and emotional involvement of parents in children's lives in the development of self-control, the researchers also included an eight-item "parental neglect scale" that included items measuring direct control (e.g., parents making sure the respondent went to school) and social support (e.g., parent provided comfort). These measures allowed a pretty solid test of the general theory in that parental efforts could be correlated with self-control, which in turn could be related to criminal behavior.

The findings and results of the study are fairly clear and supportive of Gottfredson and Hirschi's theory. First, parental neglect was a significant predictor of self-control in all 32 countries, explaining between 15 and 39% of the variation in self-control. Second, self-control was significantly related to violent crime in all 32 countries, and self-control was significantly related to property crime in 28 of the 32 countries.

While the researchers found considerable support for Gottfredson and Hirschi's general theory of crime across both Western and non-Western nations, they do point out a few caveats. First, the measure of criminal peers was also found to be a relatively robust predictor of crime across nations. Second, even though self-control was largely associated with violence and property crime across countries, there was considerable variation in its predictive ability—that is, the effect of self-control was not constant across cultures, as predicted by the theory.

This study and the others described above, taken together, suggest that self-control is a relatively strong correlate of crime and deviance across 32+ nations. Although empirical evidence is not perfectly consistent across countries, overall there appears to be general support across various forms of deviance.

Testing Differential Association and Social Learning Theories Outside of the United States

Like social and self-control theories, tests of differential association and social learning theories have mostly been conducted in the United States. However, some recent efforts have moved beyond the confines of this country. Not far from the United States is the French- and English-speaking country to the north, Canada. There Gallupe and Bouchard (2013) examined social learning theory and substance use through an investigation of party-going among adolescents in a large Canadian city. A total of 829 students were surveyed and 411 of them reported on their behavior at a total of 775 parties. Three hundred and sixty-one students reported on multiple parties, which allowed the researchers to investigate changes in party characteristics and how that affected substance use. The key social learning variable was reinforcement, and this was measured by the number of close friends who drank alcohol or used marijuana at the party and the amount of alcohol and marijuana these friends used. In both the cross-sectional and semi-longitudinal analyses (change), reinforcement variables were found to be relatively strong predictors of both alcohol and marijuana use, thus showing support for differential association/social learning theories.

Moving across the ocean, we find that differential association/social learning theories have also been tested in Europe. By the year 2000, there had been only a few ethnographic and interview-based studies of youth deviance conducted in France, and no systematic self-report studies, so Hartjen and Priyadarsini (2003) initiated a study to test theories in rural France, focusing heavily on differential association/social learning theory. They argued that France is a particularly interesting country to utilize self-reported methods because,

> France appears to have an extremely benevolent and tolerant approach to misbehaving youth. Very few are ever incarcerated and, if so, not for very long. Every effort is made by officials from police to judges to divert misbehaving juvenile from official processing or punitive action. (Hartjen & Priyadarsini, 2003, p. 389)

With official counts of criminal sanctions being so low, self-report research is likely to detect much more deviant behavior and should be a better indicator of misbehavior. Hartjen and Priyadarsini surveyed male and female junior high and high school students ranging in age from 13–18 from three schools. All three schools were located in a single, ethnographically homogeneous, rural town in France.

The survey they used was based on the National Youth Survey, which was translated into French. They included two measures of delinquency—a total delinquency scale based on 50 items and a "petty delinquency" scale that included minor misbehaviors. Measures based on differential association/social learning theories included

> attitudes towards deviance [measured as negative attitudes towards deviance or prosocial attitudes], peer involvement [measured as positive peer involvement], exposure to delinquent peers, and an index of exposure to delinquent peers [created by combining peer involvement with exposure to delinquent peers]. (p. 393)

Positive peer involvement and prosocial attitudes were negatively related to both total and petty deviant behaviors among both males and females in the sample, while exposure to delinquent peers was positively related to both measures of deviant behavior among both groups. Interestingly, there were no differences in the effects of the differential association/social leaning variables across gender, suggesting that the theory is generalizable and not unique to male or female respondents.

In one of the more impressive and truly international inquiries, Antonaccio and her colleagues (2011) have tested several theories including social learning theory in three key cities in three European countries that have "exhibited widely publicized actions to preserve their unique national cultural patterns" (p. 1203). The cities were Athens, Greece; Nizhni Novgorod, Russia; and Lviv, Ukraine. In an effort to maintain causal order in a cross-sectional study, the researchers asked questions about the likelihood of committing violent and property crimes in the future and about past experiences reinforcing violent behavior and property crime (via social learning theory). They argue that using projected offending has been found to be as valid as using self-reports of prior deviant behaviors and comes as close to maintaining the causal ordering of the model as one can get with a cross-sectional design.

Under the supervision of the research team, trained local interviewers conducted face-to-face interviews with individuals from randomly selected households in Athens ($n = 400$), Lviv ($n = 500$), and Nizhni Novgorod ($n = 500$). In analyses of the data set as a whole (merging data from the three cities), they found that reinforcement was significantly associated with projections of both violent behavior and property crimes after controlling for a number of other variables. Indeed, reinforcement was the strongest predictor across models. Similarly, when the analyses were disaggregated by city (analyzed separately), the social learning measure of reinforcement was positively related to both property and violent crime projections. Again, in virtually all of the models, reinforcement was the strongest predictor.

Differential association/social learning theories have also been tested in Asian countries. Kim and her colleagues (Kim et al., 2010; Kim et al., 2013), for example, have provided at least two tests of social leaning theory in South Korea, both focused on substance use. In the first study they analyzed data from the Korea Youth Panel Survey, which was a longitudinal study of two cohorts (second graders and junior high students) beginning in 2003 (Kim et al., 2013). They used the first two waves of data collected in 2003 and 2004. There was only minor attrition from the study (<10%), resulting in 3,188 student respondents. Substance use, the dependent variable, was measured with self-reported items indicating how often they had drunk alcohol or smoked cigarettes in the past year. Three concepts emerged that were most clearly derived from social learning theory: (1) a differential peer association measure based on six items indicating how many of their close friends engaged in delinquent activities, (2) differential association intensity indicated by a single item indicating how important one's reputation with deviant peers was, and (3) peer substance use measured with two items indicating how many close friends used tobacco and how many used alcohol. Interestingly, in a multivariate model, substance use was unrelated to substance use by peers and peer delinquency, but it was positively related to deviant peer intensity increasing the odds of using substances by 21%. In this carefully collected data from a nationally represented sample of young South Koreans, we find only modest support for social learning theory. In fact, controls for parental attachment and supervision, usually associated with social control/bond theory, were more powerful predictors of substance abuse.

The second study (Kim et al., 2013) was more ambitious theoretically and empirically. In this study Kim and colleagues attempted to test Akers' full social structure social learning model to predict alcohol use. The data came from a self-report study of high school students in Busan, South Korea, a large metropolitan area in the southeast tip of the Korean Peninsula. Data were collected from just over 1,000 high school students. The data analyses clearly show support for the standard social learning theory. Kim and colleagues (2013, p. 908) found that alcohol use increases when students:

1. Have a greater proportion of peers who use alcohol

2. Have fathers who use alcohol

3. Have definitions favorable to alcohol use

4. Have a greater chance of imitating use of alcohol by behavioral models

Furthermore, they found that, consistent with Akers' SSSL theory, the effects of several of the structural-level variables, significant when only they were in the model, were mediated by the social learning variables. Specifically, the effects of population size, residential mobility, type of school, and religiosity were explained by social learning variables. Even the strong gender effect, which remains significant in the final model, is largely explained by the social learning variables. Given the more rigorous measurement of the key constructs and analyses conducted in the previous study, we believe the evidence lends considerable support for Akers' SSSL theory.

◈ A Global Perspective on Social Disorganization Theory

Social disorganization theory is clearly an American-born theory, rooted in the Chicago School of Sociology. Indeed, stemming from the original theoretical and empirical work by Shaw and McKay (1942/1969) in the early 1900s, work in this tradition continues to the present day (e.g., Sampson, 2012). Of course, the theory has been tested in other major U.S. cities, such as New York, Chicago, and St. Louis, among others. The theory was originally developed to explain neighborhood variation in delinquency and crime across relatively small macro units, but there is clearly reason to believe that the same general structural characteristics (i.e., economic deprivation, population instability, and racial/ethnic heterogeneity) may operate at other levels to explain various forms of crime and deviance. For example, social disorganization theory has also been applied to schools, cities, and states within the United States. There is also reason to believe that social disorganization is a general macro-level theory of crime that can be applied to other countries and across nations that vary in levels of informal social control.

Recently, several efforts to test the theory at the neighborhood level in other countries have been published, and it appears that social disorganization has the potential to explain levels of deviant behavior outside the United States. In the next section, we describe studies that focus on neighborhood-level analyses across cities outside the United States.

Tests of Social Disorganization in Cities Outside the United States

Breetzke (2010) argues that South Africa provides an excellent setting to test social disorganization theory. He states that

> the recent political history of South Africa is inherently intertwined with social disorganization and community fragmentation. While a few examples may exist elsewhere, no other country in the world has endured such a direct and sustained attack on the social fabric of its society through state laws and policies aimed at enforcing and accentuating spatio-social segmentation. (p. 447)

To test social disorganization theory in this context, Breetzke collected data in the city of Tshwane, one of the six largest metropolitan areas in South Africa. The level of analysis was the census-defined "suburb," with the number of households in each suburb ranging from 150–300.

Three years of violent crime data (2001–2003), including "murder, attempted murder, sexual offenses assault with the intent to cause grievous bodily harm and common assault," was culled from the Crime and Information Analysis Centre (Breetzke, 2010, p. 448). Address-based data were geocoded and aggregated to the suburb level. These were matched with other 2001 census measures, including ethnic heterogeneity, socioeconomic deprivation, family disruption, and residential mobility (Breetzke, 2010, p. 448). Several of these variables were quite different in nature from those found in the United States or had potentially different meanings from our understanding in the West. For example, in addition to unemployment (a common measure used in tests of social disorganization theory in the United States), the measure of socioeconomic disadvantage included "type of dwelling, source of water, toilet facilities, refuse or rubbish removal, and energy or fuel for lighting, heating and cooking" (Breetzke, 2010, p. 448). These items are largely irrelevant in industrialized developed nations and were specifically designed by the Nation's Development Program (2003) to assess socio-economic development in South Africa. Interestingly, given the heterogeneous nature of the country, there was plenty of room to measure various forms of racial and ethnic heterogeneity (as the country has four official racial groups and nine distinct ethnic groups) and linguistic heterogeneity (as the country has eleven official languages). The authors chose to focus simply on the percentage black, given the history of apartheid that segregated "Black African, Colored, Asian, or Indian" individuals who were viewed as nonwhites (Breetzke, 2010, p. 448).

Results were mixed. On the one hand, consistent with social disorganization theory both measures of socioeconomic deprivation (unemployment and the deprivation index) were statistically and positively related to rates of violent crime. Similarly, residential mobility (the percentage of the population that had moved in the past 5 years) was positively related to the rate of violent crime. However, the percentage of the suburb characterized as black or nonwhite actually trended in a negative direction and was not statistically significant. This was also the case for the percentage of female-headed households. The race finding is particularly interesting given the history of South Africa and its policy of total segregation. One would think with this shift in policy that desegregated communities would have higher violent crime rates. There may be something statistically odd going on here, but not enough information was provided on the distribution of this variable to comment further. However, given the heterogeneous nature of the country, more work should look at finer measures of racial/ethnic and linguistic heterogeneity.

The fact that the percentage of households headed by women was unrelated to violent crime might be explained by the measurement of the variable. Black South Africans often work far from the home and are gone for long periods of time, even though their household census designation is in the home. Thus, because two of the empirical inconsistencies with social disorganization theory may have to do with poor measurement and statistical anomalies, we suggest that the bulk of the evidence supports the predictive ability of social disorganization, at least across suburbs of Tshwane, South Africa.

Moving to Asia, Zhang and colleagues (2007) studied household burglary victimization across neighborhoods in Tianjin, China. The results were interesting, and while somewhat different from what researchers have found in the West, in some ways still supportive of social disorganization theory. First, inconsistent with social disorganization theory, poverty was unrelated to burglary, and residential stability was positively associated with burglary. The former may have something to do with the lack of attractive targets in impoverished neighborhoods cancelling out the safer but wealthier neighborhoods. The latter seems somewhat intractable given the various possibilities. Alternatively, collective efficacy was, as expected, negatively associated with burglary, as was the presence of formal agents of social control (the visibility of the police). The perceived effectiveness of neighborhood mediation groups was not a significant predictor of burglary, but this may reflect the amount of mediation going on. That is, if there are many problems, there may be more information to base judgment on (though mediation may appear less effective because there are many problems), but, when there are few disputes, there is little to base judgment on. Given these concerns, perceptions of mediation groups may not be the best indicator of the semi-public control the researchers wanted to measure. These finding are supportive of newer versions of social disorganization theory that focus on collective efficacy (social cohesion and informal social control) and social control from the public sector (i.e., the police).

As mentioned, social disorganization theory has mostly been tested in the United States and mostly in urban areas. While a few empirical tests of social disorganization theory in rural areas of the United States have been conducted and have supported the theory (Barnett & Mencken, 2002; Osgood & Chambers, 2000), not much has been done outside the country. However, Jobes and his colleagues (2004) provided one such test in New South Wales, Australia. They obtained crime data from the New South Wales Bureau of Crime Statistics and census data from the Australian Bureau of Statistics for 123 local geographic areas. These are the smallest "municipal" units defined by the census and include on average less than 50,000 residents. Crime data included rates of assault, breaking and entering, malicious damage to property, and motor vehicle theft. The researchers collected 19 different measures from the census that fell under five dimensions of social disorganization theory: (1) low socioeconomic status (e.g., unemployment, poverty); (2) residential instability (e.g., living at a different address, living in own home); (3) ethnic heterogeneity (e.g., proportion indigenous); (4) family disruptions (e.g., divorce, sole parent); and (5) population size and density.

Across dimensions of crime the social disorganization variables explained a good deal of the variation—between 20 and 45% across models. This is similar to analyses conducted in rural areas in the United States, suggesting that not only is the theory generalizable, its ability to explain variation is about the same across these two countries. Dimensions of social disorganization particularly predictive of the various crimes included measures of ethnic heterogeneity, residential instability, and family disruption.

Another study in Australia, though not directly testing social disorganization theory per se, does offer some insight on the predictors of indigenous violence among the Australian Aboriginals. Using the National Aboriginal and Torres Strait Islander Survey (NATSIS), Snowball and Weatherburn (2008) examined a number of theoretical explanations to assess violence among Aboriginals. This is a large survey, not specifically designed to test any one theory, but several items pertained to social disorganization. Given what was available, and based on social disorganization theory, the authors expected that "violent victimisation would be higher amongst Indigenous Australians who:

- Are not socially involved in their communities
- Are sole parents
- Have high rates of geographic mobility (as measured by the number of times they moved house
- Are member or have relatives who are member of the stolen generation" (p. 222)

With the exception of the first expectation, the results were largely supportive of social disorganization theory. In contrast to the researchers' expectations, Aboriginals who were involved in their communities were actually more likely to be victimized than those who were more socially isolated. This may have to do with the different environmental and social settings those in the community find themselves in. Alternatively, the odds of a sole parent being victimized were 39% higher than those with a partner, and the odds of members of the stolen generation (or having relatives who were members) being victimized were 71% higher than others. Finally, each additional geographic move increased the odds of being victimized by 33%. Although this is an individual-level examination of a macro-level theory, the data seem to support social disorganization theory. Taken in total, we find significant support for social disorganization theory outside the United States and across several countries.

Cross-National Tests of Institutional Anomie Theory

In trying to understand the high rates of crime in the United States, Messner and Rosenfeld (2007) argued that societies that value economic institutions (e.g., capitalism and the accumulation of wealth) over non-economic institutions (e.g., education, the family) will have higher rates of crime. Several studies have examined their theory by analyzing subnational macro social units within the United States, including counties (Maume & Lee, 2003) and states (Chamlin & Cochran, 1995). Some support for the theory has been found.

A few studies have begun to investigate the merits of the theory using cross-national tests, which would seem to be the most appropriate test of the theory as it was originally developed to explain the high rates of crime in the United States relative to other nations. Messner and Rosenfield (1997) provided the first empirical test of their theory by linking it with the concept of **decommodification**—the movement away from pure market economies to ones that provide political institutions (such as the welfare state) to protect individuals from the harsh realities of pure capitalism. They argue that "a greater degree of decommodification indicates a lower level of economic dominance in this particular institutional interrelationship" (p. 1397). They created a measure of decommodification that reflects "the ease of access to welfare benefits, their income-replacement value, and the expansiveness of coverage across different statuses and circumstances" (pp. 1398–1399) across 45 nations. These nations varied widely, ranging from developed nations such as the United States and Japan to developing nations such as El Salvador and Sri Lanka. Messner and Rosenfield found support for their hypothesis that countries that have moved away from a pure market economy have lower homicide rates.

Savolainen (2002) extends this work by suggesting that a more "critical test of the institutional anomie theory should estimate the moderating effect of the institutional context on the relationship between economic inequality and serious crime, preferably at the cross-national level of analysis" (p. 1026). That is, other institutions should affect the strength of the relationship between economic inequality and crime. He found not only a direct effect of decommodification on homicide rates, but also an interaction effect with measures of income inequality. Savolainen (2000) concludes that "nations that protect their citizens from the vicissitudes of market forces appear to be immune to the homicidal effects of economic inequality" (p. 1021).

Cochran and Bjerregaard (2012) provide the most recent cross-national test of institutional anomie theory with a new complex measure of structural anomie based on measures of economic freedom, wealth, and income inequality. Controlling for measures of other social institutions, such as the family (divorce rates), the polity (lack of voter turnout), and educational spending, they found that their measure of structural anomie was a robust predictor of both the homicide rate and rates of theft. Taken together, this emerging line of research suggests relatively strong support for institutional anomie theory in a cross-national setting.

Critical Collective Framing Theory and the Genocide in Darfur

While much of the sociological research to date has focused on what leads up to genocide (Gurr & Harff, 1994; Horowitz, 2001); the problem of defining genocide (Chirot & Edwards, 2003); typologies of genocide (Chirot & McCauley, 2006); and the disputed scales of genocide (Hagan et al., 2006), Hagan and Rymond-Richmond (2008) examined the genocide in Darfur from the perspective of critical collective framing theory. Their focus was on "the dehumanizing racial motivations and intentions that explain how a government mobilizes and collaborates in the ideological dehumanization and criminal victimization of a racial group" (p. 876). They found that, indeed, there was an emergence of collective racial motivation and intent with respect to the killings in Darfur that was indicated through the use of racial epithets preceding and during attacks.

This dehumanization process placed black African groups in Darfur outside a bounded universe of moral obligation and left them vulnerable to targeted genocidal victimization. Treatment of groups as dehumanized and contemptible makes them vulnerable to displacement and destruction. We found compelling evidence that collective processes of racial motivation and intent influenced the severity of victimization across settlements, above and beyond this influence at the individual level, and that this collective frame mediated the concentration of attacks on densely settled areas and particular African groups. (Hagan & Rymond-Richmond, 2008, p. 895)

In other words, by framing a group as subhuman (deviant), it makes this group vulnerable to violence in general, and, in the case of Darfur, genocide in particular.

RECENT STUDY IN DEVIANCE

The Cycle of Violence in Spain

By I. Ibabe, J. Jaureguizar, & P. Bentler, 2013, Risk factors for child-to-parent violence, in *Journal of Family Violence, 28(5)*, 523–534.

Does *violence breed violence?* Is there a *cycle of violence,* or an *intergenerational transmission of violence?* That is, do parents teach violence to their children through their own use of violence? Many have linked the empirical correlation between parental deviant behavior, including violence, and children's deviant behavior to social learning theory. Parents may model the behavior and children imitate it. Children may see parental violence work—that is, the parent gets what he or she wants through the use of violence, and this produces an anticipated reinforcement effect that encourages violence. In examining risk factors for child-to-parent violence (CPV), Izaskun Ibabe, Joana Jaureguizar and Peter Bentler studied this link among 485 young male and female children in the Basque Country of Spain. The found interparental violence and parent-to-child violence to be strong predictors of CPV among this sample, suggesting that parents may model violent behavior, reinforce violence as a means of achieving desired outcomes, and, in the end, bring about the *cycle of violence.*

◈ Social Control in Global Context

Discussing social control in global context is a daunting task. Just as there are many, many types of deviant acts depending on the cultural context, there are many different and varied reactions to human behaviors and statuses. Rather than attempt to give a comprehensive overview of the extreme differences in both informal and social control across the globe—a herculean, if not impossible task—in this section, we offer a few examples of how perceived deviance is responded to in different cultural settings. We chose these few examples to illustrate that the systems in America are culturally specific and are not necessarily the best or only way to react to deviance. Our hope is that your curiosity will be sparked by these differences and you will pause to question and research social control as you continue your education.

When we think about social control, what often comes to mind is the reaction to an act—it might be a criminal act, a social faux pas, or the violation of a society's unwritten rules that trigger a reaction from the community. If you think back to what you learned about labeling theory (Chapter 8), however, you will recall sometimes people are punished, oppressed, and sanctioned purely because of who they are. The following examples take two master statuses—that of being a woman and that of identifying as gay or as a gay rights activist—and show how simply existing within those statuses can lead to deadly consequences in some parts of the world.

Social Control of Girls and Women

The book *Half the Sky,* written by husband and wife journalist team Nicholas D. Kristof and Sheryl WuDunn (2009), vividly documents the oppression and control of women and girls across the globe. The authors focus their book on three particular kinds of abuse: "sex trafficking and forced prostitution; gender based violence, including honor killings and mass rape; and maternal mortality, which still needlessly claims one woman a minute" (p. xxi).

Kristof and WuDunn tell stories of young girls in Cambodia, Nepal, Thailand, and Malaysia who were kidnapped, raped, and sold into brothels where they were regularly drugged, beaten, and forced to live as prostitutes and/or modern-day slaves. Girls who were brave enough and risked their lives to escape found no help from local police, who sent them back to the brothels (p. 7).

The authors go on to report on many different kinds of punishments and threats that women endure in other nations. Women perceived to be "loose" or "bad" in Pakistan had their faces destroyed by acid or had their noses cut off as a form of punishment (p. 75). Girls in Iraq were killed by family and religious leaders if it was believed they lost their virginity before marriage (p. 82). In Darfur, militia gang-raped and mutilated women from African tribes, and the Sudanese government responded by punishing women who reported the rapes or sought medical attention (p. 83). In the Congo, rape was used as a terror tactic to control civilian populations; Congolese militia raped women with sticks or knives and were known to fire their guns into women's and girls' vaginas (p. 84). A teenage soldier in Congo explained that rape was routine, saying if he and his fellow soldiers saw girls, it was their right to rape and violate them (p. 86).

As terrifying as it may be, some girls living in restrictive and punitive cultures take great risks to fight for better lives. Malala Yousafzai, a Pakistani schoolgirl, received widespread attention—both positive and negative—when she began speaking out against Taliban oppression when she was only 11 years old. She began her individual form of resistance by writing her thoughts and experiences in a blog using a pseudonym to protect her identity; gradually, she became a more public figure and made media appearances advocating for education for girls. When she was just 14 years old, Malala was targeted and shot in the head and neck by a Taliban gunman while on the school bus home. In part because of her public persona and status as a martyr, she was fortunate enough to get specialized medical care and recover from her wounds.

▲ **Photo 13.1**   Malala Yousafzai was targeted by the Taliban and nominated for a Nobel Peace Prize as a teenager for her courage in advocating for education for girls in Pakistan.

Source: ©Claude Truong-Ngoc/ Wikimedia Commons.

Malala was nominated for the Nobel Peace Prize and won the European Union's highest human rights honor, the Sakharov Prize, in 2013 at just 16 years old. Her bravery has been lauded by the international press, and she has inspired other young girls to fight against oppression and for education and opportunities. "I Am Malala" became the slogan for a campaign to demand global access to education for children. Malala herself continues to face threats from the Taliban; the goals she risks her life for may seem quite simple to those who grew up in the United States and accept such circumstances as their birthright. In Malala's words, "I hope that a day will come when the people of Pakistan will be free, they will have their rights, there will be peace, and every girl and every boy will be going to school" (quoted in Williams, 2013).

Social Control of Homosexuality

Although the United States continues grappling with evolving norms and attitudes around the issues of homophobia, the bullying of gay teens, and the legality of gay marriage, simply being gay is not a crime, and threats and cruelty are not formally sanctioned. The same cannot be said in other countries. Homosexuality is illegal in most African countries, and homosexual acts are punishable by 14 years to life in prison in Uganda (Walsh, 2011). The Anti-Homosexuality Bill proposed in Uganda in 2009 included harsh sanctions for anyone engaging in gay sex or protecting the privacy of those who do; the bill featured the following provisions:

- Gays and lesbians convicted of having gay sex would be sentenced, at minimum, to life in prison
- People who test positive for HIV may be executed
- Homosexuals who have sex with a minor, or engage in homosexual sex more than once, may also receive the death penalty
- The bill forbids the "promotion of homosexuality," which in effect bans organizations working in HIV and AIDS prevention
- Anyone who knew of homosexual activity taking place but did not report it would risk up to three years in prison. (Ahmed, 2009)

The Anti-Homosexuality Bill prompted an international reaction; European nations threatened to cut aid to Uganda if such laws were passed, and the bill was shelved. While the bill was not passed into law, harsh and deadly informal sanctions are still a real threat to gays and gay rights activists in Uganda. A Ugandan tabloid published a front-page story targeting the "top 100 homosexuals," complete with photographs and addresses of those on the list. David Kato, a gay rights activist, told reporters that he feared for his life after his name was published on the list; he was right to be afraid—within the year, Kato was bludgeoned to death in his home (Walsh, 2011).

Social Control of Crime: Extremes in Prison Conditions Internationally

Scandinavia has long been considered the gold standard in terms of creating and maintaining humane prisons that work to rehabilitate offenders and keep crime and incarceration rates low. Indeed, Scandinavian prisons were designed to be constructive and productive, built on the belief that a prison should not be a place of suffering, fear, and deprivation, but instead should be one of redemption, learning, training, and cure, until ultimately, with the commitment to normalization, it replicated the conditions of the outside world rather than shutting them out (Pratt & Eriksson, 2011, p. 20).

Prisons in the United States vary markedly in their quality, and few compare favorably to prisons in Norway or Sweden. Yet there are basic minimum standards for the treatment of prisoners, with codified rules and written documentation that are part of "a culture of audit and control" (Birckbeck, 2011, p. 3180). When documented standards are not met in the United States, litigation is a possibility, and the courts may step in to order changes. Many countries in Latin America and the developing world do not have this type of quality control, and prisons are often overcrowded, unsanitary, and unsafe. Here we offer comparison of prisons in Norway and prisons in Latin America to show these two extremes.

Norway—The Best Prisons in the World?

The goal of many Scandinavian prisons is to make life for prisoners as normal as possible. Loss of liberty is the primary punishment. Arne Nilsen, the governor or head of Bastoy prison island, explained how his philosophy that a prison should be "an arena of developing responsibility" was put into practice:

> In closed prisons we keep them locked up for some years and then let them back out, not having had any real responsibility for working or cooking. In the law, being sent to prison is nothing to do with putting you in a terrible prison to make you suffer. The punishment is that you lose your freedom. If we treat people like animals when they are in prison they are likely to behave like animals. Here we pay attention to you as human beings. (quoted in James, 2013a)

The Norwegian penal system has no death penalty or life sentences; the maximum sentence that can be handed down in Norway is just 21 years. This maximum sentence can be extended only if the inmate is deemed to be an imminent threat to society (Sutter, 2012). With this sentencing structure, Norwegian society is forced to confront the fact that most prisoners, however heinous their crimes, will one day be released back into society (Hernu, 2011). In fact, more than 89% of Norway's sentences are for less than one year of confinement, as compared to U.S. federal prisons where only 2% of sentences are for one year or less (Sutter, 2012).

Two examples—one of a closed prison and one of a more open and transitional prison—help to show Norway's commitment to rehabilitating and reintegrating all of its offenders, even those who have committed very serious crimes. Inmates may still suffer the pains of imprisonment (as discussed in Chapter 11), but they can gain skills, maintain contact with their families, and practice responsible and conforming living even while incarcerated.

Halden is Norway's most secure prison and its second largest, holding about 250 men. While Halden does have a 20-foot cement wall around the perimeter, life inside is meant to mimic a small village. Prison cells in Halden are similar to dorm rooms and have windows, adjoining bathrooms, and flat-screen televisions. There is a two-bedroom house on the prison grounds where prisoners can host their families overnight. There are jogging trails, sports fields, and a recording studio (Adams, 2010).

Bastoy prison island in Norway looks virtually nothing like an American prison. While it might be compared to Alcatraz due to its location on a 1-square mile island, Bastoy operates under a much different philosophy. Bastoy offers prisoners trust and responsibility, giving them the chance to become educated, learn new skills, work at varying jobs around the island, grocery shop and cook meals, live

▲ Photo 13.2 While still somewhat isolated from the rest of society, Norway's island prison offers prisoners some freedom and responsibility, helping them to prepare for the transition back to their home communities.

Source: ©Ninic/iStock.

semi-independently in small houses around the island, and generally prepare themselves for their full transition back into the community upon their release. Prisoners farm and grow much of their own food, and families can share weekly visits in private rooms. Prisoners, including those convicted of serious violent crimes such as murder and rape, can apply for transfer to Bastoy from more traditional, close-custody prisons when they have 5 years left on their sentence and can show "determination to live a crime-free life on release" (James, 2013a). Most prisoners that come to Bastoy have served time in higher-security prisons—such as Halden—in Norway; they recognize the privileges and relative freedom that Bastoy offers and view finishing their sentences there as a valued opportunity.

Bastoy, which holds approximately 120 male prisoners without the use of concrete walls, razor wire fences, or bars, is one of the cheapest prisons in Norway to run (James, 2013b). Inmates work 9 hours a day, earning approximately $10 per day. Guards work alongside them on a daily basis, yet carry no weapons. At night, only a handful of corrections officers stay on the island with their charges. Correctional officers in Norway are highly trained in comparison to much of the rest of the world; it takes at least 2 years of practical and theoretical training to be a prison guard in Norway. Prisoner officer training in the United Kingdom, in comparison, lasts only 6 weeks.

The methods used in the Scandinavian prisons, and especially those in Norway, appear to be working. The reoffending average across Europe is approximately 70–75%. In Denmark, Sweden, and Finland, the average is 30%. In Norway, it is 20%. The reoffending rate for those released from Bastoy prison island is just 16% and is the lowest in Europe (James, 2013a).

Prisons in Latin America

Prisons in Latin America tend to be characterized by mass overcrowding, filthy conditions, and the presence of powerful prison gangs. Supervision can be difficult as there are higher numbers of inmates per staff member and there is very little technology to help with surveillance in Latin American prisons as compared to the United States (Birkbeck, 2011, p. 312). In such conditions, violence and chaos can rule the institutions.

The Economist reported in a 2012 article titled "A Journey Into Hell" that

in Honduras a fire killed more than 350 inmates at a jail in the central town of Comayagua in February. In the same month in Mexico three dozen imprisoned members of the Zetas, a drug gang, murdered 44 other inmates at a jail at Apodaca, near Monterrey, before escaping. Last month at least 26 prisoners died in a battle between gangs inside Yare jail in Venezuela. The authorities later seized a small arsenal from prisoners, including assault rifles, sniper rifles, a machine-gun, hand-grenades and two mortars. A similar number died in a riot at El Rodeo, another Venezuelan prison, last year, which saw gang bosses hold out against thousands of national-guard troops for almost a month.

A fire begun during a fight between inmates at San Miguel prison in Santiago, Chile's capital, in December 2010 killed 81 prisoners and injured 15. Survivors said a group of inmates used a homemade flame-thrower, fashioned from a hosepipe and a gas canister, to set fire to a mattress barricade erected by a rival group in their barred cell. San Miguel was not a high-security jail, and the victims of the worst prison fire in Chile's history were all serving sentences of five years or less, for crimes such as pirating DVDs and burglary. (© The Economist Newspaper Limited, London [06 May 2014].)

Lurigancho, Peru's largest prison, is considered to be one of the world's most dangerous. The inmates essentially run the institution while corrupt and outnumbered guards regularly accept bribes from both inmates and visitors alike. Inmates with resources can purchase food, drugs, nice clothing, conjugal visits, and influence over their fellow inmates. Those without resources are left to try to eke out a miserable existence within the prison's walls.

In Venezuela, penal confinement is prescribed for all felony convictions, and there is no possibility of sentencing to probation. While there are more avenues for parole and early release from prison (Birkbeck, 2011) than in the United States, inmates' time served in prison may turn into a *de facto* death penalty: Venezuela had more than 500 prison deaths in 2011. Prisons in Latin America do have the potential benefit of more permissive visiting policies. In Mexico and Bolivia, for example, families and children may actually live in the prisons with their incarcerated parent(s) for an extended period of time. Visits are much less regimented and allow for significant mingling with members of the outside community, helping to ease the social isolation often experienced by prisoners. With the philosophy of internment—where detaining the offenders is the primary goal—what happens inside the facility is irrelevant; inmates must rely on self-government, for better or worse. There is little public scrutiny unless inmates escape or are killed in dramatic circumstances.

Social Control of Mental Illness

Communities both define and react to mental illness in very different ways. In many countries, there is not much of a safety net for those with mental illness. In China, for example, there is no national mental health law, and insurance rarely covers psychiatric care. Even when families and individuals are motivated to seek professional help, there are few educated psychiatrists to care for the population. The *New York Times* focused attention on a tragic case that illustrates the immensity of the problem:

A Lancet study estimated that roughly 173 million Chinese suffer from a mental disorder. Despite government efforts to expand insurance coverage, a senior Health Ministry official said last June that in recent years, only 45,000 people had been covered for free outpatient treatment and only 7,000 for free inpatient care because they were either dangerous to society or too impoverished to pay.

The dearth of care is most evident when it comes to individuals who commit violent crimes. For example, after Liu Yalin killed and dismembered an elderly couple cutting firewood in a Guangdong Province forest, he was judged to be schizophrenic and released to his brother.

Unable to afford treatment, the brother flew Mr. Liu to the island province of Hainan, in the South China Sea, and abandoned him, a Chinese nongovernment organization, Shenzhen Hengping, said in a recent report.

Last year, the tragedy was multiplied when—left without care or supervision—Mr. Liu killed and dismembered an 8-year-old Hainan girl. (LaFraniere, 2010)

In poor countries, the government returns severely mentally ill people to their families, and the families are generally at a loss as to how to care for them. With few resources, information, or help available in their communities, families must sometimes resort to locking up and shackling relatives who pose a threat to themselves and others.

In Kenya mentally ill family members are tied up daily by their relatives in order to keep them from running away or harming themselves. Family members are consumed with the task of caring for their mentally ill loved ones. They may find themselves entirely alone in their efforts, shunned by the community because of the unpleasant noise and stench. While one-fourth of patients visiting Kenyan hospitals or clinics complain of mental health problems, the Kenyan government spends less than 1% of its health budget on mental health (McKenzie & Formanek, 2011).

Social Control and Reintegration: Restorative Justice

Howard Zehr, one of the early proponents of restorative justice, explains the basic principles of the concept as follows: Crime is a violation of people and of interpersonal relationships; violations create obligations; and the central obligation is to put right the wrongs (Zehr, 2002, p. 19). While he uses an American lens to discuss these principles, Zehr suggests that there are deep roots for the concept in many different cultures, expressed in different languages. He writes, "Many cultures have a word that represents this notion of the centrality of relationships: for the Maori, it is communicated by *whaka-papa*; for the Navajo, *hozho*; for many Africans, the Bantu word *Ubuntu*" (Zehr, 2002, pp. 19–20).

After spending a decade studying restorative justice, primarily in South Australia, Kathleen Daly found that there is little empirical evidence as to what actually happens in youth justice conferences and how participants feel about the process and outcomes. Daly argues that there is a complex definition and meaning of restorative justice:

Restorative justice is not easily defined because it encompasses a variety of practices at different stages of the criminal process, including *diversion* from court prosecution, actions taken *in parallel* with court decisions, and meetings between victims and offenders *at any stage* of the criminal process (for example, arrest, pre-sentencing, and prison release). For virtually all legal contexts involving individual criminal matters, restorative justice processes have only been applied to those offenders who have *admitted* to an offence; as such, it deals with the penalty phase of the criminal process for admitted offenders, not the fact-finding phase. Restorative justice is used not only in adult and juvenile criminal matters, but also in a range of civil matters, including family welfare and child protection, and disputes in schools and workplace settings. (Daly, 2002, p. 57)

New Zealand's youth justice system, which emphasizes diversion, family involvement, and restorative justice principles, has been a model for other jurisdictions worldwide. From approximately

1990–2010, New Zealand dealt with most youth offenders—nearly 80% of apprehensions—through diversion rather than prosecution (Lynch, 2012). With the use of restorative justice,

> the victim of the offence may be part of the process, giving him or her tangible power in the resolution of the offence. True participation by victims (and by the community) can reduce the public appetite for punitiveness. (Lynch, 2012, p. 512)

Similarly, Bazemore (1998) advocates for a variation of restorative justice featuring a system of earned redemption that would allow offenders to earn trust back from the community by making amends to those they harmed.

In Africa, using the *ubuntu* principle, the goals of justice-making include the restoration of victims, the reintegration of the offender back into the community, and the restoration of relationships and social harmony undermined by the conflict. All stakeholders should have equal access and participation in the conflict resolution process (Elechi, Morris, & Schauer, 2010, p. 73); this process has the power to reinforce the values of the community. Elechi et al. (2010) argue that the African Indigenous Justice System is "an opportunity for the resocialization of community members and the relearning of important African values and principles of restraint, respect, and responsibility" (p. 74), and, further, when communities rely on themselves to solve problems, both individual and collective accountability may be improved as a result (p. 83).

Different cultures and individuals may embrace a wide variety of restorative justice principles and techniques, but what sets these efforts apart from the criminal justice system in the United States is the focus on the reparation of harm and the restoration of the offender rather than on retribution for the harm caused.

Explaining Deviance in the Streets and Deviance in the Suites: Human Trafficking: Crossing Boundaries and Borders

We have chosen to discuss **human trafficking** because it is a deviance that is both big business and found on the streets. While some human trafficking occurs across state or regional lines, a great proportion of it is transnational and global.

Human trafficking is a crime that "recognizes no race, gender, or national boundary" (Zhang, 2010, p. 15) although it is generally visited on the least powerful: children, women, and people of color. According to the Trafficking Victims Protection Act, human trafficking is "the act of recruiting, harboring, transporting, providing, or obtaining a person for compelled labor or commercial sex acts through the use of force, fraud, or coercion" (U.S. Department of State, 2013, p. 29). While most envision that human trafficking means transporting a victim from one country to another, the official definition does not require the victim to be transported:

> Human trafficking can include but does not require movement. People may be considered trafficking victims regardless of whether they were born into a state of servitude, were transported to the exploitative situation, previously consented to work for a trafficker, or participated in a crime as a direct result of being trafficked. At the heart of this phenomenon is the

traffickers' goal of exploiting and enslaving their victims and the myriad coercive and deceptive practices they use to do so. (U.S. Department of State, 2013, p. 29)

Children and adults who are victims of human trafficking are coerced into being soldiers, sold for hard labor or sex, or forced into domestic labor, prostitution, or marriage. Others find themselves working in mines, plantations, or sweatshops (United Nations Global Initiative to Fight Global Trafficking [UN.Gift], 2008). Many initially go with their captors willingly because of promises of a better job or an escape from a hard life, only to be turned into slaves once they arrive at their new destination. These experiences are illustrated by the stories of three trafficking victims below:

> Ximena: "When you're a kid, it's easy to be deceived. Each Sunday when I walked down from the town, where my mum had a business, they would urge me to go with them, telling me that I would have a really good time, that it was better to go with them than to keep on working. On my 12th birthday, they came back for me. My mum was away at work, so I took the chance and escaped with them. . . . Five months later I regretted being there, but there was no chance of leaving. Besides, they told my mum that I was dead, that they had already killed me." (UN. Gift, 2008, p. 2)
>
> Luana: "A friend of mine told me that a Spanish group was hiring Brazilian girls to work as dancers on the island of Lanzarote. My friend Marcela and I thought it was a good opportunity to earn money. We didn't want to continue working as maids. For a short while we only danced. But later they told us there had been too many expenses. And we would have to make some extra money." (UN.Gift, 2008, p. 5)
>
> Marcela: "We were trapped by criminals and forced into prostitution in order to pay debts for the trip. We had up to 15 clients per night. The use of condoms was the client's decision, not ours. The criminals kept our passports and had an armed man in front of the 'disco' to make sure we never escaped. But a woman helped us. We went to the police and told everything." (UN. Gift, 2008, p. 5)

According to The United Nations Global Initiative to Fight Human Trafficking (UN.Gift, 2008) human trafficking is a billion-dollar industry. The UN acknowledges, however, that our understanding of human trafficking is negligible—there is no broad agreement on how to count individuals that have been trafficked, and therefore the estimates from various organizations often contradict each other. One organization estimates that at least 2.5 million people are victims of human trafficking, with an estimated 130,000 in sub-Saharan countries, 200,000 in countries with economies in transition, 230,000 in the Middle East or Northern Africa, 250,000 in Latin American and the Caribbean, 270,000 in industrialized countries, and over 1.4 million in Asia and the Pacific (International Labour Organization, 2005). A second estimate suggests that at least 800,000 people are smuggled across national borders every year, with millions more trafficked in their own countries (Department of State, 2007). And the nongovernmental organization Free the Slaves estimates that there are between 21 and 30 million people in slavery globally (Free the Slaves, 2013).

The elusive nature of human trafficking is illustrated in the small number of human trafficking incidents that are investigated and confirmed in the United States, in comparison to the estimated number of human trafficking cases that are believed to exist. The U.S. Department of Justice reports that in the United States, just over 2,500 cases were investigated by federally funded human trafficking task forces between 2008 and 2010 (Banks & Kyckelhahn, 2011). And in very few of these cases could law enforcement confirm the victim's characteristics (see Table 13.2).

Table 13.1   Victim Characteristics in Cases Confirmed to Be Human Trafficking by High Data Quality Task Forces, by Type of Trafficking

Victim characteristic	Total[a]	Sex trafficking	Labour trafficking
Sex			
Male	49	27	20
Female	477	432	43
Age			
17 or younger	257	248	6
13–24	159	142	17
25–34	68	46	22
35 or older	27	12	15
Unknown	16	12	3
Race/Hispanic origin			
White[b]	106	102	1
Black/African American[b]	167	161	6
Hispanic/Latino origin	129	95	34
Asian[b, c]	26	17	9
Other[b, d]	35	23	11
Unknown	63	61	2
Citizenship			
U.S. Citizen/U.S. National	346	345	1
Permanent U.S. resident[e]	6	6	0
Undocumented alien[f]	101	64	36
Qualified alien[e]	19	1	15
Temporary worker	2	0	2
Unknown	50	41	9
Number of victims identified	527	460	63

Source: Banks, D., & Kyckelhahn, T. (2011). Characteristics of suspected human trafficking incidents, 2008–2010. Bureau of Justice Statistics. Washington DC: U.S. Department of Justice. Retrieved from http://www.bjs.gov/content/pub/pdf/cshti0810.pdf

Note: Analysis restricted to cases opened and observed between January 2008 and June 2010 in high data quality task forces. See definition of high data quality task forces on page 5.

[a]Includes cases of unknown trafficking type.

[b]Excludes persons of Hispanic or Latino origin.

[c]Asian may include Native Hawaiian and other Pacific Islanders or persons of East Asian or Southeast Asian descent.

[d]Includes persons of two or more races.

[e]Permanent residents and qualified aliens are legal residents in the U.S., but do not have citizenship.

[f]Undocumented aliens reside in the U.S. illegally.

Ideas in Action: What Can Be Done About Human Trafficking?

While the challenges to eradicate human trafficking are significant, at least they are known and can be addressed. The United Nations suggests that these challenges include the following:

- Lack of knowledge: there are still huge gaps in knowledge even about the extent of human trafficking and modern-day slavery.
- Lack of a national legal framework, policy, and capacity to respond: while human trafficking is acknowledged as a crime, there is little systematic legal response or public policy to address it.
- Limited protection of and assistance to victims: social service and law enforcement agencies need training in order to better identify and respond to victims of human trafficking.
- Limited international cooperation: as probably the best example of deviance or crime that crosses national borders, there is surprisingly less cooperation than one would hope between countries in identifying and stopping human trafficking. (UN.Gift, 2008, p. 1)

Another challenge that has been identified involves the definition of human trafficking. Human trafficking laws in many countries require that the person accused of human trafficking be proven to have "bought or sold" another human being. But the reality is that most human trafficking victims are never bought or sold in the traditional sense. Because no transaction occurs and no money changes hands, the vast majority of human trafficking victims are not acknowledged or protected by such laws. Broadening language in countries that rely on the provision of buying and selling individuals would mean that more offenders would be prosecuted and more victims acknowledged (U.S. Department of State, 2013).

Finally, Zhang (2010) makes five suggestions for public policies to address human trafficking:

- Law enforcement should focus on disruption tactics that make the business of human trafficking harder to sustain.
- Increase the financial cost to the business of human trafficking; a legal outcome should be asset forfeiture for anyone found guilty of human trafficking.
- Law enforcement agencies, medical providers, and social services providers need to be systematically educated on how to recognize trafficking victims.
- Engage in a campaign that increases public awareness of the existence of human trafficking and that reaches victims of trafficking and makes them aware of who they can contact for help.
- Effect an increase in political will measured by resource allocation that will secure and offer long-term solutions to human trafficking.

NOW YOU . . . THINK ABOUT GLOBAL DEVIANCE

It is often easy to pass judgment on other countries for their beliefs and practices, and, in most instances when we are passing judgment, we are implicitly or explicitly defining those practices as deviant. It is your turn to explore and critique these differences.

1. Choose a country.

2. Find a practice or behavior that the laws in your chosen country or individuals in the country define as deviant that the United States or individuals in the United States would be less likely to define as deviant.

3. Find a practice or behavior that laws in the United States or individuals in the United States define as deviant that your chosen country or individuals in the country would be less likely to define as deviant.

4. Find a practice or behavior that is defined as deviant in both your chosen country and the United States.

5. Why is it that these practices or behaviors may or may not be defined as deviant? Does it matter who engages in the practice for it to be defined as deviant? Who benefits from these definitions of deviance or nondeviance? Why might this behavior be deviant in one country and not in another?

Conclusion

We hope you have enjoyed this exploration into the many, many forms of deviance and the varied ways that societies first define deviance and then react to such acts or characteristics. While we understand that we may be considered deviant ourselves due to our years focusing on the topic, we find all of this material so fascinating that we have devoted our careers to studying it, researching our favorite theories and subtopics, and writing this textbook to share with you. Whether you choose to join us in a career related to deviance, crime, delinquency, or mental health, or whether you can simply now check this off your list of required classes, we hope that after reading this book you will bring a lingering curiosity and a more complex understanding of the causes and reactions to deviant behavior into all of your future endeavors.

EXERCISES AND DISCUSSION QUESTIONS

1. You are part of a research team that will be studying human trafficking links between China, Mexico, and the United States. Explain the research challenges/issues you will need to be aware of as you plan your study.

2. Choose a country whose prison system has not been discussed in this chapter. Research its forms of social control. Compare and contrast these forms of social control to the U.S. prison system.

KEY TERMS

Decommodification   Human trafficking

Glossary

Age-crime curve: an observed relationship between the likelihood to engage in crime and age. The relationship is low in the early childhood/adolescent years, peaks in late adolescence, and then declines as individuals age out of adolescence.

Anomie: a state of normlessness where society fails to effectively regulate the expectations or behaviors of its members.

Attachment: "emotional" component of the social bond that says individuals care about what others think.

Belief: component of the bond in social control theory that suggests the stronger the awareness, understanding, and agreement with the rules and norms of society, the less likely one will be to deviate.

Body modification: includes piercings, scarification, extreme tattooing, and reconstructive and cosmetic surgery.

Broken windows theory: basically the notion that social and physical disorder lead to greater disorder and other forms of crime and deviance.

Central business district: the commercial area of a city where most of the business activity occurs.

Civil commitment: a process whereby offenders, particularly sex offenders, who are perceived to be a risk to the community can be held indefinitely after completing the sentences handed down by the criminal justice system.

Collateral consequences of imprisonment: damages, losses, or hardships to individuals, families, and communities due to incarceration of some members.

Collective efficacy: conditions of some neighborhoods or groups where there is trust, cohesion, and a willingness to act for the common good.

Commitment: "rational" component of the social bond that says individuals weigh the costs and benefits of their behavior.

Concentric zones: a model of urban cities, generally consisting of and moving out from the central business district, the zone in transition, zone of the working class, residential zone, and commuter zone.

Conflict: a theoretical perspective that considers how society is held together by power and coercion for the benefit of those in power (based on social class, gender, race, or ethnicity).

Conflict subcultures: from Cloward and Ohlin's theory—conflict subcultures develop in disorganized neighborhoods where young people are deprived of both conventional and illegitimate opportunities; frustration and violence are defining characteristics.

Content analysis: involves reviewing records of communication and systematically searching, recording, and analyzing themes and trends in those records.

Covert observation: refers to public observation where the researcher does not let the human subjects under study know that he or she is a researcher and that they are being studied.

Criminal career paradigm: a view that there are some criminals who offend at high rates across their life courses.

Criminal subcultures: from Cloward and Ohlin's theory—criminal subcultures develop in poor neighborhoods where there is some level of organized crime and illegitimate opportunity for young people growing up in the area.

Critical conception: the conception of deviance that critiques the existing social system that creates norms of oppression.

Critical race theory: a theoretical perspective that examines the use of law, the legal order, and institutions in maintaining white privilege and supremacy.

Cross-sectional designs: involves data that are collected at only one point in time, such as a survey distributed in a classroom.

265

Cultural deviance theory: a theory emphasizing the values, beliefs, rituals, and practices of societies that promote certain deviant behaviors. Related, subcultural explanations emphasize the values, beliefs, rituals, and practices of subgroups that distinguish them from the larger society.

Decommodification: the movement away from pure market economies to ones that provide political institutions (such as the welfare state) to protect individuals from the harsh reality of pure capitalism.

Definitions: attitudes, values, orientations, rationalizations, and beliefs related to legal and moral codes of society.

Deinstitutionalization: encourages keeping offenders or the mentally ill in the community, to the extent that doing so is a reasonable option. The idea is that there is less disruption, labeling, and stigma if the individuals can be treated outside of prisons, mental hospitals, juvenile facilities, and so on.

Demedicalization: occurs when behaviors are no longer assigned or retain medical definitions. As one example, homosexuality was once defined as a form of mental illness, but it has been demedicalized and is no longer considered a medical issue.

Desistance: the process of ending a deviant career or career in deviance. This can be abrupt (e.g., "quitting cold turkey") or a gradual process (e.g., a self-help recovery process where individuals alternate between periods of use and abstinence).

Dialectical materialism: the belief that nature (the material world) is full of contradictions (conflict) and that through a process of negotiating those contradictions, we can arrive at a new reality.

Differential association: social interactions with deviant as opposed to conventional others.

Differential location in the social structure: social and demographic characteristics of individuals that define or influence their position or role in the larger social structure (e.g., age, sex, socioeconomic status).

Differential reinforcement: the balance of rewards and punishments (anticipated and/or actual) that follow from deviant behaviors.

Differential social location in groups: one's position or role in the social groups he or she is part of.

Elite deviance: criminal and deviant acts committed by large corporations, powerful political organizations, and individuals with prestige and influence; may result in physical harm, financial harm, or moral harm.

Escalation: some deviant behaviors accelerate or intensify over time, such as persistent drug use that may increase in frequency or quantity.

Ethics in research: much effort has gone into the ethical implications of researching human subjects, which can be quite complex when studying deviant behavior. Generally, the subject should be asked if he or she consents to participate and his or her confidentiality should be protected.

Ethnography: the study and recording of human society and subcultures.

Experiments: often considered the "gold standard" in research, experimental designs generally require subjects to be randomly assigned to a treatment or control condition.

External control: formal controls that society places on an individual to keep him or her from engaging in crime or deviance.

False consciousness: laborers' lack of awareness of the exploitation they are experiencing at the hands of the owners of the means of production and capitalism.

Felon disenfranchisement: the loss of the right to vote in local and national elections after conviction for a felony offense; laws vary by state.

Feminist criminology: a theoretical perspective that defines gender (and sometimes race and social class) as a source of social inequality, group conflict, and social problems.

Field research: generally involves getting out into the environment and studying human behavior as it exists in the "real world."

Folkways: everyday norms that do not generate much uproar if they are violated.

General strain theory (GST): Robert Agnew's version of strain theory; suggests that strain at the individual level may result from the failure to achieve valued goals and also from the presence of negative relations/stimuli.

Human agency: the capacity of people to make choices that have implications for themselves and others.

Human subjects: living persons being observed for research purposes.

Human trafficking: the illegal movement of people, usually for the purposes of forced labor or sexual exploitation.

Imitation: observing behavior and reenacting modeled behavior in actuality or in play.

Individual efficacy: an individual's ability to achieve specific goals.

Institutional review board: an independent group that reviews research to protect human subjects from potential harms of the research.

Institutional anomie theory: from Messner and Rosenfeld— argues that the major institutions in the United States, including the family, school, and political system, are all dominated by economic institutions; the exaggerated emphasis on monetary success leads to crime and deviance.

Institutionalization/prisonization: when individuals who have been confined to a prison, mental hospital, or other total institution become so used to the structure and routine of the facility that they lose the confidence and capability to exist independently in the outside world.

Instrumental Marxism: the theory that the state (e.g., politicians or the police) is an *instrument* of the capitalists.

Internal control: rules and norms exercised through ourconscience.

Involvement: component of the social bond that suggests the more time spent engaged in conforming activities, the less time available to deviate.

Laws: the strongest norms because they are backed by official sanctions (or a formal response).

Liberal feminism: focuses on gender role socialization and the roles that women are socialized into.

Life course perspective: a theoretical perspective that considers the entire course of human life (through childhood, adolescence, adulthood, and old age) as social constructions that reflect the broader structural conditions of society.

Longitudinal data: comes from a series of observations of the same phenomena over time.

Low self-control: the inability of an individual to refrain from impulsive behavior designed to increase immediate gratification.

Master status: a status that proves to be more important than most others.

Medicalization of deviance: a process by which nonmedical problems and behaviors become defined and treated as medical conditions; examples might include medical illness, hyperactivity, alcoholism, and compulsive gambling.

Mores: "moral" norms that may generate outrage if broken.

Nonintervention: the policy of avoiding intervention and action for as long as possible. For example, labeling theorists often suggest we should tolerate some level of minor deviance and misbehavior before taking official action and labeling individuals deviant.

Normative conception: the conception of deviance that assumes there is a general set of norms of behavior, conduct, and conditions on which all individuals can agree.

Norms: rules of behavior that guide people's actions.

Onset/initiation: the beginning of a career in deviance; this career can be short- or long-lived.

Operationalization: refers to the process that a researcher uses to define how a concept is measured, observed, or manipulated in a study.

Overt observation: refers to studies where the researcher makes human subjects aware that they are being observed.

Pains of imprisonment: as described by Gresham Sykes, the pains of imprisonment include deprivation of liberty, deprivation of goods and services, deprivation of heterosexual relationships, deprivation of autonomy, and deprivation of security.

Parental efficacy: parents' ability to control their children's behavior through parent–child attachment, rules, supervision, and also social support.

Participant observation: research activity where the researcher is actively involved in the behaviors being studied. For example, a recovering alcoholic researcher might study the behaviors of others in AA meetings.

Peacemaking criminology: a theoretical perspective focused on the belief that there must be a new way of seeing and organizing the world around compassion, sympathy, and understanding.

Persistence: subsequent to onset or initiation, the continuation of some deviant behaviors over time.

Physical deviance: generally thought to be of two types: (1) violating norms of what people are expected to look like and (2) physical incapacity or disability.

Physical disorder: condition of some neighborhoods with high levels of, for example, litter, graffiti, vandalism, and "broken windows."

Polygamy: a subculture in which men are allowed and encouraged to take multiple wives.

Population turnover: Also referred to as residential instability and often measured as the percent of the population that did not reside in the neighborhood five years earlier.

Positive deviance: a concept that is still under debate but generally understood as intentional behaviors that depart from community norms in honorable ways.

Positivist perspective: A deterministic approach that focuses on "factual" knowledge acquired through observation and measurement.

Postmodern feminism: questions the idea of a single "truth" or way of knowing and understanding.

Poverty: a lack of resources or financial well-being.

Prevention programs: any number of programs and policies geared at keeping individuals away from crime and deviance and on a conforming path.

Primary deviance: common instances where individuals violate norms without viewing themselves as being involved in a deviant social role.

Protective factors: factors that reduce the impact of risk factors and protect or prevent individuals from turning to crime or deviance. Protective factors are not simply the opposite of risk factors.

Pure observation: form of study in which participants do not see the researcher or even know they are being observed.

Quasi-experimental designs: whereas experimental designs generally require random assignment to a treatment or control condition, quasi-experiments usually relax this requirement.

Racial/ethnic heterogeneity: refers to a mixture of different races and ethnicities in a given area.

Radical feminism: focuses on the sexual control of women, seeing their oppression as emerging from a social order dominated by men.

Rehabilitation programs: programs that are focused on changing individual behavior after an individual has already engaged in deviant behavior.

Reinforcement: an act or thing that strengthens or encourages a behavior.

Reintegrative shaming: a reaction to deviant behavior that views the offender as a good person who has done a bad deed; this process encourages repair work and forgiveness rather than simply labeling the individual as a bad person.

Relativist: assumes that the definition of deviance is constructed based on interactions with those in society.

Residual rule breaking: deviance for which there exists no clear category—acts that are not crimes yet draw attention and make the societal audience uncomfortable.

Response rate: the number of people in a survey divided by the number of people in the defined sample.

Restorative justice: typically involves bringing victims, offenders, and community members together in a mediated conference where the offenders take responsibility for their actions and work to restore the harm they have caused, often through restitution to the victim and service to the community.

Retreatist subcultures: from Cloward and Ohlin's theory—similar to Merton's adaptation of retreatism, a subculture based around drug use, drug culture, and relative isolation from the larger society.

Risk factors: factors that place certain individuals at greater risk for engaging in deviant (often unhealthy) behaviors.

Sample: a group of people taken from a larger population and studied or surveyed.

Scientific method: analysis and implementation of a rigorous, replicable, and objective strategy to gain information about our world.

Secondary data: data collected by other researchers that may be used or reanalyzed by another researcher.

Secondary deviance: when an individual engages in deviant behavior as a means of defense, attack, or adjustment to the problems created by reactions to him or her.

Self-fulfilling prophesy: once an individual is labeled, that individual's self-conceptions may be altered, causing him or her to deviate and live up to the negative label.

Self-injury: harming oneself by cutting, burning, branding, scratching, picking at skin or reopening wounds, biting, hair pulling, and/or bone breaking.

Sexual deviance: largely determined by community, culture, and context, sexual deviance may include exotic dancers, strippers, sex tourism, anonymous sex in public restrooms, bisexuality, online sexual predators, prostitutes, premarital chastity, and many others.

Social bonds: bonds to conformity that keep individuals from engaging in socially unacceptable activities.

Social cohesion: neighborhoods characterized by positive social interaction, trust, and a sense of community.

Social consensus: general agreement by the group.

Social construction: subjective definition or perception of conditions.

Social contract: the process by which individuals give up some personal freedoms and abide by general rules of conduct in order to live in a community and enjoy the protection and companionship of the group.

Social disorder: conditions of some neighborhoods with high levels of, for example, unmonitored youth misbehaving, drug dealers, people openly and illegally using alcohol or other drugs, and fighting.

Social disorganization: neighborhoods that lack the ability to control delinquent youth and other potentially problematic populations.

Social structure: organization of society, often hierarchical, that affects how and why people interact and the outcomes of those interactions.

Socialist feminism: focuses on structural differences, especially those we find in the capitalist modes of production.

Sociological imagination: the ability to see the link between our personal lives and experiences and our social world.

Specialization: a primary interest and focus on one form of deviant behavior (e.g., marijuana use), to be contrasted with "generality of deviance" (e.g., drug use, theft, and violent behaviors).

Status frustration: a concept from Albert Cohen, suggesting the strain that working-class boys feel when measured against middle-class standards they have trouble meeting.

Stigma: a mark of deviance or disgrace; a negative label or perceived deviance often leads to stigma that may then reduce an individual's life chances.

Strain: lack of opportunities for conventional success may lead to strain, which can manifest in anger, frustration, and deviance.

Structural impediments: obstacles on the road to conforming success—for example, lack of education, poor access to legitimate careers, and so on.

Structural Marxism: a theory that law is less about maintaining power and benefits for the ruling class and more about maintaining the interests of the *capitalist system.*

Subcultures: a distinct group within the larger culture that has its own subset of norms, values, behaviors, or characteristics.

Supervision: a process in which an individual's actions are either directly or indirectly known by (usually) a parent or guardian.

Suppression: the act of inhibiting, restraining, or stopping something, such as an activity or a behavior, by authority or force.

Survey: a form of research in which participants are asked a question or questions in order for the researchers to gather information.

Symbolic interactionism: a micro-level, relativist sociological perspective that is focused on individuals and the meanings they attach to objects, people, and interactions around them.

Theoretically defined structural variables: measures based on social theories of deviance such as anomie/strain, social disorganization, or patriarchy, among others.

Theory: a set of assumptions and propositions used for explanation, prediction, and understanding.

Total institutions: institutions such as prisons, jails, and mental hospitals in which all aspects of life are conducted in the same place, in the company of a group of others, with tightly scheduled activities that are closely supervised and monitored.

Trajectory: a series of linked states or patterns under some domain of behavior. For example, students reading this book are likely to be in an educational trajectory seeking a degree in higher education.

Transition: a turning point within a long-term trajectory, such as dropping out of school, divorce, or desistance from a particular form of deviant behavior.

Zone in transition: an area of a city that usually borders the central business district. The name comes from the notion that the poorest groups (often recent immigrants) are forced to live there, and as they secure financial stability, they move out, so it is an area in transition of different populations.

References

Abbey, A., Pilgram, C., Hendrickson, P., & Buesh, S. (2000). Evaluation of a family-based substance abuse prevention program for the middle school year. *Journal of Drug Education, 30,* 213–228.

Abel, R. (1982). The contradictions of informal justice. In R. Abel (Ed.), *The politics of informal justice: Vol. 1. The American experience* (pp. 267–320). New York: Academic Press.

Adams, M. S., Robertson, C. T., Gray-Ray, P., & Ray, M. C. (2003). Labeling and delinquency. *Adolescence, 38*(149), 171–186.

Adams, W. L. (2010, July 12). Sentenced to serving the good life in Norway. *Time.com.* Retrieved from http://content.time.com/time/magazine/article/0,9171,2000920-1,00.html

Adler, F. (1975). *Sisters in crime: The rise of the new female criminal.* New York: McGraw-Hill.

Adler, P. A. (1993). *Wheeling and dealing: An ethnography of an upper-level drug dealing and smuggling community* (2nd ed.). New York: Columbia University Press.

Adler, P. A., & Adler, P. (1983). Shifts and oscillations in deviant careers: The case of upper-level drug dealers and smugglers. *Social Problems, 31*(2), 195–207.

Adler, P. A., & Adler, P. (2007). The demedicalization of self-injury: From psychopathology to sociological deviance. *Journal of Contemporary Ethnography, 36*(5), 537–570.

Agnew, R. (1985). Social control theory and delinquency. *Criminology, 23,* 47–61.

Agnew, R. (1992). Foundation for a general strain theory of crime and delinquency. *Criminology, 30*(1), 47–87.

Agnew, R. (1997). Stability and change in crime over the life course: A strain theory explanation. In T. P. Thornberry (Ed.), *Developmental theories of crime and delinquency, advances in criminological theory* (Vol. 7, pp. 101–132). New Brunswick, NJ: Transaction.

Agnew, R. (2006). *Pressured into crime: An overview of general strain theory.* Los Angeles: Roxbury.

Aguirre, A., Jr. (2000). Academic storytelling: A critical race theory story of affirmative action. *Sociological Perspectives, 43*(2), 319–339.

Ahmed, S. (2009, December 8). Why is Uganda attacking homosexuality? *CNN.com.* Retrieved from http://www.cnn.com/2009/WORLD/africa/12/08/uganda.anti.gay.bill/

Akers, R. L. (1985). *Deviant behavior: A social learning approach* (3rd ed.). Belmont, CA: Wadsworth.

Akers, R. L. (1996). Is differential association/social learning cultural deviance theory? *Criminology, 34*(2), 229–247.

Akers, R. L. (1998). *Social learning and social structure: A general theory of crime and deviance.* Boston: Northeastern University Press.

Akers, R. L., & Cochran, J. K. (1985). Adolescent marijuana use: A test of three theories of deviant behavior. *Deviant Behavior, 6*(4), 323–346.

Akers, R. L., & Sellers, C. (2004). *Criminological theories: Introduction, evaluation, and application* (4th ed.). Los Angeles: Roxbury.

American Civil Liberties Union (ACLU). 2007. *Firestorm: Treatment of vulnerable populations during the San Diego fires.* San Diego, CA: Author.

Andersen, C. (1999). Governing aboriginal justice in Canada: Constructing responsible individuals and communities through "tradition." *Crime, Law & Social Change, 31,* 303–326.

Anderson, E. (1999). *Code of the street: Decency, violence & the moral life of the inner city.* New York: W. W. Norton.

Anderson, G., Hussey, P., Frogner, B., and Waters, H. (2005). Heath spending in the United States and the rest of the industrialized world. *Health Affairs, 24,* 903–914.

Anderson, L., Snow, D. A., & Cress, D. M. (1994). Negotiating the public realm: Stigma management and collective action among the homeless. *Research in Community Sociology, 1,* 121–143.

Antonaccio, O., Botchkovar, E. V., & Tittle, C. R. (2011). Attracted to Crime: Exploration of Criminal Motivation Among Respondents in Three European Cities. *Criminal Justice & Behavior, 38*(12), 1200–1221.

Arter, M. L. (2008). Stress and deviance in policing. *Deviant Behavior, 29,* 43–69.

Arthur, M. W., Briney, J. S., Hawkins, J., Abbott, R. D., Brooke-Weiss, B. L., & Catalano, R. F. (2007). Measuring risk and protection in communities using the Communities That Care Youth Survey. *Evaluation & Program Planning, 30*(2), 197–211.

Ashworth, A. (1993). Some doubts about restorative justice. *Criminal Law Forum, 4,* 277–299.

Atkinson, M. (2011). Male athletes and the cult(ure) of thinness in sport. *Deviant Behavior, 32*(3), 224–256.

Atkinson, M., & Young, K. (2008). *Deviance and social control in sport.* Champaign, IL: Human Kinetics.

Bader, C. D. (2008). Alien attraction: The subculture of UFO contactees and abductees. In E. Goode & D. A. Vail (Eds.), *Extreme deviance* (pp. 37–65). Thousand Oaks, CA: Pine Forge Press.

Baker, L. M., Dalla, R. L., & Williamson, C. (2010). Exiting prostitution: An integrated model. *Violence Against Women, 16*(5), 579–600.

Bandura, A., Caprara, G-V., & Zsolnai, L. (2000). Corporate transgressions through moral disengagement. *Journal of Human Values, 6*(1), 57–64.

Banks, D., & Kyckelhahn, T. (2011). Characteristics of suspected human trafficking incidents, 2008–2010. Bureau of Justice Statistics. Washington DC: U.S. Department of Justice. Retrieved from http://www.bjs.gov/content/pub/pdf/cshti0810.pdf

Barak, G. (1991). Homelessness and the case for community-based initiatives: The emergence of a model shelter as a short-term response to the deepening crisis in housing. In H. E. Pepinsky & R. Quinney (Eds.), *Criminology as peacemaking* (pp. 47–68). Bloomington: Indiana University Press.

Barlow, Hugh D. and Decker, Scott H. 2010. Criminology and Public Policy: Putting Theory to Work. Philadelphia: Temple University Press.

Barnoski, R. (2005). *Sex offender sentencing in Washington state: Does community notification influence recidivism rates?* (Document No. 05–08–1202). Olympia: Washington State Institute for Public Policy.

Bartollas, C., Miller, S. J., & Dinitz, S. (1976). *Juvenile victimization: The institutional paradox.* New York: John Wiley.

Bates, K.A. and Swan, R. S. (2010). "You CAN Get There from Here, But the Road Is Long and Hard: The Role of Public, Private and Activist Organizations in the Search for Social Justice" pgs. 439–450 in Bates, K.A. and Swan R.S. (Eds. 2nd Edition) *Through the Eye of Katrina: Social Justice in the United States.* Durham: Carolina Academic Press.

Bazemore, G. (1998). Restorative justice and earned redemption: Communities, victims, and earned reintegration. *American Behavioral Scientist, 41*(6), 768–813.

Becker, H. S. (1953). Becoming a marihuana user. *American Journal of Sociology, 59*(3), 235–242.

Becker, H. S. (1973). *Outsiders.* New York: Free Press. (Original work published 1963)

Beckett, K., & Herbert, S. (2010). *Banished: The new social control in urban America.* Oxford, UK: Oxford University Press.

Beirne, P. (1979). Empiricism and the critique of Marxism on law and crime. *Social Problems, 26,* 373–385.

Bender, K., Thompson, S. J., McManus, H. H., Lantry, J., & Flynn, P. M. (2007). Capacity for survival: Exploring strengths of homeless street youth. *Child & Youth Care Forum, 36*(1), 25–42.

Bendle, M. F. (1999). The death of the sociology of deviance? *Journal of Sociology, 35,* 42–59.

Bennett, T., Holloway, K., & Farrington, D. (2006). Does neighborhood watch reduce crime? A systematic review and meta-analysis. *Journal of Experimental Criminology 2*(4), 437–458.

Benson, M. L., Wooldredge, J., & Thistlethwaite, A. B. (2004). The correlation between race and domestic violence is confounded with community context. *Social Problems, 51*(3), 326–342.

Bentham, J. (1970). *An introduction to the principles of morals and legislation* (J. H. Burns & H. L. A. Hart, Eds.). London: Athlone Press. (Original work published 1789)

Berg, M. T., & Rengifo, A. F. (2009). Rethinking community organization and robbery: Considering illicit market dynamics. *Justice Quarterly, 26,* 211–237.

Bernard, T., Snipes, J., & Gerould, A. (2009). *Vold's theoretical criminology.* Oxford, UK: Oxford University Press.

Bernasco, W., & Block, R. (2009). Where offenders choose to attack: A discrete choice model of robberies in Chicago. *Criminology, 47*(1), 93–130.

Birkbeck, C. (2011). Imprisonment and internment: Comparing penal institutions north and south. *Punishment & Society, 13*(3), 307–332.

Blalock, H. M., Jr. (1967). *Toward a theory of minority group relations.* New York: John Wiley.

Blevins, K. R., & Holt, T. J. (2009). Examining the virtual subculture of johns. *Journal of Contemporary Ethnography, 38*(5), 619–648.

Blumstein, A. (1995). Youth violence, guns, and the illicit-drug industry. *Journal of Criminal Law and Criminology, 86,* 10–36.

Blumstein, A., & Cohen, J. (1979). Estimation of individual crime rates from arrest records. *Journal of Criminal Law and Criminology, 70,* 561–585.

Boeringer, S., Shehan, C. L., & Akers, R. L. (1991). Social context and social learning in sexual coercion and aggression: Assessing the contribution of fraternity membership. *Family Relations, 40,* 558–564.

Bohm, R. M. (1982). Radical criminology: An explication. *Criminology, 19,* 565–589.

Bohm, R. M. (1997). *A primer on crime and delinquency.* Belmont, CA: Wadsworth.

Bonger, W. A. (1916). *Criminality and economic conditions.* Boston: Little, Brown.

Braithwaite, J. (1989). *Crime, shame and reintegration.* Melbourne, Australia: Cambridge University Press.

Braithwaite, J. (2000). Shame and criminal justice. *Canadian Journal of Criminology, 42*(3), 281–298.

Braithwaite, J. (2002). Setting standards for restorative justice. *British Journal of Criminology, 42,* 563–577.

Braithwaite, J., & Mugford, S. (1994). Conditions of successful reintegration ceremonies: Dealing with juvenile offenders. *British Journal of Criminology, 34*(2), 140–171.

Braswell, M. C., Fuller, J., & Lozoff, B. (2001). *Corrections, peacemaking, and restorative justice: Transforming individuals and institutions.* Cincinnati, OH: Anderson.

Breetzke, G. (2010). Modeling violent crime rates: A test of social disorganization in the city of Tshwane, South Africa. *Journal Of Criminal Justice, 38*(4), 446–452.

Bridges, G., & Crutchfield, R. (1988). Law, social standing, and racial disparities in imprisonment. *Social Forces, 66,* 699–724.

Broidy, L. (1995). Direct supervision and delinquency: Assessing the adequacy of structural proxies. *Journal of Criminal Justice, 23,* 541–554.

Brown, J. D. (1991). The professional ex-: An alternative for exiting the deviant career. *Sociological Quarterly, 32*(2), 219–230.

Brownell, K. D., Marlatt, G., Lichteustein, E., & Wilson, G. (1986). Understanding and preventing relapse. *American Psychologist, 41*(7), 765–782.

Browning, C. R. (2002). The span of collective efficacy: Extending social disorganization theory to partner violence. *Journal of Marriage and Family, 64*(4), 833–850.

Burgess, R. L., & Akers, R. L. (1966). A differential association reinforcement theory of criminal behavior. *Social Problems, 14,* 128–147.

Burgess-Proctor, A. (2006). Intersections of race, class, gender, and crime: Future directions for feminist criminology. *Feminist Criminology, 1*(1), 27–47.

Bursik, R. J., Jr. (1988). Social disorganization and theories of crime and delinquency: Problems and prospects. *Criminology, 26*(4), 519–551.

Cain, M. (1974). The main theme of Marx' and Engels' sociology of law. *British Journal of Law and Society, 1*(2), 136–148.

Campbell, D. T., & Stanley, J. C. (1963). *Experimental and quasi-experimental designs for research.* Chicago: Rand McNally College.

Campos, R. (2012). Graffiti writer as superhero. *European Journal of Cultural Studies, 16*(2), 155–170.

Cancino, J. M. (2005). The utility of social capital and collective efficacy: Social control policy in nonmetropolitan settings. *Criminal Justice Policy Review, 16*(3), 287–318.

Capaldi, D. M., Kim, H. K., & Owen, L. D. (2008). Romantic partners' influence on men's likelihood of arrest in early adulthood. *Criminology, 46*(2), 267–299.

Castle, T., & Hensley, C. (2002). Serial killers with military experience: Applying learning theory to serial murder. *International Journal of Offender Therapy and Comparative Criminology, 46*(4), 453–465.

Cernkovich, S. A., & Giordano, P. C. (1987). Family relationships and delinquency. *Criminology, 20,* 149–167.

Cernkovich, S. A., Giordano, P. C., & Rudolph, J. L. (2000). Race, crime, and the American Dream. *Journal of Research in Crime and Delinquency, 37*(3), 131–170.

Chambliss, W. J. (1964). A sociological analysis of the law of vagrancy. *Social Problems, 12*(1), 67–77.

Chambliss, W. J. (1969). *Crime and the legal process.* New York: McGraw Hill.

Chambliss, W. J. (1973, November/December). The Roughnecks and the Saints. *Society,* pp. 24–31.

Chambliss, W. J. (1975). Toward a political economy of crime. *Theory and Society, 2,* 149–170.

Chambliss, W. J. (1978). *On the take: From petty crooks to presidents.* Bloomington: Indiana University Press.

Chambliss, W. J. (1999). *Power, politics, and crime.* Boulder, CO: Westview.

Chambliss, W. J., & Seidman, R. B. (1971). *Law, order and power.* Reading, MA: Addison-Wesley.

Chamlin, M. B., & Cochran, J. K. (1995). Assessing Messner and Rosenfeld's Institutional Anomie Theory: A Partial Test. *Criminology, 33*(3), 411–429.

Chamlin, M. B. (2009). Threat to whom? Conflict, consensus, and social control. *Deviant Behavior, 30,* 539–559.

Chappell, A., & Lanza-Kaduce, L. (2010). Police academy socialization: Understanding the lessons learned in a paramilitary-bureaucratic organization. *Journal of Contemporary Ethnography, 39*(2), 187–214.

Chesney-Lind, M., & Shelden, R. (2003). *Girls, delinquency and juvenile justice.* Belmont, CA: Wadsworth.

Chesney-Lind, M. (1988). Girls and status offenses: Is juvenile justice still sexist? *Criminal Justice Abstracts, 20,* 144–165.

Chesney-Lind, M. (1997). Female offenders: Girls, women, and crime. Thousand Oaks, CA: Sage.

Chesney-Lind, M., & Shelden, R. (1998). Girls, delinquency, and juvenile justice (2nd ed.). *Pacific Grove,* CA: Brooks/Cole.

Chirot, D., & Edwards, J. (2003). Making sense of the senseless: Understanding genocide. *Context, 2*(2), 12–19.

Chirot, D. & McCauley, C. (2006). *Why not kill them all? The logic and prevention of mass political murder.* Princeton, NJ: Princeton University Press.

Ciclitira, K..(2004). *Pornography, Women, and Feminism: Between Pleasure and Politics. Sexualities, 7,* 281–301.

Clear, T. R. (2007). *Imprisoning communities: How mass incarceration makes disadvantaged neighborhoods worse.* New York: Oxford University Press.

Clemmer, D. (1958). *The prison community.* New York: Holt, Rinehart & Winston. (Original work published 1940)

Clinard, M. B., & Meier, R. F. (2010). *Sociology of deviant behavior.* Belmont, CA: Wadsworth.

Cloward, R. (1959). Illegitimate means, anomie, and deviant behavior. *American Sociological Review, 24*(2), 164–176.

Cloward, R., & Ohlin, L. (1960). *Delinquency and opportunity: A theory of delinquent gangs.* New York: Free Press.

Cochran, J. K., & Bjerregaard, B. (2012). Structural Anomie and Crime: A Cross-National Test. International *Journal Of Offender Therapy & Comparative Criminology, 56*(2), 203–217.

Cohen, A. K. (1955). *Delinquent boys: The culture of the gang.* New York: The Free Press.

Coker, D. (2006). Restorative justice, Navajo peacemaking, and domestic violence. *Theoretical Criminology, 10,* 67–85.

Cole, D. (1998). *No equal justice: Race and class in the American criminal justice system.* New York: New Press.

Comfort, M. L. (2002). "Papa's house": The prison as domestic and social satellite. *Ethnography, 3*(4), 467–499.

Comfort, M. L. (2003). In the tube at San Quentin: The "secondary prisonization" of women visiting inmates. *Journal of Contemporary Ethnography, 32*(1), 77–107.

Comfort, M. L. (2008). *Doing time together: Love and family in the shadow of the prison.* Chicago: University of Chicago Press.

Conrad, P. (1992). Medicalization and social control. *Annual Review of Sociology, 18,* 209–232.

Cragg, W. (1992). *The practice of punishment: Towards a theory of restorative justice.* London: Routledge.

Crenshaw, K., Gotanda, N., Peller, G., & Thomas, K. (1995). Introduction. In K. Crenshaw, N. Gotanda, G. Peller, & K. Thomas (Eds.), *Critical race theory: The key writings that formed the movement* (pp. xiii–xxii). New York: New Press.

Cretacci, M. A., Fei Ding, M. L., & Rivera, C. J. (2010). Traditional and bond measures of self-control and their impact on deviance among Chinese University students. *International Journal Of Criminal Justice Sciences, 5*(1), 220–238.

Cretacci, M., & Cretacci, N. (2012). Enter the Dragon: Parenting and Low-Self Control in a Sample of Chinese High School Students. Asian *Journal Of Criminology, 7*(2), 107–120. doi:10.1007/s11417-012-9129-z

Cullen, F. T. (2011). Beyond adolescent-limited criminology: Choosing our future—The American Society of Criminology 2010 Sutherland Address. *Criminology, 49*(2), 287–330.

Cullen, F. T., & Agnew, R. (2006). *Criminological theory past to present: Essential readings* (3rd ed.). New York: Oxford University Press.

Cullen, F. T., & Agnew, R. (2011). *Criminology theory: Past to present, essential readings* (4th ed.). New York: Oxford University Press.

Cullen, F. T., & Messner, S. F. (2007). The making of criminology revisited: An oral history of Merton's anomie paradigm. *Theoretical Criminology, 11*(5), 5–37.

Dai, B. (1937). *Opium addiction in Chicago.* Shanghai: Commercial Press.

Daly, K. (2002). Restorative justice: The real story. *Punishment & Society, 4*(1), 55–79.

Daly, K., & Chesney-Lind, M. (1988). Feminism and criminology. *Justice Quarterly, 5,* 497–538.

Daniel, M. (2006, April 17). Suspect had three guns on bus. *Boston Globe.* http://www.boston.com/news/local/massachusetts/articles/2006/04/17/suspect_had_three_guns_on_bus/

Davies, S., & Tanner, J. (2003). The long arm of the law: Effects of labeling on employment. *The Sociological Quarterly, 44*(3), 385–404.

Davis, L. M., Bozick, R., Steele, J. L., Saunders, J., & Miles, J. N. V. (2013). *Evaluating the effectiveness of correctional education: A meta-analysis of programs that provide education to incarcerated adults.* Santa Monica: Rand Corporation.

DeJong, W. (1987). A short-term evaluation of project DARE (Drug Abuse Resistance Education): Preliminary indications of effectiveness. *Journal of Drug Education, 17,* 279–294.

DeKeserdy, W., Ellis, D., & Alvi, S. (2005). *Deviance and crime: Theory, research and policy.* Cincinnati, OH: Anderson.

De Li, S. (2004). The impacts of self-control and social bonds on juvenile delinquency in a national sample of midadolescents. *Deviant Behavior, 25*(4), 351–373.

Dishion, T. J., Patterson, G. R., & Kavanagh, K. A. (1992). An experimental test of the coercion model: Linking theory, measurement, and intervention. In J. McCord & R. E. Tremblay (Eds.) *Preventing antisocial behavior: Interventions from birth through adolescence* (pp. 253–282). New York, NY: Guilford Press

Downing, S. (2009). Attitudinal and behavioral pathways of deviance in online gaming. *Deviant Behavior, 30*(3), 293–320.

Du Bois, W. E. B. 1901. "The Spawn of Slavery: The Convict-Lease System in the South." *The Missionary Review of the World* 14:737–745.

Dumb Laws. (2013). The Dumb Network. Retrieved from http://www.dumblaws.com/law/1917

Dunlap, E., Johnson, B., & Manwar, A. (1994). A successful female crack dealer: Case study of a deviant career. *Deviant Behavior, 15,* 1–25.

Durkheim, É. (1951). *Suicide.* New York: Free Press. (Original work published 1897)

Eddy, J. M., & Chamberlain, P. (2000). Family managment and deviant peer association as mediators of the impact of treatment condition on youth antisocial behavior. *Journal of Consulting and Clinical Psychology, 68*(5), 857–863.

Edwards, M. L. (2010). Gender, social disorganization theory, and the locations of sexually oriented businesses. *Deviant Behavior, 31*(2), 135–158.

Eidelson, J. (2013). Workers Tell OSHA They Were Locked Inside Target Stores Overnight. *The Nation.* Retrieved from http://www.thenation.com/blog/172426/ohsa-charges-workers-were-locked-inside-target-stores-overnight#axzz2Y3PU7d8m

Einstadter, W., & Henry, S. (1995). *Criminological theory: An analysis of underlying assumptions.* Fort Worth, TX: Harcourt Brace College Publishers.

Einwohner, R. L. (2003). Opportunity, honor, and action in the Warsaw ghetto uprising of 1943. *American Journal of Sociology, 109*(3), 650–675.

Elechi, O. O., Morris, S. V. C., & Schauer, E. J. (2010). Restoring justice (ubuntu): An African perspective. *International Criminal Justice Review, 20*(1), 73–85.

Elliot, D. S., & Menard, S. (1996). Delinquent friends and delinquent behavior: Temporal and developmental patterns. In J. D. Hawkins (Ed.), *Delinquency and crime: Current theories* (pp. 28–67). New York: Cambridge University Press.

Ellsworth-Jones, W. (2013). The story behind Banksy. *Smithsonian* magazine. Retrieved from http://www.smithsonianmag.com/arts-culture/The-Story-Behind-Banksy-187953941.html?c=y&page=1

Emergency Response and Research Institute. 1991. Fire Violations Kill Twenty-Five in Chicken Plant. Retrieved from http://web.archive.org/web/20061205035348/http://emergency.com/nc-fire.htm

Empey, L. T., & Erickson, M. L. (1972). *The Prove Experiment: Evaluating community control of delinquency.* Lexington, MA: Heath.

Empey, L. T., & Lubeck, S. G. (1971). *The Silverlake Experiment: Testing delinquency theory and community intervention.* Chicago: Aldine.

Ennett, S. T., Tobler, N. S., Ringwalt, C. L., & Flewelling, R. (1994). How effective is drug abuse resistance education? A meta-analysis of project DARE outcome evaluations. *American Journal of Public Health, 84,* 1394–1401.

Environmental Protection Agency. (2011). Climate change, basic info. Retrieved June 30, 2011, from http://www.epa.gov/climatechange/basicinfo.html

Enzmann, D., & Podana, Z. (2010). Official Crime Statistics and Survey Data: Comparing Trends of Youth Violence between 2000 and 2006 in Cities of the Czech Republic, Germany, Poland, Russia, and Slovenia. *European Journal On Criminal Policy & Research, 16*(3), 191–205.

Erikson, K. T. (1966). *Wayward puritans: A study in the sociology of deviance.* New York: Macmillan.

Fairbanks, A. M. (2012). Seeking arrangement: College students using "sugar daddies" to pay off loan debt. Huffington Post. Retrieved from http://www.huffingtonpost.com/2011/07/29/seeking-arrangement-college-students_n_913373.html?page=1

Fan, S. (1997). Immigration law and the promise of critical race theory: Opening the academy to the voices of aliens and immigrants. *Columbia Law Review, 97*(4), 1202–1240.

Faris, R. E. L., & Dunham, H. W. (1939). *Mental disease in urban areas.* Chicago: University of Chicago Press.

Farley, M., & Barkan, H. (1998). Prostitution, violence, and post-traumatic stress disorder. *Women and Health, 27*(3), 37–49.

Farrington, D. (1986). Age and crime. *Crime and Justice, 7,* 189–250.

Farrington, D., Gallagher, B., Morley, L., Ledger, R., & West, D. J. (1985). *Cambridge study in delinquent development: Long term follow-up, first annual report to the Home Office.* Cambridge, UK: Cambridge University Press.

Federal Bureau of Investigation. (2004). Uniform Crime Reporting Handbook. U.S. Department of Justice. Retrieved from http://www2.fbi.gov/ucr/handbook/ucrhandbook04.pdf.

Federal Bureau of Investigation. (2011). Crime in the United States, 2010. U.S. Department of Justice. Retrieved from http://www.fbi.gov/about-us/cjis/ucr/crime-in-the-u.s/2010/crime-in-the-u.s.-2010/property-crime/larcenytheftmain

Feld, B. C. (1977). *Neutralizing inmate violence: Juvenile offenders in institutions.* Cambridge, MA: Ballinger.

Ferguson, K. M., Bender, K., Thompson, S., Maccio E.M., Xie, B., and Pollio, D. (2011). Social Control Correlates of Arrest Behavior Among Homeless Youth in Five U.S. Cities. *Violence and Victims,* 26:648–668.

Ferrell, F., & Hamm, M. S. (1998). *Ethnography at the edge: Crime, deviance, and field research.* Boston: Northeastern University Press.

Fields, G., & Phillips, E. E. (2013, September 25). The new asylums: Jails swell with mentally ill. *The Wall Street Journal.* Retrieved from http://online.wsj.com/article/SB10001424127887323455104579012664245550546.html

Fleisher, M. S. (1995). *Beggars and thieves: Lives of urban street criminals.* Madison: University of Wisconsin Press.

Fleming, C. B., Catalano, R. F., Oxford, M. L., & Harachi, T. W. (2002). A test of generalizability of the social development model across gender and income groups with longitudinal data from the elementary school developmental period. *Journal of Quantitative Criminology, 18*(4), 423–439.

Frailing, K., & Harper, J. (2010). The social construction of deviance, conflict and the criminalization of midwives, New Orleans: 1940s and 1950s. *Deviant Behavior, 31*(8), 729–755.

Free the Slaves. (2013). About slavery. Retrieved from http://www.freetheslaves.net/page.aspx?pid=348

Fremont Arts Council. (2010). Fremont Solstice Parade. Retrieved October 14, 2010, from http://fremontartscouncil.org/events/summer-solstice-parade/

Fremont Fair. (2010). Fremont Fair homepage. Retrieved October 14, 2010, from http://www.fremontfair.org/

Frericks, P., R. Maier, and W. de Graaf. (2009). Toward a Neoliberal Europe?: Pension Reforms and Transformed Citizenship. *Administration & Society, 41,* 135–157.

Frieswick, K. (2012, May 29). Ex-cons launching lives as entrepreneurs. *Inc.com.* Retrieved from http://www.inc.com/magazine/201206/kris-frieswick/catherine-rohr-defy-ventures-story-of-redemption.html/3

Fuller, J., & Wozniak, J. F. (2006). Peacemaking criminology: Past, present, and future. In F. T. Cullen, J. P. Wright, & K. R. Blevins (Eds.), *Taking stock: The status of criminological theory* (pp. 251–276). New Brunswick, NJ: Transaction.

Gabbidon, S. L. (2003). "Racial profiling by store clerks and personnel in retail establishments: An exploration of 'shopping while black.'" *Journal of Contemporary Criminal Justice* 19(3):345–364.

Gallupe, O., & Bouchard, M. (2013). Adolescent parties and substance use: A situational approach to peer influence. *Journal Of Criminal Justice, 41*(3), 162–171.

Gastil, R. D. (1971). Homicide and a regional culture of Violence. *American Sociological Review* 36: 412–437.

Gastil, R. D. (1978). Comments. *Criminology, 16*(1), 60–64.

Gauthier, D. K., & Chaudoir, N. K. (2004). Tranny boyz: Cyber community support in negotiating sex and gender mobility among female to male transsexuals. *Deviant Behavior, 25*(4), 375–398.

Gellman, B.,, and Poitras, L. (2013, June 6). U.S., British intelligence mining data from nine U.S. Internet companies in broad secret program. *The New York Times.* Retrieved from http://www.washingtonpost.com/investigations/us-intelligence-mining-data-from-nine-us-internet-companies-in-broad-secret-program/2013/06/06/3a0c0da8-cebf-11e2-8845-d970ccb04497_story.html

Gerstein, J. (2011). "Eric Holder Accused of Neglecting Porn Fight." Politico. Retrieved from http://www.politico.com/news/stories/0411/53314.html

Ghosh, B. (2012, August 11). Tag, you're it: Graffiti artists can't stop. *SF Gate.* Retrieved from http://www.sfgate.com/art/article/Tag-you-re-it-graffiti-artists-can-t-stop-3781992.php

Giordano, P. C., Longmore, M. A., Schroeder, R. D., & Seffrin, P. M. (2008). A life-course perspective on spirituality and desistance from crime. *Criminology, 46*(1), 99–132.

Glueck, S., & Glueck, E. (1950). *Unraveling juvenile delinquency.* Cambridge, MA: Harvard University Press.

Goffman, A. (2009). On the run: Wanted men in a Philadelphia ghetto. *American Sociological Review, 74,* 339–357.

Goffman, E. (1961). *Asylums.* Garden City, NY: Anchor Books.

Goffman, E. (1963). *Stigma: Notes on the management of spoiled identity.* Englewood Cliffs, NJ: Prentice Hall.

Goode, E. (1991). Positive deviance: A viable concept? *Deviant Behavior, 12*(3), 289–309.

Goode, E. (2005). *Deviant behavior* (7th ed.). Upper Saddle River, NJ: Pearson Education.

Goode, E. (2008a). *Deviant behavior* (8th ed.). Upper Saddle River, NJ: Pearson Prentice Hall.

Goode, E. (2008b). The fat admirer. In E. Goode & D. A. Vail (Eds.), *Extreme deviance* (pp. 80–90). Thousand Oaks, CA: Pine Forge Press.

Gottfredson, M., & Hirschi, T. (1986). The true value of lambda would appear to be zero: An essay on career criminals, criminal careers, selective incapacitation, cohort studies and related topics. *Criminology, 24,* 213–234.

Gottfredson, M. R., & Hirschi, T. (1990). *A general theory of crime.* Stanford, CA: Stanford University Press.

Gowan, T. & Whetstone, S. (2012). Making the criminal addict: Subjectivity and social control in a strong-arm rehab. *Punishment & Society,* 14(1), 69–93.

Gourley, M. (2004). A subcultural study of recreational ecstasy use. *Journal of Sociology, 40*(1), 59–74.

Gove, W. R. (1975). The labeling theory of mental illness: A reply to Scheff. *American Sociological Review, 40,* 242–248.

Government Accountability Project. (2013). GAP Statement on the Espionage Charge Filed Against Edward Snowden. Retrieved from http://www.whistleblower.org/blog/44-2013-2804-gap-statement-on-the-espionage-charge-filed-against-edward-snowden

Greene, J. M., Ennett, S. T., & Ringwalt, C. L. (1999). Prevalence and correlates of survival sex among runaway and homeless youth. *American Journal of Public Health, 89*(9), 1406–1409.

Greene, J., Ringwalt, C., Kelley, J., Iachan, R., & Cohen, Z. (1995). *Youth with Runaway, Throwaway, and Homeless Experiences . . . Prevalence, Drug Use, and Other At-Risk Behaviors.* Administration for Children and Families. Youth Services Bureau.

Greenhouse, S. (2004). Workers Assail Night Lock-Ins By Wal-Mart. *The New York Times.* Retrieved from http://www.nytimes.com/2004/01/18/us/workers-assail-night-lock-ins-by-wal-mart.html?pagewanted=all&src=pm

Greenberg, D. (1985). Age, crime, and social explanation. *American Journal of Sociology, 91,* 1–21.

Greenwald, G., MacAskill, E., Poitras, L. (June 9, 2013). "Edward Snowden: the whistleblower behind the NSA surveillance revelations". *The Guardian* (London). Retrieved from http://www.guardian.co.uk/world/2013/jun/09/edward-snowden-nsa-whistleblower-surveillance

Greenberg, D. F., Kessler, R. C., & Loftin, C. (1985). Social inequality and crime control. *Journal of Criminal Law and Criminology, 76,* 684–704.

Greenwood, P. W. (1992). Substance abuse problems among high-risk youth and potential interventions. *Crime and Delinquency, 38,* 444–458.

Griffin, C., Bengry-Howell, A., Hackley, C., Mistral, W., & Szmigin, I. (2009). "Every time I do it I absolutely annihilate myself": Loss of narratives (self-)consciousness and loss of memory in young people's drinking. *Sociology, 43*(3), 457–476.

Grinberg, E. (2010). No longer a registered sex offender, but the stigma remains. CNN.com. Retrieved February 15, 2010, at http://www.cnn.com/2010/CRIME/02/11/oklahoma.teen.sex.offender/index.html

Gunther, A. (2011) "Greening our food deserts from the ground up." *Huffington Post*, 10/03/2011; http://www.huffingtonpost.com/andrew-gunther/la-green-grounds_b_993247.html

Gurr, T. R., & Harff, B. (1994). *Ethnic conflict in world politics.* Boulder, CO: Westview Press.

Gusfield, J. (1967). Moral passage: The symbolic process of public designations of deviance. *Social Problems, 15*(2), 1785–1788.

Gusfield, J. (1968). On legislating morals: The symbolic process of designating deviance. *California Law Review, 56*(1), 54–73.

Haas, H., Farrington, D. P., Killias, M., & Sattar, G. (2004). The impact of different family configurations on delinquency. *British Journal of Criminology, 44*(4), 520–532.

Hackney, S. (1969). Southern violence. *American Historical Review, 74,* 906–925.

Hagan, J. (1985). *Modern criminology: Crime, criminal behavior, and its control.* New York: McGraw-Hill.

Hagan, J. (1989). *Structural criminology.* New Brunswick, NJ: Rutgers University Press.

Hagan, J., Gillis, A. R., & Simpson, J. (1985). The class structure of gender and delinquency: Toward a power-control theory of common delinquent behavior. *American Journal of Sociology, 90,* 1151–1178.

Hagan, J., Gillis, A. R., & Simpson, J. (1990). Clarifying and extending power-control theory. *American Journal of Sociology, 95*(4), 1024–1037.

Hagan, J., & Palloni, A. (1986). Crimes as social events in the life course. *Criminology, 26,* 87–100.

Hagan, J., & Rymond-Richmond, W. (2008). The collective dynamics of racial dehumanization and genocidal victimization in Darfur. *American Sociological Review, 73*(6), 875–902.

Hagan, J., Schoenfeld, H., Palloni, A., Cook, K. S., & Massey, D. S. (2006). The Science of Human Rights, War Crimes, and Humanitarian Emergencies. *Annual Review Of Sociology,* 323–349

Hagan, J., Shedd, C., & Payne, M. R. (2005). Race, ethnicity, and youth perceptions of criminal injustice. *American Sociological Review, 70,* 381–407.

Hagan, J., Simpson, S., & Gillis, A. R. (1987). Class in the household: A power-control theory of gender and delinquency. *American Journal of Sociology, 92*(4), 788–816.

Halcon, L. L., & Lifson, A. R. (2004). Prevalence and predictors of sexual risks among homeless youth. *Journal of Youth and Adolescence, 33*(1), 71–80.

Halkitis, P.N. & Palamar, J. J. (2008). Multivariate modeling of club drug use initiation among gay and bisexual men. *Substance Use and Misuse* 43: 871–879.

Hall, S., Critcher, C., Jefferson, T., Clarke, J., & Roberts, B. (1978). *Policing the crisis.* London: Macmillan.

Hallstone, M. (2002). Updating Howard Becker's theory of using marijuana for pleasure. *Contemporary Drug Problems, 29,* 821–845.

Hamm, M. S. (2004). Apocalyptic violence: The seduction of terrorist subcultures. *Theoretical Criminology, 8*(3), 323–339.

Hammer, H., Finkelhor, D. & Sedlak, A. J. (2002). "Runaway/Thrownaway Children: National Estimates and Characteristics." National Incidence Studies of Missing, Abducted, Runaway, and Thrownaway Children. Office of Juvenile Justice and Delinquency Prevention: U.S. Department of Justice. Retrieved from https://www.ncjrs.gov/pdffiles1/ojjdp/196469.pdf

Haney, L. A. (2010). *Offending women: Power, punishment, and the regulation of desire.* Berkeley: University of California Press.

Harcourt, B. (2001). *The illusion of order.* Cambridge, MA: Harvard University Press.

Harris, A. J., & Lurigio, A. J. (2010). Introduction to special issue on sex offenses and offenders: Toward evidence-based public policy. *Criminal Justice and Behavior, 37*(5), 477–481.

Hartjen, C. A., & Priyadarsini, S. S. (2003). Gender, Peers, and Delinquency. *Youth & Society, 34*(4), 387.

Hayes, T. A. (2010). Labeling and the adoption of a deviant status. *Deviant Behavior, 31,* 274–302.

Hayes-Smith, J., & Whaley, R. B. (2009). Community characteristics and methamphetamine use: A social disorganization perspective. *Journal of Drug Issues, 39,* 547–576.

Haygood, W. (2002). Still Burning: After a deadly Fire, A Town's Losses Were Just Beginning. *The Washington Post.* Retrieved from http://web.archive.org/web/20061208182200/http://www.fedlock.com/public_relations/Still_Burning.htm

Haynie, D. L. (2002). Friendship networks and delinquency: The relative nature of peer delinquency. *Journal of Quantitative Criminology, 18*(2), 99–134.

Heimer, K., & Matsueda, R. L. (1994). Role-taking, role commitment, and delinquency: A theory of differential social control. *American Sociological Review, 59*(3), 365–390.

Herman-Kinney, N. J., & Kinney, D. A. (2013). Sober as deviant: The stigma of sobriety and how some college students "stay dry" on a "wet" campus. *Journal of Contemporary Ethnography, 42*(1), 64–103.

Hernu, P. (2011, July 2011). Norway's controversial "cushy prison" experiment—could it catch on in the UK? *Mail Online.* Retrieved from http://www.dailymail.co.uk/home/moslive/article-1384308/Norways-controversial-cushy-prison-experiment—catch-UK.html#ixzz2i10120Gy

Higgins, G. E., Tewksbury, R., & Mustaine, E. E. (2007). Sports fan binge drinking: An examination using low self-control and peer association. *Sociological Spectrum, 27*(4), 389–404.

Hinton, S. E. (1967). *The outsiders.* New York: Penguin.

Hirsch, M. L., Conforti, R. W., & Graney, C. J. (1990). The use of marijuana for pleasure: A replication of Howard Becker's study of marijuana use. *Journal of Social Behavior and Personality, 5,* 497–510.

Hirschfield, P. (2008). The declining significance of delinquent labels in disadvantaged urban communities. *Sociological Forum, 23*(3), 575–601.

Hirschi, T. (1969). *Causes of delinquency.* Berkeley: University of California Press.

Hirschi, T., & Gottfredson, M. R. (1995). Control theory and life-course perspective. *Studies on Crime Prevention, 4*(2), 131–142.

Hochman, D. (2013, May 3), "Urban gardening: An Appleseed with attitude." *New York Times,* May 3, 2013; http://www.nytimes.com/2013/05/05/fashion/urban-gardening-an-appleseed-with-attitude.html?pagewanted=all&_r=0.

Hochstetler, A., Copes, H., & DeLisi, M. (2002). Differential association in group and solo offending. *Journal of Criminal Justice, 30*(6), 559–566.

Hoffman, A. (1971). *Steal This Book.* Pirate Editions, Grove Press.

Hoffman, A. (2002). *Steal This Book.* New York: Four Walls Eight Windows.

Hold, T. J., & Copes, H. (2010). Transferring subcultural knowledge on-line: Practices and beliefs of persistent digital pirates. *Deviant Behavior, 31*(7), 625–654.

Homeboy Industries. (2012). The Homeboy Museum: Thursday, May 10, 2012. Retrieved September 28, 2013 from http://www.homeboystories.blogspot.com/

Homeboy Industries. (2013a). Home. Retrieved September 28, 2013 from http://www.homeboyindustries.org/.

Homeboy Industries. (2013b). What We Do. Retrieved September 28, 2013 from http://www.homeboyindustries.org/what-we-do/.

Hopkins, R. B., Paradis, J., Roshankar, T., Bowen, J., Tarride, J., Blackhouse, G., & Longo, C. J. (2008). Universal or Targeted Screening for Fetal Alcohol Exposure: A Cost-Effectiveness Analysis. *Journal of Studies on Alcohol & Drugs, 69:* 510–519.

Horowitz, D. (2001). *The deadly ethnic riot.* Berkeley: University of California Press.

Hudson, B. (1998). Restorative justice: The challenge of sexual and racial violence. *Journal of Law and Society, 25*(2), 237–256.

Huiras, J., Uggen, C., & McMorris, B. (2000). Career jobs, survival jobs, and employee deviance: A social investment model of workplace misconduct. *The Sociological Quarterly, 41*(2), 245–263.

Humphreys, L. (1970). *Tearoom trade: Impersonal sex in public places.* Chicago: Aldine.

Hunt, P. M. (2010). Are you kynd? Conformity and deviance within the Jamband subculture. *Deviant Behavior, 31*(6), 521–551.

Hunter, S. K. (1993). Prostitution is cruelty and abuse to women and children. *Michigan Journal of Gender & Law, 1,* 91–104.

Inderbitzin, M. (2006). Lessons from a juvenile training school: Survival and growth. *Journal of Adolescent Research, 21,* 7–26.

Inderbitzin, M. (2007). Inside a maximum-security juvenile training school: Institutional attempts to redefine the American dream and normalize incarcerated youth. *Punishment & Society 9*(3), 235–251.

Inderbitzin, M., & Boyd, H. (2010). William J. Chambliss. In K. Hayward, S. Maruna, & J. Mooney (Eds.), *Fifty key thinkers in criminology* (pp. 203–208). New York: Routledge.

International Labour Organization. (2005). *A global alliance against forced labour.* Geneva: International Labour Office.

Irvine, C. (2008, October 27). Tattooed leopard man leaves hermit lifestyle behind. Telegraph.co.uk. http://www.telegraph.co.uk/news/newstopics/howaboutthat/3265474/Tattooed-Leopard-Man-leaves-hermit-lifestyle-behind.html

Jackson, P., & Carroll, L. (1981). Race and the war on crime: The sociopolitical determinants of municipal police expenditures in 90 non-southern cities. *American Sociological Review, 46,* 390–405.

Jacobells v. Ohio, 378 U.S. 184, 197 (1964).

James, E. (2013a). The Norwegian prison where inmates are treated like people. *The Guardian.* Retrieved from http://www.theguardian.com/society/2013/feb/25/norwegian-prison-inmates-treated-like-people

James, E. (2013b). Bastoy: The Norwegian prison that works. *The Guardian.* Retrieved from http://www.theguardian.com/society/2013/sep/04/bastoy-norwegian-prison-works

Jang, S. J., & Smith, C. A. (1997). A test of reciprocal causal relationships among parental supervision, affective ties, and delinquency. *Journal of Research in Crime and Delinquency, 34,* 307–337.

Jencks, C. (1994). *The Homeless.* Cambridge, MA: Harvard University Press.

Janus, M., Burgess, A., & McCormack, A. (1987). Histories of sexual abuse in adolescent male runaways. *Adolescence, 22,* 405–417.

Jensen, G. F. (2007). The sociology of deviance. In C. D. Bryant & D. L. Peck (Eds.), *The handbook of 21st century sociology* (pp. 370–379). Thousand Oaks, CA: Sage.

Jobes, P. C., Barclay, E., & Weinand, H. (2004). A structural analysis of social disorganisation and crime in rural communities in Australia. *Australian and New Zealand Journal of Criminology, 37*(1), 114–140.

Johnson, R. E. (1986). Family structure and delinquency: General patterns and gender differences. *Criminology, 24,* 65–84.

Jones, A. L. (1998). Random acts of kindness: A teaching tool for positive deviance. *Teaching Sociology, 26*(3), 179–189.

A journey into hell. (2002, September 22). *The Economist.* Retrieved from http://www.economist.com/node/21563288

Junger, M., & Marshall, I. H. (1997). The interethnic generalizability of social control theory: An empirical test. *Journal of Research in Crime and Delinquency, 34,* 79–112.

Junger-Tas, J. (1992). An Empirical Test of Social Control Theory. *Journal Of Quantitative Criminology, 8*(1), 9–28.

Kaufman, J. G., & Widom, C. S. (1999). Childhood victimization, running away, and delinquency. *Journal of Research in Crime and Delinquency, 36*(4), 347–371.

Kempf-Leonard, K., & Johansson, P. (2007). Gender and runaways: Risk factors, delinquency, and juvenile justice experiences. *Youth Violence and Juvenile Justice, 5,* 308–327.

Kemple, J. J., & Scott-Clayton, J. (2004). *Career academies: Impacts on labor market outcomes and educational attainment.* San Francisco, CA: Manpower Demonstration Research Corporation.

Kennedy, Bruce. (2013). Why do companies still lock workers inside? China's deadly factory fire joins an ever-growing list of example sin which employees have no means of escape despite workplace laws. *MSN Money.* Retrieved from http://money.msn.com/now/post.aspx?post=d8522b07-db76-4a0f-b8f5-b0b1c2392923

KFMB-News 8. (2010). Man flashes undercover cop during sting operation at Lake Murray. Retrieved October 14, 2010, from http://www.cbs8.com/global/story.asp?s=12842252

Kim, E., Akers, R. L., & Yun, M. (2013). A Cross-Cultural Test of Social Structure and Social Learning: Alcohol Use among South Korean Adolescents. *Deviant Behavior, 34*(11), 895–915. doi:10.1080/01639625.2013.782–787

Kim, E., Kwak, D. H., and M. Yun. (2010). "Investigating the Effects of Peer Association and Parental Influence on Adolescent Substance Use: A Study of Adolescents in South Korea." Journal of Criminal Justice 38:17–24.

Kipke, M. D., Unger, J. B., O'Connor, S., Palmer, R. F., & LaFrance, S. R. (1997). Street youth, their peer group affiliation and differences according to residential status, subsistence patterns, and use of services. *Adolescence, 32*(127), 655–669.

Kitsuse, J., & Spector, M. (1973). Toward a sociology of social problems: Social conditions, value-judgments, and social problems. *Social Problems, 20*(4), 407–419.

Kitsuse, J., & Spector, M. (1975). Social problems: A reformulation. *Social Problems, 21*(2), 145–159.

Klein, H., & Shiffman, K. S. (2008). What animated cartoons tell viewers about assault. *Journal of Aggression, Maltreatment & Trauma, 16*(2), 181–201.

Klein, J. D., & St. Clair, S. (2000). Do candy cigarettes encourage young people to smoke? *British Medical Journal, 321,* 362.

Kobrin, S. (1959). The Chicago Area Project. *Annals of the American Academy of Political and Social Science, 322:* 20–29.

Kokaliari, E., & Berzoff, J. (2008). Nonsuicidal self-injury among nonclinical college women: Lessons from Foucault. *Affilia: Journal of Women and Social Work, 23*(3), 259–269.

Kornhauser, R. R. (1978). *Social sources of delinquency: An appraisal of analytic models.* Chicago: University of Chicago Press.

Kotlowitz, A. (1988). *There are no children here: The story of two boys growing up in other America.* New York: Anchor.

Kovandzic, T. V., Vieraitis, L. M., & Boots, D. P. (2009). Does the death penalty save lives? New evidence from state panel data, 1979 to 2006. *Criminology and Public Policy, 8,* 803–844.

Krakauer, J. (1996). *Into the wild.* New York: Anchor.

Kristof, N. D., & WuDunn, S. (2009). *Half the sky: Turning oppression into opportunity for women worldwide.* New York: Vintage Books.

Krohn, M. D. (1999). On Ronald L. Akers' Social learning and social structure: A general theory of crime and deviance. *Theoretical Criminology, 3*(4), 437–493.

Krohn, M. D., & Akers, R. L. (1977). An alternative view of the labeling versus psychiatric perspectives on societal reaction to mental illness. *Social Forces, 56*(2), 341–361.

Krohn, M. D., & Massey, J. (1980). Social control and delinquent behavior. *Sociological Quarterly, 21,* 529–543.

Kubrin, C. E. (2008). Making order of disorder: A call for conceptual clarity. *Criminology & Public Policy, 7*(2), 203–213.

Kubrin, C. E., Stucky, T. D., & Krohn, M. D. (2009). *Researching theories of crime and deviance.* New York: Oxford University Press.

Laforgia, M. (2011, May 21). Huge doses of potent antipsychotics flow into state jails for troubled kids. *The Palm Beach Post.*

LaFraniere, S. (2010, November 10). Life in shadows for mentally ill in China. *New York Times.* Retrieved from http://www.nytimes.com/2010/11/11/world/asia/11psych.html?pagewanted=all&_r=0

Langman, L. (2013). Occupy: A new social movement. *Current Sociology, 61*(4), 510–524.

Lankenau, S. E. (1999). Panhandling repertoires and routines for overcoming the nonperson treatment. *Deviant Behavior, 20*(2), 183–206.

Lanza-Kaduce, L., Capece, M., & Alden, H. (2006). Liquor is quicker. *Criminal Justice Policy Review, 17*(2), 127–143.

LaPrairie, C. (1998). The "new" justice: Some implications for aboriginal communities. *Canadian Journal of Criminology, 40*(1), 61–79.

Laub, J. H., & Sampson, R. J. (1988). Unraveling families and delinquency: A reanalysis of the Gluecks' data. *Criminology, 26,* 355–379.

Lefkowitz, B. (1997). *Our guys: The Glen Ridge rape and the secret life of the perfect suburb.* Berkeley: University of California Press.

Leiber, M. J., & Stairs, J. M. (1999). Race, contexts, and the use of intake diversion. *Journal of Research in Crime and Delinquency, 36*(1), 56–86.

Lemert, E. (1951). *Social pathology.* New York: McGraw-Hill.

Levit, N. (1999). Critical of race theory: Race, reason, merit, and civility. *Georgetown Law Journal, 87,* 795.

Liazos, A. (1972). The poverty of the sociology of deviance: Nuts, sluts, and preverts. *Social Problems, 20,* 103–120.

Link, B. G., Phelan, J. C., Bresnahan, M., Stueve, A., & Pescosolido, B. A. (1999). Public conceptions of mental illness: Labels, causes, dangerousness, and social distance. *American Journal of Public Health, 89*(9), 1328–1333.

Liska, A. E., & Messner, S. F. (1999). *Perspectives on crime and deviance* (3rd ed.). Englewood Cliffs, NJ: Prentice Hall.

Lowenkamp, C. T., Cullen, F. T., & Pratt, T. C. (2003). Replicating Sampson and Groves's test of social disorganization theory. *Journal of Research in Crime and Delinquency, 40*(4), 351–373.

Lu, Y., Yu, Y., Ren, L., & Marshall, I. (2013). Exploring the Utility of Self-Control Theory for Risky Behavior and Minor Delinquency Among Chinese Adolescents. *Journal Of Contemporary Criminal Justice, 29*(1), 32–52.

Lucas, A. M. (2005). The work of sex work: Elite prostitutes' vocational orientations and experiences. *Deviant Behavior, 26*(6), 513–546.

Luhman, R. (2002). *Race and ethnicity in the United States: Our differences and our roots.* Fort Worth, FL: Harcourt College.

Lukács, G. (1971). *History and class consciousness: Studies in Marxist dialectics.* Cambridge: MIT Press. (Original work published 1920)

Lynch, N. (2012). Playing catch-up? Recent reform of New Zealand's youth justice system. *Criminology & Criminal Justice, 12*(5), 507–526.

Maass, A., Cadinu, M., Guarnieri, G., & Grasselli, A. (2003). Sexual harassment under social identity threat: The computer harassment paradigm. *Journal of Personality and Social Psychology, 85*(5), 853–870.

MacKinnon, C. (1984). Not a Moral Issue. *Yale Law & Policy Review, 2,* 321–345.

Madden, M., & Lenhart, A. (2009). *Teens and distracted driving: Texting, talking and other uses of the cell phone behind the wheel.* Washington, DC: Pew Internet and American Life Project. Retrieved January 20, 2011, from http://pewinternet.org/Reports/2009/Teens-and-Distracted-Driving.aspx

Maier, S. L., & Monahan, B. A. (2010). How close is too close? Balancing closeness and detachment in qualitative research. *Deviant Behavior, 31*(1), 1–32.

Mannheim, K. (1959). *Ideology and utopia: an introduction to the sociology of knowledge, A harvest book; HB 3.* New York: Harcourt Brace. (Original work published 1936)

Mantsios, G. (2010). Making class invisible. In D. Newman & J. O'Brien (Eds.), *Sociology: Exploring the architecture of everyday life readings* (8th ed., pp. 236–241). Thousand Oaks, CA: Pine Forge Press.

Manza, J., & Uggen, C. (2006). *Locked out: Felon disenfranchisement and American democracy.* New York: Oxford University Press.

Martin, D. (2002). Spatial patterns in residential burglary: Assessing the effect of neighborhood social capital. *Journal of Contemporary Criminal Justice, 18*(2), 132–146.

Martin, J., & O'Hagan, M. (2005, August 30). Killings of 2 Bellingham sex offenders may have been by vigilante, police say. *Seattle Times.* http://community.seattletimes.nwsource.com/archive/?date=20050830&slug=sexoffender30m

Maruna, S. (2011). Reentry as a rite of passage. *Punishment & Society, 13*(1), 3–28.

Marx, K. (1992). *Capital: Volume 1: A critique of political economy.* London: Penguin. (Original work published 1867)

Marx, K. (1993). *Capital: Volume 2: A critique of political economy.* London: Penguin. (Original work published 1885)

Marx, K., & Engels, F. (1957). *The holy family.* London: Lawrence and Wishart.

Marx, K., & Engels, F. (1961). *The communist manifesto.* In A. P. Mendel (Ed.), *Essential works of Marxism* (pp. 13–44). Toronto: Bantam. (Original work published 1848)

Matsueda, R. L. (1992). Reflected appraisals, parental labeling, and delinquency: Specifying a symbolic interactionist theory. *American Journal of Sociology, 97*(6), 1577–1611.

Mauer, M. (2005). Thinking about prison and its impact in the twenty-first century: Walter C. Reckless Memorial Lecture. *Ohio State Journal of Criminal Law, 2,* 607–618.

Mauer, M. (2009). Racial Impact Statements: Changing Policies to Address Disparities. *Criminal Justice, 4:* 19–22.

Maume, M. O., & Lee, M. R. (2003). Social Institutions and Violence: A Sub-National Test of Institutional Anomie Theory. *Criminology, 41*(4), 1137–1172.

Mayo, H. B. (1960). *Introduction to Marxist theory.* New York: Oxford University Press.

McCarthy, B., Hagan, J., & Woodward, T. S. (1999). In the company of women: Structure and agency in a revised power-control theory of gender and delinquency. *Criminology, 37,* 761–788.

McCleary, R., & Tewksbury, R. (2010). Female patrons of porn. *Deviant Behavior, 31*(2), 208–223.

McCord, J. (1978). A thirty-year follow-up of treatment effects. *The American Psychologist, 33,* 284–289.

McCormack, A., Janus, M., & Burgess, A.W. (1986). *Runaway youths and sexual victimization: Gender differences in adolescent runaway populations. Child Abuse & Neglect, 10,* 387–395.

McKenzie, D., & Formanek, I. (2011, February 25). Kenya's mentally ill locked up and forgotten. CNN.com. Retrieved from http://www.cnn.com/2011/WORLD/africa/02/25/kenya.forgotten.health/index.html

McLorg, P. A., & Taub, D. E. (1987). Anorexia nervosa and bulimia: The development of deviant identities. *Deviant Behavior, 8*(2), 177–189.

Meisner, J. (2013). Sister escaped "Trigger Town," but bleak fate snared brother. Adapted from http://articles.chicagotribune.com/2013-04-14/news/ct-met-brother-sister-trigger-town-20130414_1_grammar-school-drugs-family-friend

Menardi, R. (2013, May 9). Catherine Rohr helps former felons defy odds, start businesses. *Silicon Prairie News.* Retrieved from http://www.siliconprairienews.com/2013/05/catherine-rohr-helps-former-felons-defy-odds-start-businesses

Meranze, M. (2009, Aug. 24). California's crisis: Coming to a neighborhood near you. *The Huffington Post.* Retrieved Sept 15, 2009 from http://www.huffingtonpost.com/michael-meranze/californias-crisis-coming_b_267461.html.

Merry, S. E. (1989). Myth and practice in the mediation process. In M. Wright & B. Galaway (Eds.), *Mediation and criminal justice: Victims, offenders, and community* (pp. 239–250). London: Sage.

Merton, R. K. (1938). Social structure and anomie. *American Sociological Review, 3*(5), 672–682.

Merton, R. K. (1957). *Social theory and social structure* (Rev. and enlarged ed.). Glencoe, IL: Free Press.

Merton, R. K. (1964). Anomie, anomia, and social interaction: Contexts of deviant behavior. In M. B. Clinard (Ed.), *Anomie and deviant behavior.* New York: Free Press.

Messmer, H., & Otto, H.-U. (Eds.). (1992). *Restorative justice on trial: Pitfalls and potentials of victim-offender mediation: International research perspectives.* Amsterdam: Kluwer.

Messner, S. F., & Rosenfeld, R. (2007). *Crime and the American Dream* (4th ed.). Belmont, CA: Wadsworth.

Messner, S. F. & Rosenfeld, R. (2007). Political restraint of the market and levels of criminal homicide: A cross-national application of Institutional-Anomie Theory. *Social Forces* 75:1393–1416.

Mestrovic, S. G., & Lorenzo, R. (2008). Durkheim's concept of anomie and the abuse at Abu Ghraib. *Journal of Classical Sociology, 8*(2), 179–207.

Meyer, A. G. (1963). *Marxism: The unity of theory and practice.* Ann Arbor: University of Michigan Press.

Milkman, R. (2012). Revolt of the college-educated millennials. *Contexts, 11*(2), 12–21.

Miller, J. G. (1998). *Last one over the wall* (2nd ed.). Columbus: Ohio State University Press.

Mills, C. W. (2000). *The sociological imagination.* Oxford, UK: Oxford University Press. (Original work published 1959)

Miner, H. (1956). "Body Ritual Among the Nacirema." *American Anthropologist 58*(3): 503–507.

Minor, K., & Morrison, J. T. (1996). A theoretical study and critique of restorative justice. In B. Galaway & J. Hudson (Eds.), *Restorative justice: International perspectives* (pp. 117–133). Monsey, NY: Criminal Justice Press.

Mitchell, K. (2001). Transnationalism, neo-liberalism, and the rise of the shadow state. *Economy and Society, 30*(2), 165–189.

Moffitt, T. E. (1993). "Life-course-persistent" and "adolescence-limited" antisocial behavior: A developmental taxonomy. *Psychological Review, 100,* 674–701.

Moffitt, T. E. (2003). Life-course-persistent and adolescence-limited antisocial behavior: A 10-year research review and a research agenda. In B. B. Lahey, T. E. Moffitt, & A. Caspi (Eds.), *Causes of conduct disorder and juvenile delinquency* (pp. 49–75). New York: Guilford.

Moffitt, T. E. (2006). Life-course-persistent versus adolescence-limited antisocial behavior. In D. Cicchetti & D. Cohen (Eds.), *Developmental psychopathology* (2nd ed., pp. 570–598). New York: John Wiley.

Monk-Turner, E., Edwards, D., Broadstone, J., Hummel, R., Lewis, S., & Wilson, D. (2005). Another look at handwashing behavior. *Social Behavior and Personality: An International Journal, 33*(7), 629–634.

Monroe, J. (2004). Getting a puff: A social learning test of adolescents smoking. *Journal of Child & Adolescent Substance Abuse, 13*(3), 71–83.

Monto, M. A., Machalek, J., & Anderson, T. L. (2013). Doing art: The construction of outlaw masculinity in a Portland, Oregon, graffiti crew. *Journal of Contemporary Ethnography, 42*(3), 259–290.

Morash, M. (1999). On Ronald L. Akers' social learning and social structure: A general theory of crime and deviance. *Theoretical Criminology, 3*(4), 437–493.

Moyer, I. L. (2001). *Criminological theories: Traditional and nontraditional voices and themes.* Thousand Oaks, CA: Sage.

Moynihan, C. (2013, January 28). In "Occupy," well-educated professionals far outnumbered jobless, study finds. The *New York Times.* Retrieved from http://cityroom.blogs.nytimes.com/2013/01/28/in-occupy-well-educated-professionals-far-outnumbered-jobless-study-finds/?ref=occupywallstreet

Mudge, S. (2008). The state of the art: What is neo-liberalism? *Socio-Economic Review, 6,* 703–731.

Muftic, L. R. (2006). Advancing institutional anomie theory: A microlevel examination connecting culture, institutions, and deviance. *International Journal of Offender Therapy and Comparative Criminology, 50*(6), 630–653.

Mumola, C. J. (2000). *Incarcerated parents and their children* (Bureau of Justice Statistics Special Report, NCJ 182335). Washington, DC: Bureau of Justice Statistics.

Murphy, S., Waldorf, D., & Reinarman, C. (1990). Drifting into dealing: Becoming a cocaine seller. *Qualitative Sociology, 13,* 321–343.

NASP. (2013). National Learning & Resource Center: Shoplifting Statistics. Retrieved from http://www.shopliftingprevention.org/WhatNASPOffers/NRC/PublicEducStats.htm

National Health Care Anti-Fraud Association. (2010). The problem of health care fraud. Washington, D.C.: Retrieved September 27, 2013 from http://www.nhcaa.org.

Neff, J. L., & Waite, D. E. (2007). Male versus female substance abuse patterns among incarcerated juvenile offenders: Comparing strain and social learning variables. *Justice Quarterly, 24*(1), 106–132.

Netter, S. (2010, September 16). Student's body modification religion questioned after nose piercing controversy. abcnews.com. http://abcnews.go.com/US/students-body-modification-religion-questioned-nose-piercing- controversy/story?id=11645847&page=1

Neve, L., & Pate, K. (2005). Challenging the criminalization of women who resist. In J. Sudbury (Ed.), *Global lockdown: Race, gender, and the prison-industrial complex* (pp. 19–34). London: Routledge.

Newman, G. (2008). *Comparative deviance: Perception and law in six cultures.* Piscataway, NJ: Transaction Press.

Nixon, K., Tutty, L., Downe, P., Gorkoff, K., & Ursel, J. (2002). The everyday occurrence: Violence in the lives of girls exploited through prostitution. *Violence Against Women, 8,* 1016–1043.

Nye, F. I. (1958). *Family relationships and delinquent behavior.* New York: John Wiley.

Office of the Attorney General Grant Wood. (1997). *Results of the Chandler Survey.* Phoenix, State of Arizona.

Ogden, S. (2005). The prison-industrial complex in indigenous California. In J. Sudbury (Ed.), *Global lockdown: Race, gender, and the prison-industrial complex* (pp. 57–66). London: Routledge.

O'Hagan, M., & Brooks, D. (2005, September 7). Man says he'll plead guilty to killing sex offenders. *Seattle Times.* http://community.seattletimes.nwsource.com/archive/?date=20050907&slug=sexoffender07m

Ogas, O., & Gaddam, S. (2011). *A Billion Wicked Thoughts: What the Internet Tells Us About Sexual Relationships.* New York, New York: Penquin Group.

O'Malley, P. M., & Johnston, L. D. (2007). Drugs and driving by American high school seniors, 2001–2006. *Journal of Studies on Alcohol & Drugs, 68*(6), 834–842.

Orcutt, J. D. (1983). *Analyzing deviance.* Chicago: Dorsey.

Oselin, S. S. (2009). Leaving the streets: Transformation of prostitute identity within the prostitution rehabilitation program. *Deviant Behavior, 30,* 379–406.

Osgood, D. W., & Chambers, J. M. (2000). Social disorganization outside the metropolis: An analysis of rural youth violence. *Criminology, 38*(1), 81–115.

O'Shea, T. C. (2006). Physical deterioration, disorder, and crime. *Criminal Justice Policy Review* 17:173–187.

Özbay, Ö. (2008). Self-control, gender, and deviance among Turkish university students. *Journal Of Criminal Justice, 36*(1), 72-80.

Özbay, Ö., & Köksoy, O. (2009). Is Low Self-Control Associated With Violence Among Youths in Turkey?. *International Journal Of Offender Therapy & Comparative Criminology, 53*(2), 145–167.

Pager, D. (2007). *Marked: Race, crime, and finding work in an era of mass incarceration.* Chicago: University of Chicago Press.

Pager, D., & Quillian, L. (2005). Walking the talk? What employers say versus what they do. *American Sociological Review, 70,* 355–380.

Park, K. (2002). Stigma management among the voluntarily childless. *Sociological Perspectives, 45*(1), 21–45.

Paternoster, R., & Bushway, S. (2009). Desistance and the "feared self": Toward an identity theory of criminal desistance. *Journal of Criminal Law and Criminology, 99*(4), 1103–1156.

Patterson, G. R., & Dishion, T. J. (1985). Contributions of families and peers to delinquency. *Criminology, 23,* 553–573.

Patterson, G. R., Dishion, T. J., & Bank, L. (1984). Family interaction: A process model of deviancy training. *Aggressive Behavior, 10*(3), 253–267.

Payne, B. (2013). *White-Collar Crime: The Essentials.* Thousand Oaks: Sage.

Payne, A., & Welch, K. (2010). Modeling the effects of racial threat on punitive and restorative school discipline practices. *Criminology, 48,* 1019–1062.

Pepinsky, H., & Quinney, R. (1991). *Criminology as peacemaking.* Bloomington: Indiana University Press.

Percival, G. L. (2010). Ideology, diversity, and imprisonment: Considering the influence of local politics on racial and ethnic minority incarceration rates. *Social Science Quarterly, 91,* 1063–1082.

Petts, R. J. (2009). Family and religious characteristics' influence on delinquency trajectories from adolescence to young adulthood. *American Sociological Review, 74*(3), 465–483.

Piquero, A. R., Daigle, L. E, Gibson, C., Piquero, N. E., & Tibbetts, S. G. (2007). Research note: Are life-course-persistent offenders at risk for adverse health outcomes? *Journal of Research in Crime and Delinquency, 44,* 185.

Platt, T. (1974). Prospects for a radical criminology in the United States. *Crime and Social Justice, 1,* 2–10.

Ploeger, M. (1997). Youth employment and delinquency: Reconsidering a problematic relationship. *Criminology, 35*(4), 659–675.

Pornhub. (2013). Pornhub 2013 Year in Review. Retrieved from http://www.pornhub.com/insights/pornhub-2013-year-in-review/

Porter, B. E., & England, K. J. (2000). Predicting red-light running behavior: A traffic safety study in three urban settings. *Journal of Safety Research, 31,* 1–8.

Pratt, J., & Eriksson, A. (2011). "Mr. Larsson is walking out again." The Origins and development of Scandinavian prison systems. *Australian & New Zealand Journal of Criminology, 44*(1), 7–23.

Pruitt, M. V. (2008). Deviant research: Deception, male Internet escorts, and response rates. *Deviant Behavior, 29*(1), 70–82.

Pruitt, M. V., & Krull, A. C. (2011). Escort advertisements and male patronage of prostitutes. *Deviant Behavior, 32*(1), 38–63.

Quinn, A. (2013). *Book News: Inmate Fights for His Right to Read Werewolf Erotica. The Two-Way: Breaking News from NPR.* Retrieved from http://www.npr.org/blogs/thetwo-way/2013/06/13/191237331/book-news-inmate-fights-for-his-right-to-read-werewolf-erotica?sc=ipad&f=1008

Quinney, R. (1963). Occupational structure and criminal behavior: Prescription violation by retail pharmacists. *Social Problems, 11,* 179–185.

Quinney, R. (1970). *The social reality of crime.* Boston: Little, Brown.

Quinney, R. (1995). Socialist humanism and the problem of crime: Thinking about Erich Fromm in the development of critical/peacemaking criminology. *Crime, Law, and Social Change, 23,* 147–156.

Quinney, R. (1997). The way of peace: On crime, suffering, and service. In H. E. Pepinsky & R. Quinney (Eds.), Criminology as peacemaking (pp3-13). Bloomington: Indiana University.

Rampona, J. (2004, November 28). What happens to the homeless? Criminalizing the necessary and life-sustaining actions of homeless people adds to the burden of living in constant exposure to the elements. *Arkansas Democrat-Gazette.*

Rankin, B. H., & Quane, J. M. (2002). Social contexts and urban adolescent outcomes: The interrelated effects of neighborhoods, families, and peers on African-American youth. *Social Problems, 49*(1), 79.

Rankin, J. H., & Kern, R. M. (1994). Parental attachments and delinquency. *Criminology, 32,* 495–515.

Rankin, J. H., & Wells, L. E. (1990). The effect of parental attachments and direct controls on delinquency. *Journal of Research in Crime and Delinquency, 27,* 140–165.

Raphael, J., & Shapiro, D. L. (2004). Violence in indoor and outdoor prostitution venues. *Violence Against Women, 10*(2), 126–139.

Rebellon, C. J., Straus, M. A., & Medeiros, R. (2008). Self-Control in Global Perspective. *European Journal Of Criminology, 5*(3), 331–361.

Reed, M. D., & Rountree, P. W. (1997). Peer pressure and adolescent substance use. *Journal of Quantitative Criminology, 13*(2), 143–180.

Reiling, D. M. (2002). The "simmie" side of life: Old order Amish youths' affective response to culturally prescribed deviance. *Youth & Society, 34*(2), 146–171.

Reiman, J., & Leighton, P. (2009). *The rich get richer and the poor get prison: Ideology, class, and criminal justice* (9th ed.). Englewood Cliffs, NJ: Prentice Hall.

Reitman, J. (2013, December 4). Snowden and Greenwald: The men who leaked the secrets: How two alienated, angry geeks broke the story of the year." *Rolling Stone.* Retrieved from http://www.rollingstone.com/politics/news/snowden-and-greenwald-the-men-who-leaked-the-secrets-20131204

Rhoades, K. A., Chamberlain, P., Roberts, R., & Leve, L. D. (2013). MTFC for high-risk adolescent girls: A comparison of outcomes in England and the United States. *Journal of Child & Adolescent Substance Abuse, 22*(5), 435–449.

Riley, N. (1995). Hamlet: the Untold Tragedy. *The Organica News.* Retrieved from http://web.archive.org/web/20070107011410/http://www.organicanews.com/news/article.cfm?story_id=103

Robinson, M. M., & Murphy, D. (2009). *Greed is good: Maximization and elite deviance in America.* Lanham, MD: Rowman & Littlefield.

Rogers, T. (August 28, 2011). Why do college students love getting wasted? *Salon.* Retrieved from http://www.salon.com/2011/08/28/college_drinking_interview/

Romero, M. (2006). Racial profiling and immigration law enforcement: Rounding up of usual suspects in the Latino community." *Critical Sociology* 32:447–473.

Ronai, C. R., & Ellis, C. (1989). Turn-ons for money. Interactional strategies of the table dancer. *Journal of Contemporary Ethnography, 18,* 271–298.

Rosenbaum, D. P. (2007). Just say no to DARE. *Criminology & Public Policy, 6*(4), 815–824.

Rosenfield, S. (1997). Labeling mental illness: The effects of received services and perceived stigma on life satisfaction. *American Sociological Review, 62*(4), 660–672.

Rosenhan, D. L. (1973). On being sane in insane places. *Science, 179,* 250–258.

Rosenthal, E. (1994). Irked by Medicare limits, doctors ask elderly to pay up. *New York Times.* Retrieved September 28, 2013 from http://www.nytimes.com/1994/02/15/nyregion/irked-by-medicare-limits-doctors-ask-elderly-to-pay-up.html?pagewanted=all&src=pm

Rothe, D., & Mullins, C. W. (2009). Toward a criminology for international criminal law: An integrated theory of international criminal violations. *International Journal of Comparative and Applied Criminal Justice, 3*(1), 97–118.

Rothe, D. L., & Kauzlarich, D. (2010). State-level crime: Theory and policy. In H. D. Barlow & S. Decker (Eds.), *Crime and public policy: Putting theory to work* (2nd ed., pp. 166–187). Philadelphia: Temple University Press.

Rousseau, J. (1987). *The basic political writings.* (D. A. Cress, Trans.). Indianapolis, IN: Hackett Publishing Company.

Rowe, D. C. (2002). *Biology and crime.* Los Angeles: Roxbury.

Rubington, E. S., & Weinberg, M. S. (2008). *Deviance: The interactionist perspective.* Englewood Cliffs, NJ: Prentice Hall.

Rutter, M., & Giller, H. (1984). *Juvenile delinquency: Trends and perspectives.* London: Guilford.

Ruvolo, J. (2011). The Internet Is for Porn (So Let's Talk About It). *Forbes.* Retrieved from http://www.forbes.com/sites/julieruvolo/2011/05/20/the-internet-is-for-porn-so-lets-talk-about-it/

Sallman, J. (2010). Living with stigma: Women's experiences of prostitution and substance use. *Affilia, 25,* 146–159.

Sampson, R. (1999). On Ronald L. Akers' social learning and social structure: A general theory of crime and deviance. *Theoretical Criminology, 3*(4), 437–493.

Sampson, R. J. (2012). *Great American city: Chicago and the enduring neighborhood effect.* Chicago, IL: Chicago University Press.

Sampson, R. J., & Groves, W. B. (1989). Community structure and crime: Testing social-disorganization theory. *American Journal of Sociology, 94*(4), 774–802.

Sampson, R. J., & Laub, J. H. (1993). *Crime in the making: Pathways and turning points through life.* Cambridge, MA: Harvard University Press.

Sampson, R. J., & Laub, J. H. (1994). Urban poverty and the family context of delinquency: A new look at structure and process in a classic study. *Child Development, 65,* 523–541.

Sampson, R. J., & Laub, J. H. (1995). Understanding variability in lives through time: Contributions of life-course criminology. *Studies on Crime and Crime Prevention, 4*(2), 143–158.

Sampson, R. J., & Raudenbush, S. W. (2004). Seeing disorder: Neighborhood stigma and the social construction of "broken windows." *Social Psychology Quarterly, 67,* 319–342.

Sampson, R. J., Raudenbush, S. W., & Earls, F. (1997). Neighborhoods and violent crime: A multilevel study of collective efficacy. *Science, 277,* 918–924.

Sanders, T. (2007). Becoming an ex-sex worker. *Feminist Criminology, 2*(1), 74–95.

Sarkis, C. (2012, December 20). 10 weird laws from around the world. *USA Today.* Retrieved from http://www.usatoday.com/story/travel/destinations/2012/12/19/10-weird-laws-from-around-the-world/1779931/

Savolainen, J. (2000). Inequality, Welfare State, and Homicide: Further Support for the Institutional Anomie Theory. *Criminology, 38*(4), 1021[en dash]1042.

Scarce, R. (2008). Earth first! Deviance inside and out. In E. Goode & D. A. Vail (Eds.), *Extreme deviance* (pp. 177–188). Thousand Oaks, CA: Pine Forge Press.

Scheff, T. J. (1966). *Being mentally ill: A sociological theory.* Chicago: Aldine.

Schlossman, S, and Sedlak, M. (1983). The Chicago Area Project Revisited. *Crime and Delinquency 29:* 398–462.

Scholinski, D. (with Adams, J. M.). (1997). *The last time I wore a dress: A memoir.* New York: Riverhead Books.

Schur, E. M. (1973). *Radical non-intervention: Rethinking the delinquency problem.* Englewood Cliffs, NJ: Prentice Hall.

Schur, E. M. (1983). *Labeling women deviant: Gender, stigma and social control.* Philadelphia: Temple University Press.

Schwendinger, H., & Schwendinger, J. (1970). Defenders of order or guardians of human rights? *Issues in Criminology, 5,* 123–157.

Shane, S., and Somaiya, R. (June 16, 2013). "New Leak Indicates U.S. and Britain Eavesdropped at '09 World Conferences". The New York Times. Retrieved from http://www.nytimes.com/2013/06/17/world/europe/new-leak-indicates-us-and-britain-eavesdropped-at-09-world-conferences.html?_r=0

Sharp, S. (1998). Relationships with children and AIDS—Risk behaviors among female IDUs. *Deviant Behavior, 19,* 3–28.

Shaw, C. A., & McKay, H. (1969). *Juvenile delinquency in urban areas.* Chicago: University of Chicago Press. (Original work published 1942)

Shteir, R. (2011). *The Steal: A Cultural History of Shoplifting.* New York: The Penguin Press.

Silver, E. (2000). Extending Social Disorganization Theory: A Multilevel Approach to the Study of Violence Among Persons With Mental Illness. *Criminology, 38*(4), 1043–1074.

Simmons, J. L. (1965). Public stereotypes of deviants. *Social Problems, 13*(2), 223–232.

Simon, D. R. (2008). *Elite deviance* (9th ed.). New York: Pearson Education, Inc.

Simon, R. J. (1975). *The contemporary woman and crime.* Rockville, MD: National Institute of Mental Health.

Simons, R. L., Simons, L., Burt, C., Brody, G. H., & Cutrona, C. (2005). Collective efficacy, authoritative parenting, and delinquency: A longitudinal test of a model integrating community and family level processes. *Criminology, 43*(4), 989–1029.

Skipp, C. (2009, July 25). A bridge too far. *Newsweek.* http://www.newsweek.com/2009/07/24/a-bridge-too-far.html

Skogan, W. (1990). *Disorder and decline: Crime and the spiral of decay in American neighborhoods.* New York: Free Press.

Smart, C. (1977). Criminological theory: Its ideology and implications concerning women. *British Journal of Sociology, 28,* 89–100.

Snowball, L., & Weatherburn, D. (2008). Theories of Indigenous Violence: A Preliminary Empirical Assessment. Australian & *New Zealand Journal Of Criminology (Australian Academic Press), 41*(2), 216–235.

Sokol-Katz, J., Dunham, R., & Zimmerman, R. (1997). Family structure versus parental attachment in controlling adolescent deviant behavior: A social control model. *Adolescence, 32,* 199–216.

Solomon, G.S., Joseph B. Ray (1984). "Irrational Beliefs of Shoplifters". *Journal of Clinical Psychology 40*(4): 1075–1077.

Soothill, K., Fitzpatrick, C., & Brian, F. (2009). *Understanding criminal careers.* Cullompton, UK: Willan.

Spitzer, R. L. (1976). More on pseudoscience in science and the case for psychiatric diagnosis: A critique of D. L. Rosenhan's "On being sane in insane places" and "The contextual nature of psychiatric diagnosis." *Archives of General Psychiatry, 33*(4), 459–470.

Spitzer, S. (1975). Towards a Marxian theory of deviance. *Social Problems, 22*, 638–651.

Spitzer, S. (1983). Marxist perspectives in the sociology of law. *Annual Review of Sociology, 9*, 103–124.

Spreitzer, G. M., & Sonenshein, S. (2004). Toward the construct definition of positive deviance. *American Behavioral Scientist, 47*(6), 828–847.

Stark, R. (1987). Deviant places: A theory of the ecology of crime. *Criminology, 25*(4), 893–909.

Steffensmeier, D. J., Allan, E. A., Harer, M. D., & Streifel, C. (1989). Age and the distribution of crime. *American Journal of Sociology, 94*(4), 803–831.

Steinhauer, J. (2007, April 29). For $82 a day, booking a stay in a 5-star jail. *New York Times.* Retrieved from http://www.nytimes.com/2007/04/29/us/29jail.html?pagewanted=all&_r=1&

Stern, G. M. (2013, September 30). John Jay College tries to help prisoners turn lives around. *New York Business Journal.* Retrieved from http://www.bizjournals.com/newyork/news/2013/09/30/john-jay-college-tries-to-help.html?page=all

Stiles, B. L., & Clark, R. E. (2011). BDSM: A subcultural analysis of sacrifices and delights. *Deviant Behavior, 32*(2), 158–189.

Stillman, S. (2013). "A reporter at large: Taken." *The New Yorker,* August 12 & 19: 49–61.

Strang, H., & Braithwaite, J. (2001). *Restorative justice and civil society.* Cambridge, UK: Cambridge University Press.

Sudbury, J. (Ed.). (2005). *The global lockdown: Race, gender, and the prison-industrial complex.* London: Routledge.

Sullivan, L. (2010, October 28). Prison economics help drive Arizona immigration bill. NPR online. Retrieved February 3, 2011, from http://www.npr.org/templates/transcript/transcript.php?storyId=130833741

Sullivan, M. L. (1989). *"Getting paid": Youth crime and work in the inner city.* Ithaca, NY: Cornell University Press.

Sumner, W. G. (1906). *Folkways: A study of the sociological importance of usages, manners, customs, mores, and morals.* Boston: Ginn & Company.

Sutherland, E. H. (1934). *Principles of criminology.* Philadelphia: Lippincott.

Sutherland, E. (1940). White-collar criminality. *American Society of Criminology, 5,* 1–12.

Sutherland, E. H. (1947). *Principles of criminology* (4th ed.). Philadelphia, Lippincott

Sutherland, E. H. (1949a). *Principles of criminology* (4th ed.). Philadelphia: Lippincott.

Sutherland, E. H. (1949b). *White collar crime.* New York: Holt, Rinehart & Winston.

Sutter, J. D. (2012, May 24). Welcome to the world's nicest prison. CNN.com. Retrieved from http://www.cnn.com/2012/05/24/world/europe/norway-prison-bastoy-nicest/index.html

Sykes, G. M. (1958). *The society of captives.* Princeton, NJ: Princeton University Press.

Sykes, G. M., & Matza, D. (1957). Techniques of neutralization: A theory of delinquency. *American Sociological Review, 22*(6), 664–670.

Szalavitz, M. (2012, September 28). College binge drinking: How bad is the problem really? *Time* magazine. Retrieved from http://healthland.time.com/2012/09/28/college-binge-drinking-how-bad-is-the-problem-really/

Tannenbaum, F. (1938). *Crime and the community.* Boston: Ginn.

Taylor, E. (1998). A primer on critical race theory. *Journal of Blacks in Higher Education, 19,* 122–124.

Taylor, I., Walton, P., & Young, J. (1973). *The new criminology.* New York: Harper Torchbooks.

Taylor, P. (1991). Fire at Chicken Processing Plant Kills 25: Disaster: Witnesses say locked doors added to death toll at North Carolina facility that had never been inspected for safety; 49 workers hurt. *Los Angeles Times.* Retrieved from http://articles.latimes.com/1991-09-04/news/mn-1562_1_chicken-processing-plant

Thio, A. (2009). *Deviant behavior.* New York: Allyn & Bacon.

Thompson, W. E., Harred, J. L., & Burks, B. E. (2003). Managing the stigma of topless dancing: A decade later. *Deviant Behavior, 24*(6), 551–570.

Thornberry, T. P., Lizotte, A. J., Krohn, M. D., Farnworth, M., & Sung Joon, J. (1994). Delinquent peers, beliefs, and delinquent behavior: A longitudinal test of interactional theory. *Criminology, 32*(1), 47–83.

Tong, R. P. (1998). *Feminist thought: A more comprehensive introduction.* Boulder, CO: Westview.

Tonry, M. (2011). *Punishing race: A continuing American dilemma.* New York: Oxford University Press.

Trammell, R. (2009). Values, rules, and keeping the peace: How men describe order and the inmate code in California prisons. *Deviant Behavior, 30,* 746–771.

Traub, S. H., & Little, C. B. (1985). *Theories of deviance* (3rd ed.). Itasca, IL: F. E. Peacock.

Tuggle, J., & Holmes, M. (1997). Blowing smoke: Status politics and the Shasta County smoking ban. *Deviant Behavior, 18*(1), 77–93.

Turk, A. T. (1969). *Criminality and legal order.* Chicago: Rand McNally.

Turk, A. T. (1976a). Law as a weapon in social conflict. *Social Problems, 23,* 276–291.

Turk, A. T. (1976b). Law, conflict and order: From theorizing toward theories. *Canadian Review of Sociology and Anthropology, 13*(3), 282–294.

Turk, A. T. (1977). Class, conflict, and criminalization. *Sociological Focus, 10,* 209–220.

Turk, A. T. (2002). Crime causation: Political theories. In J. Dressler (Ed.), *Encyclopedia of crime and justice* (2nd ed.). New York: Macmillan References USA.

Tyler, K. A., Hoyt, D. R., Whitbeck, L. B., & Cauce, A. M. (2001). The impact of childhood sexual abuse on later sexual victimization among runaway youth. *Journal of Research on Adolescence, 11*(2), 151–176.

Uggen, C., & Inderbitzin, M. (2010). The price and the promise of citizenship: Extending the vote to non-incarcerated felons. In N. A. Frost, J. D. Freilich, & T. R. Clear (Eds.), *Contemporary issues in criminal justice policy: Policy proposals from the American Society of Criminology Conference* (pp. 61–68). Belmont, CA: Cengage/Wadsworth.

Uggen, C., Manza, J., & Thompson, M. (2006). Citizen, democracy, and the civic reintegration of criminal offenders. *Annals of the American Academy of Political and Social Science, 605,* 281–310.

Umbreit, M. (1994). *Victim meets offender: The impact of restorative justice and mediation.* Monsey, NY: Criminal Justice Press.

United Nations Global Initiative to Fight Human Trafficking. (2008). Human trafficking: An overview. United Nations Office on Drugs and Crime. Retrieved from http://www.ungift.org/docs/ungift/pdf/knowledge/ebook.pdf

U.S. Department of State. (2007). Trafficking in persons report 2007. Retrieved from (http://www.state.gov/g/tip/rls/tiprpt/2007/).

U.S. Department of State. (2013). Trafficking in persons report 2013. Retrieved from http://www.state.gov/documents/organization/210737.pdf

Vander Ven, T. (2011). *Getting wasted: Why college students drink too much and party so hard.* New York: NYU Press.

VanNostrand, L., & Tewksbury, R. (1997). The motives and mechanics of operating an illegal drug enterprise. *Deviant Behavior, 20,* 57–83.

Van Voorhis, P., Cullen, F. T., Mathers, R. A., & Garner, C. C. (1988). The impact of family structure and quality on delinquency: A comparative assessment of structural and functional factors. *Criminology, 26,* 235–261.

Vaughan, D. (2004). Theorizing disaster: Analogy, historical ethnography, and the Challenger accident. *Ethnography, 5*(3), 315–347.

Vazsonyi, A. T., Pickering, L. E., Junger, M., & Hessing, D. (2001). An Empirical Test of a General Theory of Crime: A Four-Nation Comparative Study of Self-Control and the Prediction of Deviance. *Journal Of Research In Crime & Delinquency, 38*(2), 91–131.

Vazsonyi, A. T., & Klanjsek, R. (2008). A test of self-control theory across different socioeconomic strata. *Justice Quarterly, 25*(1), 101–131.

Venkatesh, S. (2008). *Gang leader for a day: A rogue sociologist takes to the streets.* New York: Penguin Books.

Veysey, B. M., & Messner, S. F. (1999). Further testing of social disorganization theory: An elaboration of Sampson and Groves's "community structure and crime." *Journal of Research in Crime and Delinquency, 36*(2), 156–174.

Vold, G. B. (1958). *Theoretical criminology.* New York: Oxford University Press.

Wacquant, L. (2000). The new "peculiar institution": On the prison as surrogate ghetto. *Theoretical Criminology, 4,* 377–389.

Walsh, A. (2000). Behavior genetics and anomie/strain theory. *Criminology, 38*(4), 1075–1107.

Walsh, T. (2011, January 27). Ugandan gay rights activist bludgeoned to death. CNN.com. Retrieved from http://www.cnn.com/2011/WORLD/africa/01/27/uganda.gay.activist.killed/index.html

Warner, B. D., & Pierce, G. L. (1993). Reexamining social disorganization theory using calls to the police as a measure of crime. *Criminology, 31*(4), 493–517.

Warr, M. (1993). Parents, peers, and delinquency. *Social Forces, 72,* 247–265.

Warr, M. (2002). *Companions in crime: The social aspects of criminal conduct.* Cambridge, UK: Cambridge University Press.

Watson, B. (2013). Fremont's pay-to-stay jail offers a more pleasant prison experience. DailyFinance.com. Retrieved from http://www.dailyfinance.com/2013/08/06/freemont-calif-offers-pay-to-stay-nicer-jail-cells/

Weeks, A.H. (1958). *Youthful Offenders at Highfield.* Ann Arbor: University of Michigan Press.

Weinberg, M. S. (1966). Becoming a nudist. *Psychiatry: Journal for the Study of Interpersonal Processes, 29,* 15–24.

Weinberg, M. S., Williams, C. J., & Pryor, D. W. (2001). Bisexuals at midlife: Commitment, salience, and identity. *Journal of Contemporary Ethnography, 30*(2), 180–208.

Wells, L. E., & Rankin, J. H. (1988). Direct parental controls and delinquency. *Criminology, 26,* 263–285.

West, C. (1995). Forward. In K. Crenshaw, N. Gotanda, G. Peller, & K. Thomas (Eds.), *Critical race theory: The key writings that formed the movement* (pp. xi–xii). New York: New Press.

West, S. L., & O'Neal, K. K. (2004). Project DARE outcome effectiveness revisited. *American Journal of Public Health, 94,* 1027–1029.

Western, B. (2006). *Punishment and inequality in America.* New York: Russell Sage Foundation.

Whaley, R., Smith, J. M., & Hayes-Smith, R. (2011). Teenage drug and alcohol use: Comparing individual and contextual effects. *Deviant Behavior, 32*(9), 818–845.

Williams, C. J. (2013, October 7). Malala's year: Shot for defying Taliban, now considered for Nobel. *Los Angeles Times.* Retrieved from http://www.latimes.com/world/world now/la-fg-wn-malala-yousafzai-taliban-20131007,0,876137.story

Wilson, J. Q., & Kelling, G. (1982). Broken windows: The police and neighborhood safety. *Atlantic Monthly, 249,* 29–38.

Wolfgang, M. E., & Ferrcuti, F. (1967). *The subculture of violence: Towards an integrated theory in criminology.* Beverly Hills, CA: Sage.

Wright, E. R., Gronfein, W. P., & Owens, T. J. (2000). Deinstitutionalization, social rejection, and the self-esteem of former mental patients. *Journal of Health and Social Behavior, 41*(1), 68–90.

Wright, J., & Cullen, F. T. (2001). Parental efficacy and delinquent behavior: Do control and support matter? *Criminology, 39*(3), 677–705.

Wright, M. (1996). *Justice for Victims and Offenders: A Restorative Response to Crime.* (2nd edition) Winchester, England: Waterside Press.

Yacoubian, G. S., Jr., & Peters, R. J. (2005). Identifying the prevalence and correlates of ecstasy use among high school seniors surveyed through 2002 Monitoring the Future. *Journal of Alcohol & Drug Education, 49*(1), 55–72.

Yip, A. K. T. (1996). Gay Christians and their participation in the gay subculture. *Deviant Behavior,* 17(3), 297–318.

Zehr, H. (1990). *Changing lenses: A new focus for crime and justice.* Scottsdale, PA: Herald Press.

Zehr, H. (2002). *The little book of restorative justice.* Intercourse, PA: Good Books.

Zhang, L., Messner, S. F., & Liu, J. (2007). A Multilevel Analysis of the Risk of Household Burglary in the City of Tianjin, China. *British Journal of Criminology, 47*(6), 918–937.

Zhang, S. X. (2010). *Sex trafficking in a border community: A field study of sex trafficking in Tijuana, Mexico.* San Diego, CA: San Diego State University.

Index

About the Authors

Michelle Inderbitzin primarily studies prison culture, juvenile justice, and transformative education. She has published papers in *Punishment & Society, Journal of Adolescent Research, The Prison Journal, Journal of Offender Rehabilitation, International Journal of Offender Therapy and Comparative Criminology,* and *Criminology & Public Policy*, and is currently working on research about prison education, broadly defined. Dr. Inderbitzin earned her PhD in Sociology from the University of Washington and has been a faculty member at Oregon State University since 2001. Along with her on campus classes on crime and deviance, she regularly teaches classes and volunteers in Oregon's maximum-security prison for men and in state youth correctional facilities.

Kristin A. Bates is Professor of Sociology and Criminology and Justice Studies at California State University San Marcos. Her current research examines the impact of suppression policies such as Civil Gang Injunctions on communities, families, and individuals. She has co-authored several books, including an examination of social justice in the United States using Hurricane Katrina as the case study, deviance and social control, and juvenile delinquency. She earned her PhD in Sociology from the University of Washington in 1998 and has been a faculty member at Cal State San Marcos ever since.

Randy Gainey is Professor of Sociology and Criminal Justice at Old Dominion University. He has coauthored several books focused on family violence, deviance and social control, and policing drug use. His recent research has focused on sentencing, neighborhood organizations as controllers or enablers of deviance, and the use of electronic monitoring with GPS for supervising high risk sex offenders and high risk gang offenders on parole. He earned his PhD in Sociology from the University of Washington in 1995 and has been a faculty member at Old Dominion University ever since.

ⓈSAGE researchmethods

The essential online tool for researchers from the world's leading methods publisher

Find exactly what you are looking for, from basic explanations to advanced discussion

More content and new features added this year!

"I have never really seen anything like this product before, and I think it is really valuable."

John Creswell, University of Nebraska–Lincoln

Discover **Methods Lists**— methods readings suggested by other users

Watch video interviews with leading methodologists

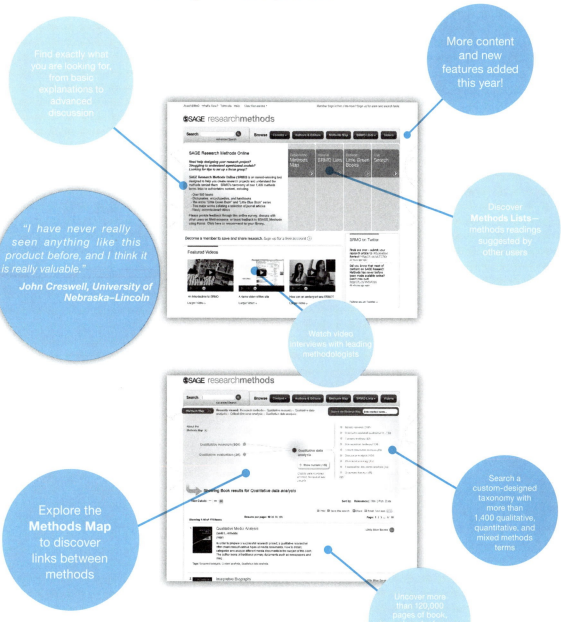

Explore the **Methods Map** to discover links between methods

Search a custom-designed taxonomy with more than 1,400 qualitative, quantitative, and mixed methods terms

Uncover more than 120,000 pages of book, journal, and reference content to support your learning

Find out more at
www.sageresearchmethods.com